WHATEVER HAPPENED TO SLADE?

First edition copyright © 2023 Omnibus Press
This edition copyright © 2024 Omnibus Press
(A division of the Wise Music Group
14–15 Berners Street, London, W1T 3LJ)

Cover image © Gered Mankowitz / Iconic Images
Cover designed by Amazing15

Picture research by the author

PB ISBN 978-1-9158-4149-0
HB ISBN 978-1-7830-5554-8
Special edition ISBN 978-1-9158-4128-5

A catalogue record for this book is available from the British Library.

Typeset by Evolution Design & Digital Ltd (Kent)
Printed in Turkey

www.omnibuspress.com

WHATEVER HAPPENED TO SLADE?

WHEN THE WHOLE WORLD WENT CRAZEE

DARYL EASLEA

FOREWORD BY BOB GELDOF

OMNIBUS PRESS

London / New York / Paris / Sydney / Copenhagen / Berlin / Madrid / Tokyo

For Dave Kemp

Also by the Author

Everybody Dance: CHIC and the Politics of Disco
The Story of the Supremes
Talent is an Asset: the Story of Sparks
Madonna: Blond Ambition (with Eddi Fiegel)
Crazy in Love: the Beyonce Knowles Biography
Cher: All I Really Want to Do (with Eddi Fiegel)
Without Frontiers: the Life and Music of Peter Gabriel
Michael Jackson: Rewind: The Life and Legacy of Pop Music's King
The Supreme Record Company: the Story Of Decca Records 1929 – 2019
(co-editor, contributor)

Haiku Does It Feel
By Paul Cookson

If Don's the heart beat
Dave's the hair style, Nod's the voice
Then Jim is the soul

If Don's the thunder
Dave's the lightning, Nod's the storm
Then Jim is the calm

If Don's the waistcoat
Dave's the boots, Nod's the top hat
Jim wears the trousers

Contents

Contents

Foreword by Bob Geldof

In a posh restaurant with a bunch of rock'n'roll friends last week, we started talking about the huge sound that Oasis made. It was agreed that it was essentially The Beatles meets the Pistols and then amped up a bit more. 'A good bit of Slade in the mix too,' I volunteered fairly meekly fearing instant scorn from the stellar assembly. 'Fucking sure,' said Noel and a great chorus of enthusiastic approval erupted.

There then followed a sort of late-night Sladeathon with competing musos citing favourite tracks, B-sides, 'things they were doing when they first heard 'Gudbuy T'Jane'', or whatever. Which was very dull gruel for the visiting Americans who weren't musicians and had never heard of one of the great British bands and their singer with the ridiculously loud harsh bellow. Like someone had taken John Lennon aside and turned him up to 11 just before his final take on 'Twist and Shout'.

Slade have slipped between the cracks of pop history. They shouldn't have been allowed to. Maybe it was the time that was in it as they say. They've been lumped in with all the confused shit of the early seventies when pop seemed to have lost its way and Bolan, Bowie and Roxy were doing their damnedest to right the good ship rock'n'roll back on to its correct and steady road to righteousness. We have thankfully forgotten the depth of awfulness that was Mud, The BC Rollers, The Rubettes (ffs!!), Showadafuckingwaddy, etc… but we should not forget Slade. The crack they slipped down was the gulf between the pasticheurs of the above and the utter fabulousness of Marc, David and the Roxy boys. We need to haul them back out.

It was true that pop (as happens frequently) needed to go back to something approaching its essential stripped-down, dangerous, sexy, beautiful boy self but there was nothing in the least bit threatening in the sexless tripe of the manufactured clones playing their Pap Pop. Then along comes some very loud bawdy Black Country blokes, throwing aside their dubious earlier bovver boy outfits in exchange for equally crap but boisterous and positive sequins, satins and silver 13 floor platform boots and shit haircuts and screaming that we needed to 'feel the noize'. FEEL! There you go. That's the essential key. You don't just parrot this music. Feel it or fuck off.

Now if you're the Stop/Go guy at the crossroads of the being-built M25/M23 interchange and the demand to 'feel the noize' booms out of the transistors beside your lunch sandwiches and dusty summer haul road then that, friends, is precisely what you do come the earliest Saturday available!

Glam was glam because it sought an ironic 'look' and stripped-down noise and sense ('Get It On', 'Cum On Feel the Noize', 'Jean Genie', etc.) that was the possible route back past the dull, charmless drudgery of endless muso noodling prog, earnest 'head' music and shit third-rate blues bands as featured every Sunday afternoon at the London Roundhouse Implosion sessions and back to an earlier period of youth, style and rooted rebel fun when good music was great and everyday and singable.

Slade was part of that. They should be revered. Here's a book that does that.

Bob Geldof, April 2023

It's Christmassss!

The phenomenon of the pop Christmas hit, and indeed, the race to top the festive singles chart in the UK, is a relatively recent occurrence.

Christmas songs are, of course, almost as old as the Christian festival itself. Popular hymns and carols have been handed down through generations. When the sheet music boom took off from the 1920s, running in tandem with advances in the recording and motion picture industries, the festive hit became an industry standard; Irving Berlin's 'White Christmas' (as famously sung by Bing Crosby) and Mel Tormé's 'The Christmas Song' (sung by Nat King Cole) are but two poignant and powerful examples of the potency of the medium.

The seasonal novelty song was a staple of the late fifties – Alma Cogan emphasised the giggle in her voice with 'You Should Never Do a Tango with an Eskimo', 10-year-old Gayla Peevey wanted nothing more than a 'Hippopotamus for Christmas' and Michael Holiday ran willing listeners through 'The Christmas Alphabet'. Aside from these, though, Christmas records were often simply jazzed-up versions of popular standards, and carols, the original Christmas singles.

Although producer and songwriter Phil Spector had (uncommercially, at the time) trailblazed within the genre in 1963 with his album *A Christmas Gift for You*, it was not until John Lennon and Yoko Ono recorded 'Happy Xmas (War Is Over)' in 1971 with, ironically, Spector as producer, that the concept of a modern, contemporary, yuletide pop song with gravitas was entertained. Although Elvis Presley had offered 'Blue Christmas' in 1957, and several Christmas albums, The Beatles – who enjoyed four festive chart-toppers – thought so little of the form, they had honoured the holidays only by making flexi-discs of skits and song snatches strictly for their fan club between 1963 and 1969. From 'Happy Xmas (War Is Over)' onwards, an open (festive?) season began. As an ex-Beatle was experimenting with the form, all the acts that looked up to Lennon clamoured to get their own yuletide sound.

Kathleen Ganner, the mother-in-law-to-be of Slade bassist, violinist and co-writer, Jim Lea, thought that Slade should write their own Christmas hit. When she teased Lea at the breakfast table that 'White Christmas' had sold more than any Slade hit, although he was disgruntled stating that Slade were a rock band, not a Christmas band, she planted a seed with him. And so, in September 1973, Slade – Dave Hill, Noddy Holder, Jim Lea and Don Powell – went into the Record Plant studios on 321 West 44th Street, New York, and recorded their contribution to the festive canon.

'Merry Xmas Everybody' was an amalgam of two songs that the band's principal songwriters, Lea and Holder, had previously written; Holder added the lyric, an accessible, everyman celebration of the Christmas season that was so obvious and simple, it was akin to a nursery rhyme. The initial version committed to tape was rejected by the group; another was recorded not in the studio itself, but in the adjacent hallway to get the suitable acoustics. A harmonium that was being used by John Lennon, who'd been in another studio in the complex recording his *Mind Games* album, was utilised at the suggestion of Lea, giving the song its most distinctive introduction. Released three months later, on 7 December 1973, the record was to become Slade's biggest hit single, and the one for which they will forever be remembered.

For many, there is but one image of the group, whether it is a genuine or a received memory. It was captured in a television studio in West London, and it involves balloons, fake snow and four men in their late 20s stomping around singing a modern folk song. The men look like a very seventies take on something quite Dickensian: frontman Holder as an ebullient be-mutton-chopped gang leader, with guitarist Hill as an Artful Dodger and bass player Lea and drummer Powell lurking behind them, like two malevolent street urchins primed to mete out retribution. 'Merry Xmas Everybody', with its simple blend of hope, nostalgia and cheer, struck a chord with the people of Great Britain who propelled it to that year's Christmas number one, and in many respects, it began the modern – and uniquely British – obsession with the record that tops the charts at the festive season and all its attendant ballyhoo.

*   *   *

Although they had their apprenticeship in the beat boom of the sixties, and a hard-rocking third act in the eighties, Slade are inextricably linked with the 1970s. And 1973 in particular. Britain was in the middle of economic and social turmoil; the Conservative government, led by Prime Minister Edward 'Ted' Heath, was at loggerheads with the National Union of Mineworkers headed by militant leader Mick McGahey. Although the three-day weeks that have become so much a cornerstone of mid-century UK folklore did not actually occur until early 1974, the union tactic of power cuts – which had run intermittently since 1972 – had led to uncertainty and food shortages. Much is on record about how 'Merry Xmas Everybody' lifted morale and helped provide old-fashioned Christmas cheer amid the gloom of the political unrest.

'We were right in the middle of a disastrous period politically. There were power cuts every day and half the work force seemed to be on strike,' Noddy Holder said in Alwyn W. Turner's book *Crisis? What Crisis? Britain In The 70s.* 'Merry Xmas was a happy uplifting record. I'm sure that's part of the reason why so many people liked it.'

People did like it, and they liked Slade, too. They enjoyed unparalleled success in 1973. It was the apex of their mainstream appeal. The year is now seen in the annals of rock history as one of the 'album': but if global successes such as *The Dark Side of the*

Moon by Pink Floyd and Mike Oldfield's debut masterpiece, *Tubular Bells*, ruled the album charts, then the battleground of youth, the singles charts, were governed by Slade, enjoying three UK number one singles and one number two. That said, Slade put in their time on the LP listings as well – and they spent six weeks at the top of the albums chart, too – a feat *The Dark Side of the Moon* was never to achieve, and *Tubular Bells* was not to do until the following year.

Since its initial twenty-five-week run in the charts as 1973 became 1974, 'Merry Xmas Everybody' has been reissued frequently, and since the era of downloading and subsequently, streaming, it has revisited the Top 75 each year since 2007.

* * *

During the confusion surrounding the rules throughout the Covid-19 pandemic in the UK in 2020, when it appeared that there may be Christmas social 'bubbles', *The Sun* newspaper's front-page headline on 25 November trumpeted – 'Here It Is… Mini Christmas'. With this, there was a classic picture of Holder, mirrored hat and all, with then Prime Minister Boris Johnson's face superimposed onto it. It was, forty-seven years later, still a soothing balm for a troubled time, underlining quite how profound an effect the original had on those at the time who were now grown up and in positions of power.

In the UK in July 2021, as lockdown concluded, Holder starred in an advert for food chain Pret A Manger, as they brought their Christmas sandwich back for a limited time to celebrate. On 6 July of that year, he made a personal appearance at the Wardour Street branch of Pret – a four-minute walk from the site of the former Marquee Club where, five decades earlier, Holder was making his name with Slade – giving away 100 sandwiches. In 2022, Iceland, a leading frozen food retailer in the UK, employed Holder along with actor Brian Blessed to take part in a campaign that put Christmas on hold due to the World Cup being held in Qatar in November and December. Iceland Foods marketing director Caspar Nelson was to say, 'We've taken the unusual step of silencing the Christmas legend. With the World Cup kicking off on Sunday, we need the nation to be putting their energy into supporting the England and Wales football teams.' Holder was by now, unquestionably, 'the Christmas legend'. To coincide, 'Merry Xmas Everybody' was released by BMG in a 12-inch splatter vinyl version, which was to reach number two in the Official Chart Company's vinyl chart. Slade's relationship with the festive season was further underlined in the UK as 2022 became 2023 when the British Heart Foundation used another of Slade's 1973 chart-toppers, 'Cum On Feel the Noize', in their seasonal TV advert.

But it is 'Merry Xmas Everybody', at the time of writing, that is the reason most people know Slade; one record from a twenty-five-year career that has come to define them. ''Merry Xmas Everybody' has kept Slade on the radio, at least once a year,' says Bob Stanley writing in *Yeah Yeah Yeah: The Story of Modern Pop*, 'and it reminded everyone how much dunderheaded, giddy fun they had been in the first place. If you took a survey tomorrow, Slade could well be the best-loved band in English pop history.'

It's time to explore why Slade, of all their seventies peers, are still so warmly recalled and how, importantly, they are so much more than their ubiquitous Christmas chart smash.

A Once Colossal Presence

Uncouth
Lacking good manners, refinement, or grace.
'He is unwashed, uncouth, and drunk most of the time.'

Yob
British slang
'An aggressive and surly youth, esp a teenager.'

I'm in Bilston, West Midlands, on the afternoon of Bonfire Night, 2017, at The Robin 2, the 700-capacity venue that rose from the ashes of The Robin Hood, a beloved pub on the fringes of Brierley Hill, a suburb of the Black Country that borders the unruly modern monolith to Mammon, the Merry Hill Shopping Centre. Opened in 1985, the retail hub – complete with its own monorail – replaced Merry Hill Farm and the Round Oak steelworks. At The Robin, Jim Lea, the least visible member of Slade, took to the stage of the rammed-to-the-gunwales venue to promote the DVD of his solitary live solo gig that he had performed there in 2002. What strikes you first is the incredible fervency of the audience.

It is clear that I am not like many of those in the room. Eyed, perhaps, with an initial suspicion; an outsider at a family gathering, the stranger in town; a few tentatively speak to me to investigate who this newcomer from the south may be. Having explained who I am and what I'm doing, the universal warmth and embrace of all was immediate and touching, and the message was crystal clear: anyone who wants to spread the word about 'our' band has got to be alright. Later, in 2021, I was a talking head on Channel 5's *Britain's Biggest Hits – The 70s*, and for my discussion on the Slade entries of 1971 to 1974, I was billed as this book's author. Immediately to the wise keepers of the Slade flame, there were certain enquiries as to my identity on social media, mainly along the lines of 'who does he think he is?' and asking if I had been one of the 'magic 500' (the number of die-hard fans who supported Slade in their lean years 1977–1979). I was not one of the 'magic 500', nor would I pretend to be. But many rushed to support me.

It's hard to find anyone who doesn't like at least a fraction of Slade's work. Often seen today as a jokey, blokey cartoon, Slade were, in their way, as revolutionary as T. Rex or Roxy Music in synthesising the past and present for the future in the early seventies. However, instead of the mystical effeteness of a Marc Bolan or Bryan Ferry out front, here was Noddy Holder, an exceptionally loud fellow with huge muttons and a top hat with mirrors on it. Bovver rock at its very best, Slade's work was peerless.

But, Slade are, to use that very 21st-century phrase, 'hidden in plain sight'. While their peers became enormously revered (Bolan, David Bowie), largely forgotten (Sweet, Mud) or disgraced (Gary Glitter), Slade have become, as time passes, something of a mystery. Their once colossal presence in UK culture – seventeen consecutive Top 20 chart hits and six number one singles – has been reduced to a handful of artefacts left in the seventies tomb after the explorers' departure. Among these trinkets are the singer's mirrored top hat; the guitarist's custom-built instrument with the words 'Super Yob' emblazoned on it; and a 45 offering a message of hope and cheer to the entire world, a communication of unity and joy to celebrate the festive season.

And that is about it.

This cartoon outline of the band perpetuates, often happily propagated by their singer, Holder, who has become one of the UK's best-loved personalities. This populist caricature is both a blessing and a curse: the former, as they are remembered far more and with greater affection than their peers; the latter, as they are recalled only as the larger-than-life exaggeration they were to become.

As Bob Stanley notes further, 'Noddy Holder had a voice like John Lennon screaming down the chimney of the QE2; rosy-cheeked bassist Jim Lea looked as if he lived with his mum and bred homing pigeons; Dave Hill on guitar had the most rabbit face in the world; while drummer Don Powell chewed gum and stared into space.' Yet, this cartoon analogy is not entirely without merit – in this 21st-century age of the emoji or Funko plastic figures, pop stars who can be exaggerated and reduced to a sketch are the ones not only most likely to stick in the memory, but also, importantly, translate to a new generation – witness the Freddie Mercury moustache; the Elton John glasses; the Amy Winehouse beehive – add to that Holder's mirrored coachman's hat and Hill's 'metal nun' outfit.

To add to this, in the well-shared, woke homilies of 21st-century Britain, fear of the seventies 'back in the day' and 'things being different then' is, with good reason, acute. Slade have a bitter-supping vulgarity, a blur of grainy, un-PC memories of bovver boys and laddishness, Brut 33, backstreet boozers with their pickled eggs and Big D cardboard peanut displays. Slade are more difficult to carry forward than the long-lasting, genteel middle and upper classness of Pink Floyd or Genesis, or the forces of grown-up darkness of Led Zeppelin or Black Sabbath. Slade seemed uncouth (for example, one of their tracks has a throaty belch in its middle), encapsulating stomping boots, misspelling, and an unruly yobbery that seemed more in common with the football terrace than the common room.

So, and perhaps because of this, the comedic, festive public image of Slade remains strong, as does the potency of their Christmas hit. But beyond that, little. The *Slade In England* site – one of many lovingly detailed and updated by an army of Slade fans – is clear on the reason for the dimly held view of the group:

Slade collectively made some astonishingly bad career decisions along the way, selling their souls in the 'glam' era to the teeny girl magazines, appearing on countless kiddies TV shows broadcast at a time of day when those watching didn't know or care who they were, and the people who they wanted to know of their new single were at work... with that there now is a general public perception that Slade were a bunch of jolly japesters, tinsel clad gurning buffoons with little or no merit as a band.

Tinsel-clad gurning buffoons they were not, but this populist power and memory of Slade keeps the group and its members popping up across the UK media, illustrated in early 2020 when Dave Hill allegedly 'sacked' Don Powell from the version of Slade the two members had put together in 1992. The amount of column inches that this garnered in the UK press showed the residual interest in the band. This was underlined further by the release of *Cum On Feel the Hitz – The Best of Slade*, later that year, which entered the UK charts at number eight, despite it being the fifth hits collection released on behalf of the group. It was the first, however, to be released after the vinyl revival of the 2010s. It was time again to buy the record you'd replaced with a CD.

A Boxing Day headline in 2021 in the *Daily Mirror* screamed, 'Slade planning to reform original line-up to perform for Glastonbury's legends slot.' The item continued, 'Noddy himself has vowed to get the original band back together to storm the iconic Pyramid Stage to take the legends slot – but might have an uphill struggle to reunite the feuding members.' Holder allegedly continued, 'It would be amazing if we could work out our differences. I think we'd probably all have to go in on a coach each. Or we'd all have to have a changing room or caravan each.' Again, it illustrates how delighted the British press were to publish a Slade story. The story was entirely refuted within days, by which time, the group's work had seen an appreciable rise in streaming numbers. All good for business.

* * *

Whatever Happened to Slade?: When the Whole World Went Crazee has taken an age to come together – it's a desire to tell the story as

4

truly, honestly and objectively as possible. Noddy Holder's two autobiographies, next to Don Powell's and Dave Hill's, as well as Chris Charlesworth's long out-of-date and out-of-print 'bible', *Feel the Noize!*, from 1984, and Chris Selby and Ian Edmundson's exemplary 2018 book *The Noize* (revised 2020) are incredible captures of different aspects of the group. If it's warm anecdotes from those that were there, there are the autobiographies; and there is little I can reveal that hasn't been covered in forensic detail in *The Noize*. In 1975, Futura published *The Slade Story* by George Tremlett, a fascinating, sophisticated populist take on the group in a series of cheap music biographies. Like Charlesworth's book a decade later, it captured the group on the verge of something. *Slade in Flame* was just released, and America beckoned. *Feel the Noize!* continued this feeling of expectation as it appeared with 'Run Runaway'. The US, so resistant to the group's appeal, was finally being won over by their charms. Now, all of that is far in the past. There is still a phenomenal story to be told against the backdrop of the hard facts and personal reminisces. This is the first biography written with perspective and long after the band's heyday (and with fresh material and insights).

Whatever Happened to Slade?: When the Whole World Went Crazee sets out to chart the fortunes of a group who frequently appeared out of step with the time they were in and their position in the music industry in the seventies. 'They were a proper geezer's band, but they dressed like the Diddymen, didn't they?' Noel Gallagher said in 1999. It will get behind this often unintentionally hilarious facade and tell the tale of a hard-grafting, genuinely working-class, provincial band that enjoyed mass popularity and widespread acclaim in the first half of the seventies, whose desire to break America was so strong that it cost them their UK career; and their influential afterlife. Drawing on hours of new interviews and meticulous research, *Whatever Happened to Slade?: When the Whole World Went Crazee* chronicles a different time, of dancehalls and working men's clubs, places to play, three TV channels, three-day weeks, live scenes, community, class and camaraderie amid the brutality of the architecture, politics and inequality of seventies Britain.

PART ONE
BEGINNINGS

CHAPTER 1

Beginnings

The Black Country is a vast expanse of urban and suburban land in the UK Midlands that is today known mostly for being a spiralling maze of motorway, bridges and junctions; a place of arrivals and departures, but most often, passing travel. The fact that it is often the midway point of country-traversing journeys leads to a sense that it is overlooked. A great deal of it seems to be under a motorway flyover. This liminal space is, in fact, an area of great variation and splendour. North and west of Birmingham, the area incorporates south Staffordshire and east Worcestershire. Fringed by areas of outstanding natural beauty, its two major conurbations are Wolverhampton and Walsall, separated since 1968 by the M6 motorway. Walsall is at the region's epicentre, a settlement that grew prosperous from the leather industry, while Wolverhampton is a thriving city that burgeoned in the Industrial Revolution with steelworking and coal mining.

It was Elihu Burritt, Abraham Lincoln's United States Consul in Birmingham, who popularised the idiom 'the Black Country' in his book *Walks in the Black Country and its Green Border-land*, published in 1869. The phrase had been in use for several years – to reference where the coal seam met the surface. Burritt stated that the region was, 'black by day and red by night' and that it 'cannot be matched, for vast and varied production, by any other space of equal radius on the surface of the globe'. The name stuck. Viewed as one of the Industrial Revolution's supremely important bases, the area was principal in its pioneering use of coke smelting in iron production, glass-making and the epicentre of the canal system, England's major transport artery before the advent of the railways.

It has been said that Mordor, in J. R. R. Tolkien's *The Lord of the Rings* took its inspiration from the area, with 'Mor-Dor' in the novel's Sindarin language meaning 'black land'. A lot of the music that originates from this and the wider area could be described as intense: Rob Halford from Judas Priest was a Walsall son; Robert Plant, born in West Bromwich; Roy Wood from Kitts Green; Jeff Lynne from Erdington; Kevin Rowland from Wednesfield; the Campbell Brothers from Birmingham; even Martin Degville from Sigue Sigue Sputnik; and, given that the music – heavy metal – they became synonymous with and possibly invented, Black Sabbath, whose sound reflected the industry of the area. And as with every thriving industrial hub, ale and entertainment was needed, to give thirsty workers respite in evenings and at weekends. The area's blurring into Birmingham meant there was a huge circuit to fill. Each suburb had a separate identity and venues in which to play.

There was a post-war music-hall joke about Wolverhampton, that Jim Lea's brother, Frank, a man with deep connections to the band, shared in 2023. It was said that when the Germans were bombing everywhere, they flattened Coventry. Then they went to Birmingham because of the industry, 'but when they got to Wolverhampton, they never did anything to it because they thought it had already been done, and when they did bomb it, they caused five pounds worth of damage'. This was the area where Slade were to have and maintain their foundations, and no matter how far they were to travel, their roots remained here. The very fact that only two of the group left the Black Country permanently speaks volumes: the loyalty, the sense of place and relationship with the area. This very provinciality would act as a blessing and a curse: it offered them an unparalleled closeness to their fanbase, with a loyalty that lasts to this day; but also, a distance to the London-based music industry – outsiders on a smash-and-grab raid.

* * *

The four members of Slade grew up in the immediate post-Second World War era, with its considerable aftershocks of poverty and ration books. Donald George Powell is the backbone of the group, and the first member of the future Slade to join The Vendors. The rest of the band was to coalesce around him. Powell was born on Chapel Street, Bilston, on 10 September 1946, to steelworker Walter (Wally) and his wife Dora, who worked at Woden Transformers on Moxley Road. One of five children, Powell had an elder sister, Carol, and a younger brother, Derek, and finally in 1953, Marilyn (who Powell called 'Mash'). A younger sister, Christine, died in babyhood. Like many of Walter Powell's generation, he fought in the war (as a Desert Rat), and like many who returned, refused to accept his medals because of the deep trauma the war had caused.

In 1957, Don Powell joined the local Boy Scouts, and it was here that he learned to play the drums, fashioning sticks from the base of an artificial Christmas tree. 'I painstakingly with my boy scout's pen knife carved them out,' Powell says. 'The first time I hit a drum, they broke. Talk about disappointment, I'd spent months doing these things. I was almost crying.' Powell attended Etheridge Secondary Modern School, where he met his future best friend, Graham Swinnerton. Pretty soon, the pair were inseparable. Hardly enamoured with academia, Powell flourished in athletics and boxing, winning the school's prize for the 100-yard dash. He was a member of the Bilston Athletics Club. 'My big ambition as a kid was to run in the Olympics, nothing else got in the way,' Powell told writer Mark Blake. 'I trained solidly seven days a week, really going for it. Then it all changed. Then girls got on my mind, and everything went out the window.'

A severe ear infection put paid to his boxing career: he fought at middleweight level. Although not academic, Powell was entranced by reading: 'Bilston had a really good library. I used to go there every day to do my homework,' Powell says. 'I knew having a brother and two sisters, there'd be no peace at home. When I finished college, I used to go and sit in there for a couple of hours and do my homework because of the peace and quiet.'

Powell went to Wednesbury Technical College, to study metallurgy at the recommendation of his father, and spent eighteen months on day release at a foundry, British Insulated Callender's Cables (BICC). 'Metallurgy fascinated me, and nothing could take my attention off work,' he told biographer George Tremlett in 1974. 'Then, I spent six months working on the analysis of brass, iron and steel, wearing a white coat every day, testing metals in a laboratory. It was a very responsible job, really, and I think I would probably have made a career of it if I hadn't become a musician – it's still something I could go back to if I ever wanted to.'

Powell was never to return to the laboratory, the boxing ring or the racetrack, but his strength of character redefined the role of the strong silent type and ensured the group would be able to withstand calamity.

* * *

Born in Flete House, Hobleton, Devon, on 4 April 1946, David John Hill moved with his parents to Penn on the outskirts of Wolverhampton when he was a year old. His father Jack, who was a mechanic, met his mother, Dorothy, while working in munitions factories during the war. He had already been married and she had had a child out of wedlock. Because of the scandal that surrounded such a union, the couple relocated to Devon.

Growing up in Rindleford Avenue on the Warstones Estate in Penn, Hill attended Springdale Junior School on Warstones Drive and then Highfields Secondary School on Boundary Way, and was, by all accounts, what used to be referred to as a 'handful'. Partly, this was due to Dorothy's health. At a time when mental illness was an enormous stigma, she would spend time away at hospital leaving Jack to look after him and his younger sister Carol. 'I was quite shy at school,' Hill told Mark Blake:

> I didn't have the sort of hair you could get a Cliff Richard or Tony Curtis. I was a bit of an oddity. My ears have always been slightly large, so when you had short hair, there was ribbing. I went through stuff at school, fancying someone and they don't want to go out with you. I was on other side of the playground, and my sister said I was a bit of a loner. It's hard for people to believe I was shy, but I lacked confidence.

Salvation came for Hill in his mastering of a musical instrument. 'I learned to play guitar when I was 13 or 14,' Hill told the *Birmingham Mail*. 'I had found an instrument which I had fallen in love with. It was from the Kays Catalogue and came in a cardboard box. I played it upside down because I was left-handed. The Beatles hadn't made it and so there were no left-handed guitars.'

At school, he learned to play guitar thanks to biology teacher Brian Close, who taught Hill to play right-handed. 'I was brought up on Chuck Berry and Buddy Holly and later The Shadows, certainly the early rock'n'roll of Little Richard,' Hill was to say. His first local group was The Shamrocks, which developed into The Young Ones, named after the Tepper/Bennett-written Cliff Richard hit from January 1962. However, as pop music was not a serious career option in the early sixties, Hill took a job as an office junior at Tarmac's head office in Ettingshall, turning up on his Velocette motorcycle. With Brian Maclaghlan, Tony Bate, John Bradford, Keith Evans and Tony Cater, The Young Ones became Brad Ford and the Sundowners.

'I was thinking of a life not a career,' Hill said to Mark Blake. 'I asked Mum and Dad the question – sending my sister out of the room – saying I really wanted to go professional. They were forward-thinking parents. Mum was slightly cautious because she'd got me the job at Tarmac and then Dad said, keep the night school on and do it. It was almost like, put my fist in the air – yes! Which means I can grow my hair; cover my dodgy ears and look like George Harrison with the moptop. It changed my life. I went on the road with Don in The Vendors. Never mind playing, which was fantastic, it was the freedom of doing something you really want to do.'

Dave Hill would for many years be talismanic for Slade. As Rob Chapman states in his 2002 essay on the group, 'In the early seventies there was a Dave Hill in every town. For every suburban Bowie-ite, following their master through every image change, or Rod Stewart lookalike adorned in silk scarves and rooster barnet, there was always that goofy grinning kid with the-not-quite-right hair, or clothes, or manner, or anything.' Dave Hill would play an enormous part in the mythology of Slade.

* * *

Neville John Holder was born at 31½ Newhall Street, in Caldmore, Walsall, on 15 June 1946, the only child of Jack and Leah Holder. Jack had a window cleaning business and Leah worked part-time as a school cleaner. Named after Neville Chamberlain, Holder grew up living in a modest post-war semi on Gurney Road, at the heart of Beechdale Estate, two and a half miles north of Walsall city centre.

'When I was growing up all that area was green belt,' Holder told the *Express and Star* in October 2021:

> We moved there in 1953 when I was seven. At the time, the place was called Gypsy Lane Estate because there was a traditional gypsy encampment there, with families living in the traditional caravans. There were only about four or five roads built there at the time. It was a new thing in Walsall for these new estates to be built to take the populations of places like Caldmore where the properties had got old, mouldy, and damp. Across the road from where my mum and dad lived was the power station and all that area was absolutely beautiful countryside. We spent all our school holidays fishing at the lakes near the power station and Reedswood Park.

Although Holder was 'born rowdy' as he claimed, and made his debut on stage during the 'free and easy' section of the night at Walsall Labour Club at the age of 7, singing Frankie Laine's 'I Believe', he was also a hardworking, conscientious pupil. 'I loved school,' Holder told the *TES* in 2011. 'I had a great time at my infant and junior schools and passed my 11-plus, so for a year, I went to a grammar school.'

In 1946, Clement Atlee's Labour government began trialling the Comprehensive system, and by 1958 Elmore Green High School in Bloxwich became the T. P. Riley Community School. Holder was enthralled and a good pupil. 'History was my favourite,' Holder said in 2008. 'The one teacher who stood out for me was my history teacher [Mr Dickenson], an ex-army bloke who didn't stand for any messing, but he got us through our exams and made the subject interesting.' According to Holder, his nickname came at this age as well, as his school friend, John Robbins, called him it as he was always nodding off to sleep. It stuck.

Although like many of his peers he saw and loved Bill Haley and his Comets performing 'Rock Around the Clock', it was Little Richard singing 'The Girl Can't Help It' in 1957 that was to change Holder's world. Hearing Richard on record was one thing but seeing him on screen performing it in glorious DeLuxe Colour in Frank Tashlin's influential film of the same name was quite another. The 12-year-old Holder went to the Savoy Cinema on Town End Bank in Walsall, and like many in that 2,169-seater theatre that day and in similar movie houses around the country, life was never going to be the same.

Holder got his guitar as a Christmas present, and Leah knew Freddie Degville (unrelated to Beechdale Estate resident Martin Degville), a local jazz guitarist, who gave Holder his first lessons. Holder was to join the classic school band, The Rockin' Phantoms, with his friend Phil Burnell on guitar, Kenny Holland on bass and Mick Aulton on drums. It was clear that Holder had boundless stagecraft, even at this early age. Slade biographer and friend, Chris Charlesworth, noted that he was 'influenced as much by Al Jolson as he was by Little Richard'. 'My dad was a great singer and never had any aspirations to be pro, and he did the clubs but couldn't and wouldn't in that era do it professionally,' Holder said in 2019. 'You didn't if you were a window cleaner from Walsall. But he and my mum saw that I loved it.'

Holder was determined he wanted to make a go of his dream of being in a band – 'I'd already sussed out at the age of 13 or 14 that I wanted to be in the group business. Nothing else would satisfy me. I knew I had to put my foot down and say I'm leaving school,' he told Bob Houston for the *Sladest* album in 1973. 'My mum and dad didn't put the mockers on me working in clubs,' he later recalled. 'It was sad for my dad, as he had to go back to the school and do the windows and get bollocked because he had let me leave.' Holder had six O-levels, which meant that a potentially lucrative career could have beckoned.

Unlike his father, Jack, Holder was able to begin his career professionally and his professionalism would be the glue that held Slade together for twenty-five years.

* * *

Born on 14 June 1949, James Whild Lea was the final piece of The 'NBetweens jigsaw. Younger than Hill, Holder and Powell, Lea was later described by Slade's early PR Keith Altham as bearing the 'pained expression of a highly-strung young man being driven to the edge of a nervous breakdown', by the others. The three-year difference meant that Lea would at times be seen as both as the baby, but most importantly the precocious wunderkind, of the band. He was born above the The Melbourne Arms pub in Snow Hill, Wolverhampton. As a young infant, he moved to the village of Bilbrook, four and a half miles north-west of Wolverhampton city centre. Lea was one of four: elder brother Ray, Jim, then Frank and John. His parents, Frank – Chief Inspector in the engineering industry, who himself was a good singer, and Edna – who worked at Beatties department store, whose father was First Violin in the orchestra at the Hippodrome in Wolverhampton – encouraged Jim to play the violin and his grandmother, known as 'Grom', bought him one.

Initially at their house in Cherry Tree Lane, Bilbrook, the children had to share the bedroom. 'At one time, all four of us slept in the same room in bunk beds,' says brother Frank. 'Jim and me would share a bed. You know boys at that age, I used to say "Mum, can I sleep in the shallow end tonight?" There was a permanent rainbow over the bed.'

There was little question of Jim Lea's musical ability – learning violin initially, Lea passed his initial exam with first-class honours at the National College of Music in London on 19 June 1961, at the age of 12 years and 5 days old, and soon was to take a place with the Staffordshire Youth Orchestra. But it was pop music that completely engulfed the young Lea. Hearing 'Apache' by The Shadows was to change his life, and being that bit younger than his other future bandmates, at the key moment when age difference is so very important, Lea, having few outside interests, had more time to get completely lost in music. 'I was always very popular at school,' Jim Lea told the *Birmingham Post* in 2000. 'I was the kind of kid who got on with everybody. I wasn't withdrawn, I was just shy. But there was a whole world going on within me.' Buying his first guitar at the age of 12, he'd played in archetypal school band Nick and The

Axe Men who later became The Stalkers, realising that his nimble fingers from violin playing would be well suited to the bass guitar – moreover, few people wanted to be bass guitarists, opting for the flashier vocalist or guitarist role.

Lea was to remain the group's odd one out, but was a more than capable writer and arranger – the Slade sound as we know it would not be in place were it not for Lea. In a group with a Lennon and two Ringos, Lea provided not only the McCartney but the Harrison figure also.

CHAPTER 2

'NBetween Days

It is a labyrinthine journey that takes us to Slade with all the usual twists and turns of any beat scene beginning. Although it can be said that Slade began with Don Powell, it was actually Noddy Holder and Dave Hill who were out of the traps playing live first. Holder's group, The Rockin' Phantoms, used to rehearse in his parents' kitchen and made their live debut at Saint Chad's Youth Club, Bloxwich, on Monday 10 September 1962. The bug quickly bit Holder. They would then pick up paying shows at youth clubs and weddings.

The *Wolverhampton Chronicle* was to note:

> The Phantoms comprise Noddy Holder (17), lead; Phillip
> Burnell (18), rhythm; Peter Bickley (bass); Mike Alton (17),
> drums; and John E. Blue – John Cooper (17), vocalist. Their
> sound is terrific, and showmanship well above the average
> standard. The group started about 12 months ago, when the
> members brought their guitars to school. All pupils of the T. P.
> Riley Comprehensive School, Bloxwich, they decided to form
> their own combo, and have been going great guns ever since.

'A great guns beat combo' needed advertising, and a makeshift business card was made, giving Holder's parents' address, saying 'Dances, Concerts, Parties – The Phantoms, "Kings Of Rhythm".'

After a tentative show with The Young Ones at the Victory Club in Lower Penn, Dave Hill made his full live debut with the Sundowners, playing at Wednesbury Town Hall on Monday 29 October 1962. Singer John Bradford would go by the name 'Brad Ford', which led to the group being billed as Brad Ford and the Sundowners, or occasionally Devon Ford and the Sundowners.

Both Hill and Holder had racked up gigs into double figures before Don Powell took to the stage as the drummer in The Vendors. The group had been founded by singer and guitarist John Howells and guitarist Mick Marson and took their name from the first song they learned to play, the Moisés Simons-written Cuban standard 'The Peanut Vendor'. They then worked their way – like so many other bands of their era – through The Shadows songbook. Introduced by a mutual friend, Dennis Horton, Powell joined Howells and Marson in early 1963, as they had heard he had access to a drum kit. Soon Dave 'Cass' Jones had joined on bass. Rehearsing at Howells's parents' guest house, they had built up a sufficient repertoire to take to the stage on 2 March 1963, when the group played Shaw's Social Club on Waterglade Lane in Bilston.

Johnny Shane – who had led his band, The Cadillacs – joined on guitar when The Vendors were Thursday night regulars at Willenhall's St Giles' Youth Club, often in payment for being able to rehearse there. Becoming something of a base for the group, Powell recalls seeing The Rockin' Phantoms at St Giles, one of the first times he had seen Noddy Holder in action. With local agent Chalkie White, who Powell had met around Wolverhampton, looking after their bookings, The Vendors began to work on the circuit. 'He [Chalkie] wasn't in the business,' Powell told Mark Blake. 'He just wanted a sideline, he had a bit of a mouth on him so could go round the pubs and get us gigs.'

In 1963, Beatlemania had truly broken out in the UK, and pop bands were in greater demand than ever. The Vendors won a competition at St Giles' to support The Hollies at nearby Willenhall Baths that November, where larger dances were held a couple of times a year. It offered Powell a chance to meet Bobby Elliott, The Hollies' drummer, who would become one of Powell's great influences, and to see a band on the verge of breaking into the big time, with two Top 30 singles and their new single, 'Stay', heading for the Top 10.

With Johnny Shane's departure in November, a need to untether John Howells from his instrument, Chalkie White told the band they needed a proper guitarist. Dave Hill, since the Sundowners split in May 1963, had been playing with John Bradford in Big Roll 7, a showbiz covers band featuring Mac Wooley on drums. Being younger than the other members, Hill felt increasingly out of place. White clocked Dave Hill and recommended him to Johnny Howells.

On 22 November 1963, before The Vendors were about to take the stage at Beacon Youth Club, on the New Invention housing estate in Willenhall, Powell was at John Howells's home when he noticed Howell's father, Ted, looking devastated. 'I asked, "Are you OK?",' Powell says. 'He said, "Some bastard's shot Kennedy." I never took any notice at the time, my interest has become phenomenal.' It was around this time that Dave Hill joined The Vendors.

As New Year 1964 dawned, at the Three Men In A Boat pub opposite future singer Noddy Holder's house in Bloxwich, Don Powell and Dave Hill began playing together in a new line-up of The Vendors – Marson, Howells, Jones, Powell and Hill. 'I used to come out of Tarmac dressed in a suit,' Hill said in 2021. 'Then this J2 van comes round to pick me up to take me to a show, and I've got my change of costume in there. So, I've suddenly become Superman. I've suddenly become an extrovert.'

As their local popularity and confidence grew, The Vendors went into Domino Sound Studio in Albrighton, a studio favoured by local groups, to record. Owned by Andy McLachlan, the bassist with The Tremors, the group recorded the quaint-in-era Hill-Howells original 'Don't Leave Me Now', and capable takes on The Platters' 'Twilight Time', Buddy Holly's 'Take Your Time' and The Shadows' 'Peace Pipe'. The tracks highlight Hill and Powell's skills, and as Howells was to say, 'the complexity of arrangement... prevented many other bands from attempting this kind of material. From now on, that complexity would work in our favour.'

On 8 November 1964, at the Ship & Rainbow, Wolverhampton, The Vendors played their first show with their new name of The

'NBetweens, something that sounded all together more beaty for the new world of Beatlemania. The Ship & Rainbow had a large upstairs room and played host to many upcoming bands from the area.

By that December, The 'NBetweens had become the go-to group for providing support when bigger local bands and those further afield came to the region. In that month alone, they played with Spencer Davis, The Moody Blues, Zoot Money and Alexis Korner. 'We could play for a month around that particular area and not go back to the same place,' Powell says. 'Be it only pubs and clubs, but that's what it was like in those days. A phenomenal number of gigs there. Unbelievable.'

The Vendors signed to Wolverhampton's The Astra Agency, founded in 1963 by agents and promoters Len Rowe and Stan and Peter Fielding. With offices in Princes Street, Wolverhampton, they became the foremost booking agents in the West Midlands. The agency had set up the R&B club at the Ship & Rainbow the following year. Maurice Jones began to manage the group, moonlighting from working at John Thompson engineering works in Bilston.

* * *

By mid-1964, Noddy Holder's group, The Rockin' Phantoms, had become The Memphis Cut-Outs, and continued playing halls, youth clubs and working men's clubs. After accruing enough money from his short day-job stint as a car parts salesman, Holder bought a semi-acoustic Hofner and an amp. However, things were quickly to turn up a notch for the Cut-Outs when they were approached by Steve Davies, known professionally as Steve Brett, whose original backing band, The Mavericks, had recently disbanded.

Brett was a charismatic frontman, had been on TV, and was well regarded on the Midland scene, with his musical blend of country, R&B and soul. Represented too by The Astra Agency, The Mavericks boasted a full gig list and a better class of venue than the Cut-Outs had been used to. They went from playing the Jubilee Hall in Brewood in August 1964 to supporting Johnny Kidd & the Pirates at the Birmingham Show, and then the Civic in Wolverhampton with all the biggest groups of the area. Before Brett took to the stage, the Cut-Outs repertoire would warm the audience up, with, as Holder described, a 'good time party set', before Brett would appear for something a little easier and more countrified.

Brett's popularity was sufficient to secure a deal with Columbia Records, with three singles all recorded at Hollick & Taylor (Grosvenor Road) Studios in Handsworth. 'Wishing'/'Anything That's Part of You', 'Sad, Lonely and Blue'/'Candy', and 'Chains on My Heart'/'Sugar Shack' were all released in 1965 in January, May and September. All the A-sides were written by Brett alone and were not without merit – 'Wishing' could almost be a dry run for The Velvet Underground; 'Sad, Lonely and Blue' is a sprightly romp; 'Chains on My Heart' was lachrymose balladry. However, his take on Jimmy Gilmer and the Fireballs' 'Sugar Shack' showed the groove in The Mavericks, with Phil Burnell and Noddy Holder's guitars interlocking. As Brett had a mutual connection with Joe Meek, the group also ventured for a session at the mercurial producer's studio in his flat on London's Holloway Road. 'Chains on My Heart' sounds like a Meek production as it stands. The bathroom and hallway sessions remain unreleased.

*   *   *

The 'NBetweens had two shots at recording at Pye Studios in 1965, after being offered a recording contract for Barclay Records by session drummer Bobby Graham. Graham was one of the crack team of British players, who'd been on numerous number ones. He had been in The Outlaws, the conglomerate of musicians that included Chas Hodges and Ritchie Blackmore, who'd played extensively with Joe Meek. The 'NBetweens played an audition at Le Metro club in Birmingham. On 17 July, the group – Johnny Howells on vocals, Mick Marson on guitar, Dave 'Cass' Jones on bass and Hill and Powell – assembled at Pye Studios in Great Cumberland Place, just north of Marble Arch. The building was the third of the 'big three' studios (the others being EMI's facility at Abbey Road, St John's Wood, and Decca's at Broadhurst Gardens, West Hampstead). The group assembled in Studio Two, the smaller of the two rooms, the same place where The Kinks had recorded 'All Day and All of the Night' and 'Tired of Waiting'.

The initial recordings, 'Can Your Monkey Do the Dog', 'Respectable' (a rather fine version of The Isley Brothers' 1959 single), 'I Wish You Would' and 'Ooh Poo Pa Doo' were scrapped, yet an acetate of 'Ooh Poo Pa Doo' surfaced and a cassette with all four tracks on it finally appeared on *The Genesis of Slade* CD in 2000. Graham recalled the group in early October 1965, to record a further four songs that ultimately did get released in France in December of that year – 'Feel So Fine', 'Take a Heart', 'Little Nightingale' and 'You Don't Believe Me' – these tracks were to turn up on an ultra-rare EP on Barclay Records that was released in France only.

Noddy Holder played eight weeks in Cologne and Frankfurt in late 1965 with Steve Brett and the Mavericks, and all his experience came to bear: 'I was known around the Midlands for doing all sorts,' he told Mark Blake. 'I could sing standards, rock'n'roll, soul, blues and wanted to be all things to all men.' Holder was also accomplished in extra-curricular activities: it was a well-documented time of some debauchery, where Holder gained his drinking legs and also his ability to defecate on a sheet of glass over a bath with a fetish-loving club owner underneath for a week's wages.

'Steve Brett would do Elvis, Jim Reeves and George Jones, stuff I wasn't acquainted with at that time. We did the American bases in Germany, and they loved it,' Holder told Blake. 'Hamburg, Cologne. I was singing rock'n'roll and soul, James Brown and Sam & Dave. But I then later discovered the stuff Steve been bringing to us was bloody good. You forget as a young kid how good that is.'

Holder had a chance meeting on the ferry across to Germany with Don Powell and Dave Hill, who were going over to play in Dortmund with The 'NBetweens. As the group were one of the principal professional rivals to The Mavericks on the scene, a respectful distance had been kept. Holder and Powell were on nodding terms, but little else. As Holder wrote in his autobiography, he'd spotted Hill around and about, as he 'used to pose around Wolverhampton in a cloak, looking like a Shakespearian actor'. On the ferry, they had a few drinks together and Powell and Hill talked with Holder about the possibility of joining them, as they felt, in the wake of The

Beatles, the days of bands with a named frontman were over. But, for the time being, The 'NBetweens singer Johnny Howells was still very much at the helm. Holder was becoming disenchanted with The Mavericks, as well, but if he joined The 'NBetweens, Holder would have again been second fiddle, so he declined the offer.

By Christmas 1965, Holder had left Steve Brett and the Mavericks, and spent the first months of 1966 doing some roadying for his friend Robert Plant. 'I used to ferry him around the Wolverhampton scene in my dad's window-cleaning van when he was in The Tennessee Teens,' Holder told *The Guardian* in 2015. In early 1966, too, Holder met up with Don Powell and Dave Hill in Wolverhampton. At Beatties department store's coffee shop, they asked Holder if he would be interested in joining the group. This time, he was.

CHAPTER 3

Bloodnok's Rock'n'Roll Call

W here had Jim Lea been during all this? While Hill, Holder and Powell were earning their spurs, the answer was simple – Lea had been at school and playing in his hobby bands Nick and The Axe Men and The Stalkers. Although shy, Lea was confident in his ability and realised that others in his orchestra were keener on Rachmaninov than The Rolling Stones. Lea was aware of The 'NBetweens around town and was greatly enamoured by Johnny Howells's performances. 'I used to go and watch The 'NBetweens and they were phenomenal,' Jim Lea said in 2022. 'I wasn't fully grown, and I looked like a child. I always used to stand in front of the stage and watch the band and I didn't realise that I was terrifying them. They thought I was some sort of Child of the Damned or something.'

After a busy start to the year of gigs, bassist Dave 'Cass' Jones left The 'NBetweens in early 1966 to go into the wholesale fruit business, and Hill and Powell thought this could be an opportune moment to shake up the group. Perhaps they could even stage something of a coup and move the group in a more Beatles and Stones direction than the blues, creating a four-piece, without Mick Marson and Howells. On Thursday 27 and Friday 28 January 1966, the group took out an advert in the *Express and Star* for a new bass player; on Saturday 12 February 1966, at the Blue Flame Club, auditions for the new bassist were held. The secretary at Astra, Carole Williams, sat in the hall taking down all the details of those auditioning.

Young Jim Lea responded to the advert and turned up at the Blue Flame on a bus from Bilbrook with his bass in a polythene bag. He was the final player to be auditioned. Although he was 16, it was clear to Powell and Hill that Lea's musical ability was second to none. 'There was a lot of aggression in me,' Lea told the *Birmingham Mail* in 2000. 'But psychological paradoxes are usually at the centre of everything. I was auditioning for a band, but I played bass because I didn't want to be noticed too much.' And play bass he could, a little like John Entwistle from The Who, one of his heroes. Despite his rawness and his youth, he certainly had something.

'A guy looking like a blond Mick Jagger was playing, singing 'My Girl'. It sounded fantastic. Unbeknown to me, they told him he'd got the job,' Lea said to the *Lancashire Post* in 2018. 'But then I walked up there. Don asked, "is there anybody else out there?" He was told, "There's a little kid with a bass as big as him in a polythene bag." They agreed to get me up, let me play, then send me home. They didn't reckon with what they were going to get.' The band ran through 'See Saw' by Don Covay and Otis Redding's 'Mr Pitiful'. Powell and Hill were impressed with the fact Lea could play violin; when Lea said he didn't play the cello, Powell quipped, 'is that because the spike would stick in your neck?' The ice was broken.

Although Holder had tentatively agreed to join Hill and Powell, the day after Lea's audition, Holder placed an ad in the *Express and Star* looking for vocal work. Holder had wished to be sole vocalist, not back-up to Howells, as he was in the same position as he had been with Steve Brett. 'Nod wasn't as loud and raucous as he became, but he still reminded me of John Lennon,' Don Powell says. But the promise of change was in the air, and Holder would replace Mick Marson when he decided to move on.

Just under a month later, on 3 March, Jim Lea was asked to join the band. The key question was if Lea had a girlfriend. He hadn't at this point, although he was smitten with Louise Ganner at his school. Hill was a firm believer that girlfriends get in the way of the progress of a band. Lea was in. The four players who were to become

Slade enjoyed a covert four-piece session together. 'The day that Dave, Don and Noddy came over to my house and asked me to join the new group was an exciting day for me,' Lea told *The 'NBetween Times* site. 'We went straight from Codsall over to the Three Men In A Boat and performed together. It was just round from Noddy's house. That first session definitely gelled together from the very first beat. It was great.' The writing was on the wall for Marson and Howells, as a new group was coalescing without them.

When his opportunity came to join The 'NBetweens, all those close to Jim Lea were shocked: 'The Rolling Stones were on the news,' younger brother Frank Lea says, 'because they'd pulled up in the van and took a piss up a wall of a petrol station and it made headlines. So, when James walked out of school to join a band, it was a big deal, because he was always near the top of the class and the musician playing with the teachers. He was the big guiding light you know. My mum was very disappointed.' Jim Lea expanded on this at the Wolverhampton Art Gallery in 2022: 'I walked down the driveway of Codsall School. No pupils were allowed to walk down that drive, you had to go down this little sort of path. But I walked down it on my own. I just thought, "I'm off to join the circus."'

Dave Hill's idea for two lead guitars blurring the convention of lead and rhythm, which had been the norm for so long in beat music, could be realised, especially with a bassist with the musical skills of Lea. As Lea was noticeably younger than the others, Powell and Hill used to call him Little Plum because he had a red nose, or Bloodnok, Peter Sellers' character in *The Goon Show*. 'I found out later they thought I looked like a puppet because I'd got rosy cheeks,' Lea said in 1984. 'I was only 15. Pimply and was just totally oddball to everyone else that came to the audition.' After a few shows with Lea on bass, Mick Marson's departure was announced on 24 March. Holder then joined the band.

'I grew up in the 1950s with rock'n'roll,' Holder told Mark Blake. 'That was what I brought to the band – the rock'n'roll, the black music. Little Richard my upbringing. When I joined them, they were basically a blues band. I was the last guy to come in, they already got Jim. I think Dave and Don wanted to open up a bit and stretch their legs a bit further than just playing 12-bar blues.'

'Saturday Night Dancing' was the name of the event where The 'NBetweens with Lea and Holder made their debut on 19 March 1966 at Walsall Town Hall. For four shillings, the programme also included a buffet and the 'ever-popular Morgan Fayne Soul Band'. A show the group supposedly played at Walsall Town Hall on 1 April 1966, has gone down in Sladelore as the date when they first came together, prompting Holder's thoroughly showman-like response, 'it was April Fool's Day and we've been playing the fool ever since'. However, the band were on stage at Newcastle's Atlantic Ballroom that night. They devised a way, as Holder had done with the Cut-Outs and Steve Brett, to play as a four-piece first, and then Johnny Howells would come on and sing the bluesier numbers. However, this arrangement wasn't to last. Howells decided to leave the group he had founded to take a more blues-oriented path. The news was made public in May 1966, and he played his final show with them at the Locarno Ballroom in Swindon on 25 June, honouring the bookings that had been agreed. The night after, at the Silver Blades Ice Rink on Pershore Street, Birmingham, the four-piece line-up that became Slade played together in public for the first time.

Like The Beatles (a group with whom Slade would frequently be compared) losing Pete Best, at grassroots level around Wolverhampton, there was some consternation at what had happened to 'their' group. For many, Howells, with his characteristic voice and large frame to match his personality, WAS the band. While Astra got further bookings for the new group, in July 1966, The 'NBetweens played a week at the Star Palast in the Gaarden district of Kiel in Germany. The club had opened in 1964, and played host to many of the leading names in the business at this point. Although it was just a week (and Powell, Hill and Holder had already played there with their old bands), The 'NBetweens could say they'd put in their time in Germany.

* * *

Fate has often intervened, good and bad, in Slade's story.

On Monday 29 August 1966 (ironically, the day The Beatles played their last ever concert at San Francisco's Candlestick Park), The

'NBetweens got a show performing with Crispian St Peters at the Tiles Club at 78/89 Oxford Street, London. Opened that February as 'the underground city for the new generation', the venue was adjacent to a shopping arcade with book and record shops and boutiques. Crispian St Peters, born Robin Smith, had recently enjoyed a Top 3 hit with 'You Were on My Mind', and was a moderately hot ticket, a good performer for The 'NBetweens to be billed with. 'Members of the youth club back home got a coach trip to see us,' Don Powell recalls. 'When we came on, they were all shouting.'

Like many events in the group's career, a degree of happenstance brought them in touch with some of music's most quicksilver figures. None more so than the mercurial US record producer, impresario and scenester, Kim Fowley, who just happened to be in that night looking for some hip young UK talent to promote. 'Kim Fowley's in the audience thinking "what's going on here?"', Powell said, noting the response of the youth club.

Fowley came up to The 'NBetweens after their performance and said, 'YOU GUYS PROJECT' and stated that he could make them stars. 'He believed in us so much,' Powell says. With his eccentric demeanour and broad American accent, it was like a scene from a film. Fowley had made a name for himself either co-writing, arranging, or producing a string of novelty hits such as 'Alley-Oop' by the Hollywood Argyles and 'Nut Rocker' by B. Bumble and the Stingers. He was also notorious for releasing the single 'The Trip', delivered in, as pop culture historian and writer Jon Savage says, his 'customary hoarse style'.

Fowley's charisma and already considerable track record garnered the band a deal with Columbia Records. Founded in the UK in 1925 as an offshoot of its US parent company, it was a prestigious imprint of EMI, merged with the company in 1931. It was known to all the band as being the label that Cliff Richard and The Shadows released their records on. Holder, of course, was no stranger to the label, as they had released the Steve Brett and the Mavericks tracks. And so, in autumn 1966, The 'NBetweens recorded six tracks with Fowley at Regent Sound on Denmark Street, London's Tin Pan Alley.

Regent Sound was the fabled studio where The Rolling Stones had recorded their early albums instead of Decca's main studios at Broadhurst Gardens. 'You Better Run', a cover of The Young Rascals' US Top 20 hit, produced by Fowley, was chosen as the A-side. Written by Eddie Brigati and Felix Cavaliere, the song was a popular beat cover at the time – borne out by the fact that Robert Plant's outfit, Listen, released a cover version of the same record a week before The 'NBetweens on CBS.

The 'NBetweens' version of 'You Better Run' was backed with the group and Fowley-penned 'Evil Witchman', a swaggering studio romp with Holder in full pleading mode, a riff on The Artwoods' 'I Take What I Want'. Four other tracks were recorded during these sessions – a cover of Otis Redding's 'Security'; a strong take on 'Hold Tight', the Dave Dee, Dozy, Beaky, Mick & Tich hit written by Ken Howard and Alan Blaikley; the supremely zany, in-era self-penned (with Fowley) 'Ugly Girl', concluding with Fowley drawling, 'buy our next record, it's ever groovier than this one.' Finally, 'Need' was a high-powered two minutes of garage. All in all, it was an extremely respectable, credible session. There have been a lot worse ways to commence a career.

'You Better Run' came out on Columbia Records (DB 8080) on 2 December 1966, and, in Wolverhampton, it became a huge local hit, beating Listen's version and giving The 'NBetweens their first number one – albeit merely in the West Midlands, keeping the national chart-topper, Tom Jones's 'Green, Green Grass of Home' off the summit. 'Maurice [Jones] sent me out with Nod and Dave to take posters to record shops in the Midlands. They were supposed to go in and talk the talk, but they stayed in the van and sent the girl in,' Astra's Carole Williams was to say.

That was the sum total of The 'NBetweens dalliance with Kim Fowley. The next group to receive the Fowley touch were more out-of-town scensters, The Soft Machine, from Canterbury in Kent. The group had made a name for themselves on the London underground scene, often mentioned in the same breath (and appearing on the same bill as) The Pink Floyd. Fowley produced 'Feelin' Reelin' Squealin'' for Polydor. Released in February 1967, the A-side, 'Love Makes Sweet Music', was produced by Bryan 'Chas' Chandler, until recently a member of The Animals, and now getting into management with his acts The Soft Machine and, with

Chandler's discovery from the US, Jimi Hendrix, whom he'd paired with UK musicians to form The Jimi Hendrix Experience.

In October 1966, The 'NBetweens supported Cream at Willenhall Baths, with Robert Plant's group Listen opening. Lea was deeply impressed.

Aided by the success of 'You Better Run', gigs continued to come thick and fast for The 'NBetweens, and any sense of loss following Johnny Howells's departure was quickly forgotten. The Astra Agency, who had fought somewhat against the group being a four-piece, got them gigs, and the bill matters of 'Columbia Recording Artists' did them little harm. Maurice Jones was proving a capable manager; the first half of 1967 saw the group working several nights a week – their club gigs in the Black Country were supplemented by trips further afield to Bournemouth, a return to Tiles in London and the 400 Club in Torquay. There were a couple of prestigious support shows at Wolverhampton's Civic Hall, supporting local(ish) heroes, The Move, on 6 January, and Zoot Money and John Mayall. They quickly settled into life on the road, ably abetted by Don Powell's old friend, Graham Swinnerton, who had become the group's road manager. 'There was only Nod and Swin who could load the van,' Powell says. 'We had a little section of the van, and they knew exactly what went where otherwise it wouldn't go in, like a jigsaw.'

The 'NBetweens would often convene at The Trumpet in Bilston, a pub with a long and chequered history. Actually titled The Royal Exchange, the pub got its colloquial name from a local legend about a woman being able to get the sweetest notes from said instrument by holding it to her labia. Landlord Les Megson had taken over the licence of the pub in 1965, when it was one of the area's last remaining 'beer houses'. When Megson took over, it was empty most nights, so he began playing his favourite jazz records at loud volume, which attracted local musician Tommy Burton, who offered to play for free. The pub, no bigger than a large front room, became known as a music venue. 'It would be packed, you'd be dancing and there'd be a trombone in your ear,' Les Megson's son, Steve, who would go on to play a key role in Slade's career, said. 'Burton was a very funny man, a very crude kind of act, but you got away with it in those days. He used to sing, play piano and tell jokes. Reg Keirle was also very popular. I used to buy hundreds of records when I was a student. I came home from college one year and my dad had pinned all my records on the ceiling. My collection of rock and roll and stuff. It didn't go down very well.'

The Trumpet became Slade's unofficial HQ for the length of their career.

Because of the Columbia association, on Thursday 20 April 1967, the group had the opportunity to go to EMI's studios at Abbey Road to record 'Delighted to See You' with Norman Smith, who had acted as engineer for The Beatles and was soon to produce Columbia labelmates, Pink Floyd. The Beatles themselves were adding overdubs to George Harrison's 'Only a Northern Song' in Studio Two at the same time, and The 'NBetweens saw the Fab Four's chauffeurs asleep on the sofas in the reception area. Although Hill, Holder, Lea and Powell did not meet 'the four kings of EMI', the thrill of being in the same space was enough. 'We were like little kids, sneaking in, putting our ear to the control room door to work out what was going on,' Powell told me in 2020. 'When we heard a noise, we ran away quickly. I'll always remember, I turned round to look, and George Martin came out of the studio, and just buried his head in his hands.'

'The tracks we did there never came to anything, but it was worth it for the buzz,' Holder later said. 'The Beatles were gods to every band, and we had recorded next door to them.' Ironically, Smith had produced the group's hero, when he came to EMI Studios in December 1966. Five months before The 'NBetweens visited, Little Richard recorded a cover version of Bobby Marchan's 'Get Down With It' there, with Smith at the controls. Smith was quite the name in industry circles already: 'We kept on asking him about The Beatles,' Powell said.

* * *

While Maurice Jones managed them, Noddy Holder took care of money matters and the day-to-day nuts-and-bolts running of the group, and although there was to be no further recording activity in 1967, the group worked flat out live. Although they didn't play further afield than Stoke-on-Trent in their seventy-plus shows for the rest of the year, the group truly honed their craft, observing their support acts and those who were following them. In that period, as well as playing with the local gold standard such as The Californians and The Montanas, they worked with acts as diverse as John Mayall's Bluesbreakers, Dave Dee, Dozy, Beaky, Mick & Tich, The Alan Bown Set and Jimmy Cliff. Their popularity was thus that Carole Williams, who worked at Astra and had overseen Lea's audition with the band, ran an official fan club for the group from her home in Whitmore Reans, just outside Wolverhampton.

'It was a lovely feeling,' Don Powell says. 'It was like an unwritten thing. We all knew what our role was within the band, and we just carried on with it. Nothing was ever questioned. In the early days, all the gig contracts would come to my parents' house. Nod would look after the money and the accounts. I used to have the gigs and then I'd give everybody a list every Friday with what we were doing the next week. I'd have the contract and I'd have to sign it to send it back to the agency.'

Young Frank Lea saw this close up: 'James was three years older – when he was 16, I was 13. The band used to come around to collect James and I was 12 or 13. They were very strict on their rehearsals, they used to treat it as a job. They'd pick James up, nine o'clockish, get to the rehearsal rooms and work. As time went on, they used to come with longer hair and long Crombie coats.'

Already, the volume of The 'NBetweens became a huge talking point. Hill bought a treble booster for his guitar, and then Holder and Lea followed suit. Graham Swinnerton linked the individual speakers, so each musician came out of every speaker. Already their wall of sound seemed unique. 'Before days of monitor, everything got louder so Noddy had to sing louder,' Powell says. 'Drums weren't miked up in those days.' 'When Nod first joined, he was very much into Little Richard but his voice wasn't the way it would become,' Hill told Mark Blake. 'Certainly Tamla Motown, bit soulful, just to get heard he had to start bawling his head off. You know that singer you've got, he keeps shouting. Jim said I can hardly hear him. So, it came from necessity.'

CHAPTER 4

Club Tropicana –
Four Go Wild in the Bahamas

In late spring 1968, The 'NBetweens were offered the chance to play in a hotel in the Bahamas. Even in the 21st century, the Bahamas still conjures images of it being an opulent paradise. Although the reality may not be a patch on what people assume them to be, the archipelago of islands still feels remote and inextricably linked with money and glamour, and, out of hurricane season, a sun-soaked otherworld. At that time, the twin icons of the sixties – The Beatles and James Bond – had both recently filmed there, in *Help!* and *Thunderball*, respectively, which had showcased the clear blue skies and glass-calm ocean of the islands.

The Astra Agency received a call from Ken Mallin, a Willenhall man who'd relocated to the islands. He had become involved with a club in Freeport on Grand Bahama Island. Freeport was something of prospector's paradise – the area had only been reclaimed from the swamps in 1955 by US financier Wallace Groves, who in an agreement with the Bahamian government, was able to establish a resort in a free-trade area.

Aware of The 'NBetweens from their reputation in the Midlands, Mallin thought they would be a perfect house band. Evidently, the group had not been first choice. 'Somebody had wanted this big Midlands cabaret band, The Montanas, but couldn't get them so we went out instead,' Lea was to say. Long-term circuit rivals, The Montanas had indeed played some engagements with The 'NBetweens across the years and featured future nightclub and TV comic Ian 'Sludge' Lees on the bass. Mallin assured The 'NBetweens that 'everything would be taken care of'. It was an offer too good to be true.

And so, on 19 May 1968, Hill, Holder, Lea and Powell departed for the islands, to begin their residency. It was one thing for a band to ply their craft and get into scrapes in Germany (something they had of course done, together and apart). It was a relatively well-trodden path for British beat groups, and even then, still comparatively close enough for UK parents to rescue their offspring if the going was to get exceptionally tough. But the Bahamas? That was half a world away and these boys, barely into their 20s, were a long way from home.

Landing at Nassau on Grand Providence, they were met by Mallin at the airport, then hopped on one of the small aircraft that fly between the islands in the archipelago to Grand Bahama. Part of the deal was that the band could lodge at the Sheraton Oceanus Hotel, with all expenses paid. The four had two twin rooms with adjoining doors. However, the group were not booked to play the swanky Pirate's Den nitespot inside the hotel, their venue was instead the Tropicana Club on the Queen's Highway within the city, more for the locals and tourist service industry rather than the opulent holidaymakers taking advantage of the resort's location, less than 70 miles off the coast of Florida. They would play three shows a night – early sets would have younger US tourists in, then the later ones were strictly locals only.

For a group of young men who had barely been out of the West Midlands, it was something of an eye-opener. Hill's were wide with wonder. 'We couldn't believe it,' he wrote in *So Here It Is*. 'We're a bunch of working-class lads off council estates and before we'd got the band going, it was a bit exotic to go the other side of Wolverhampton. Now we're being asked to go to the Bahamas.'

Powell adds, 'Four bloody scumbags from Wolverhampton in the fucking Bahamas on the beach every day! We'd never even been in a hotel before.' Letters would intermittently come home updating family on the group's well-being.

In between the group's three sets, cabaret acts would appear. There was Eric Roker the stoned compere and bongo player ('He smoked SO much dope and drank pure spirit,' Powell recalls), Prince Badou, the fire-eater, Madame Fru-Fru, a belly dancer and a snake charmer. There was also a man who painted himself either silver or gold, depending on different sources. US artists would fly over – the group played with William Bell, with his guitarist Harold Beane who would go on to play with Funkadelic, and Florida-based girl vocal trio The Twans. The Twans featured soul singer Berry Wright's sister Jeanette, and their super-rare 45, 'I Can't See Him Again', was written by Henry Stone, later the founder of the influential TK label. All the time, The 'NBetweens would play, improvise, support, often in chaotic conditions. Jim Lea recalls, 'We were very much out on a limb and in between acts, we used to have to play 'Green Onions' while the next act was coming on. Nod used to go and have to pull the cage up for Madame Fru-Fru to dance in.'

Roker, who passed away in 2019, and was a member of Boss & the Conch Shells, has a notable footnote in the Slade story – as the man who introduced the group to marijuana.

After a month playing – and enjoying unparalleled quantities of room service – The 'NBetweens learned that the Tropicana Club had changed hands, and their benefactor, the mysterious Mr Mallin, had disappeared. It transpired that only their flight and the first two weeks' accommodation had been paid for. As a result, they were confronted by disgruntled hotel management. The band had run up an enormous account that needed paying. 'The manager sent for us and showed us this stupendous hotel bill,' Powell says. 'All we could do was start laughing. We had no money, so there was nothing we could do about it. He said, "This is no laughing matter".'

To add to this, in mid-June there had been protests by Afro-Caribbean Bahamian natives railing against the whites-only employment policy of the hotels, which saw several hotel lobbies being charged through, threatening holidaymakers. There was something wrong in paradise. The group sent letters to Astra asking for help, but nothing came of them. It must have been a wrench too for the parents and siblings: all, but maybe not younger Lea brother, Frank, 'I didn't give a shit. I just went to school; we had a field at the back of our house and I was out there playing football all the time – that was all I was bothered about.'

Dan Darrow, the hotel manager, moved Hill, Holder, Lea and Powell out of their accommodation to something rather less hospitable, down in staff quarters, and the group had to continue working at the club until their debt was cleared. Their scheduled mid-July 1968 return date was cancelled. 'The four of us were living in one room with four beds, a fridge and a toilet, that's it,' Hill wrote. 'It sounds horrendous, but I think that was what made Slade. That's how we got really close. We had to spend that much time cooped up in that room together that we came out of it so tight.'

What was equally surreal was that, at the same time, Andy Scott, who would go on to be guitarist in Slade's main 1973 glam rivals, Sweet, was also on Grand Bahama in his then-outfit, The Elastic Band. 'Don and I have reminisced many times about the fact that how could it happen that when he was in The 'NBetweens, and I was in a band that had just changed its name to The Elastic Band, we could find ourselves on the same island in the Bahamas. They were there for virtually as long as we were.'

Both bands had their issues to deal with. 'They were staying in one of these first flash ten-storey hotels on their side of the island, but the club they were playing in was a little bit more urban,' Scott says. 'The club we were playing in was for slightly more well-heeled tourists. But the house that we were given to live in was chatelained by a Vietnam vet, who was off his head all the time, and he used to bring his biker mates to come and stay and ride their Harleys through the house.' However, the visit had enormous upsides for both bands. 'We came back to England with whole new influences,' Scott continues. 'I mean, I thought Deep Purple were an American band as they had just had a hit with 'Hush'.' What it did mean, however, was that Scott and Powell would often hang out with other members of other bands and form a deep, lasting friendship.

The opportunity for The 'NBetweens to leave presented itself when the club – which had been renamed The Pussycat A Go Go by its new owners – was to close for refurbishment for a week, and the band were required to move their equipment out. At that point, the band simply took the chance to scarper, getting their gear surreptitiously to the airport and hot-footing it back to London, leaving them with a debt in the region of £2,000. The 'NBetweens returned to the UK on 29 August, the same week The Beatles released their debut single on Apple, 'Hey Jude'. While the group they looked up to was entering its final phase, The 'NBetweens were still in their own Star-Club. 'That was our Hamburg...' Lea told Rob Chapman. 'We weren't in the fancy areas playing the casinos. We were playing the black areas. We stayed in a Holiday Inn with a fountain outside and boats. We'd never seen boats in our lives. Round our way it was cloth caps and going to work in the mist, pea-soupers at night because of the factories.'

* * *

The time in the Bahamas gave Hill, Holder, Lea and Powell an unparalleled closeness. Dave Kemp, who would later run their fan club, noticed just how tight they were when he first encountered them. 'They were really strong as a unit – they'd make all of the decisions together and they'd have to agree before they'd do anything. This came about because of the Bahamas. Because they had no food, it made them bond together and look after each other – it was all from that time – and that carried right on through to the eighties.'

Frank Lea concurs, 'You couldn't break into them four. I was with them all of the time. I was always in the group car, going with them to venues.'

There is little doubt quite how much the Bahamas sojourn shaped them – the regularity with which it would pop up in interviews, and indeed six years later in the lyrics of their number two UK hit, 'Far, Far Away'. Twenty-eight years later, Hill would talk about it during Noddy Holder's *This Is Your Life*. To add this to the experience in Germany in youth clubs and pubs in the Midlands and some of London's trendy venues, the band could consider no challenge too sizeable.

The United Services Club in Bilston was not in a sun-kissed paradise, but it was one of their regular haunts, and on Friday

6 September, with their new material they had picked up in the Bahamas and their new hippie look, it was a different 'NBetweens that took to the stage to the one that had left back in May. 'What we were doing was no different to The Beatles in Hamburg or the Stones being a travelling jukebox of blues and R&B. We were exactly the same but also doing Tamla and Soul,' Jim Lea said.

Tamla would figure in the group's next exposure. On 12 September, the *Express and Star* printed a delightful little nugget that never seemed to be referred to since: 'While in the Bahamas, The 'NBetweens were offered a contract to record for Tamla Motown. If financial considerations had not led to their refusal, they would have been the first white group to record for the Detroit organisation.'

Sadly, there is not a shred of evidence to this being correct. 'It looks like BS,' leading Motown author and former *Billboard* staffer Adam White says. 'Motown acts would occasionally play in the Bahamas (and Berry [Gordy] used to go there). That's the only possibility that exists – that someone associated with the company saw the band and expressed an interest. Personally, I don't believe it's anything but nonsense, because by 1968 in the UK, people would speculate about all sorts of British acts signing to Motown.' It was all good for business, keeping The 'NBetweens up there with The Montanas and The Californians at the top of the Black Country pop table.

CHAPTER 5

The Purse and the Mirror –
A New Name, a New Look

'Mix that hot lot together and you create a brand of musical
mayhem, extravagantly extrovert, that grabs and doesn't let go.'

Peter Jones, *Ballzy* sleevenotes, 1969

Thoroughly dispirited by their treatment in the Bahamas, The
'NBetweens split from the Astra Agency and moved to the Nita
Anderson Agency, run by husband-and-wife team Andy and Anita
(Nita) Anderson. As Andy Anderson was a serving policeman, the
business was put in his wife's name; it was here the group met Roger
Allen, who had links with producer, writer, arranger and talent scout
Irving Martin who, in turn, had links with London-based record
company, Fontana.

Allen took over from Maurice Jones as the group's de facto
manager, for the time being. Allen was the complete character,
a 'Del Boy' as Noddy Holder has called him, a Brian Epstein
figure for so many West Midlands bands. His principal turns The
Californians and The Montanas were still doing big business locally,

and making inroads nationally and internationally. It made perfect sense that The 'NBetweens should align with this set-up. However, The 'NBetweens would not completely abandon ties with Astra and would play many times at the agency's new venue, the Lafayette, or the Laf, on Thornley Street in Wolverhampton, where Jones was to build his reputation as a promoter by booking all major acts there.

'The Lafayette got really big,' Frank Lea says. 'I saw Led Zeppelin there, Jethro Tull, twice. Fleetwood Mac, everybody who was anybody played at the Laf.'

Founded in 1958, Fontana Records had its origins as an independent record label in France before becoming absorbed by Dutch giant, Philips. Alongside releasing albums on the American Vanguard label and becoming one of the first distributors of Motown in the UK, Fontana scored a string of notable pop successes in the mid-sixties, poaching Manfred Mann from Columbia, (Wayne Fontana and) the Mindbenders, and The Troggs. Not long before The 'NBetweens signed to the label, Walter Woyda, who had helped pioneer the introduction of the cassette format, joined from Philips Records as general sales and marketing manager, and the label was enjoying strong success with Dave Dee, Dozy, Beaky, Mick & Tich, the second incarnation of Manfred Mann, and Esther & Abi Ofarim, whose 'Cinderella Rockefeller' had been at number one for three weeks in spring 1968.

Fontana's A&R director, Jack Baverstock, was an established figure within London's music industry; previously working for Oriole and Embassy, he had been assistant editor at *Melody Maker* before being poached by Maurice Kinn to be part of the team that established *New Musical Express* and had assisted in introducing the Top 20 charts to the UK. Baverstock was the epitome of an old-school record company man. 'I don't believe that young people are necessarily the best judges of pop,' he told *Record Mirror* in 1967. 'You need a lot of experience behind you to cope with all the tricks in this business.' He had played his part in the careers of Dusty Springfield, The Walker Brothers and Kiki Dee.

Baverstock had gained a reputation for talent scouting – working with his younger A&R manager, Dick Leahy, he was one of the first people to recognise the potential in the young Reg Dwight, signing his first group Bluesology to Fontana in 1965. Baverstock had a reputation as a redoubtable man. Peter Daltrey from Kaleidoscope was to dismiss Baverstock as 'one of the suits at Fontana-Philips,' who 'never rated us. Jack Baverstock was never a friend of ours. We were never close to the guy. He always looked down his nose at us,' but, according to Leahy, could also be 'very nice'. Irving Martin counteracts this: 'He was a very difficult, very obtuse, very opinionated man. He wasn't a good executive. Johnny Frantz was a far better executive than Jack.'

Hearing about The 'NBetweens from Roger Allen, Baverstock was intrigued as they had built up such a strong following in the Midlands. Other bands from the area such as The Move and The Moody Blues were providing decent business for other labels, so it was time for the company to get some more Black Country action after The Spencer Davis Group had long departed its roster.

Go-between Irving Martin, a producer and writer at CBS before setting up on his own in 1968, worked with Roger Allen. 'Roger gave me not much money to find deals for acts,' Martin says. 'It was a good little gig as far as I was concerned, because I was newly independent, and I wanted a foot in the pop market. The Californians were doing quite well for them, and I was doing OK with them. They were doing better overseas than they were in the UK.' Allen told Martin to go and investigate The 'NBetweens. 'I went to see them,' Martin continues, 'a real rough, hard band. Noddy wasn't the star he became, he was much more nervous, and Jim was much more apparent as the talent. The drummer was just about keeping time, and the guitar player was sort of take it or leave it, but he had a nice personality.'

Martin fed back his comments to Jack Baverstock and arranged a session at Stanhope Place, Philips's recording studio in London's Marble Arch on 3 December 1968. 'I said, "Jack, I like this band, they've got a lot of edge," Martin says. "Why don't we bring them in?" He agreed and we did some tracks. Roger Wake was the engineer and basically, we recorded, with a few amendments. I put a rough mix down. There was an instrumental, which they all seem to like.' The tracks were the instrumental 'Blues in E' and a song they had heard in the Bahamas, 'Journey to the Centre of Your Mind' by The Amboy Dukes. It was effectively an audition. A few days passed.

'I called up Jack,' Martin continues. 'He called me back and said, "I don't like that fucking band." That's what he said to me. I said, "What was wrong with them?" He said, "It's just not Fontana; it's just not us." He told me to get on with the other albums I was looking after.'

Effectively cutting Martin out of the proceedings, Baverstock asked the group to return on 11 December to record again with Roger Wake. 'The next thing I know is they're back in the studio with Jack,' Martin says.

> I found out because they were following on a date I was doing at the studios. Jack said he didn't like them, the next thing they're doing all their bits and pieces with him. I thought to myself, 'Do I have to have a war here? Or shall I just get on with what I'm doing?' I was working for Decca, I was working for Jack, I was working for three or four other record companies as well as doing my own music. Jack was a personal friend, but obviously not as good a friend to me as I was to him. So, I let the thing go, I didn't want a war and even then, these things were expensive to argue. I had jobs in the States, I had jobs everywhere.

Irving Martin went on to be a successful producer and director globally, introducing Japanese artist Tomita to the wider world, and launching Sky TV in Europe.

A deal was struck between Baverstock and The 'NBetweens but there were two key provisos – one being that the group acquire a London-based agent to move beyond the Midlands network, and a manager who could promote them nationally. The other? To change their name. The 'NBetweens seemed routed in a long-gone beat era, and for many promoters, had been difficult to spell. Baverstock also suggested that the name implied, as Don Powell suggested in his book, 'an element of homosexuality'. As they had moved on from The Vendors when that sounded too rooted in the early sixties, so The 'NBetweens had that air of beat group. The group seriously toyed with Nicky Nacky Noo, a phrase that they had heard from Graham Bond when he played Wolverhampton, meaning 'the best'. It had been in northern parlance for some time, used by comedians such as Hylda Baker and Ken Dodd, possibly a reference to a vagina. Fortunately, The 'NBetweens decided against the name. It was an era of two-word composites: Vanilla Fudge, Iron Butterfly, Led Zeppelin, Deep Purple, Pink Floyd.

On 12 December, an announcement was made in the *Express and Star* that from New Year's Day 1969, The 'NBetweens would now be now known as Ambrose Slade, which seemed more in keeping with the time. The name allegedly originated from Baverstock's secretary, Hilary, who had a habit of naming her possessions. 'She had a purse called "Ambrose" and a mirror called "Slade", and there we were, Ambrose Slade,' Hill said. The group were hardly enamoured with the name, but they had a major London label fully invested in them.

'We didn't particularly like the name... The 'NBetweens was bad enough. It was always misspelled, as people couldn't figure it out,' Powell says, 'We were billed as Ambush Shake, Arnold Shed, Amboy Spade – it was horrible.' It's difficult to know whether the purse and mirror story is true or more Sladelore, but it makes for a great tale.

A first bit of business was to shoot some promo footage of the group, that could be used to showcase the new act to Philips employees. On 15 December, the four were filmed at London's entirely rebuilt, ultra-modernist Euston railway station which had been opened by the Queen just two months earlier. Long thought lost, the footage was found by Slade historian David Graham in 2013. It is splendid, catching the group transitioning from The 'NBetweens to Ambrose Slade; acting as a travelogue for those to be wowed by the station as much as being wowed by the band. Concrete and escalators were still enormous news, especially after the furore there had been earlier in the decade with the demolition of Philip Hardwick's Doric arch that had stood outside the station since 1837.

And so, as 1969 dawned, Ambrose Slade came into being. Their gig sheet was as full as ever as, punctuated with intermittent recording sessions until 22 February at Stanhope Place with Roger Wake engineering and co-producing for what was to become their debut album. Engineer Gary Moore offers a snapshot of the studio:

It was a very exciting place to work. Not only did you have the studio in the basement, in the building above was Philips Records. The location was also excellent, being on the corner of Stanhope Place overlooking Hyde Park and at the top of Oxford Street. The range of music recorded at Stanhope House was vast, which made working there always interesting.

'We'd never had anybody believe in us like Jack Baverstock,' Powell says. 'He just let us get on with it. He popped into the studio control room every so often with a nice smile on his face. There was one time where Jim had his violin and was doing a hoedown thing. We thought it sounded good. Jack listened and said, "Are you taking the piss out of me?" We thought, "Ah, he's right." Roger Wake taught us so much about studio things as well. Basically, the four of us went in and played together as we would on stage. It was us with Roger. He was very integral; we didn't know anything about technique or anything technical. It was exciting.'

On 28 February, Ambrose Slade went up to Pouk Hill quarry, a small, grassy area between Willenhall and Walsall with photographer Richard Stirling to shoot the photo session for their first album sleeve. An edgeland if ever there was one, by the side of the M6, this scrubby land would be where the group were asked to strip to the waists and pose against the backdrop of the snow-covered field. 'We were all freezing cold,' Holder was later to recall. 'God knows why, but the photographer wanted us to strip down to the waist and that was why I wrote the song 'Pouk Hill' about that experience.' The irony was that on the front cover, very little of the surrounding land was seen. To the rear, the group are pictured naked from the waist up on a pile of rocks, communing with nature. The track was later to be included on their compilation album, *Sladest*, where writer Bob Houston noted that Pouk Hill was 'just up the road from Noddy's gaff in Wolverhampton. Don't bother to look it up in the guides to Beautiful Britain.'

The first fruits of the deal appeared in a week ahead of the album in May 1969, with the single 'Genesis', backed with 'Roach Daddy'. 'Genesis' acts as an overture with its gentle, pulsing menace before breaking into its raucous, heavily phased chorus. As David Graham points out, it owes a debt to the track 'Portfolio' from Fairport Convention's debut album, which had been released in June 1968. 'Roach Daddy' took its name from one of the cast of characters and hangers-on in the Bahamas; it has a lovely sunshine swing to it, with Lea's piano in the mix and, given the title, lyrics about getting high.

Ambrose Slade released their LP debut on 9 May. Debut albums are often overlooked as part of the bigger journey, and of course *Beginnings* is no different, but it is positively brimming with charm. As Selby and Edmundson point out, the album was originally to be named after its lead single, 'Genesis', and labels were pressed up accordingly. However, on 28 March that year the band Genesis, Jonathan King's ex-public school protégés at Decca, released their debut album *From Genesis... To Revelation*. Although it sold next to nothing, it would have been one factor in the album changing its title to *Beginnings*.

A direct result of their time in the Bahamas, surrounding the four fledgling, band-written tracks, are a diverse selection of covers, a reflection, too, of their constant visits to the Diskery record shop on Hurst Street in Birmingham, which specialised in imports. There is a thoroughly incredible version of Marvin Gaye's 'If This World Was Mine', which had been covered by Joe Bataan and the Fania All-Stars in 1968; The Mothers of Invention's *Freak Out!* standout 'Ain't Got No Heart', and considering it had only been in the shops two months before they recorded it, The Beatles 'White Album' whimsy of 'Martha My Dear', with Lea's violin replacing McCartney's piano part. Closer to home, they covered 'Knocking Nails into My House', the B-side of 'The Skeleton and the Roundabout' by The Idle Race, giving its leader Jeff Lynne one of his first covers. 'Jeff Lynne wrote songs when nobody else wrote songs,' Hill said in 2019. 'Knocking Nails...' was Jeff's. He didn't say a lot, but you knew he could write.'

Beginnings also featured one of the hippest new sounds that the islands had heard from America, 'Born to Be Wild' by Steppenwolf (another Steppenwolf cover, 'Everybody's Next One', the B-side of 'Born to Be Wild', was also included). Originally released in the US around the time the band were playing at the Tropicana, the record was just hitting the UK singles charts at the same time as the release of *Beginnings*. This was a full four months before *Easy Rider*, the film with which the song will be forever linked, was released in the UK. Ambrose Slade was ahead of the curve.

'That album is our stage show,' Don Powell said 'That's why there's so many diverse things. We all had different tastes, which is very healthy. There's that brilliant Marvin Gaye and Tammi Terrell one on there, which is just so soulful. We heard that in the Bahamas and thought that it'd be a great stage song. Nod did a great performance on that. It was on the radio all the time, and I thought we have to learn that.' The group had a process for capturing their covers: 'We'd sit around and normally I used to get the lyrics. Play a line, needle off, write it, back on. I'd write them on a little scrap, then I'd write them out properly afterwards, so they could read them. I used to love doing that. We all had a little job within the band. Nod would do the chords and Jim would do the arrangement. Quite a good team. Dave always got out of that. He'd be eyeing the girls up,' Powell laughs. 'James used to do the arrangements from the American records,' Frank Lea says of his older brother.

Of the band's originals, aside from the two sides of the single, the instrumental 'Mad Dog Cole' – a tribute to Roger Allen – punches along sweetly, with some impressive scatting from Holder. 'Pity the Mother' is auspicious for being the first Noddy Holder/Jim Lea composition. It really is a fascinating song, with the lyrics reading something like one of Thomas Hardy's bleaker poems, dealing with a war-widowed mother raising a child living on the breadline, worried that social services may remove her offspring from her care. As she returns home from a long day, the child is soundly asleep in the warm. It's a poignant moment of respite on the album with Noddy's plaintive cry, Lea's acoustic and violin and Hill's electric power chords demonstrating that there was more to the palette than just straight-ahead rock.

With its front cover of the four semi-naked men (looking like 'any other bunch of longhairs running late for the summer of love,' as writer Simon Reynolds was to note), *Beginnings* also had some fine in-era sleevenotes to welcome the band: written by respected *Record Mirror* writer Peter Jones (who, as Billy Goodman, wrote *The True Story of The Beatles*, the first full-length book on the group), it was full of the flourish, flamboyance and fatuousness of the time. It opens: '"Stand by" they said, "for a new group that'll really blow your mind. No kidding" they said, "These boys are different. Wait till you hear them" they said, "then you'll know what it really means to flip."' The essay ends with the spectacular lines – encouraging the listener to 'open up and play this album. That's all. Then call in some friends and play it all over again. Ambrose Slade is for real.'

Being part of the Philips label meant that *Beginnings* was released in mid-October the same year in America, where so much of the music on the album originated. However, the sleeve and title were changed for the US market. Firstly, it was retitled *Ballzy*, as an accurate reflection of the music therein – aggressively bold and gutsy. Cover-wise, who needed to see a bunch of half-naked hippies who looked needy rather than gutsy, when the States had more than enough of their own. Instead of the shivering band, Don Wilson illustrated a cover that is curious at best: two red balls and their shadows on a green field, with four clouds behind it. It has an oblique, children's storybook feel. Wilson was part of the Daily Planet design team who had done work with Chess Records and would go on to draw the picture of Piccadilly Circus on *The London Howlin' Wolf Sessions*. *Ballzy* was not one of his greatest works. Again, to retain the mystery surrounding the group, the picture to the rear of the sleeve of the UK edition was done instead as a line drawing, making it difficult to differentiate between group members. In what must have been a humorous writing session, Peter Jones had to modify his turn of phrase on the sleevenotes for the US market. 'No kidding' became 'straight'; 'what it really means to flip' became 'what it really means to turn on', and, best of all, before the 'Ambrose Slade is for real' sign-off, the peak 1969 US statement, 'This album is a heavy collection of strictly good vibes.

The album came and went without much of a ripple. Those who noticed it, enjoyed. *Billboard* made it a four-star album in their 25 October issue. A pointer to the future on *Beginnings* is the group's cover of The Moody Blues' 'Fly Me High', which shows the group's capability – while the original 1967 original single is sweet, Ambrose Slade's version has the bite that would soon be emphasised further by their new manager and producer.

Beginnings was something of a false start. Those who did hear it were broadly enamoured, but for most, it simply passed them by. John Peel, who became something of a minor-key champion for Slade as the seventies progressed, wrote in 1974 that, *'Beginnings* is an extraordinary LP – I wish I didn't have to return this copy to the BBC – because it shows so clearly all those features that were to lead, several years later, to the string of huge successes that Slade have to their credit. I'm slightly embarrassed that so-called experts like myself failed to notice the signs.'

CHAPTER 6

'Tell Me the Fucking Truth, Jimmy' –
Enter Chas Chandler

Jack Baverstock knew that the one thing Ambrose Slade did need was London booking agents and management if they were to succeed. He also knew a Wolverhampton-based agency, however sizeable, would simply not be big enough for the intentions he had for his clients. To that end, he hooked the group up with the Gunnell Brothers, Richard (Rik) and his younger brother John. Now aligned with the Robert Stigwood Organisation, they had gained considerable experience managing the Flamingo and opening the Ram Jam Club in Brixton, and, with Blue Flame saxman Mick Eve, had set up management and a booking agency.

As Johnny Gunnell, younger brother John would frequently compere the nights at the Flamingo, and for those of a certain stripe, was immortalised for his introduction of the band on Georgie Fame and the Blue Flames' *Rhythm and Blues at the Flamingo*, and for writing its swinging sleevenotes. With Rik overseeing the operation in the US, John Gunnell began to look after Slade's interests in the UK. The Gunnells had Chris O'Donnell working with them: 'I knew them in all their early incarnations as they were represented by Astra and regularly worked the club scene. I saw them as Ambrose Slade in the Temple Wardour Street.'

Chas Chandler was tipped off about the group by John Gunnell and came down to Stanhope Place while they were finishing *Beginnings*.

* * *

By the time Bryan 'Chas' Chandler met Ambrose Slade, his reputation was secure as one of the key figures in sixties music. Born on 18 December 1938, Chandler grew up at 35 Second Avenue, Heaton. His first job was as a turner at the Newcastle-on-Tyne shipyards. Learning to play on a homemade guitar, Chandler had joined the Alan Price Trio on bass with vocalist Eric Burdon. Soon, with the burgeoning blues and beat boom, they became The Animals.

One of the most volatile of bands, the abrasion and tension between the personnel in The Animals that would create such a unique take on US blues would also clearly prove their downfall. Chandler, Burdon, guitarist Hilton Valentine, drummer John Steel and keyboardist Alan Price were hot-headed, and a schism immediately broke out when Price took the sole arranging credit on their cover of the traditional 'Rising Sun Blues'. 'The House of the Rising Sun', inspired by Bob Dylan, Dave Van Ronk and Nina Simone's version of the folk song, became a transatlantic number one in 1964, and according to Burdon, should have had all five names of the group on the credit. Instead, it just had keyboard player Alan Price's. The group were soon to disintegrate. Price was the first to leave in 1965 and was replaced by Mick Gallagher.

While on his final tour of the US as part of The Animals, at the recommendation of Keith Richards's then girlfriend, Linda Keith, Chandler encountered a guitarist at Café Wha in Greenwich Village. His bringing to the UK and subsequent management (with Animals manager Mike Jeffery) of James Marshall 'Jimi' Hendrix saw the shy Seattle guitarist become a superstar, helping shape progressive rock music and redefine guitar playing as he burst onto the UK scene in late 1966. A larger-than-life figure with an empathy for musicians and an uncanny ability to create a marketing stunt, Chandler leapt on publicist Keith Altham's suggestion that Hendrix set fire to his guitar during a show at the Finsbury Park Astoria, and cannily put Hendrix on a US tour with The Monkees in the secure knowledge that the contrast between the acts would somehow implode and generate headlines. By 1968, however, he became frustrated with the protracted recording sessions for *Electric Ladyland* and left the Hendrix operation.

In short, Chandler, recently married to his Swedish girlfriend, Lotte Null, was at large on the London scene looking for a new challenge, and joined the Robert Stigwood Organisation. He set up Montgrove Productions, a partnership with Stigwood – a well-established manager and industry figure – to develop new artists.

'Philips Studios in Stanhope Place was fantastic for us,' Don Powell says. 'Even Chas Chandler couldn't believe that Jack Baverstock let an unknown band use the studio, just us and staff engineer Roger Wake to make an album.'

It had been a bold move, usually more of a track record was needed for a major label to let a band go in on their own without arrangers or orchestrators or session players to make an album. Ambrose Slade clearly instilled a belief in those that ran Philips and Chandler was thoroughly impressed. In them, he recognised the spirit of the early Animals, the rough and ready attitude but also the musicianship and craft underlying it. Unlike The Animals, the band seemed to actually like each other, and their closeness offered a harmony that he had not been used to.

'The main fault was they didn't do any of their own material,' Chas Chandler told Chris Charlesworth in 1984. 'But I liked the arrangements they did of other people's songs. Watching that first night, I could reason to myself that if they can do such good versions of other people's material, they can write.'

Chandler liked what he saw but said that he needed to see Ambrose Slade live. A show was arranged, often quoted as being at the short-lived Rasputin's club, 70 New Bond Street, but Slade historian Chris Selby has still been unable to turn up hard evidence, and it seems most likely that it was Blaises on 24 January. It was at this gig that Chas decided to manage Ambrose Slade. Holder recalled: 'There were only 20 people in the place, but we were doing audience participation when everybody else was doing long solos and very introverted music. He loved us and signed us the next day.'

'He came across a bit like a guy in the film, with a cigar, hey, you're gonna be big,' Hill told Mark Blake. 'Not quite like that. Think you're great and really like to manage you. We were all thinking "is this real?"'

Chandler told the group that Lotte was about to have a baby, and to call him in two weeks' time. He wrote his number and address on a piece of paper with his address, and gave it to Jim Lea. Two weeks later, 'We all went to a phone box,' Lea said. 'I see the memory in front of my eyes – it was a blustery day and it was raining. We crammed in the box. The conversation was positive. Ambrose Slade were to be managed by Chas Chandler.

Chandler put everything on a professional footing. Graham Swinnerton, who had been their roadie since 1964, was able to quit his job at Woden Transformers, and work full-time for the group on an £18-a-week wage. 'The band bloody worshipped Chas from the word go,' Swinnerton, known to one and all as Swin, told Chris Charlesworth.

Recalling the impact the big stunts had for Jimi Hendrix, Chandler brought in PR Keith Altham and his partner Chris Williams to work with them. Altham, who, with Derek Taylor, was one of the first PRs-as-stars that was to become so commonplace in the music industry, had been an *NME* journalist and had extensively covered The Animals, and become great friends with Chandler. He had recently set up his own PR agency, Jigsaw. Altham recalls vividly their first meeting in the summer of 1969 at the Studio 51 club in Soho's Great Newport Street, especially the volume at which they played, 'making The Who sound like the Amadeus String Quartet', he was to note. Together, Chandler, Altham and Williams could cook up a few inches of good newsprint for this most unusual band.

Chandler used his connections to get Ambrose Slade a prestigious support slot at the Newcastle City Hall on 6 June 1969, supporting Amen Corner and Dave Dee, Dozy, Beaky, Mick & Tich. 'I remember that night at the Newcastle City Hall with Ambrose Slade,' Andy Fairweather Low from Amen Corner recalls. 'Terry The Pill, our manager at the time, suggested we copromote a night.

Keith Altham and Chris Williams, who later became our managers, ran a top PR company with The Who, The Moody Blues, The Beach Boys, Jefferson Aeroplane, plus many more. They also knew Chas Chandler, so they handled Ambrose Slade.'

It was a busy night, as both other bands on the bill had topped the UK chart, and were both promoting new singles – Amen Corner with 'Hello Susie' and Dave Dee, Dozy, Beaky, Mick & Tich with 'Snake in the Grass'. It was a prestigious support for Ambrose Slade. 'As for the gig, I don't remember too much except someone threw a large candy baby's dummy which hit me on the head,' Fairweather Low says. 'We didn't see or hear Ambrose Slade that night. We were too all-consumed in our wonderfulness.'

Fortunately, *The Walsall Observer* did see and hear them and printed a feature about them on 27 June, a full 'local lads done good' piece, and announcing that Chas Chandler had taken over their management.

However, Andy Fairweather Low did get to see them a month later: 'I saw them play live down at the Speakeasy. A fantastic late-night venue that was frequented by most of the London rock set. Ambrose Slade were fantastic that night. A great live band. They played 'Martha My Dear'. That really stuck in my mind, a really top version.'

* * *

It was clear that of all four group members, Chas Chandler could rely on Lea. 'When we first met Chas, none of us had telephones,' Don Powell says. 'Chas said he would put a telephone in one of our houses. Jim had the telephone. So, any messages came through from Jim's parents' house.' Chandler paid to have a telephone installed in Lea's family home, the only one of the band to have one. 'I asked Chas why I got the phone,' he told Mark Blake. 'Because I was the kid, and he said "'Cos I knew you'd always tell me the fucking truth, Jimmy."'

Jim Lea told Phil Riley at Boom Radio in 2023 what drew Chandler to Slade: 'First he saw Dave Hill, he thought he'd make a nice pop star; he was looking at Nod and said sometimes he sounded like

John Lennon when he was singing, he was very nasal; he could hear Don at the back and he knew what he was doing.' Chandler was to say that he then noticed Lea, saying "That's the guy who's making it all happen."'

Chandler also brought the respected photographer Gered Mankowitz along. Mankowitz had taken some of the most hallowed rock pictures of the era and had leapt to worldwide attention for his picture of Jimi Hendrix in military uniform, which was how manager and photographer knew each other. 'Chas Chandler was one of those clients who just left it all to me,' Mankowitz recalls. 'Ambrose Slade came to my studio in Mason's Yard. I took them down to the south coast and photographed them on the beach near Hastings. I can't remember what the inspiration for that was, but they were still quite sixties in their look, quite glittery, not glam, but had that sixties edge to them, still quite long hair, flowing scarves and things. I photographed them on the beach, and then back in my studio and we just clicked, we seemed to get on really well, we enjoyed ourselves.'

It was the start of a long professional relationship that would stretch on until the mid-eighties. However, it would be difficult to tell based on the seashore pictures. The band look absolutely freezing as the water is breaking hard against the rocks, spray erupting over the boulders. Dave Hill is in a vest and Don Powell in a smock, both with Indian-influenced necklaces on. The other two at least have jackets on, with only Holder crouching, looking toward the camera with shades on. It didn't exactly scream that audiences were viewing a new pop phenomenon. To be quite frank, there were a thousand other pop groups on either side of the Atlantic that had adopted The Beatles post-India garb of informal hippiedom to the nth degree. It was time to change tack, and get these hardworking boys noticed.

PART TWO

WHEN THE WHOLE WORLD WENT CRAZEE

CHAPTER 7

A Spot of Bovver

The skinhead and suedehead phenomenon in the UK in the late sixties can be seen as a direct working-class reaction against the hippie movement, which had been primarily led by the middle and upper classes. A fascinating adjunct to the sixties music scene, skinheads acted as a bridge into the seventies and were first mentioned in the UK press during 1968, as a development of the mod culture that had been prevalent in the middle sixties. While many mods went on to be hippies, skinheads, often aligned to a football team, were having none of that – with their hair shaved, a uniform of boots and braces, they adopted ska and rocksteady as their music of choice.

Writer James Moffatt was a jobbing Canadian-born UK writer who wrote at least 290 novels in several genres under at least forty-five pseudonyms. His most well-known pseudonym in UK youth culture was Richard Allen. Allen became the skinhead laureate, writing best-selling pulp novels *Skinhead* in 1970, *Suedehead*, the following year, and *Bootboys* in 1972. As his obituary in *The Independent* ran, 'His books were foul-mouthed, violent, racist, but they gripped readers and helped influence a generation of writers... There is hardly a style magazine that hasn't enthusiastically embraced Allen.'

Such was the climate at the turn of the seventies, skinheads were big news. And, after Ambrose Slade's single and album had flopped, it was time to see if some magic could be added. Keith Altham noted how the skinhead movement was taking off and suggested, possibly late at night and rather worse for wear, to Chandler that this may well be a way that the group could get noticed. They should cut their hair and get their bovver boots on and join the nascent skinhead movement. Chandler – who had seen at close quarters what alignment to the mods had done for The Who five years earlier – ran with the idea, and the next morning, took the boys to the barbers. Altham was later to say that he'd changed his mind, as they were far too gentlemanly to fit the bill as skinheads.

'We can't do this to them,' he told Chandler. 'They are nice guys, regular blokes.' It was too late. On 23 September, Chandler took his charges to the hairdresser, Harry's in Greek Street. Their hair had been cut; their clobber purchased. The skinhead transformation was another of Chas Chandler's great marketing coups. Another trim was made that day. Ambrose was shorn from their name. The group were now Slade.

The change of look was a shock to all that knew them, especially the reserved Jim Lea. 'James would come in from a gig dead late, and I would be asleep as I had to get up and go to school,' Frank Lea, who shared a bedroom with him, says. 'I got up one morning and instead of his flowered jacket and satin trousers on the floor, there was a pair of bovver boots, a pair of jeans and a Ben Sherman shirt instead. I could see all his curly hair had gone. My mum wasn't best pleased.'

As momentum began to gather, another player was to join the team: John Steel. After Steel left The Animals in 1966, he had reconnected with Chandler at the group's one-off reunion concert at Newcastle City Hall in December 1968. 'Chas by that time was very successful with the Hendrix Experience,' John Steel says:

He asked me to come and join him as part of his team. I took him up on it a few months later, in the second half of 1969, I moved back to London, and he had offices in Robert Stigwood's Brook Street. He introduced me to his to his new group, Slade. It was practically the day after they had their transformation into skinheads. I was confronted with four skinheads with very thick Black Country accents that I could hardly understand. We managed to communicate, but I think I had more trouble than they had.

Steel would prove invaluable in the coming years: 'I was a sort of Man Friday, if Chas wanted anything done, I could do it. I would just string along on his coattails. I didn't have any real responsibility, but it was a lot of fun. I was just a mate really, but for some reason Chas liked having me around.' It was this sort of charming self-deprecation that made Steel a key part of the organisation.

Once the boots and braces had been bought, suddenly, everyone in pop seemed to know who they were. 'Chas rang me and said, "We've got to do a new session because the boys have changed their look," Gered Mankowitz recalls. 'So, I walked up to the office and there they were in their bovver boots and skinheads.' Another session was done by legendary Beatles photographer Dezo Hoffmann, again underlining that it was only the best for Chandler's boys. Keith Altham got the group into the *Daily Express* and *Disc* magazine, calling them 'rock and roll bother [sic] boys'. *Disc* and *Music Echo* of 11 October 1969, had the cover story 'Skinheads launched on record' with a picture of Holder with his arms crossed in a typically defiant pose.

Rob Partridge interviewed Lea and Hill for *Record Mirror* in August 1969: 'Jim Lea is the group's bass guitarist. He looks like the sort of bloke you see creating a bit of "bovver" on the terraces at West Ham every week – short hair to the point of where-is-it and big boots. Big black boots. "Why the boots?" I asked. "Because that's what skinheads are about" Jim replied.' For those who knew and would know Jim Lea, this stance was about as far from the truth as possible.

'We'd always looked to image,' Holder said in 2022. 'Nobody had done the skinhead look at the time... there were a lot of bands dressing in the Carnaby Street fashions, and we thought we had to stick out from all these acts, just be different to everybody. It wasn't a violent thing at the end of the sixties, it was more or less a follow-on from what the mods were doing, they were into the ska and the reggae.'

Hill and Lea hated the look, but Holder and Powell loved it, emphasising their masculinity. 'Nobody would mess with us, because even though we weren't really frightening, we looked frightening.'

Nick Kent, writing in *NME* in 1973, provided some retrospective rationale for Chandler's decision: 'Chandler saw the skinhead phase as a working-class eruption on a par with the "mod" bust-out of ye olde mid-sixties and must have envisaged Slade as spokesmen of the current outbreak in the same way as The Who scooped the venom out of the former revolt for their own purposes.'

It's a very interesting take on just how much Slade wanted fame to do this; hair had become the most obvious badge of rebellion over the past decade; as people had grown used to hair worn long, shorn hair was so otherworldly, such a statement – by appropriating the look of the army, surely the most regimented embodiment of the establishment, and subverting it, skinheads at once seemed to suggest both order and chaos. By breaking away from the so-called rebelliousness of long hair, which had now become a form of youth conformity, Slade were seen as rebels with a different stance. But the group were playing with fire.

In the cauldron of British society post-Enoch Powell's 'Rivers of Blood' speech, there was a real feeling of inner-city tension, especially in areas with a high percentage of immigration, of which the West Midlands was one. Enoch Powell was also the MP for Wolverhampton Southwest, a constituency he had held since 1950. The speech thoroughly unsettled the more liberal factions of society. Although skinhead affiliations with the far right had yet to occur, it was easy to see how the movement was to attract disenfranchised youth.

The *Daily Mirror*, especially, ran with skinhead stories – on 5 January 1970, its front-page headline was 'Man Dies As Skinheads Mob a Pop Group Car' (Keith Moon's driver was crushed under the wheels of Moon's Bentley as skinheads mobbed it); and 11 April, 'Skinheads Soccer Riot: 60 Arrests' (Coventry fans rioting on a train near Bescot junction in Walsall after they'd beaten Wolves 1–0). On Easter Monday 30 March 1970, Southend-on-Sea's Chief Constable Freddie Bonfield called for 'decisive on the spot judgments concerning a variety of people.' He instructed all his officers to confiscate the skinheads' laces and braces.

In June 1970, Edward Heath's Conservatives won an unexpected victory at the General Election, which followed the US electing Richard Nixon as part of the swing to the right.

It wasn't just the British working-class taking part. It was a febrile time: the anti-war movement across the States; the student protests in Paris; the rioting at the Democratic Chicago Convention; the murders at Kent State University. John Lennon and Yoko Ono were making their stand for peace, but it clearly wasn't being heard.

The bubbling threat of violence seemed ever-present throughout the seventies. Football hooliganism was identified in the mid-sixties, gangs were in, and the vocabulary was reflecting this – words such as bovver, aggro, yobbo and bundle were commonplace, and there was a strong notion that a night, a Friday or Saturday, especially, wouldn't be complete without getting tanked up and ending in a massive ruck; and this would be reflected, directly or indirectly, in song – The Rolling Stones' 'Street Fighting Man', Symarip's 'Skinhead Moonstomp', and later, Bernie Taupin's glorification of pub fighting in Lincolnshire, 'Saturday Night's Alright for Fighting' ('get a little action in', indeed).

Soon, the ultraviolence of Anthony Burgess's 1963 novel *A Clockwork Orange* would be enshrined by Stanley Kubrick in his 1971 film version. With their braces and bowlers, Alex DeLarge (Malcolm McDowell) and his droogs Georgie (James Marcus), Dim (Warren Clarke) and Pete (Michael Tarn) did not look a million miles away from skinheads; and the four of them were in a pack, just like a pop group. Keith Altham had a point: Slade were far too much nice guys and regular blokes to do this. But suddenly, they were noticed.

* * *

With a new look, the name change – 'Ambrose' was far too fey for this bunch of hards – in October 1969, 'The' Slade released their first single, 'Wild Winds Are Blowing'. Chandler was sent the track – written by Bob Saker and Jack Winsley – by a publishing company, and he felt it would be ideal to launch the group. A critique of the single in *Melody Maker* puzzled Jim Lea: 'I remember Chris Welch reviewing 'Wild Winds Are Blowing', he just said two words: "Stark bilge." I don't know what it means to this day.'

On 4 November 1969, Slade made their debut on national television. There were very few outlets on which to get yourselves heard then, but because of the size and scale of these operations, get heard you could, and the opportunity to become a nationwide talking point was huge if you capitalised on your breaks accordingly. The group played two songs – 'Martha My Dear' and 'Wild Winds Are Blowing' – on the penultimate episode of BBC1's *Monster Music Mash*. Produced by Peter Ridsdale Scott, who had made his name producing *Play School*, it was part of the BBC's ongoing drive to incorporate pop into the teatime schedule. Originally entitled *Plays Pop*, it was hosted by Chas Chandler's Animals cohort, Alan Price. The show ran for six episodes, and it was an attempt to allow acts to perform live in the Manchester studio; a current single and then an album track with the purpose of allowing a band to show their capabilities. As such, a widely diverse range of acts played – including Shirley Collins, Magna Carta, Fleetwood Mac and Pentangle.

Slade's performance is fascinating, especially on 'Martha My Dear', where the disconnect between their bootboy look and the ornate whimsy of Paul McCartney's composition is enormous. Jim Lea steals the performance with his intense violin playing McCartney's piano part, and Holder playing the bass with elan. Earnestly introduced by Hill looking at least five years younger than his age, 'Wild Winds Are Blowing' is more suited to the look, and the triangle formation of Lea, Holder and Hill is powerful, especially as Holder is at the rear.

After the TV performance, the group's notoriety spread. Their long-booked show at the Chelsea College of Art on Saturday 15 November was cancelled because of their new image. Never one to hold back, Keith Altham made sure maximum coverage was gained and the story was handed to Reuters, with it making the *LA Times*. 'The group is "The Slade" which has what is known as "the skinhead look" after London's new teenage gangs who have their hair close-cut, wear heavy boots and provoke fights with long-haired hippies.'

A spokesman was on hand to say, 'This group when booked was called Ambrose Slade. They have since changed their name and image, we do not think the new image is suitable, so we cancelled the booking.'

Keith Altham was to say, 'unlike before, when they turned up at a gig or for a TV show and no one took any notice of them, now it was a case of "Look out – it's them"... Slade may have been getting noticed for all the wrong reasons, but we stuck a boot in the media's door. Now all they needed was a hit record.'

The lines were clearly drawn between skinheads, hippies and rockers. *Record Mirror* wrote, 'Skinheads are here and now. Hairies are then and there. So, it's complete. Skinheads have their own battles to fight, their own scene, their own group. It's called Slade...'

However, despite all this press and notoriety, 'Wild Winds Are Blowing' failed to chart.

* * *

On 6 March, the second of Slade's new material with Chas Chandler at the helm was released. It was not to be the hit they craved. 'The Shape of Things to Come' had been an American hit for Max Frost and the Troopers, a made-up group for the teensploitation film *Wild in the Streets* (strapline: If you're thirty, you're through!). It was the work of writing team Barry Mann and Cynthia Weil, and Slade's version later gained Mann's praise. At once, Slade's sound was more dynamic, punchy, upfront. However, the combination of their skinhead notoriety and the title's implication that the movement was soon to take over jarred with broadcasters. Supposedly, *Top of the Pops* producer Stanley Dorfman refused to have the group on the show because his son had been roughed up by skinheads. Yet the band did appear on 4 April 1970, in what was to be the first of eighty-eight performances on the show.

It was not easy being Slade: 'We haven't really got any friends in pop,' Holder told David Skan at *Record Mirror*. 'The other groups all think we are thickies, even though we have been playing together for two and a half years, they steer clear of us.' Don Powell was to say that when the group played Bournemouth that May, 'it was full of skinheads... they just saw right through us.'

Whatever Happened to Slade?

The Marquee Club in London's Wardour Street was one of the mythical venues on which seventies rock was built. And it was here, like many of their generation, that Slade were to make their name. But it was not without the mismatches that were to blight their career – on 10 April, they supported Yes. Although Yes had yet to go the full and utter airy-fairy of the following years, the audiences could not have been further apart. 'The London crowd didn't know us, and they didn't know how to take us,' Don Powell says:

> We were skinheads at the time, we supported Yes when they had the Thursday night residency. Jack Barry gave us a gig and then we eventually got the Thursday night residency ourselves. That was something special because whoever had the residency always made it. The Move, Yes and The Yardbirds had all had the residency. It was really good for us. We used to play all those tiny clubs around. I remember from the Marquee; we'd load up the van and then just drive a few hundred yards down the road and play at The Temple. We used to do the all-nighter there. We'd be asleep in the dressing room. We went home about five in the morning. No roadies then. We'd do it ourselves and then drive back to Wolverhampton.

When Slade played the Marquee for the fifth time on 15 July 1970, they were supported by a new group who'd sprung from the ashes of sixties beat combo Simon Dupree and the Big Sound. Although Gentle Giant were produced by Tony Visconti, signed to a hip underground label, they were the epitome of the esoteric. Their bass player, Ray Shulman says, 'I remember the Slade show. It was one of our first gigs. It was during their skinhead period, which at the time had pretty bad connotations and the audience was similarly attired so we felt alienated from the start. For some reason, we weren't allowed to share the grotty dressing room, so never actually met them, and had to change in the toilet. It was definitely their audience which we had to battle to convince.'

Gentle Giant underwhelmed Slade's boisterous crowd. 'The thing I do remember is, like a lot of Birmingham bands, they were incredibly tight,' Shulman continues. 'As Simon Dupree we played

68

quite a few shows with The Move which we always dreaded 'cos they were too fucking good. It's a shame we didn't actually meet because nowadays, I do enjoy Noddy's comments as a pundit.' Gentle Giant's Phil Shulman explained how these strange clashes kept happening: 'Ask people called agents. If you want to keep eating and you keep wanting to pay rent, you play the gig.' Slade had no problem in playing the gigs, building pockets on loyalty throughout the country.

Scotland especially loved them, and as a result they gigged hard and long there.

In September 1970, Slade moved across from Fontana to Polydor, the label who had been the parent of Track, with whom Chandler had had dealings through The Jimi Hendrix Experience. From their first meeting it was apparent that new Philips head Olav Wyper did not get along with Chandler. 'Chas just picked up his stuff and walked out and I trotted after him,' John Steel says. 'Chas went straight to Polydor to John Fruin, and Chas just tore strips off Wyper saying he wasn't going to have anything to do with that guy.' Over at Polydor, 'unorthodox but imaginative' label head John Fruin took them in. It also meant their base moved just over half a mile easy along Oxford Street to Polydor's HQ at 17/19 Stratford Place. Carlos Olms oversaw the recording studio there, yet the group barely used the in-house facility. Chandler was looking to the new studio opening at Olympic in Barnes.

With their new image everywhere, the band could still not achieve a hit record. Their third single and first for Polydor, 'Know Who You Are', showed the band progressing and would become a cornerstone of both their album, *Play It Loud*, and their live set. The line 'read a new book/finish the other one,' and the way it is delivered, more or less provided the template for Queen. A rewrite of *Beginnings'* instrumental opener, 'Genesis', it showed the potential of the band. Released in September 1970, despite all the ongoing hoo-ha that the skinhead look brought, the record did little.

Robert Stigwood was not as smitten as Chas Chandler with these rough and ready reprobates and left the partnership. Chandler moved out of Stigwood's offices on Brook Street and found a room at accountant Harold Waterman's office at 12 Thayer Street, just north of Oxford Street. 'We had one desk between us and one telephone and a chair for somebody to sit in if they happened to visit and some pigeons on a windowsill and that was it,' John Steel says. It was around this time that accountant Colin Newman entered Slade's orbit, one of the key presences throughout their career.

CHAPTER 8

Play It Loud

Chas Chandler was keen to bring as many onside journalists into the fray as possible. 'Hanging around with the five of them in the early seventies, especially before the hits started coming,' Chris Charlesworth says, 'it was easy to detect the group's admiration for their manager, this devoted Geordie who would scream about them from the rooftops if he thought it would advance their career.'

Polydor, led by Fruin, were happy to support Slade for as long as it took. They had seen what Chandler had done for Hendrix: 'Chas loved them. They loved him,' Chris O'Donnell says. 'It was so the bromance, they just worshipped him. He gave them time at Polydor because he'd go in, beat them up and say, "It won't happen overnight." So, Polydor invested in Chas who then in turn invested in Slade.'

'I first became aware of the band in the early seventies when I met up again with John Steel of The Animals, while pursuing the life of a musician in London with my writing partner of the time, John Turnbull,' keyboard player Mick Gallagher, who would cross their path later, says. 'I'd first met John and Chas Chandler in 1965 when I was fortunate to get the job of replacing Alan Price when he left the band. In the early seventies John was working with Chas's management company to break Slade. John and I met up and he showed me the *Melody Maker* front page photo of Slade in all their skinhead/borstal boy glory. What a brilliant piece of image making that was.'

Demoralised by the lack of success of 'Know Who You Are', Altham quit the operation, suggesting that he could take them no further. Replacing him (and his partner Chris Williams) was John Halsall who, as 'Popwire', would write 'columns from London' in various foreign publications. 'Chas called and I needed work,' Halsall says. 'I was primarily working as a freelance writer, much like Keith, whose example I followed – I knew Keith from his time as editor of *Top Pops* and *Fab208*.'

Working alone, Halsall took the position of the band's PR for the princely sum of fifteen pounds a week (around £300 today). 'Chas was a tight bugger,' he adds, 'but I knew I could use them and my connection to him as a "door opener" to other business.' Halsall realised that Slade needed a champion within the serious rock press, as at that time, the potency and importance of the music weeklies was paramount. A band could be made or broken. At the moment, Slade were broadly seen as an enormous novelty act.

Melody Maker's Chris Charlesworth would become one of the band's key champions. 'John Halsall coerced me into going to see Slade at Samantha's nightclub.' Samantha's was situated at 3 New Burlington Street, and was one of the happening early seventies clubs that were dotted around London's West End. Dave Paul was the DJ, and the booth was designed as if the decks were in an E-type Jaguar. Around early October 1970, Charlesworth first saw the band:

> I think it was a last-minute booking, unadvertised, as there was hardly anyone there, and no one looked like they had gone along to see Slade. Chas was there that night and kept buying me scotch and cokes. I met them and thought they were great. Lovely guys, very easy going, very 'natural', absolutely no side, totally unpretentious, very pleased to meet someone from *MM*. Thick Brummie accents. And terrific live, really tight and well-drilled. I didn't know then how long they'd been at it together, but all those gigs in the Midlands and that trip to the Bahamas was like The Beatles in Liverpool and Hamburg or The Who

in West London as The Detours. You simply can't beat playing
together night after night after night.

Charlesworth, who had met Chandler when he was working with
Robert Stigwood, took to the band immediately.

And Slade played; and played – honing their craft through the
now long-forgotten and often demolished ballrooms, clubs and
municipal spaces where they could gig. 'Through it all, they kept
up a stream of patter and ribaldry,' David Hepworth noted in
his book *1971 – Never a Dull Moment.* 'Nobody came away from a
Slade show without understanding that they had been entertained
and entertained by a band who didn't look down on them.' The
stagecraft they had honed throughout so many gigs was being
given extra sparkle by Chandler: 'Some of that was down to Chas.
Hendrix didn't need any help in that area. Chas schooled them a
bit,' John Steel says. 'He would say things like "Don't go on stage
wearing black. I'm not having you in black." They just jumped into
it with enthusiasm and started coming up with outrageous costumes
themselves. They didn't need much urging.'

Working as a tight unit, the synergy between the group and
their crew was second to none – Swin was in charge of the team
that included or would include sound man Ian 'Charlie' Newnham
(soon to be immortalised as 'Full Poke, Charlie' when *Slade Alive!*
was released); JJ ('Jolly John') Johnny Jones; Haden Donovan; Micky
'Sonny Boy' Legge; and Robbie Wilson, 'whose wilful disregard for
convention became a constant source of amusement for the touring
party', as Chris Charlesworth wrote in *Feel the Noize!*. Swin would drive
the band around in a Vauxhall Velox long after they would become
successful, picking them up from their homes and dropping them
off in the early morning when the gig was done.

The group also worked out just how they would behave: enough
was heard of antagonistic acts; to play that many shows, the group
had to find accord. 'We knocked that out of each other in the early
days,' Don Powell says. 'We all knew when to leave each other alone.
We all knew each other so closely and we would never ever buy each
other a drink. It was just an unwritten thing. We knew exactly what
was what. If we had to share a room, it'd probably be me and Jim.

Then Nod and Dave. Yet when we went to the Bahamas, it was me and Dave shared a room. I don't know how that came about but anyway we just knew each other so well.'

Charlesworth distinctly recalls going to see them at what now would be called a 'corporate' around this time in the City of London:

> Chas had invited me along to this ballroom as it was going to be a laugh, a posh do with debutantes and Hooray Henries, very late on a Saturday night. I think Slade were paid quite a bit plus all the booze they could drink. I got there about midnight, and they went on at about 1 a.m. for an hour. Afterwards all these posh girls in fancy frocks came into the dressing room, with blokes in dinner suits. I dimly remember leaving at around 3 a.m., extremely pissed and trying to find a cab home in the city. I didn't review it but I must have mentioned it to Chris Welch who wrote 'The Raver'.

'The Raver' was *Melody Maker*'s gossip column: '*MM*'s Chris Charlesworth becoming the rake of London. Latest escapade downing pints of champagne and scotch at Slade's raving debutante party in the City. "Never has so much been drunk by so many in such a short..."'

As Charlesworth notes, 'It was odd that Slade, of all people, were pioneering the private events gigs that bands do these days for big money!'

* * *

Slade's debut album, *Play It Loud*, was released on 28 November 1970, and, although the music was broadly in line with what the group had done before, the rebranding was huge. No more dippy hippies with their arms outstretched, here were four ruffians, captured in sepia, looking like the snap had been taken on a Black Country alley as the lads were off to either watch football, or do a shift down the steelworks in yesteryear. Gered Mankowitz, who had recently taken their first bootboy shots, took the cover not in a Bilston back passage but in Lennox Gardens Mews, in London's Knightsbridge, where he had a temporary set-up in the studio of fellow photographer, Eric Swain, after leaving his Mason's Yard address.

Engineered by George Chkiantz and produced by Chandler, the album has a clean, dry sound, quite unlike the rest of their catalogue. With no song longer than three and a half minutes, it breezes along, clearly demonstrating how tight the unit had become over its years of constant gigging. Unlike its predecessor, the covers were paired down. Aside from 'The Shape of Things to Come', there were just two amid the twelve tracks, and according to Jim Lea, both were sourced by John Steel; both relatively obscure then, and certainly long forgotten today. 'Could I' was featured on Bread's self-titled debut album. Written by Robb Royer and Jimmy Griffin, it emphasised the seldom-heard rockier side of Bread, not the world-famous ballads penned and sung by the other group member, David Gates. Equally under the radar was 'Angelina', a Neil Innes song from his short-lived post-Bonzo Dog Doo-Dah Band outfit, The World. Jim Lea was quoted in 2018: 'I had an aversion to both. But we showed willing as management had to be listened to at all times.' The three covers work perfectly on the album, which feels far less a showcase for the work of others than *Beginnings* had.

The writing partnerships on the album were predominately Lea, Powell and Holder writing together, providing 'Raven', 'See Us Here', 'One Way Hotel', 'Know Who You Are' and 'Pouk Hill'; and without Holder, Lea and Powell alone wrote 'Dapple Rose', 'I Remember', 'Dirty Joker' and 'Sweet Box'. 'Dirty Joker' fully underlines the techniques that Chandler brought to the recording studio – whereas Roger Wake's capture of the band on *Beginnings* was straightforward, here the difference can be heard, using techniques he had used in the studio with Hendrix. Lea's bass is captured like a lead instrument, thundering into its solo on 'Dirty Joker', and is quite breathtaking. US critic Dan Epstein said of 'Sweet Box', 'with thumping caveman beats, power-drill guitars and a lyric so lubricious that it barely qualifies as a double entendre, 'Sweet Box' could almost pass for a great lost Troggs single.' 'Sweet Box' is intriguing, eastern-influenced, complete with shouted words from the cover of a magazine of sewing patterns.

'Pouk Hill' demonstrates Holder's talent for storytelling developing. Clearly inspired by The Beatles' 'Penny Lane', which managed to turn a roundabout and a bus station into a seemingly blissful wellspring of paradisiacal love, here Holder and Powell recount that day. People are passing and see the boys prancing around in the cold with their tops off. In the song, they take this anonymous clump of land, and say that it 'is tall, always will be', and that it is 'older than you and me'. John Peel wrote in 1974:

> 'Pouk Hill' is a glance back to the Midlands tradition of Idle Race and Move records, a sometimes tender, sometimes fey, little song of real charm. 'Dirty Joker' is something of a curiosity, opening, as it does, with the type of guitar, bass, drums sound that distinguishes the best dance records coming from Black America in 1974. Both this track and 'Sweet Box' which follows and also closes the LP, illustrate yet again the powers of invention within the band. The sudden shifts of emphasis, the impressive skills, are of the type that have made such bands as Yes and Genesis so widely popular with the LP buying audience.

'Dapple Rose' is a standout, the tender story of an ageing horse, tethered near the back of Powell's house. 'I was writing lyrics at the time because I'm totally tone deaf, there's no way I can sing,' Don Powell said. 'I used to go to Jim's house in Broadway in Codsall and I'd sort of sing what I thought was right and it was a load of dribble and then Jim was very patient with me trying to work things out.' Powell was an evocative lyricist.

The band thought sufficiently of the album that four of the tracks made it to their 1973 compilation album, *Sladest*, aside from the two singles that were on *Play It Loud*: 'The Shape of Things to Come', 'Know Who You Are', 'One Way Hotel' (Powell's critique of the hotels the band frequently found themselves in), and 'Pouk Hill', the ode to the quarried land near Bloxwich where the band found themselves February of the year before, half-naked for Richard Stirling's photoshoot for *Beginnings*.

It was also imperative that Slade really take a crack at writing their own songs. 'Chas sat down with them,' booking agent Chris

O'Donnell says. 'He got Jim and Noddy together. It's like Loog Oldham sitting in the flat in Marylebone and saying, "Mick and Keith, write a song or you're going nowhere." John and Paul: it's only four years where they go from 'Hello Little Girl' to 'Sergeant Pepper'. You have to give somebody the opportunity to do that. It's a latent thing in them. You've just got to bring it out. He just keeps on saying I think you're capable of writing better. So arguably, you need time to be able to do that. He definitely identified Jimmy as the talent show. And Noddy had the voice. It's the classic one without the other would have been respected but together…'

'Chas pushed us into it,' Holder said in 2019. 'It wasn't the first song Jim and I had written together; that was 'Pity the Mother' on our very first album. Chas said to get a hit, it has to be our own song. Jim was writing with Don primarily and I was on my own and bits with Dave and come in on Jim and Don's songs as well. Then Chas said I want Noddy and Jim to write one. He said, "Come to me with a hit record."'

* * *

'People thought we were just a put-together group and we became known as just a skinhead group,' Holder said in 1971. 'No one wanted to listen to our music. At first the knocks didn't bother us but when they went on and on, and the people knocking us were the ones who hadn't bothered to listen to us, it got a bit much.'

Growing out their hair, their look was something in between – Holder keeping the shorter trousers and braces, but adding his huge flat cap. 'We grew our hair down the back, a bit like the skinhead girls – the feather-cut thing,' Holder said in 2005. 'We replaced the Doc Martens with platform boots. We became more colourful.'

'The hairstyle developed,' Dave Hill told Mark Blake. 'Short hair, not having a full fringe like Beatles, but a short fringe and long at the sides. Chas let us grow our hair again. I think the skinhead look did work but not get the success. Funny hairstyles, mine like a short pageboy look. Marc Bolan was in the charts and I figured out I could put a bit of glitter on my forehead where the gap was.'

Despite their leanings to be the same as Black Sabbath or The Who, the band could not be offered up as hard rockers but then, on the other hand, as Bob Stanley notes, 'with no hint or possibility of pin-up potential, they saw the Titus Groans and the Amazing Blondels, the prog noodlers, the folk archaeologists and the questing space rockers and thought, sod this, let's get pissed and have a really, really good time.'

And so, for the next three years, Slade were to own that parallel strand of a 'really, really good time' that lay far beyond the castle walls of the idea of taste suggested by the music press. But for it to find traction, they needed a record that matched their looks and captured fully the thrill of their live show.

CHAPTER 9

Get Your Boots On

Stomp

verb

To walk with intentionally heavy steps, especially as a way of showing that you are annoyed.

In the 1970s, the shiny shop window of BBC1's *Top of the Pops* was the one where the latest sounds and fashions would be dressed and careers could be made or broken. Devised by producer Johnnie Stewart, the programme was first broadcast from Manchester on New Year's Day 1964, and by the turn of the decade, the show had relocated to London, broadcasting in colour – for those who could afford such luxury – from BBC TV Centre in White City.

If their performance of 'The Shape of Things to Come' was a false start from April of the previous year, when Slade appeared on *Top of the Pops* with 'Get Down and Get With It' in July 1971, they were in transition from their skinhead phase towards their glam look. As a result, it was an unholy fusion of thrift store meeting high couture, which struck a chord out in the provinces. Whereas it was hard to emulate the boa of Bolan, Holder's flat cap could be found easily lurking at the back of your father's wardrobe. It also chimed with a renaissance in looking backwards to the Edwardian era – Gilbert O'Sullivan had also pioneered the flat cap look; Edwardian paraphernalia such as the Pears Soap and vintage Coca-Cola advertising signs and TV phenomenon *Upstairs Downstairs* chimed with the British public. This reached its apogee with the 1974 Hovis advert, directed by a young Ridley Scott, that although shot in the Golden Hill area of Shaftesbury in Dorset, created a universal view of the north, with its sepia and hard-won pleasures. The move from austerity to glitter seemed to happen overnight.

Lea told the BBC for the 1999 *It's Slade* documentary that, 'When we first went to *Top of the Pops*, the sets were being held together with tape, it was all a bit tatty and it wasn't that wonderful ball that we saw on TV – you could see the cracks, the joins and see it being stuck together – such is the arrogance of youth, I looked at this, and I thought, we can take this, we can do this.' And it was very true, they could. And they did. Heavier rock was very much the thing, and the appropriation of US music was hardly anything new – but to be done in such very spectacular style.

The BBC was initially wary of the group's charms, as Jim Lea told writer Mark Paytress, 'Jimmy Young said he'd never heard such a row in all his life, although I suppose that was image building stuff as he represented the older generation and we were kids. Tony Blackburn machine-gunned our first hit live on air. Ed Stewart said we'd never make it. Tommy Vance hated our guts to begin with. John Peel was always suspicious of us. And Noel Edmonds used to call us Never, as in "Slade? Never!"'

'Get Down and Get With It' (or by its original title, 'Get Down With It') was one of Little Richard's later records; a 1967 cover version of a 1964 Bobby Marchan song, recorded at EMI Studios in Abbey Road. The band heard it played regularly by DJ Crusoe (John Robinson) at the Connaught in Wolverhampton and would witness the raucous reaction to it. 'We started doing it,' Holder told Chris Charlesworth. 'The skinheads used to love that bit at the finish where you put your hands in the air and take your boots off and all that.'

'At a pub we did regularly in Wolverhampton a guy played records between the bands,' Holder added to Dave Ling in 2022. 'When

I heard this bloody great song I asked: "Is this the Little Richard version of 'Get Down and Get With It?" He replied that it was, and when I asked where I could get hold of it, he gave me his own. For donkey's years, right until the end of our career, that's the song we closed the set with before the encores.'

'I saw them live when they were still doing the psychedelic thing. I mean, they were fantastic,' Frank Lea says. 'I saw them again at the Connaught Hotel, and they were fucking brilliant. It was the first time I heard 'Get Down and Get With It'. It just stood out a mile. It was unbelievable.' Chas Chandler saw it in the set and thought the way forward would be to capture it exactly as it was played on stage, captured live with much multi-tracked hand-clapping and boot-stomping. It was made in the big room at Olympic, where The Rolling Stones, The Who and Led Zeppelin had recorded, and cut as live, with all the excitement of a Slade performance, and for the first time, Automatic Double Track (ADT) was used on Holder's voice. 'He had a big voice anyway,' Jim was to say, 'but this made him sound colossal.' It was a prime example of Chas Chandler's maxim: 'Make the best possible record as cheaply as possible. The most important rule in the industry.'

Released on 21 May, the rousing call-to-arms was an amazing introduction of Slade to the wider world. To support this mighty A, there were not one, but two songs on the B-Side – both rare Dave Hill/Noddy Holder collaborations, 'Do You Want Me' was a sultry number, taking its feel (if sounding nothing like) Elvis Presley's 'Crawfish'. 'A slinky, haunting celebration of fleshy pleasures,' as Slade writer Chris Ingham put it. The other track, 'Gospel According to Rasputin' is dark and progressive, with vocal harmonies on a par with Crosby Stills & Nash; Venice Beechdale, if you will.

To coincide with the release, the group appeared on *Whittaker's World of Music* on London Weekend Television on Saturday 22 May, on a bill with Freda Payne and Joe Brown. Host, genial singer and whistler, Roger Whittaker, looks like a man possessed as he says, 'and now, 'Get Down and Get With It' with SLADE!' The camera pans right to reveal Holder in red shirt, patterned tank-top and cloth cap, performing the opening yell. The band, in a curious selection of outfits (Jim's purple cape!) mime to the single with

81

the camera adoring one particular go-go dancer. It was impossible not to be thoroughly gripped by such an uproarious performance. The theatre where the band lift their hands in unison to clap is still tremendous, all these years on. Subtle it wasn't. By mid-June it started climbing the UK charts, and although it only reached a peak position of number sixteen, it was to remain on the charts for fourteen weeks.

Mark Paytress captures the record's opening perfectly in *Glam: When Superstars Rocked The World*: Holder's 'opening "Well, all right!" rap had the gospel energy of Little Richard and the call-to-arms rabble-rousing of Plastic Ono-era Lennon.' Such upfront-ness had not been heard for a while in pop. As Paytress continues, 'Slade ramped up the excitement.' 'After 'Get Down', says Jim Lea, 'we decided to make the whole show like that – cut out the clever stuff and rave it up. I don't think anybody else in the world was doing that, only in soul revues. It was like gospel. Everybody sing along.' This gospel call-and-response, that was to become so central to their records and performances, created a bootboy evangelical church, and Holder was a combination of high priest, market trader and ringmaster.

''Get Down and Get With It' doesn't really indicate where Slade are gonna go, beyond the stompiness of it,' notes music writer and Slade fan Alexis Petridis. 'But it tells you a lot about where Slade came from: they've done the classic tough sixties apprenticeship: *Slade Alive!* is like that as well. It's very much if you're playing working men's clubs and and one-night stands and Hamburg, that's the song you want in your back pocket. That is going to go down a storm in front of a load of off-duty soldiers or whatever.'

As if to further emphasise their role as outsiders, Slade always stayed at The Edward Hotel in Spring Street, opposite Paddington Station. It was near where their print champion, Chris Charlesworth, lived. 'I lived in a shared flat in Bayswater and occasionally went to the Edward to have a drink with them,' he says. 'They were very frugal and the Edward was cheap. They actually came round my flat one night after they'd recorded a *TOTP* at Shepherd's Bush, all four of them,' Charlesworth says. 'It was funny, because one of my flatmates' girlfriends was a fan and I was in the kitchen with them having a beer and she walked in. She couldn't believe her eyes. They signed their autographs for her. Then we went off back to the Edward where there was a bar and no one bothered them. I remember you could get a roast chicken dinner there for just over £1.'

At this time, Slade began to make inroads in Europe. That July, while the band were driven by Swin and the road crew drove the van, Chris Charlesworth crunched into the back of Chas Chandler's wine-coloured Aston Martin DB5 and was driven, with Lotte, from The Hague to Amsterdam where the band were playing four days. 'In Amsterdam we stayed in a hotel called The 13 Balkans, right in the centre, the red-light area,' Charlesworth recalls. 'Chas said it was where he always stayed. One thing was for sure, the brandy was dirt cheap there.' The brandy flowed so freely it became impossible for some of the party to sample the city's obvious delights.

Slade had arrived – but the trick, of course, was to follow it up. And follow it they did. Their next single brought all the experience, craft and musicianship of the past five years together, combined with all of Chandler and Halsall's marketing nous; although Halsall was more discreet in his approach to PR than his predecessor. 'Altham was good at that. I wasn't,' Halsall recalls. 'At the sharp end, I primarily dealt with John Steel who was a nice policeman as opposed to Chas's nasty policeman, lovely bloke.'

CHAPTER 10

Misspelt Youth

'Coz I Luv You' was a masterful stroke of pop writing, a confluence of glam and folk-rock with an unmistakable melody. It was the first time, at Chas Chandler's insistence, that Jim Lea and Noddy Holder actually sat down and wrote together. Lea went over to Holder's house in Gurney Road one night with a shuffle rhythm he had; Leah Holder made them a cup of cocoa and the two of them set about writing what was to become their first number one single.

'Half an hour later, cocoa was drunk, and 'Coz I Luv You' was born,' Lea said on *It's Slade*. 'Jim came round my mum's house and brought his violin with him and we came up with 'Coz I Luv You' in twenty minutes, the whole song,' Holder told Mark Blake. 'We based it on a sort of riff we used to tune up with in the dressing room. I was a big Django and Stéphane fan and the guy who taught me guitar in the fifties could play like Django, taught me that style and to tune the violin. We go into a jazzy riff and Jim played Grappelli fiddle. It is a dead simple ditty. I don't think we even played it to the band.' Lea and Holder took the track to Chas Chandler and played it to him on acoustic guitar and violin. 'He went, I don't think you've written your next hit,' Holder continues. 'I think you've written your first number one. We went, oh fuck off, Chas, no way. You think a number one takes you hours. We didn't think a twenty-minute ditty would be the way to fame and fortune.'

Although it was hardly the galumphing oafishness of 'Get Down and Get With It', retaining its use of multi-tracked stomping and clapping gave it a uniquely otherworldly edge, emphasised further by the use of echo on the handclaps that were down in the corridor at Olympic. 'We were called to Chas's office when he mixed 'Coz I Luv You' and he put it on,' Dave Hill said. 'I took an acetate of it home – Chas was always saying, Go and play it to your family. I put it on my dad's stereo. My sister, Carol, being very musical and a dancer and showbizzy, was absolutely gobsmacked. She said, "it sent me all funny. I'm tingly. Amazing record."' The reaction in the Lea household was slightly different: 'James came back from London one day, he walked up the garden and told me to listen to their new record, 'Coz I Luv You',' Frank Lea says. 'I said it was great – anyway, I'm off to play football on the field.'

'To Slade-ify, we put boot stomping, handclapping and chanting and give it the magic and brought it into a rockier vein,' Holder told Mark Blake. 'Radio took to it right away. First week released, we were amazed, in two weeks it was number one. He could spot them, and that was the good thing about Chas. He loved getting stuff down quick. He grew up in the rock'n'roll era with The Animals. When he played with them, they were one or two takes to get their hits. We had the benefit of his experience, not a technical chap at all. He left that to the engineer.'

That engineer was Alan O'Duffy, working with the group for the first time, based at Olympic Studios at Barnes, West London. 'It was an extraordinary time,' O'Duffy reflects on the era:

> That world doesn't exist any longer. Musicians moving from one session to another; ten sessions a week, two sessions a day. The string players would go from a session in Olympic in Barnes, to Abbey Road, and they go to the Royal Festival Hall to play something the same night. That was the world and it revolved around maybe 200 people. In the rhythm section there was maybe twenty-five people who were employed non-stop: adverts, television, films and pop records. My world was sitting in a studio and working with these guys, I was being used by the talent who came

in the door, make something absolutely beautiful, get paid thirty quid and go home.

The chanting on 'Coz I Luv You' as the song progresses sounds like a pop audience had inadvertently stumbled into a Romani encampment late at night, when the party was in full swing. There was the element of Russian folk song in its make-up as well, which had been in the popular imagination since Mary Hopkin had sung 'Those Were the Days', adapted from a Russian romance song from the twenties.

The Guardian wrote about 'Coz I Luv You' in 2011, 'It was all about the stomp: 'Coz I Luv You''s bootboy rhythm anchored its swirling, menacing violin line and the two combined to give this single – Slade's first number one – its frightening, primitive edge.' It was the use of violin that was so striking – the instrument that been Lea's secret weapon all along; and its use in pop and rock had been sparing – Denny Laine had incorporated strings after leaving The Moody Blues in his Electric String Band, and The Who's 'Baba O'Riley' showcased Dave Arbus's violin playing. Arbus, from the band East of Eden, Dave 'Swarb' Swarbrick from Fairport Convention and Darryl Way from Curved Air had been instrumental in helping the 'fiddle' leave the string section of an orchestra behind, finding a ground between classical, folk and rock.

Jim Lea, however, made the violin something altogether darker on 'Coz I Luv You', offering a generous nod to French virtuoso Stéphane Grappelli. Holder and Lea would often jam the gypsy jazz of guitarist Django Reinhardt and violinist Grappelli in dressing rooms before taking to the stage. Barney Hoskyns wrote in his book *Glam! Bowie, Bolan and the Glitter Rock Revolution* that it was 'an eccentric record which sounded like Family's Roger Chapman fronting a gypsy string band'.

There was also a treat on the flipside, one to immediately confuse the group's newfound fans – 'My Life is Natural', a rare Holder-only composition, is up there with their greatest material, illustrating perfectly how much the group could give The Who a fine run for their money. Chris Ingham described it as 'grave, disturbing and both metrically and morally elusive'. A possible paean to the need for a new saviour, its rich 12-string and Dave Hill power-chords make it one of Slade's best B-sides.

When the group appeared on *Top of the Pops*, Holder was wearing his outsized Baker Boy hat, and looked every inch the gang leader; for those who had witnessed 'Get Down and Get With It', it showed there was another string to their bow. Lea's fiddle playing influenced the future Dexys Midnight Runners violinist Helen O'Hara, then a 15-year-old school orchestra classical violinist:

> When I heard it on the radio, my ears absolutely latched on to the violin. A few months previously, I'd heard Rod Stewart's 'Reason to Believe'; that was more what you'd expect in a way, a slightly folky, softer sound. But I didn't know who played it. And it wasn't really important, because it was all about Rod Stewart. The difference with Slade was that Jim was part of the group. So, when I saw them on TV, he made the violin cool, because up until then, it was pretty non-existent apart from him because of background orchestras or quartets in pop music. And then suddenly *this*, the bass guitarist of the group was playing a violin. And it was the way he was playing it as well, that got me. He was playing it like he was a guitarist, rhythmically, playing at the same time as the guitarist on each beat. That was unusual. I thought that's a rhythmic, percussive bit and then of course, he had his solo.

> Two further things deeply impressed the young O'Hara, 'Jim was digging in,' she says. 'Also, he looked great. He looked like a pop star, and moved about a lot. He was really owning that fiddle in Slade, which you'd think wouldn't work, but of course it did. It was written in a key that's really good for the violin, A minor and D minor. So, he could play two strings at the same time, which would make it bright and strong. A talented guy. I'm a massive fan. He's probably the one who set me on the way really.'

'Coz I Luv You' reached number one on 13 November 1971, taking over from another record that predominantly featured a violin, Rod Stewart's 'Maggie May'. Stewart was another performer whose time was right after years of slogging around in the clubs and halls in a variety of acts. 'Coz I Luv You''s four weeks at number one was brought to a close when Benny Hill's 'Ernie (The Fastest Milkman in the West)' reached the top on 5 December. Although he hadn't been over-enamoured when he first heard 'Coz I Luv You', Frank Lea had an epiphany when he heard of its number one position: 'I was doing some plumbing at the time. I used to have a radio, and it came on and I was so excited, I just left my tools, left everything and I thought, that's it, I'm off. I left the people with no water, no nothing, that was it! I said I want to be a roadie, so it was Swin, Charlie and me.'

'Coz I Luv You' is a beguiling and long-lasting song, catching the group before the stomping really set in. Tim Rice, who aside from songwriting, is an avid chart-watcher and one-time compiler of *The Guinness Book of Hit Singles* concurs, 'I remember seeing James Blunt in concert in America, and he's sang 'Coz I Luv You'. He did a really good version, but the song is so good. [Slade's songs] have suffered a little because not enough people have done them in a more contemporary style.'

Although the group had ultimately failed in appropriating the skinhead look as a gimmick, it launched something far more copyable within its fledgling fanbase: misspelling their song titles. 'We thought 'Because I Love You' was a wet title for a song and so we used the spelling that would be on toilet walls in the Midlands and that made it more hard-hitting,' Holder said. It was said that to demonstrate, Holder wrote 'Coz I Luv You' on a wall and Chas Chandler saw it and thought it would be a good idea to retain the spelling – 'bog wall easy speek' as it became known: 'It became our gimmick – Black Country slang – years before textspeak,' Holder said in 2016. John Peel wrote that their grammatical slips 'predated the gangsta rap enthusiasm for phonetic spelling by close to three decades'. As writer Simon Reynolds notes in *Shock and Awe: Glam Rock and Its Legacy*, the titles were 'a jovial gesture of delinquent solidarity with kids who left school at fifteen with zero qualifications and a life of labour ahead of them.'

The spelling was a coup that aligned the band to a generation of school children, especially as the word 'luv' was used in teenage relationships as a far less heavy version of full-blown 'love'. Holder's choice of lyrics too acted the way that the expression of sentiment in a greeting card does for emotionally illiterate men. It's a giddy encapsulation of the intensity of early love, and the line, 'only time can tell if we get on well' embodied both the hope and the transitory nature of youthful passion. There was a beating heart underneath the exaggerated masculinity.

It has been said many times that this corruption of spelling was to fall foul with education authorities: 'There was a huge outcry,' Holder said, 'but later they taught it in schools to kids with learning difficulties – phonetic learning.' Mrs Norma Adams was the head of maths at Woodfield Avenue Junior School in Penn. 'Some kids copied the spellings, but it wasn't a big problem for us. Later, I'd see Dave walking down the corridor sometimes, as his daughter, Jade, was at the school and he'd always say, "hello love".'

Realising it was a rich seam, all of the subsequent Slade singles for the next twenty-four months had some curious spelling; it was not dissimilar to the 'Chaucer in Bloxwich' line that Slade historian Chris Selby uses. Although Slade had, in some circles, been something of a – if not laughing stock – certainly a raised eyebrow in the music press, 'Coz I Luv You' made people sit up and listen. Tony Stewart wrote about the group in *NME* at the end of 1971, and the subheading posited the pertinent question, 'Is this the death knell for "heavy listening" music? It could be... for bands like Slade are proving that fans want to rave instead of sitting around and being grave.' For Slade, the next eighteen months would be nothing but raving.

Disc and Music Echo reported on 13 November 1971, that the Slade skinhead era had passed, and that Noddy Holder's only concession were his boots. 'Gone the rest of the uniform – the super-crewcut "barnet". Regulation braces, the aggressive attitude, replaced in turn by shoulder-length locks, red velvet jacket and a softly-spoken almost apologetic air.' The paper went to on to somewhat fetishise his footwear; 'he still sports the infamous "bovver" boots. Though now they are more fashionable than functional. A deep red in colour, wet-look in style and highly polished to make a regimental sergeant-major's heart proud.' The article concludes with the line 'this aside, Slade are certainly "Skinhead" no more.'

Because of Slade's reputation as a live act, their gig sheet was booked six months into the future, which meant even though they were now a number one act, they honoured the gigs for the fee that had been agreed: 'The only thing that changed was the adulation of the fans, and being on TV regular,' Holder told Billy Sloan on BBC Radio Scotland in 2022. This led to some of the most memorable shows the group had ever played.

Holder cites the gig at the Boston Gliderdrome in Lincolnshire as the night when the mania began. 'Coz I Luv You' had just got to number one – Holder fell on stage and was virtually pulled apart by excited teenage girls. It was also at this show that a bouncer talked about another group being 'crazy with whisky', which gave him an idea for near-future reference.

'Chas had been slogging away beating his head against a brick wall as far as interest in Slade was concerned,' John Steel says. 'Until that point when we got that tickle in the charts. Then number one, and then of course *everybody* wanted to be friends with Chas and friends with Slade.'

In 1998, when glam rock started to be revaluated properly, Barney Hoskyns wrote his book *Glam! Bowie, Bolan and the Glitter Rock Revolution*, published on no less an imprint than Faber & Faber. He spoke for many on the impression that the group caused: 'For all their glam togs, there was precious little effeminate about Slade. Many more would follow in the group's clodhopping footsteps. From the Sweet to the Spiders From Mars to Arthur Harold Kane of the New York Dolls: brickies in eyeliner seemed almost as endemic to glam as swishing queens.'

CHAPTER 11

Gutbust Concrete Sledgehammer – Slade Alive!

1972 proved a cornucopia of success for groups and artists who had been working hard in semi-obscurity since the mid-sixties. Marc Bolan had gone early and started this path; his first single had been released in 1965, six years before his first number one with 'Hot Love' in 1971; Sweet had been a variety of outfits before their first single on Fontana in 1968; Elton John had first recorded with Bluesology in 1965, and had released his first solo single in 1968; David Bowie was first on record in 1964 with Davie Jones and the King Bees, and although 'Space Oddity' had been Top 10 in 1969, it was this year where he truly found his feet, and Ziggy Stardust was born. Slade had travelled a very similar path, but, unlike the others, didn't change their sound, and hardly changed their approach, which is why they were to resonate with the masses, at least for a while.

Another group of fellow travellers were Status Quo, who had actually achieved chart success with the whimsical psychedelia of 'Pictures of Matchstick Men' and 'Ice in the Sun' in 1968, but had been listing commercially since; then they struck upon a hard blues-boogie style that was beginning to gain ground. 'I remember them being in the skinheads and the braces and they looked quite aggressive, which is kind of weird when you think of H,' Francis

Rossi says of Slade. 'We were working and we decided we were going to see them and they were in Hereford.'

Quo had played the Training College in the town earlier on the evening of Friday 7 January 1972 and crossed the two miles across town to the Flamingo Ballroom, where Slade were headlining. 'There's always this myth in showbiz that everyone gets along. They used to perhaps many years ago in the late sixties. Then there became that competition with Slade. We heard 'Get Down and Get With It' and went, "Fucking hell that's good. *Shit!*" Then we were in a room together, having a joint and a chat and I just found them all very agreeable. We got on from that day on, then we did the tour together.' The band would tour together the coming May, beginning a long-lasting alliance.

It was all about the build now; their next single, 'Look Wot You Dun', was released at the end of January. A follow-up to a number one is always difficult but 'Look Wot You Dun' was enough like 'Coz I Luv You' to offer a trademark sound, but also developed the formula. The initial idea for the single came from Powell, who took it to Jim Lea, who then developed it further with Holder.

Recorded at Olympic in late 1971, Dave Hill had to borrow a guitar from Peter Frampton, who was working on his first solo album, *Wind of Change*, in the other room. The piano-driven 'Look Wot You Dun' certainly has a Plastic Ono Band swing to it, another hard rock take on gypsy jazz, with Powell contributing heavy breathing on the chorus, and arguably Hill's greatest guitar solo on record. The Olympic corridor clapping and stomping was still very much in effect.

'Look Wot You Dun' went to number four in March 1972, behind three enormous records of its day – Chicory Tip's Moog-based Giorgio Moroder-penned novelty, 'Son of My Father'; Don McLean's overrated music lecture 'American Pie'; and Harry Nilsson's epic reading of Badfinger's 'Without You'. 'Look Wot You Dun' was a solid, if slightly copycat, follow-up. The Beatles influence continued on the Lea/Powell-written B-side 'Candidate', with its harmonies and 'Paperback Writer'-esque riffing, its very looseness and immediacy is one of the reasons that Slade's flips are so well-regarded by the cognoscenti.

'There's this sort of interstitial period where they do 'Look Wot You Dun' and they're sort of searching for a direction,' Alexis Petridis says. "Look Wot You Dun"'s got that fat, kind of compressed, very Slady sort of sound to it without the sort of instrumentation that you expect on a Slade record. When they hit it, the reason it works is because I think glam, generally speaking, is a collision of two opposing things. It's old rock and roll, whether it's 'Drive in Saturday', or 'Jeepster', a lot of it sounds like it could have been made in the fifties but done in this totally artificial way deliberately, wilfully artificial production.'

Slade's relentless schedule meant they covered all bases; by the end of January, they had played eighteen shows, from Plymouth to Newcastle. 'I remember being at the Tricorn Club in Portsmouth, a great place,' Frank Lea says. 'I used to go round the front to listen to the sound. They used to play two or three songs back to back, to open the set, giving you the full power surge and then a new track appeared – 'In Like a Shot from My Gun'. You could see the way that they were going, it was a great transformation. You could see what was going to happen – it was fascinating to watch.' The group took time out to record a session for Stuart Henry's *Sounds of the 70s*. It was all go.

Frank Lea began to travel in their car with them:

I used to be in the group car quite a bit. But I had the sense to keep me gob shut. Because I had a brother in the band, I didn't want to be seen as siding with him. I used to say to James, you're weird, you lot are. Because the band would come in the car and pick us up. We'd get in and out, and nobody spoke. After the gig, they'd speak a bit then shut up. When we got home and got out of the car, nobody would 'say see you tomorrow.' Jim said, we'll see each other tomorrow so there was no need to say it. It was still strange. Because you're all close friends, like a marriage.

The group hardly ever socialised together, mainly because they spent quite so much time together.

* * *

95

Slade played the Lanchester Arts Festival in Coventry on Thursday 3 February 1972, as part of a seven-day music, poetry, comedy and theatre festival across multiple venues in the city, which had been established by Ted Little at Lanchester Polytechnic (now Coventry University) in 1969. The 1972 line-up included Chuck Berry, Billy Preston and – as a replacement for David Bowie – Pink Floyd, performing their new suite, *Eclipse: A Piece for Assorted Lunatics*. A news story in *NME* the previous week summed up how the group were thought of at this time: 'Slade are riding in on the "scream-scene" smacking audiences in the head and groin and sending them freaking up and down the aisles. Though they lack subtlety (and why shouldn't they?), this one-time band of skinheads have proved that technical brilliance is no substitute for an acute awareness of rollicking good music.'

Slade were on the bill with Billy Preston and Chuck Berry at Coventry's famous Locarno Club perched high above the concrete of the city centre. American comedian Uncle Dirty (aka actor Bob Altman) opened the bill with his laconic and, for the times, risqué humour, and then Slade began at full tilt. Charles Shaar Murray wrote in *Cream*: 'Almost before they have played a note, Noddy Holder is ordering the people to "really let rip" and after the first number he berates "all you miserable fuckers down there – you look as if you're shitting yourselves! Get off your arses and let rip!" After the second he tells the fringe of leapers at the rim of the crowd to move in and stomp all over those sitting down.'

Billy Preston continued the night, then the Roy Young Band played a set before Chuck Berry, who, with Young's rhythm section, ran through all his old favourites. Speaking of risqué, Berry brought the house down with an eleven-minute version of 'My Ding-A-Ling', his cover of Dave Bartholomew's 1952 song that he'd recorded as 'My Tambourine' on his *From St. Louie to Frisco* album in 1968. It was impossible not to get caught up in its double entendre-heavy call-and-response. All four members of Slade took part and revelled in the spectacle.

'For sure,' Powell adds, 'we all stayed and watched the MAN.' Berry's set overrun, meaning the following Pink Floyd show commenced at midnight; audience members who had tickets for both had to leave the venue to come back in again, which caused a great deal of consternation. Watching Chuck Berry gave Jim Lea an idea, and it was a big one. He saw Berry's showmanship, how he was stopping to let the crowd sing. 'I thought it was amazing,' he told *Record Mirror* in 1984. 'It wasn't just a few people, it was everyone. I thought it was amazing and I thought – why not write the crowd into the songs.' This idea become the bedrock of Slade's imperial phase.

Tony Stewart wrote about Slade's performance at Coventry in *NME* the following week, 'Slade were not too happy about going on first, I believe. As usual they worked hard at stirring the audience up, with Noddy Holder telling them to stand up and let rip. His coarse remarks shook a few people off their rumps, and I must admit to being an ardent fan of the band after such a showy and exuberant set. Their sound was something to be admired, with thudding bass and drums, and some piercing lead licks coming through.' Their act was now being honed to perfection – they were match fit through a great deal of practice.

* * *

Whereas 1971 had been all about the single, 1972 was about Slade making their definitive album. Somewhere out on an Italian promo jukebox single, there is a double A-side of James Brown's 'I Got Ants in my Pants, Pt I' backed with Slade's 'Cum On Feel the Noize'. Such unusual pairings of artists on the label's current roster were not unusual in that country. Yet, after deeper thought, it is not that wayward a union. Aside from the commonality of being on Polydor, both artists were remembered primarily as singles artists, and both their definitive albums were recorded in concert. James Brown's, of course, was recorded at Harlem's Apollo Theater on 24 October 1962, and Slade, with *Slade Alive!* recorded at Command Studios, Piccadilly almost nine years to the day later, 19–21 October 1971. Chas Chandler understood just how powerful the group were live, and to really show the record-buying public their capabilities, he would harness this potential – showing his charges being closer to Led Zeppelin or The Who than T. Rex. *Slade Alive!* would make some established heads turn.

Command Studios had an illustrious history – it had been the Allied Forces Network HQ, and during the Second World War had been the British version of New York's Stage Door Canteen, offering servicemen and guests a night of free entertainment. Bing Crosby, Fred Astaire and Glenn Miller all performed, as did Julie Andrews who made her stage debut there. It became a BBC facility after the war and converted to a recording studio in 1970. The main room could accommodate live performances and was accessed through a door next to Air France in Piccadilly.

'Chas's idea with *Slade Alive!* was to get a "live" recording but in a studio,' John Halsall says. 'I organised the audience by competition and also ran the contest for the cover design – was great fun and worked well.' An advert was placed in the music press:

See Slade Free! at Command Studios, 101 Piccadilly, W.1
October, 19th, 20th, 21st, Recording a live album to follow their
latest single Coz I Luv You (Available October 8th) Send s.a.e for
two tickets to POPWIRE (Dept Sl). 44, Park Road, London NW1
4SH – First 500 applications only

'I believed that their greatest asset was their live performance,' Chas Chandler said in 1984. 'They had two years without a hit and the only thing that was going positively was they were always being booked back at gigs. They were earning their living as musicians working very hard, five nights a week, eleven months a year. They were being musicians full-time and expanding their art if you like, playing everything that came along.'

Recorded by Barry Ainsworth with Chandler overseeing the proceedings, *Slade Alive!* is an absolute blast – the choice of material is exhilarating. Ten Years After's 'Hear Me Calling' had been a live favourite of Slade for years, it's light and airy take on heavy blues was similar in approach to that of Canned Heat. 'It was our live set at that time,' Holder told Dave Ling. 'We played lots of covers, including songs by The Moody Blues, Frank Zappa and The Idle Race, even Ted Nugent. But when Chas Chandler found us, he encouraged us to write our own. So *Slade Alive!* was very, very raw… It's the sound of a rock'n'roll band in full force.'

'Darling Be Home Soon', written by John B. Sebastian as a tender, loving song, is suddenly enlivened by Holder's loud belch at the exact moment where the song goes down to a tender denouement. 'That was a total accident,' Holder told Dave Ling in 2022, 'but after that album came out and was so successful, I had to do the same thing every night. If I didn't then the fans would go berserk.' Burping is not in the lingua franca of rock – at once it endeared the group to thousands of urchins whose party piece at the school disco was their ability to belch the alphabet. 'We haven't always used vulgarity,' Holder said in 1971 to *NME*. 'It stemmed from when we got smashed one night and it just came out. It went down a storm and we've used it ever since. We just pummel their brains until they give in. It's a kind of release valve.'

The album also featured 'In Like a Shot from My Gun', 'Know Who You Are', 'Keep On Rocking' and a thumping version of 'Get Down and Get With It'. However, it was all about the closer: 'This song's our regular finisher, this is another leaper, another one to really let rip in, it's from Steppenwolf, the one and only, and this is 'BORN TO BE WILD',' Holder screams.

It was fortuitous that the song that they had heard in the Bahamas in 1968, as it was freshly released in the States, would in the intervening years become such a well-known song, loaded with meaning as it opened the 1969 counterculture classic film, *Easy Rider*, and now at this point a record that everyone would be able to identify with. As a result, as you can imagine, the crowd completely lose themselves to the incredible groove that it makes. The power and the force of the group is just astounding. The end of 'Born to Be Wild' provides a template for The Jesus and Mary Chain, The Sex Pistols and punk. The wall of feedback and abandonment is unlike what anyone who thought of them as a singles band would do.

A reporter at the *Derby Telegraph*, Richard Cox, was so smitten with the band when he'd seen them play in Derby in December 1970, he joined a bus-load of East Midlands fans down to the night that ultimately became the recording. The horde arrived, saturated in booze and clearly were ready to party. The noise of the crowd, and their familiarity with the material made the listener feel that they should quickly join in on the celebration. There was also plenty to read, too, when the album came out. Housed in gatefold sleeve, de rigueur for the time, with the prize-winning stoner cartoon artwork on the inner sleeve with thirty-two quotes extolling the group's virtue. The most telling quote was from Paul McCartney, taken from the *Aberdeen Press* from December 1971, discussing his new group, Wings: 'I don't want Wings to get hoisted into the superstar bracket like The Beatles were: T. Rex and Slade can have that.'

Slade Alive! was released at the tail end of March 1972 and was an interesting album to be the breakthrough by the band but it certainly wasn't a varnished recording. There would be little doubt what you were getting into when you bought a Slade record. 'And I finally got a credit!' John Halsall beams. '*Slade Alive!* is a true recreation of concert visceral release, possessing much of the spirit of those two other great concert LPs, *Rockin' The Fillmore* (by the Pie) and *Five Live Yardbirds*, with none of the phoney baloney Bangla Desh faked applause; this is the genuine thing from start to finish.' They got on the radar of Lester Bangs, no less, who talked in *Phonograph Record* in his usual spiel that:

> What SLADE ALIVE! is gutbust concrete sledgehammer get it off junk jive for right now, rendered as deftly as (to quote *Time* magazine on the Dave Clark Five in 1964) 'a jackhammer battering ugly holes in the shaded street of a respectable suburb, overturning the Welcome Wagon sending 39 Hospitality Hostesses still clutching their address books tumbling out onto the "raw" concrete to crack their skulls and lay in the cruel sun and wonder.' Other words, it's gooder'n shit.

There were inroads made gently in the States. *Slade Alive!* made ripples in the right circles: Jon Tiven wrote in *Rolling Stone*, 'Despite what you may have heard of "skinhead rock" or "Seventies teddies", Slade is exactly the opposite of a gimmick band. You'll not find synthesizers, guillotines, or the like near these four fine fellows, but you will find screaming young 'uns and loud, raucous rock & roll in the immediate vicinity of any Slade appearance.'

Interestingly, *Slade Alive!* was very different to their singles. Certainly, those teenyboppers who were getting into Slade through

'Coz I Luv You' and 'Look Wot You Dun' were suddenly introduced to harder rock than some of their older brothers favoured, with nasty walls of guitar and a bass'n'drums that shake foundations.

Furthermore, *Slade Alive!* also underlined the strong sense of contract with group and audience. Slade are there to entertain, but fans are part of that deal – not just to be diverted, but to lose themselves completely. It's like a ritual, taking music back to its most primaeval form. And this is something that Holder would cultivate, as the years went by: the preacher is visiting your town, and he's going to share his experience and rock'n'roll knowledge with his flocks. There was this hardworking rhythm section behind him. And then, in Dave Hill, there was this permanent curio, a heavy rock guitarist in his big old boots and outfits. It was an amazing entrée, being the first album most people had heard by Slade. The sleeve design, with press cuttings from their work so far, made the listener feel that they should know more already – but worry not, here's a handy guide. So, while listening to this noise, their history can be boned up on.

Its raucous sound travelled well. 'I am convinced that while Slade were nothing short of a phenomenon in Australia from the middle of 1972 for around a year or so, they were a phenomenon built on word of mouth – on the back of the *Slade Alive!* album,' Australian fan Stephen Cross said. 'Although I was stuck in the backwoods and neither heard nor saw anything about Slade in the media, there obviously were articles and reviews in the few Australian music magazines around back then, such as *Go-Set*. The singles clearly received airplay on the Sydney/Melbourne/Adelaide music radio stations enabling them to climb the charts.'

The group began to be featured throughout the music press as redoubtable regulars. Dave Hill was asked to be guest reviewer in *Melody Maker*'s 'Blind Date' feature. He was played another band who were breaking through. He was intrigued: 'This sounds like something from Crimson. That sax player must definitely be the sax player from Crimson. It's the same style. I don't find anything in the voice, but there is something about it. There are a lot of influences in it. This must be a very mixed-up band. I don't know who it is but it's very interesting.' The interesting band were Roxy

Music, who had just recorded their debut album in Command Studios.

* * *

In May 1972, Slade moved up to the bigger stages, with Status Quo supporting on their first proper headline UK tour. Mel Bush took over from the Gunnells. Bush had a great reputation as a large-scale promoter. He was later to represent David Essex who said, 'he seemed honest, down to earth and enthusiastic... a wonderful and trusting relationship.'

'He did Zeppelin, he bought David Cassidy over,' Don Powell says. 'He was fantastic for us.'

Status Quo and Slade had a tremendous affinity; although there was a time to plan and then a time to party, Slade would prepare before the concert: 'I didn't see that as Nod being moody. That's a true consummate professional,' Francis Rossi says.

'Our very first UK tour was us and Quo, like a co-headline thing,' Powell says. 'They were just starting to come up again and we were just starting to make a name for ourselves. It was Mel Bush's idea. He said to put the two together and it was Chas's idea to have the tickets all around 50p. And with Quo, we've been best friends ever since.'

CHAPTER 12

A *Disturbance in Gandalf's Garden –*
The Great Western Festival, May 1972

Slade looked an interesting booking at the Great Western Festival. The festival was the brainchild of Welsh actor and businessman Stanley Baker, known primarily in the UK for his appearance in the 1965 film classic, *Zulu*. Baker was something of a renaissance man; through Oakhurst, the film company he set up with Michael Deeley, he had produced *Robbery* and *The Italian Job*. Baker was also part of the consortium that set up Harlech Television; an entrepreneur who ultimately had to take roles in questionable movies to keep his companies afloat. 'By the early 1970s my dad had more or less stopped acting to concentrate on producing films,' his eldest son, Martin Baker, recalls. 'Barry Spikings and Michael Deeley persuaded my dad that there was money to be made in promoting a music festival.'

Another partner in the festival was Lord Harlech himself, David Ormsby-Gore, who had been the British Ambassador to the United States at the time of the Cuban Missile Crisis and Kennedy's assassination. 'Dad formed Great Western Festival Company with Lord Harlech as a director and raised money from different sources for the project and at the age of 19, I joined the organisation team,' Martin Baker continues.

The Great Western Festival was held over Whitsun weekend in late May 1972. In the preceding months it had been subject to all manner of controversy as its organisers searched for somewhere to stage the event; sites in Essex and Kent had both been considered before outcries from the locals. 'We were stopped by the council from mounting the festival in Bishopsbourne in Kent,' Martin Baker says. 'We first looked at a site at Hunt's Farm in Tollesbury in Essex, but after the locals had hung and burned dummies made out to be my dad and Lord Harlech, we quickly abandoned that plan.'

In mid-April, a site was found on farmland of Tupholme Manor Park near the village of Bardney, ten miles west of Lincolnshire's county town. 'The booking team was led by John Martin, assisted by Brian Adams and Ed Bicknell (later to become Dire Straits manager). They chose a mainly rock group line-up, but my dad was keen to also have supporting groups that needed a break and asked me who I would suggest. I had recently become a fan of Slade and played him 'Coz I Luv You' and 'Look Wot You Dun'. He loved the sound of Noddy Holder, so the group were consequently added to the bill.'

Baker's wife, actor Ellen Martin (Lady Baker), visited the site by helicopter to see her husband and son before heading to Spain with her younger children. She was surprised her husband had moved into rock music as 'our generation was Frank Sinatra and Elvis Presley. Barry Spikings was much more into music and festivals.' Intermittent reports of the festival were relayed to her.

The lead-up to the festival was fraught with difficulties. The site was based around the 12th-century monastery Tupholme Abbey, which after the dissolution of the monasteries became a hall to a local family. After they left in the 19th century, it became farmland, and cottages were built around the ruins of the hall. By the time of the festival, the houses were derelict, and were, naturally, perfect squats for the weekend. As so much consternation had been caused by the festival's staging, security measures were tight. There was a short documentary made, and the police briefing is superb to view as a curio:

> You know the type of people you're going to deal with: you'll find long-haired, sometimes dirty, people gathered around in very large numbers. On their appearance you might tend, all being squares or mostly being squares, like me, to take a dislike to them. This is wrong, because from our experience... 90–95 per cent of them are coming along for a reasonably quiet, peaceful weekend, aside from the pop music that is, of course.

The locals feared 'being invaded by drug-taking hippies and the damage these so-called hooligans would cause,' Baker continues. 'Councillors sought a High Court injunction to stop the festival taking place over Whitsun bank holiday, which Dad saved by paying a bond of £10,000 against any potential damage caused.' It was one thing calming the locals; calming the weather was quite another: 'There was a terrible storm on the day of the festival. That storm absolutely collapsed the festival; and Stanley spent an enormous amount of money on rescuing people and sending them back to Scotland and wherever. It became a rescue mission,' Ellen Baker says. 'A gale force eight wind blew up and brought a deluge of rain, which blew the main stage down,' son Martin adds. 'We had to work overnight to re-erect it. The rain lasted on and off all weekend, and turned the site into a swamp, which resulted in tens of thousands of people not coming. However, during the weekend about 50,000 did come and the groups valiantly performed on the wind-swept stage.'

Among the acts on the bill were the *Monty Python's Flying Circus* team. Michael Palin wrote in his diary as he left for the site on that Sunday morning, 'the Sunday papers are full of reports of mud, and tents blowing down and general bad times from Bardney.' As Palin, who with his Python pals were to follow Slade on stage at the festival, surmised, the festival was something of a 'test case' as to whether landowners would give their acres to the great unwashed, in the wake of the Isle of Wight, Weeley and the recent Bickershaw festivals.

Slade would be on the bill on the Sunday with The Persuasions, the Average White Band, Brewer's Droop, Lindisfarne, and, as a replacement for the advertised bill toppers Sly and the Family Stone, The Beach Boys in full high hat and big beard phase.

Two days before their festival appearance, Slade released their next single. 'Take Me Bak 'Ome' removed any of the subtleties of 'Coz I Luv You' and 'Look Wot You Dun'. It was a straight-ahead stomper, a tremendous paean to the homesickness they felt and resistance to Chas Chandler's suggestion they relocate to London. 'With 'Take Me Bak 'Ome', I had some lyrics and Nod put the laddishness into it,' Jim Lea told Mark Blake. 'I was cerebral and philosophical, so Nod bought that to the writing. It was easier for people to identify with than what I was coming up with.'

And so, with a new laddish anthem in hand, at dusk on Sunday 28 May, Slade took to the stage at the Great Western Festival (known colloquially as the Lincoln Festival). Martin Baker recalls:

> I remember being with my dad in his huge caravan that Billy Smart of the circus had lent us, and hearing the conversation he had with Slade's manager, Chas Chandler, who was concerned that the group wouldn't go down well with the hippie crowd because they were thought of as just a silly pop group. To give the group a better chance, Chas wanted to delay their performance until the stage lights were needed, but my dad pointed out that would leave a fifteen-minute gap in the schedule, but in any case, the light was beginning to fade, and Chas reluctantly agreed for them to go on.

It was a gamble. Looking now at the bill of the four-day event, it seemed that Slade had little in common with many of the acts. Footage of the festival shows bedraggled youth wandering by stalls selling loons and patches, and with names like Gandalf's Garden and Festival Sleep Shop. Although Helen O'Hara wasn't at the festival, her view, as a then archetypal 16-year-old hippie-in-waiting, summed up how swathes of the crowd were feeling: 'I wouldn't have admitted then that I liked their songs. I recognised the great songs and the melody and this totally individual sound and look, especially

Noddy's voice, but I wouldn't have acknowledged it to my friends. As a teenager, there's some things that I'd secretly think like that, but your peer group would have ditched you.'

'When Slade hit the stage, it was still raining and the reaction from the crowd was anything but welcoming,' Martin Baker says. After a characteristically under-enthusiastic introduction from John Peel, 'some people even booed them'.

The band stood there in the gathering dusk. Although it was the Age of Aquarius, Holder knew that on a Bank Holiday Sunday, a good festival crowd would be ready to party. Summoning the spirit of all those boozers, WMCs, the Bahamas and Command Studios, he announced, 'Look I know it's pissing down, but stamp your feet and have a good time!'

'The group launched into a rocking set and Noddy did his best to encourage the audience to get up and enjoy themselves,' Martin Baker says. 'Suddenly, the rain stopped and the stage lights were turned on. After a very wet day this was the first time the audience didn't have to find shelter and they soon began to get up and boogie. Slade belted out one rocker after another.' All the hits and favourites came out, stunning the hippies.

'That gig stands out more than anything to me,' John Steel recalls. 'It was terrific – they just blew the place away. We were down in the front and, to this day, I can see the Polydor sales team, all these guys, record pluggers doing ring-a-ring-a-roses dancing around because they knew this was something special.'

'When they came to the end of their set, my dad, who was standing on the side of stage with Chas Chandler, waved to them to carry on,' Martin Baker says. 'Noddy Holder then told the audience that he was inviting my dad on stage and that they should thank him for organising the event. As my dad came on to stage, Noddy Holder started playing the theme music from the film *Zulu* and the rest of the band took it up,' Martin Baker says. 'My dad was absolutely delighted and thanked the audience for attending during such bad weather and behaving so well.'

'As soon as they came off, Stanley was in the dressing room, telling the guys what a great show they'd done,' John Steel adds. 'He was a very nice guy.'

Martin Baker was there as well: 'After the performance, I remember being backstage and seeing Chas Chandler being absolutely ecstatic about their performance and grabbing some music journalist and telling him that he couldn't write anything bad about his boys now because they had stolen the show.'

'Slade stormed the Great Western Festival and it was a pivotal moment in their story,' Mark Ellen, in attendance on the day as an 18-year-old hippie, was later to write. 'They'd converted the press, chucked a big brick in the pond and showed the vogueish rock underground they could wipe the floor with the lot of them.'

Although the Great Western Bardney Pop Festival ultimately lost Baker and Ormsby-Gore £200,000, it made Baker something of a folk hero, especially after his standing ovation granted by Holder. The festival was heavily in the news. Because of the controversy surrounding it, the police presence was huge, and it was one of the first times helicopters were used to survey the crowd. *Nationwide* covered its aftermath – reporter Bob Langley walked across the fields, strewn with debris, calling it 'a virtual ocean of saturated litter'. However, Baker's message of calm and respect for the neighbouring areas was borne out. Two nearby farmers, looking like they had stepped out of a Thomas Hardy novel, decreed that the festival-goers 'behaved alright'. They were 'as good as lads in our own village'.

Stanley Baker was delighted to see these kids 'be together and enjoy the music – and this is going to happen for a long, long time to come'. It also set his kid Martin off on his course: 'GWF was a breakthrough for me. Before the festival I had worked as a runner on *The Italian Job* and two Hammer horror films,' Baker recalls. 'During the festival I met a number of record company press people who told me that they need promotional films for their artist singles. Directly after the festival I joined Eyeline Films and started a forty-year career in making promotional films, concert videos and biographies.'

Another band on the verge of mass-breakthrough, Genesis, made their large-scale festival debut that day as well. Both would enjoy a level of popularity throughout the seventies. Historian Dominic

Sandbrook calls Slade and Genesis two emblematic bands of their era, yet between them 'yawned a vast cultural chasm'. Both had frontmen who enjoyed dressing up – Holder's silver-disc top hat was somewhat less than Peter Gabriel's batwings and shaven head. Holder, as Sandbrook notes, 'was the son of a Wolverhampton [sic] window cleaner, whose skinhead band had become the epitome of cheerful, unpretentious glam rock'. While Gabriel went to Charterhouse and drew inspiration from Arthur C. Clarke, Holder was 'content, he said, to be a "black country yobbo".'

* * *

Noddy Holder was all over the music press the following week. He was here to disturb the mellow vibes and bring his own party. Although Holder would be far more known for his coachman hat and his Baker Boy, he was wearing a bowler when Slade broke through fully into the credible papers. Subversives wearing bowlers in the early seventies were *au courant*, taking a badge of the establishment and disrupting it. The hat was central to what quickly became Holder's favourite film, *Cabaret*, the Bob Fosse-directed version of John Kander and Fred Ebb's 1966 musical that set the rise of the Nazis against the decadent final days of the Weimar Republic. Liza Minelli's Sally Bowles frequently steals the show wearing one.

Yet a darker connotation graced the front cover of *Melody Maker* the following week. Under the headline 'A Nice One', the paper proclaimed that Holder – in the bowler and braces – looked like something out of *A Clockwork Orange*. The film, which had been released that January, had created something of a storm. A percentage of the audience felt it was simply an instruction manual for violent behaviour, and its satire and moral ambiguity was lost on them. When copycat crimes broke out in the UK, Stanley Kubrick asked for the film to be withdrawn, something that only came to light when the NFT wanted to screen it as part of a retrospective of the director's works.

When John Steel saw the *Melody Maker* with Holder on the front page, with his arms outstretched, 'That was when I thought "This is going somewhere."' The fact that *Slade Alive!* was the album that returnees from the festival could buy was perfect timing: those who had stomped in the mud could replicate the set at home in the warm and dry, and being housed in a gatefold sleeve meant the heads could identify with it amid their *Meddles* and *Five Bridges Suites*.

The festival and its reviews had an enormous impact on their new single 'Take Me Bak 'Ome'. It thoroughly grasped Slade's desire to be back where they came from: 'Chas was always trying to get us to hang around in London and we wanted to go back home,' Don Powell said. 'After *Top of the Pops* or whatever – straight back home. It was just like an unwritten thing. We never thought about it, but at the time, London didn't hold any attraction for us.'

''Take Me Bak 'Ome' was very much how the band felt,' Steve Megson says. 'They didn't like being big superstars, they liked going back home and they used to go to my dad's pub as a consequence and celebrate their hit records.'

'Take Me Bak 'Ome' entered the chart at number twenty-five at the end of May; the following week it rose to number fourteen, before pinging up to number three and hitting number one at the start of July. The group performed the song on the short-lived London Weekend Television entertainment show *2Gs and the Pop People*. It was here that Dave Kemp, a man who would become instrumental in keeping the Slade name alive, first encountered the band. It was also where one of the magic 500, Stu Rutter, came in: ''Take Me Bak 'Ome' was the one that got me hooked on Slade after being aware of 'Coz I Luv You' and 'Look Wot You Dun'. It has a subtle intro, a great riff and when they played it live it always got a roar of approval where it became an immense epic including Jim playing his bass with his teeth. I don't think they ever dropped it from the set.'

Its solitary week at number one was due to the unstoppable force that was Donny Osmond and his impassioned take on Paul Anka's 'Puppy Love'. While the older brother was off with his Floyd, the young sister had The Osmonds, the early teens flocked to Slade.

Chas Chandler attained the amazing Slade sound, how loud those records came across, with a studio trick. 'When I was recording the band, I'd put gaffa tape over the VU meters, which pissed off the engineers, as they couldn't see what levels were going down on to the tape,' he told Polydor executive Dennis Munday in the nineties.

110

Slade as they are forged in the public consciousness: (clockwise from left) Don Powell in his waistcoast and plasters; Noddy Holder, the ringleader with his muttons and mirrors; Jim Lea, thoughtful, seemingly in a different band and Dave Hill, 'H', the Superyob himself, stealing the show. GETTY IMAGES

It's behind you. The 'Nbetweens outside The Tiger, North Street, Wolverhampton, 1965. (L-to-R) Dave 'Cass' Jones (bass), Dave Hill (guitar), Johnny Howells (vocals), Mick Marson (guitar)Don Powell (drums). CHRIS SELBY ARCHIVE

The 'NBetweens, 1966. Guitarist and vocalist Noddy Holder has arrived after four years on the scene, most recently in Steve Brett and the Mavericks, while 16-year-old virtuoso Jim Lea has joined Powell and Hill straight from Codsall School. CHRIS SELBY ARCHIVE

Rock music: Ambrose Slade in their finery, somewhere near Hastings in 1969. With a name change, the experience of three months in a Bahamian nightclub, an imminent LP and the interest of Chas Chandler, things were truly beginning. GERED MANKOWITZ/ICONIC IMAGES

The Trash Aesthetic: looking at the shock value of Skinheads, PR Keith Altham suggested to Chas Chandler that his young charges align themselves with this new working-class movement, and they went from hippies to bootboys overnight. Altham had only been joking. GERED MANKOWITZ/ ICONIC IMAGES

The Great Western Festival, 1972. Putting Slade on a bill with a bunch of 'serious' artists was always going to be a risk, certainly as they had just enjoyed their first No I single and were perceived as a pop act. The group were on their mettle . . . BARRY PLUMMER

. . . aided by the rain stopping, and their stage lights coming on, Slade brought the house down. At the end of their set, Holder enticed organiser Stanley Baker out on to the stage to take his praise. BARRY PLUMMER

The height of 'you write 'em, I'll sell 'em.' T. Rex may have had their 'Metal Guru', but Slade had their own 'metal nun' – the name Steve Marriot allegedly gave the Steve and Barbara Megson-designed outfit that Dave Hill wore on *Top of the Pops*. MICHAEL PUTLAND/GETTY IMAGES

'The communication Nod has with those kids is . . . unique. The kids identify with him . . . it's like there's one of them up there and he's talking their language. He's not talking down to them, he's talking to them.' Promoter Mel Bush, 1975. GETTY IMAGES

The Guv'nor and his mate: Chas Chandler and John Steel pictured in 1983. 'I was a sort of Man Friday,' Steel says. 'If Chas wanted anything done, I could do it. I would just string along on his coattails. I didn't have any real responsibility, but it was a lot of fun. I was just a mate really, but for some reason Chas liked having me around.' Steel would prove invaluable to the *Slade in Flame* project. MIRRORPIX

Less than 53 hours after playing Earls Court, at 1am on July 4 1973, Don Powell's Bentley glanced off a wall, spun several times and crashed, going through a hedge and bringing down part of the perimeter wall of Wolverhampton Grammar School. Powell would be fighting for his life and his girlfriend, Angela Morris, died. MIRRORPIX

The show must go on. As they sit atop the UK charts with 'Skweeze Me Pleeze Me', Slade honour their long-booked Isle of Man concert on Sunday 8 July, the same week as Earls Court and Powell's crash. Jim Lea's younger brother Frank deputises for Powell on drums. 'FROM PLUMBER TO DRUMMER', the papers say, much to Lea Jr's chagrin. GETTY

Don Powell's accident became global news. Powell was sent chewing gum from all over the world, with letters simply addressed to 'Don Powell, Wolverhampton'. After a prolonged coma, Powell made a full recovery, but was left with amnesia and no sense of taste and smell. MIRRORPIX

Ready to take the stage at Earls Court, July 1973. Chris Charlesworth was in awe: 'It was more of a convention than a concert, a gathering of the converted that rivalled political assemblies, royal weddings and sporting crowds in both size and fervour.' JACK KAY/GETTY

'Then, I would tell them how loud I wanted it. They didn't like it, but that's how I got the Slade sound.'

The Slade sound was not simply a wall of noise, though – the subtlety of records such as the Lea/Powell 'Wonderin 'Y', the B-side of 'Take Me Bak 'Ome', with its gentle waves of piano and guitar, was positively restrained. And the songs kept coming – Holder and Lea became a veritable songwriting machine. 'We used to learn songs in the youth centre,' Hill told Mark Blake. 'Did a new song, go up the road and have fish and chips, looking forward to getting back and rehearse and then be nervous about putting a new song in the act.' New songs were carefully aligned with the old material so attention would never be lost.

With Slade's profile raised, the shows after the festival were chaotic: The *Luton News* wrote about the group's Dunstable California Ballroom show on 24 June, with the headline, 'Near hysteria at Slade concert', it spoke of 'scenes of young girls fainting and near hysteria… as one of the largest crowds ever packed in to see top pop group Slade.'

It was said that around 3,500 people jammed the 3,000-capacity venue, and fire exits were opened as the crowd 'fought for air'. DJ Bruce Benson was reported as saying: 'It was Beatlemania all over again' and made repeated requests during the evening for people to move away from the PA should it topple. Benson added, 'I saw several girls faint. I certainly cannot remember a bigger crowd.' The crowd started a continuous 'we want Slade' chant over an hour before the group appeared on stage. Slade's lead guitarist Dave Hill said afterwards: 'The audience reaction was tremendous, but I felt really sorry for the kids. They were packed in like sardines.'

CHAPTER 13

My, My

Dave Hill became Slade's torchbearer for 'going glam'. 'The glitter thing was Bolan, really. He was the first person I'd seen with a teardrop thing under his eyes,' Dave Hill told music writer Chris Roberts. 'He came across as charismatic, which as an extrovert, I related to. You couldn't take your eyes off the guy. Nice bloke, too. 'Get It On' was a great record. He knew how to be in the camera. After that I started to put glitter under my eyes on *TOTP*.'

It was also imperative that their look remained as singular and unique as the band and their music. Again, Slade didn't look far outside their immediate circle – while David Bowie went to Mr Fish and Kansai Yamamoto, Dave Hill went to Steve and Barbara Megson, the son and daughter-in-law of Les Megson, who ran The Trumpet. 'I worked for Slade with my ex-wife from 1972 to 1975 taking them from skinhead to glam rock at the request of Chas,' Steve Megson says. 'I knew the boys well before I worked for them.'

'I'd come back to Birmingham and I was doing my MA, with my then wife, Barbara,' Steve Megson says. 'At Aston, Birmingham Art College. I was reasonably bright at school, I wasn't the highest, the flashiest kid on the block, but I was always very good at art. So I ended up going to Loughborough to do my degree in 1968. I came back and I did my post grad in printing, acrylic, painting and textiles at Birmingham, at Aston.'

Megson worked for his father behind the bar of The Trumpet. 'Every time the band had a hit record, they went there to party at my dad's, particularly if they had a number one.' It was one of these nights Megson struck up a conversation with Noddy Holder. 'I did the first costume for Dave Hill in 1972. For probably for about a year, I just worked for Dave. My brief was to take them completely away from this skinhead thing because they were really tough-looking skinheads and they did 'Take Me Bak 'Ome' and that was a kind of anthem for them.'

It was that very locality that endeared them to so many. 'It was huge for us in Bridgnorth,' future Dexys guitarist Kevin 'Billy' Adams says, 'just thirteen miles down the road from Wolverhampton, so knowing that a relatively local band had hit the big time made it all seem possible and all the more exciting.'

Dave Hill gave his verdict on David Bowie, the other breakthrough act of '71/'72 to Chris Roberts: 'David Bowie? I didn't take all that much notice of him personally. Obviously, we were aware of his success. But the girls were copying Bolan and me.'

Holder, too, has his admirers for his outfits. Simon Spence notes in *When the Screaming Stops* that later, Eric Faulkner of the Bay City Rollers was a huge fan of their sartorial elegance. 'He started to wear garishly coloured hooped socks and Dr Martens boots. The socks had been popularised by Slade singer Noddy Holder and were commonly referred to as "Slade socks".'

* * *

Slade began to build a loyal fanbase. Dave Kemp vocalises what so many fans felt: 'Whenever a new single was coming out, the programme I'd listen to on a Saturday was Emperor Rosko – he seemed to have a relationship with the band, and he'd often have the first play – I'd sit waiting through the whole show to hear that new single, with the microphone from my tape recorder.'

Rosko, now living in semi-retirement in the States, concurs: 'That was the vibrations back in the good old days. People would do that because the midday spin on *The Emperor Rosko Show* would put a record in the chart, even in the Top 10. Sometimes, even the number one with one spin on the weekend. That was the power back then when you had three to five million people listening.'

The mobilisation of the fanbase was something that Chandler positively excelled in. 'They are appealing to young teenagers with limited pocket money, people who respond quickly when they recognize genuine affection in an artiste – which Slade have,' George Tremlett opined in his fun tie-in, *The Slade Story*.

And again, there was another new single to promote, and the start of the group's unassailable run of smashes. 'Mama Weer All Crazee Now' was the first fruits of Lea's idea to inbuild chants into the group's songs. When Holder first sang the song – also partly inspired by the crowd reaction at the *NME* Poll Winner's Concert back in March – at Chandler's Lingfield barn in early summer, the lyrics were 'my my, we're all crazee now'. Chas Chandler misheard it, and encouraged the band to keep the misunderstanding in, creating one of the greatest titles in pop music.

Chandler was at the peak of his powers, adding Holder's howl in the intro which had been captured on tape during a vocal warm-up. It was a feral sound, that tapped in perfectly to the playground, the pub and the terrace. Again, the flip – 'Man Who Speeks Evil' – found Slade in experimental territory, as Slade authors and historians Chris Selby and Ian Edmundson note, a 'hidden prog style gem. The song was around in 1971 and really sounds like it firmly belongs in the middle of their *Play It Loud* album, with its highly arranged and strident instrumental passages and conflicting rhythms.' It could have sat easily on the heavier rock albums of the day.

When 'Mama Weer All Crazee Now' entered the charts at number two at the start of September 1972, behind Rod Stewart's 'You Wear It Well' at the top, it was clear that Slade had, indeed, arrived. It went to number one the following week and fought off strong competition from David Cassidy and T. Rex. Spending three weeks at the summit, it is, with the following year's 'Cum On Feel the Noize', the very zenith of the Slade yobbo anthem. The peak of, as Holder said, putting 'a smile of people's faces as well as making a statement of what we were going through at the time'. The press knew a hit when they heard one: *NME* wrote, 'Slade don't fool

115

around – this immediately comes on like a number one record and that's exactly what it's going to be… Slade personify the excitement that's obtainable only through the forty-five market.' 'O mi gord, thu av dun eet agen,' was *Record Mirror*'s verdict.

'During those couple of years, I had posters on the wall and collected flexi-discs, singles, albums and even a Slade scarf at one point,' Kevin 'Billy' Adams says. 'It overlapped with my love of Wolves too, I went to every home game during the early to mid-seventies as did a lot of my friends.'

'Slade terrified me because most of the sixth formers at my notoriously tough Saff London school dressed like them,' says singer Nick Heyward. 'I didn't buy the records but I stuck the posters up. Once I grew up a bit and got harder, I totally got it and felt brave enough to buy their records. Now I need to hear those songs more than ever. 'Coz I Luv You' is a must.'

'I was a very heterosexual young lad, and there was a sense for people slightly older, there were groups out there like Led Zeppelin, who would never play *Top of the Pops*. Slade was like having a taste of that sort of hardness,' author David Stubbs, who was 10 in 1972, says. 'A bit Dennis the Menace versus Walter the Softy. That was my relationship with pop music at the time. Little Jimmy Osmond was definitely one of Walter's gang with Bertie Blenkinsop and a lot of it has to do with that sort of gender tribalism. Slade aimed at people of my age. In a few years' time, I'm going to be having the rite of passage of listening to Genesis and Led Zeppelin, but, in the meantime, Slade are just right. Although my spelling was impeccable, I think to deliberately misspell or whatever was a real Dennis the Menace touch. It was clearly there to wind up people like my granddad.'

Life was good for Chas Chandler; he had struck gold for a third time. He and Lotte bought a modern, detached house in Lingfield in Surrey, twenty-three miles south of London. When Slade hit big, he swapped his Aston Martin DB5 for a light-blue two-door Rolls-Royce Silver Shadow. With the wind truly in their sails, Chandler unveiled the next part of his grand plan – to break the group in America.

* * *

By 1972, the USA was not necessarily a happy place. The major offensive mounted by the North Vietnamese and the Viet Cong on South Vietnam gave the clearest indication yet that the Vietnam War was not going to develop in the manner the US wished. Meanwhile, events at the Munich Olympics in September 1972 underlined that the threat of terrorism had established itself as a fact of daily life. In the early morning of 5 September, eight Palestinian terrorists broke into the Olympic Village, killed two members of the Israeli team and took nine more hostage. In an ensuing battle, all nine Israeli hostages were killed, as were five of the terrorists and one policeman. The Olympics were suspended, and a memorial service was held in the main stadium. The mood in America was edgy. It was re-election year in the US, and Richard M. Nixon was going all out to secure a second term of office. The liberal hippie dream in the States seemed over. This was the America that Slade were looking to smash into.

Musically, mainstream rock was burgeoning on FM stations, singer-songwriters with sensitivity on their sleeve; and a soulful, string-washed music that emanated in Philadelphia was being played in some of the hipper, underground establishments across America. It aimed straight for the feet. It was at these very clubs that disco began to break. Discotheques had long been out of fashion since the days of Arthur's nightclubs in the 1960s. They had become either a playground for the super-rich, or for the lowly poor. But slowly, over the decade, people began to return to them. The people who were dancing to the music in them had long been in obscurity themselves: gays, African-Americans, Italians, Puerto Ricans. Since the Stonewall Inn riot of June 1969, homosexuality had become more policed, and a subversive society was being forged. It was so far away from the mainstream. It was a long way from Bilston.

Chas Chandler was unwavering in his belief that Slade could crack America. He told Chris Charlesworth in *Melody Maker* in October 1972:

Slade are far and away better musicians than The Animals ever were. Hilton Valentine couldn't play a guitar like Dave Hill and I could never hope to be able to play bass as well as Jim Lea... My attitude as a manager is to get as much success and as much money for the act I am managing, and my experiences as a musician have helped me a lot. I never try to analyse my own actions which are mainly inspirations based on experience. That's how I picked up Slade.

'Chas could be stubborn,' Chris Charlesworth recalls. 'Didn't like to admit he was wrong and so he threw good after bad to try and prove he was right when he was wrong. That's just my opinion. However, if there was any trouble, Chas would be in there like a shot. He was big and built for it. Very brave physically, fearless almost.'

When Slade first arrived to tour America in September 1972, Polydor laid on two limousines to meet the group at LAX. This had not been communicated to the group, so they got in the minibus with the luggage, leaving their road crew to enjoy the sophistication of the cars as they arrived on Sunset Strip.

The British re-selling music to the Americans was not a new concept. Eight years earlier The Beatles had achieved it with some success. However, Slade's filter was so incredibly English, it was almost unclassifiable to the Americans. To be heard in America in the mid-seventies you had to be nondescript and let the music do all the talking (The Eagles) or so far over the top, you were unmissable (New York Dolls).

On Saturday 9 September, Slade began what was to become a four-year assault on America. At the time, few thought it would take so long. Since The Beatles 'conquered' America, there was a feeling that to be truly successful, America had to be won over. 'I remember quite distinctly Chas saying, "We're trying to launch the band in America, can you do a launch picture for me?"' Gered Mankowitz says. 'And we did that funny picture where Don's got the stars and stripes top hat and the frock coat on and they're holding Union Jacks, a very glittery picture.'

Instead of breaking them gently through the small clubs and letting the rest happen – rather like Elton John had done by playing the 500-capacity Troubadour in Los Angeles in August 1970 – Chandler went against US promoter/partner Peter Kauff's wishes and gave his charges the size of billing he felt they deserved – support to groups in arenas. Dave Hill wrote in the October/November 1972 fan club letter:

> I am writing this newsletter from the States... we are very excited over here as it's our first trip to America. We are on tour with a group called Humble Pie, who are top of the bill. There's another group second and we go on first. We have to talk a bit slower, and they don't understand everything Nod says, but we can get them clapping their hands in the end, just like home. We've travelled all over the place – this country is so big – San Diego, Long Beach, Las Vegas, Chicago, Philadelphia, New York and Boston. It's been really hard work and as we are only the support group we don't get all the special privileges as we do back home but we don't mind. It's been great fun.

Supporting Humble Pie in big arenas was an eye-opener for Slade. 'They were a great band,' Powell says. 'It was their first tour without Peter Frampton. Clem Clempson had just joined from Bakerloo from Birmingham. We also played with Peter's new band, Frampton's Camel.' It offered Chandler an opportunity to meet up again with old bandmate Mick Gallagher, now part of Peter Frampton's group: 'Slade were playing their first American tour and we met up at a reception party in New York where they were the toast of the town,' Gallagher says. 'They were bemusing everyone with their thick, incoherent Black Country accents. We played some shows with them on that tour which featured the famous mirrored top hat sported by Noddy with sensational effect.'

However, this wasn't a rowdy, booze-fuelled crowd like in the UK – these were stoners. Of course, Slade had been smokers since Eric Roker had turned them on in Freeport back in 1968, but for Slade, weed propelled them, or was something to calm them down after a performance. It certainly wasn't a way of life as it was for a lot of the US audience. If ever a group was going to harsh your mellow, it was Slade. Aware that the Humble Pie crowd were alienated by what they were hearing, during 'Darling Be Home Soon', Holder would say, 'If you want to see Pie, they'll be on soon, so why don't you just go out for a crap while we're on?'

CHAPTER 14

A Divine Mission to Wake
the Dead

British popular culture of the 1970s is a curious thing: defined by the three channels of television, and until 1973, just four national radio stations. The spectre of the Second World War loomed large over the era, only being twenty-five years in the rear-view mirror when the decade began. Most bank managers, civil servants, policemen, shop managers in their early 50s, all had a war past. There were still many alive who had lived through both wars. Sitcoms often reinforced the hierarchical structure of the services. In the wake of 1968's *Dad's Army*, there was *On the Buses* (1969), *Are You Being Served?* (1972) and *The Last of the Summer Wine* (1973). Alongside those who genuinely understood the medium, the UK media was run by a peculiar amalgam of ex-servicemen controlling something they did not entirely comprehend, resulting in fiefdoms established by experienced opportunistic and wily presenters – as in the case of then household favourites DJ Jimmy Savile, entertainer Rolf Harris and singer Gary Glitter – to pull the wool over the eyes of their superiors. Underpinning the glamour and the glitz there was something far darker and more sinister.

Mary Whitehouse was closely monitoring the permissive society; yet while Alice Cooper ('School's Out'); Sweet ('Teenage Rampage')

121

and especially the Chuck Berry track ('My Ding-A-Ling') that kept 'Gudbuy T'Jane' off number one incurred her wrath ('one teacher told us of how she found a class of small boys with their trousers undone, singing the song and giving it the indecent interpretation which – in spite of all the hullabaloo – is so obvious. She was, by no means, the only one with experiences of this kind'), Slade seemed wholesome in comparison; naughty but nice.

Slayed? – the group's first studio album since stardom – was released on 1 November 1972. The adverts were perfect – the trademark Slade fist in full evidence, emerging from a coffin, with the legend 'Slade. Their divine mission is to wake the dead.' In lower case underneath, it continued 'Slade has the power to move people, no matter what state they're in… Their latest hit, 'Gudbuy T'Jane' is a perfect example. Get *Slayed?* And come to life.'

It was Slade approaching their absolute apex, and the cover image encapsulated the group perfectly. Although the skinhead look was now far behind them, Chandler thought about the street culture's use of wearing tattoos. Long before tattoos became the fashion accessory they have become today, this was a time when they were the preserve of hardmen, navymen, fairground workers, teds and prison types, and to have them on your knuckles was proper hard or deviant. An example of the status they held in the popular imagination was underlined by the word-of-mouth cult theatre phenomenon of 1973, *The Rocky Horror Show*. When Frank-N-Furter asks clean-cut Brad Majors, 'Do you have any tattoos, Brad?', his reply of 'Certainly not!' is delivered in a manner that clearly suggests he wouldn't even consider it.

The band went to see Gered Mankowitz down at his new studio at 41 Great Windmill Street, right in the heart of London's Soho, to capture the image that was to reflect the music therein. 'That was probably the first session we did where we were shooting specifically for the cover,' Mankowitz recalls.

> I remember the technical issues, having to get the hands and the faces sharp. Wanting to make them look harder, that was all part of it. Dave doing his muscle man stuff, which was disconcerting… he was quite muscley. I love the way Don put the Slade underneath

the plasters that he had on his hand, because I don't know whether it helped him hold the sticks or whatever. It was just such a great idea. Those pictures were really just a question of trying to get the shape right, get them all in the frame and get the hands sharp and get them all... that look which sort of says, 'Are you with us or are you against us?'

Are you with us or are you against us? That was the polarity of Slade's world. It was all or nothing, an incredible, ebullient rush. *Slayed?* was both the sound and the look of a band who knew exactly what they were doing. Yet the hardness of the group always seemed tinged with a theatricality. 'I think one of the reasons for that was because Jim was always so pretty,' Mankowitz adds. 'Jim was the sort of Paul McCartney and Nod was the sort of Lennon. They were glamorous as well; it was sort of bovver with a glamour emphasis in a way. It was always very theatrical. I mean, the whole skinhead thing was a bit of theatre. They didn't really look hard, particularly Dave.'

Chris Charlesworth's celebratory sleevenotes echoed those that Tony Barrow wrote for The Beatles a decade earlier: 'Noddy, Dave, Jim and Don have forged a name for themselves in the strength of nothing else save their own personal brand of music. Comparisons are superfluous. Slade are Slade and Slade are now.' It also cemented Charlesworth as the group's writer of choice: 'My part-time job as Slade's go-to man for sleeve-note writing began in 1972 with *Slayed?* on the back of which were the first I did for anyone,' Charlesworth wrote in 2021. 'Chas paid me £20 by cheque, which is about £250 in today's money, not bad for about 300 words.'

It bore out that Chandler would only get the best in for the lads. Mankowitz speaks so warmly:

I loved working with them. They are incredibly creative, very clever and talented. Dave was often quite a handful, but he was so creative, his input was so important. He was so eccentric, he wouldn't dress in front of them, he'd dress in the toilet. Then he'd come out on his ridiculous heels. I did some backstage pictures, including pictures of them reflected in the mirror and I remember being there and him coming out of toilet in his finery.

The lyrics on *Slayed?* are like the Slade manifesto: 'Forget your inhibition, we've come to rock and rave' ('The Whole World's Going Crazee'); 'Maybe they'll care today, but not tomorrow' ('Look at Last Nite'). The album went to number one in the UK. Billy Walker reviewed it for *Melody Maker*, and the caption under the picture of Don Powell said it all: 'booze, birds, bread and love'.

'This album spoke volumes of where we had come as a band,' Dave Hill told Facebook page *Slade Are For Life – Not Just For Christmas*, in 2021. 'The hits and stage songs we covered which were great songs we did for years, Chas was really on the case when choosing the tracks with us and with all our new confidence as a band we knew where we were going so the recordings were a joy to make.'

'I'd saved enough money to buy the new *Slayed?* album in late 1972 and although I loved it, *Slade Alive!* remained my go-to album,' Australian fan Stephen Cross says. 'The enigmatic cover photo of the band on *Slade Alive!* suddenly made sense after I got *Slayed?*. They were clearly four pretty tough-looking blokes from what I could make out. No wonder the music was so tough and gritty.'

Released on 17 November, midway through the tour, 'Gudbuy T'Jane', side two track one from *Slayed?* is arguably, to these ears, the group's greatest, or joint greatest single – Powell's propulsive, thrusting drums set the tone for a great, if slightly under-the-radar stomper. The idea came to Lea when he was sitting poolside in Fresno, and was completed on the plane back to Britain. Holder drew inspiration from a TV show the group had been on in San Francisco where a girl called Jane simply sat by the compere, looking gorgeous and saying nothing. She wore a pair of shoes that she called 'forties trip', which she lost before recording and the band helped her find them. A possible suggestion as to who Jane may have been was Jane Dornacker, a US TV personality and comedienne who was an associate of The Tubes, who sadly died in 1986. Lea wrote the framework for the lyrics, which Holder completed just prior to recording. The record is tremendously loose, with a rough and ready feel, partially due to the fact that it was done in just two takes.

'I'd have been 12,' Kevin 'Billy' Adams says. 'We had music lessons from a nice man who, to be completely fair to him, had lost his enthusiasm for the job. So, after handing out the boxed glockenspiels for the afternoon, if there hadn't been too much uproar during the lesson, he'd reward us by playing a record at the end that someone had brought in. One day he played 'Gudbuy T'Jane' and that was it. I was hooked.' As the band were between Doncaster and Glasgow on tour, video directors Caravelle made a promo clip that was shown on *Top of the Pops*, one of the few non-performance videos they ever made.

'I don't know why 'Gudbuy T'Jane' is so good,' Alexis Petridis says. 'The only reason I can think that it's my favourite Slade single is because I have known it literally my entire life. I remember it when I was like three years old or something like that. My parents had it. It's the only Slade record that touches vaguely on glam notions of androgyny. There's something simultaneously indefinable and undeniable about that string of singles that they're so ridiculously exciting.'

'Gudbuy T'Jane' stalled at number two, held off the top spot by fellow Lanchester performer from earlier that year, Chuck Berry, with his 'My Ding-A-Ling', arguably one of the most irritating records known to humankind. In fact, Holder was on the recording. 'I was in the audience at the Coventry Locarno, when Chuck Berry recorded 'My Ding-A-Ling' live,' he told *The Guardian* in 2015. 'If you listen closely, you can hear me singing!' If indeed true, a fascinating detail for chart-watchers the world over. 'When you think of all those brilliant songs he wrote,' Powell sighs, 'and he gets a number one with 'My Ding-A-Ling'!!'

The B-side of 'Gudbuy T'Jane' was Slade storming away at their very best. Academic and writer Kieron Tyler wrote this incredible resume of it for *The Arts Desk* in 2015:

It's one of the greatest rock songs of the seventies. The production is dense, and the churning guitars are thick with tension. Beginning with a minor-key riff suggesting a familiarity with The Stooges' 'No Fun', the whole band lock into a groove which isn't strayed from. The tempo does not shift... Two squalling guitar breaks set the Jimi Hendrix of 'Third Stone from the Sun' in a hard rock context. Produced by former Hendrix co-manager Chas Chandler, it could be an outtake from MC5's 1971 album

High Time. Yet this was not a Detroit contemporary of The Stooges or MC5, but 'I Won't Let It 'Appen Agen' by Slade.

It was also, until 1991, the only song that Jim Lea wrote entirely alone.

The band's look developed further. Following on from the debut of the silver outfit at the Great Western Festival, Hill further utilised the Megsons for his designs, and carte blanche was given for him to go further and further. As Holder had said about seeing Hill around town in his cape back in the sixties, it was Chas Chandler who encouraged the look, right back from the early shows. Hill told Mark Blake, 'He said to me, "I notice you're quite small on stage, I think a great idea is get the biggest guitar you can and have it round your neck." Hang about, I like this guy. As soon as I started to experiment with Kensington Market clothes, Chas encouraged me. He always said whatever you do, do not wear black onstage, and I had no problem with that.'

Jim Lea was to have a problem with that, and, as a result, forever exasperated. 'When we did photo sessions, I could just about tolerate some of our daft outfits,' Lea told Keith Altham. 'Until Dave turned up one day looking like a cockerel and Nod acquired a huge tie which dragged on the ground and made him look like that old music hall comedian, Arthur English. I could handle "Arthur", but I wasn't having my photo taken with any soppy cockerel, so I walked out.'

It was this point that the image began to be everything, and in keeping with the era, one member had to be more outrageous than the rest, which fell to Dave Hill. Holder recalled in 2015, 'He'd never let us see what he was going to wear. You'd hear him rattling and rustling in the toilet and go: "Come on, H. Reveal." Then we'd be on the floor with laughter, except Jim who'd say: 'I'm not going on with him dressed like that.' H would go: "You write 'em, I'll sell 'em." And he was right.'

'I don't know how many costumes I made for them all together,' Steve Megson, who, with his then wife Barbara, says.

Every time we went on tour, I used to do about six or eight costumes for Dave Hill. Strange thing, I used to get on very well with Dave Hill because he was such a good customer, but he was a cocky monkey. He didn't really know what he wanted, but he knew what he wanted to look like. It was a great gig for me because he just trusted me. All my inspiration came from things like Native American costumes or Samurai costumes. I was in direct competition with people like Gary Glitter and David Bowie.

It wasn't just Hill in the fashion stakes: Holder first sported his mirrored hat, after getting the idea from seeing the light refract from Lulu's sparkly dress. 'It's actually an antique coachman's hat with mirrors stuck on,' Holder said in 2015. Its provenance is a potentially thorny issue. Holder said, 'I got the hat off a guy in Kensington Market called Freddie. He said: "One day I'm gonna be a big pop star like you." I said: "Fuck off, Freddie." He became Freddie Mercury.'

Like many anecdotes of the time, it all seems a little smooth; they were aware of Mercury working there, but not directly. Holder later suggested Mercury's stall was about three down from where he purchased the hat. But, it is absolutely vital to a legend to have the stories that surround it. Whoever sold it, when the spotlights hit the hat, the audience were bathed in beams of starlight. The spectacle was reaching its peak.

The tour that supported *Slayed?* was the first with the group hitting the big time. The gradual out-spill of clubs that had been the first half of the year and then the step up to the municipal halls with Status Quo in summer were all small beer to their first headliners as stars with three UK number ones under their belt. It was a perfect snapshot of where mainstream pop and rock was in late 1972. Signed to Mickie Most's RAK label, Suzi Quatro had recently moved to Britain from Detroit, and was on the verge of being fashioned as a leather-clad lady rocker, a persona quite removed from the humble, quiet 20-year-old she was. Chas Chandler was a great friend of Most's, meeting as they did when Most produced The Animals. Most was able to get Quatro as the opening act on the tour – fifteen minutes each night, £40 a night. The tour started 3 November at Newcastle City Hall. The show was sold out.

'The place was filled with screaming fans dressed in glittery clothes with top hats and platform boots,' Suzi Quatro wrote in

127

her autobiography, *Unzipped*. Streamers and handmade ribbons stretched across the balcony declaring 'We love Slade'. Noddy Holder watched Quatro perform that night; Holder later was to tell her, 'Slade fans were notorious for not liking our support acts. They would heckle and even used to throw stuff. But you won them over – I was impressed.' Within six months of these shows, Suzi Quatro would be at number one with 'Can the Can', written by the song-writing powerhouse team of Mike Chapman and Nicky Chinn. Suzi Quatro formed a long-lasting relationship with the band who kept an eye on her throughout their career, and within a year would 'Love the boys... especially Don,' Quatro said in 2023. 'We are friends.'

Principal support on the autumn tour of 1972 were charismatic Irish rockers Thin Lizzy, who although had signed to Decca in 1971, had yet to find any significant footings in the UK market. Their presence brought Slade into contact again with Chris O'Donnell, who two years earlier had been a booker at the Gunnell Agency. He was now co-managing Lizzy in collaboration with Bryan Morrison. 'Chas was big. He filled the room,' O'Donnell says:

> He was really tough. When Thin Lizzy played with Suzi Quatro and Slade, we played Newcastle. When Lizzy did their club set, Chas came in the dressing room afterwards, and said, 'You either get a grip on this as to what you're here for, or you can fuck off.' It was headmaster time. It just killed Phil Lynott. I said, 'Well, Phil, you can go one way or the other. Did you listen to what he said?' The next night, Phil stood in the wings, watching Noddy. He totally got the projection. The music will take care of itself. But first of all, you've got to get that across. You've got to give them a reason to want to listen to that music, and part and parcel of that is controlling, engaging with, and giving the audience some direction.

Again, Chandler's tough love and total belief in his charges and who they should surround themselves with paid off. 'Chas inspired you,' O'Donnell affirms. 'Phil became the person he became because of Chas on that fateful night. He may have written a hit record, he may have done something right, but he wouldn't have become the performer he became if it hadn't been for watching Noddy Holder.'

The autumn tour was an absolute hoot, and with three number one singles now under their mirrored topper, Slademania was breaking out. It was an eventful spell, complete with Dave Hill falling off his platforms at the Liverpool Stadium show on 18 November and breaking his leg. For the next few nights, Hill appeared in a throne-type wheelchair – the show must indeed go on. The hairies and the skinheads were dissipating. They were being replaced by teenage girls, not the sugar and spice types of Osmondmania or those who would fawn over David Cassidy – these were edgier, more musically inclined, those with *Alias Smith and Jones* posters on their wall, mourning Pete Duel, moving on from Bolan, not yet ready for Bowie.

The group were still living at home, but now, as the money started coming in, it was time to put down their own roots: 'It snowballed and we were still at home at our mums and dads,' Powell laughed. 'Mum would do my laundry and have me dinner waiting for me every night. Dad always used to joke, the only time I bloody eat is when you're here.'

At the end of 1972, Dave Hill went house shopping and bought a £40,000 home for himself – and when they married, his girlfriend, Janice Parton – to live in, in the affluent stockbroker belt of Solihull, twenty-three miles south-east of Wolverhampton. Hill thought it was next to a mansion. It transpired it was next to Malvern Hall, the site of Solihull High School for Girls.

CHAPTER 15

This Is What They Call a Lounge

There is little doubt that 1973 was Slade's year. In sheer terms of statistics, it is hard to beat, and from a distance of five decades, increasingly difficult to imagine. Four UK Top 3 hits, including three chart-toppers, two number one albums, a sell-out show at London's Earls Court and the beginning of negotiations for a feature film. It was also the year of a disastrous car crash that left Don Powell fighting for his life, and his girlfriend, Angela Morris, dead.

The year began with Midlands magazine programme *ATV Today* visiting Dave Hill in residence to see his new property. Years before *Through the Keyhole* or celebrities in *Hello!* opening the doors up of their beautiful home, Brenda Holton went to visit Hill at his as-yet unfurnished house. When asked how fame and adulation felt, Hill, sitting on the carpet in his living room, with a gold disc propped up strategically behind him, replied, 'It's great. Anybody who says it's not good are idiots.' He takes Holton on a tour of the house, and in a fabulous snapshot of early seventies upward mobility, he ushers her through a door, and states, 'This is what they call a lounge,' with great sincerity. The footage concludes with twenty or so schoolgirls chanting for Hill, while a teacher gingerly appears, possibly only a handful of years older than Hill himself and begins to corral the girls away.

It wasn't just the group who were getting bombarded by fans, it was the people who worked with them as well: Dr Clive Holmwood, now an associate professor of Therapeutic Arts at Derby University, but then an enthusiastic fan, recalls: 'Sometime in the mid-seventies, there was a rumour that Slade's road manager lived near us on the edge of Gornal Wood and the Straits estate and the rumour got round that Slade were visiting his house. Such was the Slade hysteria in the early days that my brother, me, and a couple of dozen teenagers descended on the manager's front garden, but Slade were nowhere to be seen. Not even sure if it was the road manager's house but when the rumour got out, we all descended.' Sadly, the truth got in the way of a good schoolboy rumour: 'Swin was Moxley; all the other crew members were in Bilston and Wolverhampton,' Powell confirms.

Slade played at London's storied Palladium Theatre on 7 January. Although Elton John and The Jackson 5 had appeared at the preceding year's Royal Variety Performance, this was the first full rock concert at the venue. Supported by Geordie, the concert was part of Edward Heath's Fanfare for Europe, to celebrate Britain's joining of the European Economic Community (EEC) on New Year's Day. The two-week cultural festival included a variety of events, as Heath would share his 'heart full of joy' at joining the community with the nation.

It was all go for the joy of joining the Common Market. There was an international friendly at Wembley: 36,500 people watched 'The Three' (the home nations and fellow EEC newcomers Ireland and Denmark) and 'The Six' (existing EEC nations Belgium, the Netherlands, Luxembourg, Italy, West Germany and France). Bobby Moore, Bobby Charlton and Franz Beckenbauer took part in an underwhelming spectacle, to be met with protestors outside the stadium complaining about joining Europe and the money it was costing. On the following day, ITV screened a 'Fanfare for Europe' edition of *Opportunity Knocks*, complete with host Hughie Green in full effect, with Katie Boyle, Petula Clark and Johan Cruyff all appearing.

The Palladium show was organised by Great Western limited, which meant the band were back in contact with actor and Bardney

organiser Stanley Baker. Baker attended the Palladium with his wife
Ellen, and their younger children, having missed out on going to
the festival the previous May. 'I remember the evening very well,
because the children and I were sitting in a box,' Lady Ellen Baker
recalls. 'Slade came on and they were wildly popular at that moment.
All the fans were stomping in time to the music and the whole upper
circle was bouncing. Slade stopped and told them not to bounce as
it will all fall down.'

'Chas asked me to introduce them on stage at the Palladium,'
Chris Charlesworth recalls. 'Terrifying! The place was heaving with
fans, and when they got going, I remember standing next to Chas
and we watched the circle moving as fans jumped up and down. We
really thought it might collapse. The Palladium was truly quaked by
Slade – the balcony was shaking so much the fire brigade were put
on standby.'

* * *

The group travelled to Australia for an eight-date tour at the end
of January, with Status Quo (a perfect fit), Lindisfarne (good time
folk) and Caravan (whimsical English prog?). 'On the surface, that
would seem like a mismatch, but it worked out pretty well,' Pye
Hastings from Caravan was to say. 'We got along really well with the
other bands and got a decent reaction from the fans.' Australian fan
Stephen Cross says, 'Over the years I've met many people – mainly
men – who saw Slade play the Melbourne Showgrounds on that first
tour in February 1973. All of them insisted it was one of the best live
shows they had ever seen!'

Australia was ready for them. Cross continues: 'Around the middle
of 1972 my neighbour across the road invited me over to listen to
a new record he'd bought. I was 11 years old, my friend four years
older. He carefully lined up the stylus on track two side two, cranked
the volume up and 'Get Down and Get With It' burst out of the
speakers. The album was *Slade Alive!* and the impact that song and
that record had on me was immediate and long lasting. Although
the local radio station did not play any Slade songs, each week they
would publish the Top 40 singles and Top 20 albums chart on a

single A5 sheet of paper. The charts were compiled by 2SM, then the big music radio station in Sydney. Every Thursday afternoon from early 1973, I would ride my bike into town after school to collect the latest chart and look at new releases in the record shop. The chart from 3 January had *Slade Alive!* at number two and 'Mama Weer All Crazee Now' debuting in the singles chart at thirty-nine. It was only then I realised how big Slade were in Australia.

'The Australian Broadcasting Commission's (ABC) television station ran a ten-minute magazine-style music show each weeknight before the 7 p.m. national news. It was called *GTK* (Get to Know) and as my dad liked to watch the news at 7, I would often take the opportunity to watch *GTK* as Dad looked up from his newspaper scowling disapprovingly. *GTK* were doing a spot on Slade – the entire segment was dedicated to Slade's Australian tour. Included was a gold record presentation at a press conference at Sydney airport, interviews with fans at the Sydney concert at Randwick Racecourse and footage from the actual show, including segments of 'Hear Me Calling', 'Mama' and 'Get Down'.'

The bands on the tour all got on well, and there was a special affinity between the Quo and Slade. Francis Rossi always used to take the mickey out of Chas Chandler:

> I always called him Chez Chandelier. There's been many moments like Mrs Bouquet and all that where they would do that with their names. 'Chas fucking Chandler, innit?' He had his own rock'n'roll name which of course wasn't real. There are various people, even Sting. You're 45 years old and you call yourself Sting? Shakin' Stevens who years ago I said, 'What's your name?' he said, 'Shaky'. I got to leave the room now. Slade were like us. Noddy was Noddy. It wasn't one of those kinds of silly affected sort of things. I think that's the tour we did in Australia where we woke up one morning and the promoters had fucked off with the money. Chas got this decrepit old fucking charabanc bus over there for us all.

It was a perfect blend of bands. 'It was a great tour and it worked so fucking well,' continues Rossi. 'We'd sing, "Slade! Wonderful

Slade!" and "Hi-ho, hi-ho, we are the Status Quo. We're number one, we'll have some fun!" There was a Lindisfarne song as well and they were good guys, too.'

Quo, unlike many of their peers, turned their back on 'going glam', possibly because they'd started as a post-psychedelic ensemble. 'We were on a plane in Australia and H's case fell out and all this fucking glitter went everywhere. Noddy was always roasting H, they'd make jokes, and he was great for that. But we came out of the 1968 stuff, which is why I think we're lucky, we transcended another decade. A journalist said to me, "I love your new image." I replied, "What do you mean?" and they said, "The jeans and all that." "Oh, is that an image?" That's not a fucking image, we couldn't afford to wear anything else.'

* * *

The recordings at this time at Olympic were a straight case of band, producer and engineer working at the peak of their game – Olympic used a square wave modulator that was inserted on vocal tracks to add to Holder's growl. Engineer Phil Chapman recalls: 'It was used to great effect on Noddy, giving him a kind of Robert Plant sound.' In a way, that explains a great deal – older brothers had Led Zeppelin; younger sisters had Slade.

'At the time when Slade were popular, I decided I didn't like them,' future King Crimson member Jakko Jakszyk says. 'Because I was a fan of Henry Cow. But actually, I always thought they were The Beatles. They had something about them that was unique, and musical, but also followed a Beatles-esque tradition with their songwriting, that I think is undeniable.'

Slade followed one important statistical Beatles-esque tradition: On 3 March, 'Cum On Feel the Noize' became the first single in the UK charts to enter at number one since The Beatles' 'Get Back' in April 1969. It ended friendly rival Sweet's reign at the top spot with 'Blockbuster!' 'Chas was really clever,' Alan O'Duffy says. 'People knew that there was this new Slade track and across the country people went into record stores to order it, so as a result of the pre-sales the record went straight in at number one.'

It is the ultimate Slade anthem – answering their critics, it is a fabulous, resonant snook-cock. The record had its basis in a show they did where the audience were so loud, Holder could feel the noise rippling up through his body. Barney Hoskyns called it an explosion of 'unbridled rock energy that teenagers could stomp to as they groped each other in the dark'.

It wasn't the first time the band tried to recreate the excitement of their live shows on record, but they certainly upped their game to create something even more exhilarating than they had recorded before. Right from Holder's 'Baby, baby, baby' (a mic check that Chandler kept in, just like George Martin keeping the count-in on The Beatles' 'I Saw Her Standing There', a decade earlier) onwards, here was the sound of a band in their pomp, full of the confidence and chutzpah of their success.

It's probably the most overdriven, manic, exciting record Slade ever made. Alan O'Duffy remembers the session:

> We were in Studio 1, and we went down the back stairs. We wanted the chorus to sound fantastic. So I got all four of them in the corridor. They sang the 'Cum On Feel the Noize' melody in the chorus, loudly, and then I triple tracked it. So, there's four blokes times three, equalling twelve voices. But each time we tracked it, I changed the perspective of the sound. So, the first sound maybe was like two metres away. The second one was maybe four metres away and the next one was maybe six down the corridor. So, each time the sound was a slightly different perspective on blokes singing in an echoey corridor. If you listen to the song, at some point, the track is fabulous, and then it comes into the chorus and without turning up the volume on the chorus, the impact of the voices is quite fantastic in stereo. It's a great noise.

The flip was another example of this infectious high-period hubris – 'I'm Mee, I'm Now, An' That's Orl' is another reaction against the criticism the group faced. Both sides are retaliatory and valiant – The A-side suggests so what if Noddy Holder has a funny face, evil mind or a lazy time, he is clearly doing much better than his critics;

the B-side goes further, being told what they do wrong, for them to be quiet, being blamed for things that go wrong, but ladies wink and everyone knows who's there. If a single 45 had to be given to earth dwellers in 1,000 years' time to explain who Slade were, it would be this.

There was an everyman touch to it all. Writer Malcolm Wyatt has called Slade 'the people's band', and this is indeed correct. There were no allusions to Jean Genet like David Bowie or Marc Bolan's coterie of the strange that populated his songs. There was no Beltane Way here, just belt and braces. 'If you think of our surroundings in the Midlands, governed by factories,' Dave Hill said in 2019. 'People listened making bolts, very productive, very sooty. Dad was a mechanic. My parents or certainly my wife's parents worked in factories while our songs blasting down the airwaves.'

'Their work was remarkable,' The *Guinness Book of Number One Hits* said. 'Not only in its cleverly crafted constitution, mixing heavy metal and a pseudo-rebellious teenage stance, but in that it enjoyed both critical and public acclaim.'

Chas Chandler mobilised the fanbase and got them all down the record shops on day of release – a Slade release had become an event. 'He was a "hands-on" manager, always there for his boys,' Chris Charlesworth says. Their TV appearances were looked forward to.

'I thought they were very good, exciting,' Tim Rice says. 'Noddy had great charm, which helped a lot. And you had the manic Dave Hill, who is quite a good guitar player to put it mildly, but oh, the dress.'

Slade was still – and remained – a cottage industry: 'Dave used to come round to us in his Jensen and park it outside my flat and all the people in the street would be looking,' Steve Megson says. 'Sometimes we'd go to his house and things. I'm talking about Dave mostly because probably for every ten costumes, eight or nine of them would be for Dave, until I did the Slade film and did all of that lark.'

To chime in with the times, Slade's greatest showman, Dave Hill, started to flirt further with the phrase 'yob', and his outfits began to enter a whole new realm in 1973. Keith Altham, back in his journalist role, wrote an in-depth feature on Dave Hill for *NME*, which was published on 24 February, just ahead of the release of 'Cum On Feel the Noize'. It was this feature that christened Hill 'Superyob' and gave him his enduring nickname. 'He comes on stage with Slade like an over-decorated, perambulating Christmas tree – smothered in silver-stars, gold and glitter from head to toe – but somehow, he never minces into the realm of the camp. What he does is counter Noddy Holder's version of a space-age bully with his own interpretation of Superyob.' Soon, Hill would be ordering his custom-made John Birch guitar with the phrase emblazoned on it and driving his Jensen Interceptor with the number plate YOB 1.

The guitar was an incredible statement, less so a fabulous working instrument. It was designed by the group's own Anthony Price (Roxy Music's designer), Steve Megson. 'I knew nothing about guitars. I'm not a musician. I got the fretboard from Dave's original guitar that he had. I made a drawing of it and measured everything. I just made the basic template and went to John Birch's workshop in Rubery. John looked at the shape and got the timber, I think it was cedar. I created the actual design and made an individual sized, exact template drawing for him for the body and for the neck of the guitar.'

Dave Hill's much-quoted adage to Lea and Holder, 'you write 'em, I'll sell 'em', was reaching its apex. It is because of Hill that the band are seen as glam, and led to the fact that now, in the wake of Marc Bolan and David Bowie as Ziggy Stardust, at least one member of a band had to flirt with campness, and/or make-up – Steve Priest of Sweet; Zal Cleminson of The Sensational Alex Harvey Band; Rob Davis from Mud. On 27 June 1973, at the very zenith of Sladeness, Richard O'Brien's *The Rocky Horror Show* opened upstairs at the Royal Court in London's Sloane Square, with Tim Curry playing the transsexual Transylvanian Frank-N-Furter, a mix of Ziggy Stardust and Hill at his most outré. Yet no matter how ridiculous Hill may appear there was not even the slightest hint of campness or queerness about him. It seemed forever that the eldest had broken into the dressing-up box. T. Rex may have had their Metal Guru, but Slade had Dave Hill, their own 'metal nun' – the name for the outfit Hill wore on *Top of the Pops* that Steve Marriott allegedly christened.

It was Hill that people wanted to copy: 'It was his flamboyance, the huge platform boots but more importantly that huge guitar sound,' Kevin 'Billy' Adams, from Dexys Midnight Runners, says. 'It made me want to take up the guitar and join a band. I even kept a small tube of glitter for a time because I thought that's what a guitarist ought to use. Still in the tube somewhere or ended up in the bin!'

'Dave Hill's beaming overbite was my guiding light and saviour growing up,' said future leader of Haircut 100, Nick Heyward.

In 1973, Duran Duran's John Taylor was then 12 when his parents took him to the Berni Inn in Solihull, where its celebrity resident was dining:

He had on a bright red velvet suit. He was the first star I'd seen. I asked for his autograph. I remember him being so tall. It probably was the platform shoes because when I bumped into him in AIR Studios, I think it was in '82, he was not all that tall as it happened. His appearance made an enormous impression on me, because this was a guy that was living outside of the rules, outside of the social mores. These characters that were on *Top of the Pops*, they almost weren't like regular people. I never really thought of pop stars as being people that you could relate to in that way. Suddenly, here was this guy with this extraordinary haircut. He was full on rock star at that moment.

All of these outfits that Hill would sport came out of a flat in Birmingham. 'One of the rooms we used as a little sweatshop,' Steve Megson says. 'We had two Frister & Rossmann sewing machines. Barbara could sew very well. I used to go to the dressmaking department of Rackhams in Birmingham and go through all the gents' patterns and all the women's patterns for dresses. I'd buy these patterns, take them home and lay them on the floor and say, "right, I'm gonna make this into a kind of Samurai costume," and start sticking bits of paper and changing the shape of the pattern. My wife taught me to sew, and we used to work together. We were young students. For the first year I was still doing my postgraduate MA at Birmingham so mixing that kind of artwork when I was in college with working on costumes at the weekends.'

'At my school in Leeds, there was never any thought of like dressing like Noddy Holder or Dave Hill,' David Stubbs writes. 'Now, that was absolutely the point. We all wore parkas. That was Slade's job, to be the aliens from planet pop. It wasn't like mods or punks or whatever, where you had that sort of sense of affinity. You know, they were very much stars working in their own galaxy.'

Rock writer Dave Ling recalls with deep affection, 'Those iconic Thursday night appearances on *Top of the Pops*. Which chart-topping song was it this week, and what on earth would Dave be wearing? Theirs was the soundtrack to a gloriously naive and responsibility-free era.'

Pete Townshend, no less, was to notice the power of Slade. Speaking in *NME* in early March 1973, he said, 'you can't really fault Slade, except that Dave Hill sometimes looks a bit too freaky. Slade and Bowie are just so important. If they weren't here now, in England, Christ Almighty, it would just be so sad. I'm so glad that they're there.'

Many, many people were glad they were here. This was the period when Slade were taken deep into the hearts of those who didn't fully know the intricacies of rock music. Kids. Something for the boys and tomboys to listen to while the girls mooned over them. 'Me and my sister were huge Slade fans,' says DJ Gary Crowley.

'My brother was the Marc Bolan/T. Rex fan, and we all shared a little bit of a love for Bowie. But he was sort of more for kids slightly older than us. Your Gary Kemps and your Dylan Jones get teary-eyed talking about him playing 'Starman' on *Top of the Pops*. When my mother left, pop music really became such a big thing for me and my sister.

'We both really lost ourselves in pop; me and my sister loved Slade. We both had our favourite members: mine was Noddy. Sue always fancied the loon pants off Jimmy Lea. Not that we would have been able to afford the records at the time, we would tape the chart rundown with Tom Browne on to the machine and listening on a BASF cassette. Slade really were on fire. Every record was an event in its own way. I borrowed *Slayed?*, but it would have been mainly about the singles really, and just looking forward to *Top of*

the Pops on Thursday night: watching them, seeing what they were
wearing and just feeding off that energy that they gave off. Me and
Sue, were big, big fans.'

The group had four such distinct personalities, four different stances
– Holder the shouty leader, Lea the enigma, Hill the showman, and
Powell the strong silent type, forever chewing gum. There was a
practical reason for this: 'It was to keep my mouth moist while I was
playing drums, as rarely I could bend down and get a drink,' Powell
says. 'Wrigley used to have an ad on TV with a big packet of gum on
a bloke's shoulders – they made me one of those.'

'I always wanted to be in Pink Floyd,' Jim Lea said in 1984.
'Mega, but completely faceless. You just make your records every
year and you didn't have to bother with all. You can walk down the
street, nobody knows who you are, that would suit me down to the
ground.'

'Each of them had a house style,' Steve Megson says,

Dave would wear very extravagant things. Dave was very short, so
he used to wear the big, tall boots. In those days everyone was
wearing them. He did some with a big American dollar sign in red
and white. We did this costume for him with reflective mirrors,
kind of feathered tassels. I'd show him some pictures from
American films. As long as it worked on stage for Dave, he was
fine. Noddy went into checks. He had his own style and always
wore tailored jackets. I had to learn to tailor, it's quite difficult.
I had a friend in Birmingham who helped me. We couldn't do a
lot of padding for them as we had to keep that straightforward,
for on stage the lights can get very, very hot, but Noddy did like
to wear a jacket and a shirt, big hats, ties and a waistcoat if he took
his jacket off. It became a bit of a thing for Noddy. Jim Lea always
only wore a little bomber jacket and some tight trousers and Don
Powell always a waistcoat and tight trousers.

Top of the Pops was the battleground for all of these personalities
and styles and other groups to strut their stuff: 'Rivalries?' Hill told
Chris Roberts, 'Only in a sense. It's a bit like tennis players. You get

on well with this other tennis player, you're friends, but when you get on that court you're going to play to win, aren't you? I wanted to make sure that whatever had been on *TOTP* before us, I'd get my bit in, bobbing around by Noddy because the singer gets the most camera.'

Slade were never particularly ones for ligging, however: 'We never felt comfortable like that,' Don Powell says. 'I don't know what it was, it's weird. Maybe we were insecure. We didn't know that any other bands would even want to talk to us. We were on *Top of the Pops* around the time that Marc Bolan would also be having number ones. Cliff Richard came to our dressing room to congratulate us, and he said, "He's not happy," meaning Marc because we'd started to take some of his thunder. Cliff was great, but everyone we've met have been lovely people. It is a nice feeling. I think probably a lot of that rubs off onto us as well.'

Steve Megson went to *Top of the Pops* with them for every performance in this period, making Hill look more and more outré. 'It was a kind of an unwritten challenge. *Top of the Pops*, made on Wednesday, on telly on Thursday. I knew that one of my tasks, as far as Dave was concerned, was to blow Gary Glitter out the water with his costume. Gary Glitter, you always knew what it was going to be – big shoulder pads, lots of sequins but there were other bands who wore really quite sophisticated things. Bowie's stuff was amazing. He had really good professional designers and he was a very clever man. He was responsible for his own image and changed his identity all the time.'

Dave Hill was thoroughly unique: 'We went to see Bowie and Mick Ronson was there and Dave didn't recognise him,' Steve Megson continues. 'I kicked Dave on his boot and said, "That's Mick Ronson you're talking to," and Dave replied, "Who's he?" I said, "He's David Bowie's lead guitarist, Dave. You're in the rock'n'roll business, you should know these things." Noddy or Jim would have known. I love Dave in many ways, he's got balls, he really goes for things. He had a character and personality but he was so egocentric. Everything was about Dave. For me as a designer, *that was perfect*.'

* * *

142

In April 1973, when the group returned for their second tour of
the States in April, esteemed journalist Lillian Roxon reviewed their
New York Academy of Music second show, where the group didn't
take to the stage until around four in the morning. Nils Lofgren's
Grin and Black Oak Arkansas supported. Writing in the *New York
Sunday News*, Roxon noted that the audience were mainly asleep by
the time Slade took to the stage. 'True, it was a bit late and Noddy
Holder, who wants the audience to be his in the first 10 seconds,
grumbled a bit, but I thought it was a miracle. In the end, the cheers
were deafening. Slade had done it again. They are going to be big
stars.'

The bands Slade played with can now be viewed as somewhat eye-
watering. On 6 May 1973 Slade played Winterland with Humble Pie
headlining, and Steely Dan opening. On 19 May, the tour rolled
into the Majestic Theatre in Dallas, where on a night off, Holder's
old Black Country pal Robert Plant and his band came to see them.
'Zeppelin occupied the Royal Box in the theatre for Slade's set,'
Mick Gallagher, keyboardist with Frampton's Camel recalls. 'They
had sent their road tech to McDonald's with an order for fifty
cheeseburgers which they proceeded to throw at Dave Hill from
their vantage point just above him. Unphased, Dave pressed on with
his mission ("you write 'em, I'll sell 'em!") to the admiration of his
tormentors.'

The banter between the bands continued backstage. Slade were
back in the UK when Robert Plant dedicated 'Heartbreaker' to
Slade at the Inglewood Forum on 3 June, with Plant saying, 'this
is for the world's worst group.' That sort of British sarcasm does
not translate well to the US – for an arena full of fervent US fans, a
statement like that could have been taken as gospel.

CHAPTER 16

Big Sound, Big Stage, Big Crowd, Big Riot

The UK tour that Slade undertook in May–July 1973 was the absolute summit of their achievement, supported by the equally singular Sensational Alex Harvey Band, the thirteen-town, fifteen-date tour covered England, Scotland and Wales. 'That was just before I started going to gigs,' Duran Duran's John Taylor says. 'That must have been really a hot fucking night.' Hot it was. On the night Taylor would have seen them had he been older than 12, at Birmingham Town Hall, the splendid 19th-century building, Don Powell passed out due to heat exhaustion.

The tour included two homecoming nights at the Wolverhampton Civic, on 3 and 5 June. On the first night, they shared some of their hospitality: 'We kept our sense of humour, the Black Country sense of humour is very down to earth. That helped for a start,' Noddy Holder told Mark Blake.

We still had a lot of our old mates there, so if we got on our high horse, they'd soon shoot us down in flames. We used to take the press on jaunts up to our hometown gigs in Wolverhampton; get a coach and have our after party at The Trumpet and go on til seven in the morning. All the London press guys couldn't believe it. Here is us, at top of the tree taking them to a spit-and-sawdust one-room pub, effing and blinding constantly. We had Annie Nightingale behind the bar – and they absolutely loved it. Everybody would get pissed out of their head and then get on the coach back to London and write up the gig. It was what we were about. Didn't want to hire the Dorchester and put on a posh do with canapés, you'd have some black pudding and be happy. That was our thing. That was fun for them as well. There weren't bands around doing that.

Gered Mankowitz was in the party also – he had been taking photographs of the Civic Hall show that would be used for the sleeve of their upcoming greatest hits album. 'I photographed them at the Civic,' Mankowitz says. 'It was the famous concert where the balcony was shaking. They had all the energy and the showmanship. The enthusiasm of the audience was just phenomenal. I think they really did think that they were going to bring the circle down. The ability of the band to bring the audience into it all the time, they communicated so brilliantly. The fact that almost every single track was an anthem of one sort or another. When people ask me who are the best live bands I've ever seen, Slade are right in there. I hung out with them after the show and we all went to this pub that they always used to go to.'

'My dad was a very convivial publican who loved jazz,' Steve Megson says. 'I remember Noddy sitting down one night with American musician Alton Purnell; three o'clock in the morning, everybody's well on and it's a lock-in. They sang 'Georgia'. Just listening to two completely different musicians, from completely different races, one a black American, playing this song. Noddy's got this lovely gravelly voice and so has this old boy, playing the piano and each singing a verse at a time. It was a treasured moment.'

* * *

To celebrate this success – a fourth UK number one single – Don Powell took receipt of a brand-new 6.2 litre white Bentley convertible, an ultimate symbol of rock'n'roll status. He posed for a picture outside the Castlecroft dealership and Shell garage on Castlecroft Road in Wolverhampton, pouring a glass of champagne from the bottle. Few pictures could more suggest that Powell had arrived and the ten-year rise to fame from the early days of The Vendors had all been worth it.

The group were surrounded by a tight-knit circle. 'Johnny Steel, Chas's right-hand man, was a very smart lad,' Steve Megson says. 'They'd have these meetings, some of which I'd sit on the outside of drinking a beer or a coke, just having a listen. For a few years, I was very much part of their entourage. I can even remember driving them in their big cars if Graham Swinnerton wasn't available.'

Slade moved back for another crack at the States. Chandler terminated the employment of John Halsall and appointed Les Perrin ('Press Agent to the stars') to oversee Slade's attempt to attempt to break America. Halsall was later to comment, 'taking them away from me to Les Perrin and trying to break them in America was Chas's and, to some degree, Slade's, downfall.' Perrin had worked with many A-listers, but was known primarily at this point for working with The Rolling Stones. 'He was a Fleet Street veteran,' Chris O'Donnell recalls. 'Mick Jagger was famously asked how someone who was part of the counter-cultural revolution had a spokesperson who is a Fleet Street hack in his 40s. Mick replied no one is learning the gig on my back. I want someone who knows the gig.' Perrin, like Altham and Halsall before him, knew quite how Slade suited the grand gesture.

Halsall – who was still on his £15-a-week salary – was devastated. 'I was fucking shattered,' he states. 'My hard work and their talent led to numerous number ones and chart singles and what did I get? A measly fifty quid severance.' He took some succour from the fact he had picked up the work he wanted from his connection with Slade. He gathered up Gerry Bron's stable (Uriah Heep, Paladin, Osibisa, Manfred Mann (and spin-offs), and then Probe (ABC/ Dunhill) which added Three Dog Night, Steppenwolf, the James Gang among others.

'Les Perrin looked after John, George and Ringo, and the Stones,' Chris Charlesworth adds. 'Chas wanted that prestige, I guess. One of the first things Les did for them was to try and make a big deal out of them going to the US for the second time in April 1973. I and a few others went to Gatwick airport but there weren't any fans there, none to speak of anyway. It was an attempt to replicate the scenes that occurred when The Beatles flew into or out of Heathrow.' A picture of the group, with Lea and Hill clinging on to Air Caledonian stewardesses, with Charlesworth standing in the middle of them, looking rather forlorn, exists.

With 'Cum On Feel the Noize' at number one, on 19 March, Jim Lea married his childhood sweetheart, Louise Ganner. Both had attended Codsall Secondary Modern School, and had met when Jim was 16 and she was 15. None of the other members of the band were invited to the wedding. 'One of the stories Jim liked to tell was that Lou's parents were sort of middle-class and didn't approve of their daughter going out with (let alone marrying) a pop musician who was the son of pub landlords,' Chris Charlesworth recalls. 'One of the best days of his life, he said, was when he arrived at Lou's parents' house in the Rolls-Royce he'd bought. "I wanted to show 'em."'

* * *

Released on 22 June 1973, their next single, 'Skweeze Me, Pleeze Me' sold over 300,000 copies in its first week in the shops, and like 'Cum On Feel the Noize', it entered the UK charts at number one, taking over from another group of sixties survivors, 10cc (of whom Eric Stewart had been another Jack Baverstock protégé in The Mindbenders). The excitement of Slade's chart achievements could be felt across playgrounds in the UK, captured beautifully by 'Slade Laureate' Paul Cookson in his poem, *Skweeze Me, Pleeze Me: June 1973*.

> As soon as we heard that 10cc's 'Rubber Bullets'
> was down at two we knew.
> We just knew.
> We didn't have to wait for the countdown.
> We just knew.

It had been on *Top Of The Pops* the previous week
And now it was straight in at number one
Just like 'Cum On Feel The Noize'.

Riproaring opening chords widened our smiles
And lit a fuse that sent us reeling and rocking
Like lighted jumping jacks around school furniture.

Jim Lea drew inspiration for the song when he heard Reg Keirle playing a call-and-response number at The Trumpet in Bilston. Both sides were recorded at A&M Studios at 1416 N. La Brea Avenue in Hollywood. If the band were going to make it in the US, they couldn't be hopping back to Olympic to record. 'Kill 'Em at the Hot Club Tonite', the flipside, again showcased the group's versatility, and their use of B-sides as a playground to experiment. If it had been hidden in the glam of 'Coz I Luv You', there was no masking of Lea and Holder's fan worship of Django Reinhardt and Stéphane Grappelli here, with the title referencing their outfit the Quintette du Hot Club de France. Reinhardt and Grappelli would frequently jam backstage to arrive at material, a practice that Lea and Holder would emulate. There was talk that this could even be an A-side at one point, something Lea completely refuted in 2022. 'There's that sort of inter-referential thing in the lyrics of 'Skweeze Me, Pleeze Me', "Why don't you learn to spell?",' Alexis Petridis says. 'That is slightly Bolanesque, of creating this kind of universe that you buy into. So it's sort of quite parochial on one level and quite global on another.'

To celebrate their fifth number one, Slade arrived at Polydor's London HQ at Stratford Place on Wednesday 27 June in Powell's white Bentley, to share cases of miniature champagne with head office staff. The group were pictured in front of the Bentley with a jeroboam of champagne, sitting on cases of Lanson.

Slade made joyous, feelgood music. Bob Geldof, then a 22-year-old wannabe musician and bohemian, was spending time in the UK, working on the construction of the very first sections of the new London orbital motorway, the M25; he was given the job of working the makeshift traffic lights while heavy plant was crossing the road.

Geldof recounted the scene in his 1986 autobiography, *Is That It*? 'It was a nice way to spend a summer, with a book, listening to Slade on Radio 1 and watching the cars go by.' Slade were fixtures on the radio that year, and would be on London's new commercial radio station, Capital, when it began broadcasting that October.

The Slade Fan Club newsletter of June-July captured this giddy peak. It featured talk of ticket sales at Earls Court; special boats being laid on from Liverpool, Fleetwood, Belfast and Dublin to take fans to their forthcoming Isle of Man shows, scheduled in July; as well as British Rail's Football Special being scheduled to run for the shows to the ports from London. It emphasised the magnitude of success they were enjoying.

Booked through Mel Bush, Slade announced a show at London's cavernous Earls Court Exhibition Centre in July 1973, intending to become the first rock group to play the space known for hosting the Boat Show, the Ideal Home Exhibition and military pageants. Although Slade had booked their show first, David Bowie, then at his first plateau, announced a concert for 12 May, becoming the first artist to play there. Pink Floyd, too, then in the early phases of megastardom promoting their two-month-old album *The Dark Side of the Moon* – the yin to Slade's yang – played a benefit for Shelter on 18–19 May. David Bowie's show was plagued by sound and stage-height issues.

'All you've got to do in a place like this is to build a big stage and light it properly,' Chas Chandler told Chris Charlesworth. 'It's as simple as that. All you got to do is make sure everyone has a good view of the group.'

Slademania was in full effect. The group stayed at the recently opened, plush Holiday Inn in Swiss Cottage, on the fringes of London's Regent's Park. They took up residence for the Earls Court show on 26 June booked through until 2 July. The hotel was besieged with fans, to the point where it was reported the manager had asked them to leave. Dave Hill told writer Chris Roberts that it was so frightening he got the giggles. George Tremlett and his wife Jane interviewed the group at the Holiday Inn, the day before the concert. He wrote in *The Slade Story*: 'My wife and I spent two hours with the group interviewing each of them separately, and one could

150

sense that they... realised that their career was reaching a peak, and apart from breaking through in the States and maybe making a film, there were few rivers yet to cross. They had reached the top.' Top-priced dockets for Earls Court were £2, then tiered down to £1.50 and, in the cheap seats, £1 (£30, £25 and £20 in 2023).

Slade sold out Earls Court and played in front of 18,000 people, who enjoyed a night of wild, unalloyed rock'n'roll. Mark Brennan, who would later curate Slade's archive for reissues, says, 'The first gig I went to was Slade supported by Alex Harvey Band at Earls Court – it was a birthday party for one of the kids at school – his parents took us – it's no wonder I'm fucking warped, is it?'

It was the very zenith of the mania. Hill recalls being told that the tube trains were full of people in glitter and top hats. The stage set was purpose built. 'We had the biggest PA ever, by WEM,' Jim Lea told Mark Blake. 'We were real big time now. Big sound, big stage, big crowd, big riot as fans broke in in the afternoon.'

Emperor Rosko introduced the band. 'My relationship with Slade was always very good,' Rosko says. 'We had a good time, had a jar, and we all liked loud music. Earls Court was the biggest indoor show I'd been to at the time. It was a good vibration, no doubt about it. You could feel the crowd. There was a very good café bar backstage and so many celebrities that night.'

Chris Charlesworth, absolutely delighted that the group he had championed for so long had finally reached the summit, wrote almost chillingly in *Melody Maker* that week:

And so we come to last night – perhaps the final and ultimate climax of the group's career. It would be difficult to imagine Slade, or any other group for that matter, emulating the barrage of fanatical acclaim that Slade won for themselves at Earls Court. It was more of a convention than a concert, a gathering of the converted that rivalled political assemblies, royal weddings and sporting crowds in both size and fervour. It was bluddy wonderful... *Melody Maker* has given me the opportunity of watching the cream of world rock talent over the past three years and, with the notable exception of Elvis Presley, I can safely say I've seen the lot. And before I joined this paper, I saw The Beatles on three occasions. But nothing has ever moved me as much as last night's bash at Earls Court. I have heard more subtle music, sure, but atmosphere scored the points last night.

Chris Charlesworth remembers Chas Chandler parking his Rolls-Royce at the back of the stage that night at Earls Court. 'Jeff Beck was there, and he got into it and threatened to drive it. Around that time, I happened to notice the car registration number CC1 on sale in *The Sunday Times* and told Chas about it. He enquired about it and told me later it had been bought by Charles Clore.' At the time, financier Clore was supposed to be the richest man in the UK. 'Chas told me he didn't fancy going up against him in a bidding war for CC1!', Charlesworth, another CC, recalls.

Nick Kent wrote of the audience in *NME*:

> There's no way around it: these glitzed-out football crowd mutants are here to make a point of havin' some fun. When the segregated football chants have ceased and the whole hall gets carried away in a spontaneous chant, almost as if to define its own potency, it sounds like a massed gathering of birds of prey calling attention to itself before it sets about its own ominously evil project. It's downright creepy.

On stage, Slade pulled off their amazing feat of doing exactly the same act but scaling it up to somewhere beyond the nth degree. Although the Megsons had some design issues to conquer for Dave Hill: 'I made this black-and-gold quilted thing for Dave Hill and it was literally based on a Samurai costume,' Steve Megson says. 'It had big things hanging from the sleeves that we had to change because he couldn't play his guitar properly.'

Holder did his full 'acceptable in the seventies' routine with the audience – 'We're going to play a game with you all now and have one minute's silence. If anybody makes a noise, they'll pay a forfeit. If it's a bloke who makes a noise, he's got to come up here on the stage and take his trousers down. If it's a young lady who makes a noise she's got to come up here and take her knickers off.' The crowd, of course, erupt. 'I recorded the group at Earls Court,' Alan

O'Duffy recalls. 'It was a real live event and very beautiful, me and The Rolling Stones mobile and all that; it was all very fun, but it was never released.'

With 'Skweeze Me, Pleeze Me' at number one, the Earls Court triumph under their belt, the band were down to take their first significant break for a considerable time. With only two concerts on the gig sheet (both at the Isle of Man, one at the beginning of the month, and one at the end), July 1973 was to be a time of rest and an opportunity to enjoy some early fruits of their labours. Noddy Holder was to spend some time in his new house, Jim and Louise Lea were off to Mallorca, and Dave Hill and Don Powell were off to Hollywood, something Powell had discussed with George Tremlett in the interviews before the Earls Court show.

CHAPTER 17

Don Powell, Wolverhampton; Frank Lea, Codsall; Granny, Rock'n'Rolling

Tuesday 26 June 1973 – 'Skweeze Me, Pleeze Me' hits number one in the UK.

Sunday 1 July 1973 – Slade play to 18,000 at Earls Court, London.

Wednesday 4 July 1973 – Don Powell is involved in a car crash in Wolverhampton.
His girlfriend, Angela Morris, is killed.

Thursday 5 July 1973 – Frank Lea has rehearsal with Slade at Wednesbury school.

Friday 6 July 1973 – Frank Lea is announced as replacement drummer for Isle of Man gigs.

Sunday 8 July 1973 – Frank Lea stands in for Don on drums at Slade's first summer gig at the Palace Lido in Douglas, Isle of Man.

Whatever Happened to Slade?

It could be said that the night of 3 July into 4 July 1973, was when glam rock died. Two events happened, one culturally and one catastrophically, involving two of the main players of the so-called movement. One hundred and thirty-six miles miles southeast of Wolverhampton, David Bowie announced from the stage of the Hammersmith Odeon that, 'Of all the shows on this tour, this particular show will remain with us the longest, because not only is it the last show of the tour, but it's the last show that we'll ever do.' In killing off the character he had created, Ziggy Stardust, so emblematic for teenagers, he left the stage, albeit temporarily, leaving the scene to all the wannabes out there. In Wolverhampton, something far more tragic was to happen.

'Me and Don were good mates,' Frank Lea says. 'We used to go out a lot on the piss. That night we went up the Lafayette and we're having a drink. Don's girlfriend, Ange, worked down at Dix and Don said he was going down, but I decided to stay put. And he said, "well, when you're ready, come down, and I'll give you a lift home," which he used to do.' Powell would drive Lea as Jim's younger brother had a ban for drink driving.

So, at around 11 p.m. on 3 July, Don Powell drove his Bentley to Dix nightclub on Temple Street to collect Angela Morris, where she worked as a secretary. Morris was best friends with Dave Hill's sister, Carol. Powell and Morris spent a couple of hours in the club, which was commemorating its first anniversary of opening that night. Still at the Lafayette, Frank Lea asked his friend Anthony Hackner to take him down to Dix nightclub to meet Powell. Lea and Hackner drove the three-quarters of a mile to Dix. 'Don used to park his car right in front of the club, so that the bouncers could slide the door open and see if the car was alright,' Lea says. But they couldn't see Powell's Bentley. Lea was perplexed: 'I said, "*for fuck's sake, he said he'd wait for me.*"' Hackner offered Lea a lift home, which he gladly accepted.

Don Powell and Angela Morris were still inside the club. Soon after 1 a.m., the pair headed home; it was alleged that if Powell had fallen short of proposing to Morris in the club that night, they had certainly talked about marriage, although Frank Lea thinks this was somewhat exaggerated to sell newspapers: 'I knew Ange very well. It's all sensationalism; it's just easier, a bigger story.'

156

On Compton Road West, Wolverhampton, the Bentley glanced against a wall, span several times and crashed, going through a hedge and bringing down part of the perimeter wall of Wolverhampton Grammar School. The car was in such as state it was impossible to ascertain who had been driving. Fortunately, two nurses on their way to work were passing, who kept Powell alive until the ambulance arrived.

Powell was rushed to Wolverhampton Royal Hospital and spent the following six days in a coma, and his heart stopped beating twice. Chas Chandler sped up from London. Doctors drilled into his skull to relieve pressure on his brain as they battled to save his life. Powell suffered from broken arms, legs and ribs. Angela Morris was not so fortunate – alive when taken to hospital, she died soon after from her injuries. She was 20 years old.

The news, understandably, made all the papers, and footage of the Bentley shows just how terrifying the accident must have been. In the days after, the spot was covered with flowers and notes, with one allegedly saying 'Next time demolish our school and not just the wall outside'. Powell was sent chewing gum from all over the world, with letters simply addressed to 'Don Powell, Wolverhampton'.

Don Powell was unaware of what had happened, although he had moments of lucidity in his hospital bed. He recalled waking and being freezing cold, wanting to pull all of the tubes and wires out that were connected to him. He knew he was in a band, and at first assumed they had all been injured returning from a show. 'I thought we'd all been in a crash, so the rest of the guys must be there somewhere,' Powell wrote. 'The next thing when I came round again, they were all sitting at the bottom of the bed in hospital gowns and that freaked me.'

What added further to the situation was that Powell struggled to remember Angela Morris. 'Pat [Leighton, ex-fiancée who had been with Powell since the mid-60s] was the one I had been engaged to, and only gradually did I understand that it was Angela who had died,' Powell wrote. 'That freaked me, because I didn't remember her. It got out in the press and, of course, her parents saw it and that was not very good. When I got out of hospital, I went to see them obviously and explained about my amnesia, that it was the reason why I didn't remember their daughter.'

'I never thought about it, I tried to put it in a box over there and see what happened,' Jim Lea said. 'Don slowly got better, his memory never did.'

Powell's amnesia is there to this day, yet it seems strange and non-linear. His grasp of detail of things in the distant past remains strong – aided by his decision to scrupulously keep a daily diary to remind him of what has happened – yet his short and mid-range memory can be all over the place. 'There's no explanation,' Powell says. 'Not long after the accident, I was asking a psychoanalyst when does the short-term memory become long-term memory. My long-term memory is impeccable. He couldn't answer me.'

* * *

There were two outstanding bits of booked business that the group had to attend to – the concerts that they were to play on the Isle of Man. Lea's brother, Frank, stood in for Don at the Lido in Douglas on 8 and 29 July. His playing was announced to the world before Powell had regained consciousness. It made perfect sense for Lea Jr to step in, as he had been on the inner circle since he was a young teen.

'Don was still in hospital, and they had two shows left on the tour, at the Isle of Man. And Slade never missed the show,' Lea says. 'That was what they were good at. When they got to number one with 'Coz I Luv You', any gigs that they had outstanding they did for the original money agreed. A lot of bands wouldn't do that. But they did, and they wanted to do the two gigs.'

Frank Lea, who had trained to be a plumber, but was now drumming in a band and roadying for Slade, was over at his brother's house on Warstones Road, ironically, doing some plumbing. 'James was talking to Nod about it in the kitchen, about a replacement – James was talking about Dave Donovan, the drummer in Rock Rebellion, the brother of Haden on Slade's roadcrew – they just wanted somebody local that they knew. I thought I know everything about them. I know when Nod burps; when a song stops and starts, because I was with them all the time. I could play drums. So, I said to James, well, "what about me?" He replied *"you?"*

158

'James spoke to the others, and we went down to the schools in Wednesbury where they used to rehearse. Don had this shuffle thing, which I didn't want to do. James took me down before the band and we ran through a few things. We then ran through a couple of songs with the band and Nod said it worked. Prior to the gig, we only went through it once, two times tops.'

Frank coming in was huge news. 'I was a double-page spread in the national papers, *The Sun, The Mirror*,' Frank Lea says. 'The headline in the *Express and Star* – how I hated that: "From Plumber to Drummer". I can't even be a substitute superstar.' Music writer Dennis Detheridge contributed to a *Melody Maker* feature after speaking with Paul McCartney when Wings played Birmingham Odeon on 6 July. 'It's a terrible business but Slade were right to carry on with a stand-in drummer,' McCartney was reported as saying. 'We used a dep for Ringo in Australia. I think how Slade have done it is great. They've done it very well. It's one of those things – either they lay off and lose momentum or they keep going with a dep, someone not as good, obviously. But the kids will dig it. They'll understand. That's the great thing about audiences. That's the good thing about working live. That's the kind of thing people do understand. They will think it's great of Slade to have even turned up. They'll appreciate that they did it.'

Appreciate it they did: 'It was a full house in Douglas, with fans who'd gone there deliberately, and they went wild because Slade had honoured the gig.' Chris Charlesworth, who travelled with them, recalled. 'It was a very emotional night.'

'When we got to the Isle of Man, we did a couple of songs for the soundcheck and then it was time to go on a bit later,' Frank Lea says. 'Which was a bit strange, very weird.'

Dave Hill was quoted about the younger Lea stepping in in the *Daily Express* the following day: 'Lots of good drummers would have given an arm to appear with us but we needed someone who can tune in to our wavelength. We've known Frank a long time... Fortunately, Frank's on no ego trip.' 'I was having a great time and helping out as well,' Lea Jr adds.

* * *

Before the band left for Douglas, Powell was taken off the critical list – he was in a terrible way and had yet to regain consciousness, but it was highly unlikely he would die.

'On Wednesday I went up to Wolverhampton and the doctors at the hospital didn't give Don a chance,' Chandler told Chris Charlesworth that July. 'I was walking around in a daze, but when I heard he was going to pull through I was the happiest man in the world.'

The impact on four friends in their mid-20s was huge. It took ages for the band to truly process it. It was a perfect example of 'keep calm and carry on' or denial in the extreme. 'It was heavy,' Jim Lea told *Record Mirror* in early October. 'Me and Nod went to see him and puked... I was really thinking positively; what are we going to do now, we've got gigs at the Isle of Man, what's happening, phone Chas, phone H (Dave), phone Nod, get things together, and I never gave a thought to what condition he was in. And I went up to see him before we went to the Isle of Man and Nod went in before me and we just puked, you know.' There was also the enormous irony that 'Kill 'Em at the Hot Club Tonite' was the B-side of the record at number one. If the title was an eerie coincidence, the line 'you write off my car' was positively spooky.

While Powell was laying his bed, Nick Kent, one of the most notorious of the rock writers, wrote a huge feature in *NME*, entitled 'The Kidz Are Alright', proclaiming: 'Slade are easily the most important rock band to appear from these fair shores since the 1970s were ushered in, far more so than all the Bowies, Bolans and Roxys whose individual ventures are little more than intriguing tangent offcuts from the dominant middle-class tradition.' In a full appreciation of the group, Kent continued, 'Bolan was busy building himself up into becoming the great white narcissistic wonder, while Slade, paradoxically, came out looking like buffoons in ludicrous fancy dress. But the trick was that you laughed with them and not at them. Their bawdiness was well in key with their image, their good-timey attitude was contagious and all the way along, the music acted as a celebration for all the shenanigans. Just like all good rock n' roll should.'

For the remainder of July, the band dispersed until the second Isle of Man gig on the 29th. Hill took the opportunity to go to

America as planned, where he married Jan in Tijuana on 23 July; the Leas took a break with Mel Bush and his family on the south coast of England. Holder pottered around the West Midlands; all of them would check in on Powell's progress. 'Don's condition is satisfactory, in fact, he's recovering quite quickly,' Holder told the papers. 'I've been along most days to see him, and he's very cheerful. He's even watching a lot of television and he's quite knocked out with some of the kiddies programmes.' It was clear that Holder was doing his utmost to paint the most positive picture.

On 12 August, Don Powell made his first appearance in public since the crash. It seems either ironic or downright insensitive through a 21st-century lens that the location of his comeback was at famed UK motor-racing circuit Brands Hatch in Kent for a Radio Luxembourg Fun Day. 'I really didn't want to go back to work; I really was not in the right frame of mind mentally or physically,' Powell said. 'The doctor in Wolverhampton sat me down and told me to do it; otherwise, I never would. He'd come across it in so many different fields. If I made a hash of it, so what, but get up and do it. In hindsight it was the best thing that ever happened to me.' The pictures on the day show him walking with a stick, his head clearly shaved and him looking rather dazed.

Recalling the night of the accident, Frank Lea says: 'Don told me "Some bastard had put their car where I was going to put mine in its usual place, so I had to park down the side of the club. That's why you couldn't see my car. But if you'd come in, I would have been there." So, if I'd gone in, we wouldn't have gone down the Compton Road, we'd have taken a different route to drop me off at my mum and dad's. Would history have been different... who knows?'

The news went global. Stephen Cross, their eager teenager fan in Australia, was distraught: 'My father announced at the breakfast table that "your Slade mate has been in a car crash". Don's crash had made the international news section of our town's local newspaper. That initial report was not positive regarding the chances of Don recovering and I remember many agonising weeks going by without knowing anything about Don's progress until, I learned somewhere that he was on the mend.'

* * *

The group returned to America in September. Three weeks before Slade began the next phase of their American adventure, on 7 September 1973, Elton John had played the Hollywood Bowl, a venue in the popular imagination that personifies stardom, introduced to the stage by Linda Lovelace, then at the height of her *Deep Throat* notoriety. After singing so passionately about the country, thanks to Bernie Taupin's lyrics, Elton conquered it almost by accident. Slade had a long way to go before reaching such lofty heights. But, they were a significant cult – they were one of the bands that were played at Rodney Bingenheimer's English Disco at 7561 W. Sunset Boulevard in LA, one of the scene's hippest and most decadent establishments. Bingenheimer was later to say, 'Everyone was dancing to the coolest music around: Bowie, T. Rex, Quatro, Slade, Mott The Hoople, Sweet, New York Dolls, Alice Cooper, Barry Blue.' Slade's reputation was steady, and quite underground in the States.

The matches and mismatches of bills provide some fascinating combinations: Slade played with Sly and the Family Stone ('We were the only white people in the audience,' says Don Powell) and Iggy Pop. A personal favourite is the union between King Crimson, Strawbs and Slade on 27 September 1973, in Detroit. Holder was to say in 1977 that, 'They don't categorise so much over there. I mean, we once appeared on the same bill as King Crimson – we're as different to them as chalk from cheese – and we still went down a storm, even though it was their audience.' John Wetton, the bassist from that line-up of Crimson, didn't see that initially; and Holder used the same tactic he'd used on the Humble Pie audience. 'It was always difficult for anyone to follow Crimson,' Wetton told Crimson biographer Sid Smith. 'We would end with 'Larks' Tongues in Aspic, Part Two' or '21st Century Schizoid Man' and it'd be difficult for people to top that, really. The sound was so brutal coming from all of us it didn't actually matter what we played because when we came on, even if we were improvising from the word go, people would just stand and say, "fucking arseholes – what is this!" It had such force and presence you couldn't argue with it really.'

Slade headlined over King Crimson that night at Detroit's Masonic Temple. 'We played our set, then Slade came on and they had to survive the boos and jeers,' adds Wetton. 'Noddy Holder, their lead singer, came up to the microphone and he said in a broad Wolverhampton accent, "If you don't like it, you can all go and have a shit!" It was superb!' Possibly this wasn't the best way to win over a US crowd.

In Los Angeles on 21 October they supported The J. Geils Band at the Long Beach Convention Centre, and Chris Charlesworth, newly appointed as *Melody Maker*'s US editor, was on hand to see them. 'It wasn't one of their better shows,' he says. 'The audience was filing in as they were playing and after forty minutes someone pulled the plug on them. It could be brutal on the US touring circuit. There wasn't the camaraderie there was in the UK.'

On this visit to the States, to understand his condition as fully as possible, Don Powell had a one-off meeting with Dr Albert Goodgold, MD, a leading neurologist in New York, and friend of US manager Peter Kauff. It was arranged for him to have Powell's accident hospital records sent to him, and he told Powell that he had to let it be. 'He said, "The worst thing you can do is fight. Try to relax. The tension makes it worse,"' Powell says. 'It's so true; I had to accept the situation. When I did that, it made it a lot better. There's nothing I can do about it. It's as simple as that. There's nothing surgery can do. It's just the way it is.'

Powell also discussed his loss of taste and smell with Goodgold:

He said I'd severed the nerves in my nose when I went through the windscreen. He said that also up there is your eyesight, sense of balance and I could have been blinded. Reading my hospital records, he told me about the nerves regarding my smell and taste would have needed to have been repaired immediately but they had their work cut out keeping me alive so, they would have been their last priority. One thing Albert did say to me after going through the hospital records, was how lucky I was to be alive, 'hats off to the medical staff who tended you.'

Powell began to gradually adjust: 'He said I'd soon get used to it. I've still got an appetite and I still enjoy food. I still feel hungry. I still think, "I fancy fish and chips or a bacon sandwich."'

'I'd put that to the back on my mind,' John Steel says. 'It's quite a shock to remember it now. But he wasn't quite the same. He forgot a lot of things. When he was back on the road, he had to write down before he went to sleep where he was, so he knew where he was when he woke up in the morning. He got very forgetful about stuff.'

* * *

Slade left a new release behind for their shell-shocked UK fans. Released on 28 September, their eagerly anticipated single, 'My Friend Stan', didn't resemble what admirers had been used to – the screaming was de-tuned, and, for only the second time as a key instrument on a Slade 45, the piano was played. Lea wanted to throw something new into the mix, worried as he was that Slade singles were simply becoming formulaic. One of the first things recorded since Powell's accident, it was only released because Chandler thought it would make a good stopgap while the group were heading to the States. Powell had to be lifted onto his drum stool to be able to play. It was recorded at Olympic. 'I was there on the day he came back to work,' Alan O'Duffy says. 'A lovely, lovely guy.'

'My Friend Stan' 'only' entered the chart at number four – remarkable for any other group, but for Slade, it seemed to come with an enormous sense of disappointment. The following week it shot up to number two, the place it would remain for a solitary week, before slipping to number three where it would stay for another two weeks. It was kept off the top spot by one of those great UK chart anomalies – 'Eye Level (Theme From The Thames TV Series *Van Der Valk*)'. Played by The Simon Park Orchestra, it brought middle-aged men in beige polo necks on to *Top of the Pops*. The intro to the ITV police series *Van Der Valk*, which starred Barry Foster as a detective in Amsterdam, the theme took its title from the horizon in the Netherlands, which is, indeed, always at eye level. The tune had been written by Jan Stoeckart for the De Wolfe Music Library under the pseudonym 'Jack Trombey' several years earlier. Like 'My Ding-A-Ling' the previous year, which had seen off the number one hopes of 'Gudbuy T'Jane', 'Eye Level' was one of those novelty records that went far beyond the fanbase of most contemporary acts. When parents and grandparents made their two-or-three-times a year purchase of a 45, it would obviously be something like 'Eye Level' as opposed to 'My Friend Stan'. It also saw off 'Ballroom Blitz' by Sweet, which 'My Friend Stan' replaced at number two. It would be David Cassidy in his teen-scream pomp with 'Daydreamer'/'The Puppy Song' that ultimately sent the benign orchestra packing.

'My Friend Stan' itself was somewhat oblique after the straightforward rocking of the past four singles. Driven by Jim Lea's pounding piano, it was a third-person song that didn't quite connect in the way the previous singles had. It was like a dip into The Beatles' repertory company of characters, Maxwell, Mr Mustard, Pam, Vera, Chuck and Dave. It was whimsical, and Slade weren't known for their whimsy. Its video, filmed at Olympic Studios, understandably skirted over Powell's accident, but had plenty of captures of Holder gurning; it also caught the band in a completely previously unseen emotion: reflection, and possibly even contemplation. Its stalling at number two led Dave Hill to arrive at another of his Sladelore one-liners: 'Piano equals failure'. Don Powell adds: "'Cum On Feel the Noize' went to number one the first day. 'Skweeze Me, Pleeze Me' went to number one the first day. When 'My Friend Stan' went to number four, it was like, that's it, they're finished!'

For young fans, it hit hard. 'I felt I was having records custom-made, bespoke for me. I got that same sense of dismay, as when Arsenal lost in the FA Cup in 1972, when 'My Friend Stan' didn't get to number one I took it to heart,' David Stubbs says.

Slade were in America on 4 October when the 500th anniversary episode of *Top of the Pops* was aired in Great Britain. Appearing after Lynsey de Paul's 'Won't Somebody Dance with Me?', the band were filmed sitting at an Italian pavement café in New York with Lea with a cigarette up each nostril. Holder stated, 'Wish we could have been there getting drunk with everybody', before breaking into a version of 'We Wish You a Merry Christmas', with the words changed to happy birthday, clearly a nod to what they had just recorded. 'At the time my legs were pretty painful (I'd broken both my legs) – they had to carry me on stage,' Powell said. 'When they'd all walk off, I'd still be sitting there – all the crowd would wonder why I was still there.'

Chandler had the idea for the group to make a Christmas record, but because of schedules and Powell's recovery, the group couldn't record in London, so Chandler had booked the group a session in New York's Record Plant, where Lea and Holder presented the Christmas song. According to Lea, Dave Hill had to be coaxed into playing, as he initially wanted to no part in the recording of a Christmas hit.

Because of Powell's condition, it was also the first Slade record where parts were recorded individually, whereas previously the group had always played as live and then overdubbed when needed. The speed with which Powell returned to the drum stool positively staggers by today's standards. Because of the effects of the crash, Powell had to record his drum parts piece by piece and were put together by Record Plant in-house engineer Dennis Ferrante.

'I knew 'Merry Xmas Everybody' was going to be massive, but I was mortified when I found out that everyone else was bringing Christmas songs out as well,' Jim Lea told *The Guardian* in 2016. It felt as if all pop stars felt a moral obligation to cheer everyone up that Christmas. As historian Alwyn W. Turner writes, Slade's contemporaries were 'busy producing foot stomping singalongs delivered in ever more extraordinary costumes, as though they wished to be the antidote to the gathering gloom.' With lines about the anticipation, families arriving, dismissive yet jiving grannies, references to 'Rudolph the Red-Nosed Reindeer', 'I Saw Mommy Kissing Santa Claus', snow, and the overall optimism, 'Merry Xmas Everybody' is undoubtedly Holder's greatest lyric.

Jim Lea said, 'I heard Elton's one, 'Step into Christmas', but I thought: "No competition." Then I heard Roy Wood and Wizzard's and the competition had arrived.' It was ironic as Wizzard had followed a similar trajectory to Slade, and the craft of leader Wood's songwriting was second to none – both were huge devotees of John Lennon and both had the idea to release their Christmas single for Christmas 1973. Wizzard manage to make Slade's record sound positively minimalist – which make both compelling and long lasting.

Based on melodies from discarded songs written six years before, 'Merry Xmas Everybody' became Slade's best-selling single. Jim Lea wrote the majority of the melody and came up with the 'so here it is' refrain. His mother-in-law had been encouraging him to write a Christmas hit, after chiding him that none of their singles were as big as Bing Crosby's 'White Christmas'. Holder's part was based on a song he had toyed with since 1967 called, 'Buy Me a Rocking Chair', which, as *Guardian* writer Dave Simpson noted, 'went in the bin when the band declared it "shit"'. The special ingredient, of course, was in Holder's lyrics. Written one night after a heavy session at The Trumpet, Holder went back to his mum and dad's and sat in the kitchen where so much writing magic had already occurred and wrote a list of all the obvious things people associate with Christmas.

'Merry Xmas Everybody' crowned 1973, a year of the highest highs and plummeting lows for Slade, selling over a million copies, with 300,000 copies sold on its day of release alone, and becoming the first Christmas record to enter the UK chart at number one. 'It was obviously a risk, but we had enough confidence in the songs to know it was going to do well,' Holder said. 'We loved the song from the minute we had written it.'

It was apparent that Slade had won the battle of the festive hits – 'Merry Xmas Everybody' went to number one while Wizzard 'only' made number four. Lea later described how he met Wood at a party that festive season, and Wood suggested to him that 'the best man had won'. Lea told him that he preferred his record, and still does. 'Merry Xmas Everybody' was the absolute view from the summit, their crowning glory. Although Slade did not know it at the time, it was to be their final number one single, with an afterlife like no other of their records.

'Slade became a really big band and a really good band. Fantastic songs, and a proper Christmas song. Not many people can do that,' Slade's one-time headliner Andy Fairweather Low says. 'I love Noddy – a top bloke. Amen Corner did all right. We did sell records. But we weren't in the same league as Slade.'

That November, Terry McCusker, the drummer with Colonel Bagshot, who had been touring with Slade in Europe, remembers hearing the record with the group present for the first time ever: 'We were in Cologne and we were invited out by the record company for dinner in a disco. It was like "here's the record". We all thought how good it was.'

Kevin 'Billy' Adams, the teenage Slade fan, would experience similar just under a decade later, when he co-wrote his group's biggest hit 'Come On Eileen'.

'It's certainly an evening reception wedding song isn't it, bizarrely enough. It's not uncommon in the music industry for a song to come to define a band. A double-edged sword, but as the years go by it starts to feel like more of a blessing than a curse. It's not something that troubles many people is it, so it seems quite churlish to complain about the kind of success that makes a band a household name. That said, I did struggle with it for years, then one day a guy that I respected pointed out the obvious, just smile and say thank you if someone says, "I like your song." No need for an "actually, we had more than one song" lecture. They bring so much joy to so many people, don't they, and that's brilliant.' Adams says: "'Merry Xmas Everybody' was huge for me, it was bought for me the Christmas it went to number one by a lovely aunt who said, "I had a listen and it's not for me, but I hope you like it.'''

'Back then, when you were a kid, you've got two good days of the year: your birthday, the second best, and Christmas Day, the best,' David Stubbs says. 'And everything coalesces. The presents that you get that Christmas Day are going to last you until your birthday; you're playing Monopoly 450 times. I'll never have Christmases as good as the Christmas I had at that particular time. They just stood out like a glistening ball against the rest of the dross; and Slade personified that – they were the perfect group to deliver the greatest ever Christmas song. It's just the sheer, absolute merriment of it.'

Although streaming services are but one measure of success, the single has lost some ground in recent years, but still stands there as a testament to another time, another place. Despite its late release, it still managed to be not only the twelfth best-selling single of 1973 (with 'Cum On Feel the Noize' at number six, and 'Skweeze Me, Pleeze Me' at eleven and even dear old 'Stan' down there at twenty-eight) but also the fifteenth best-selling single of 1974 – beating 'Far Far Away' by thirteen places. ''Merry Xmas Everybody' is staggeringly great,' Tim Rice, no stranger to a pop hit, adds. 'I mean, to rival 'White Christmas' from Wolverhampton is just brilliant.'

There was also a fine piece of Slade subversion going on: 'Lately I been a winner,' sings Holder on the record's flipside, 'ladies all cook me dinner'. 'Don't Blame Me' is possibly one of the most raucous B-sides to such a much-loved, in-every-household single. Recorded for the upcoming album and chosen in short order by the record company and Chandler's office as a flip was needed quickly, Hill's guitar is wild, and Holder is at his shouting best. The end is almost unpleasant to listen to. So, there was no selling out afoot. As Chris Ingham writes, 'Holder's voice sounds less like a tool of singing and more like a weapon of mass destruction.' Slade weren't going soft. Yet.

Three weeks before 'Merry Xmas Everybody' entered the world, *Sladest* was released. Originally flagged to fan club members as *The Best of Slade*, the album managed to pull off the feat of appearing like a brand-new album while containing only previously released material. As an album, it hangs together arguably the best of any of their works. It was certainly rewarded by its UK chart performance, following up *Slayed?* at number one, by topping the charts across Christmas 1973 and remaining in the charts for twenty-four weeks. What it did was marry tracks from the earliest albums and make them sound entirely contemporary alongside their recent hits. It acts as an ideal resume of the group to this point – in a gatefold sleeve with an eight-page booklet with sleevenotes by former *Melody Maker* chief sub Bob Houston, a respected writer with only a handful of notes to his name. One can only wonder what teenage fans made of Houston's work:

> Slade emerged from their Wolverhampton fastness like Atilla The Hun hightailing down the Appian Way towards a moribund and defenceless Rome. As rock became more ethereal, more intellectual, all down to sitting round a BBC studio to watch the latest American aesthete unburden his soul, perhaps we tended to forget that out there, north of Potters Bar and east of Portland Place, the dark people were huddled around their trannies, thirsting for something to get them going.

The cover of *Sladest* was another Slade classic image. Gered Mankowitz took a soft-focus approach, with white scarves as the principal fashion statement, a lot mellower than previously seen on *Slayed?*. For the first time, the group looked pensive. People also commented that, as this was the first time many had seen Powell since his accident, it appeared as if his arm was in a sling. 'I asked them to all wear their scarves differently and that's how Don, because hands are so important to the drummer, that's how he did it,' Mankowitz recalls. 'The accident was deeply distressing to everybody and anybody who knew them. It was shocking, terrible. That session was the first after the accident and Don didn't have any short-term memory at all. He must have said, half a dozen times, "Oh, Gered, great to see you," and then he'd wander off and have a cup of coffee, and then appear again and say, "Gered, great to see you!"' The package exuded opulence: four 12x12 portraits of the group, plus live pictures and Houston's critique.

'The idea of doing these great big faces was, again, giving the fans this closeness because it's a larger-than-life-sized face,' Mankowitz says.

This close proximity using the 12-inch square and when you opened it, in the booklet there's a picture of them against the silver foil background, which is one of my favourite sessions with the band. Just a black and white. I just thought their look at that point was an absolute peak of where everybody knows exactly what they are and the way they've dressed themselves absolutely embellishes and encapsulates exactly what they are. It's a perfect look. I think they're at their perfection in terms of visual image. I love that session. I remember going through about 100 packets of Bacofoil in order to get the whole studio covered.

This really was peak 1973 – there seemed to be foil everywhere. Although tin foil had been around since the start of the 20th century, Bacofoil was a relatively new addition to kitchens, the company being established a little over a decade before. At school, at the Christmas end of term, everybody seemed to be mummified in aluminium. It was easy to copy these heroes. There was no foil in any mother's kitchen that lead-up to Christmas.

Michael Gray, reviewing the album in *Let It Rock*, said that Slade reminded him of 1963: 'not because their music is that regressive,' he qualifies, 'but because the pattern is the same: Lennon-McCartney/Jagger-Richard (or Nanker-Phelge, as they preferred in those far-off days), meet Lea-Holder.' He then simply listed their achievements, as if to say to all those who thought they were flash in the pan:

'Coz I Luv You' – Silver Disc; 4 weeks at No 1

'Look Wot You Dun' – Silver Disc

'Take Me Bak 'Ome' – Silver Disc

'Mama Weer All Crazee Now' – Silver Disc; 3 weeks at No 1

'Gudbuy T'Jane' – Silver Disc

'Cum On Feel the Noize' – Silver Disc; straight to, and 4 weeks at, No 1

'Skweeze Me, Pleeze Me' – Silver Disc; straight to, and 3 weeks at, No 1

The release of *Sladest* and the crowning of 'Merry Xmas Everybody' was, with hindsight, the absolute peak of Slade: the confidence they had, their very unassailability, a moment in time. It wasn't just a sympathy vote for Don Powell – although many were truly shocked – it was just a case of 'our' band basking in the recognition it richly deserved.

'I bought *Sladest* when it came out,' Kevin 'Billy' Adams says. 'My first ever album, and would have to take it to a friend's house to give it a play, until I had my own record player for Christmas when I was 13. The best memories of lying back on the bed, headphones on, lost in my record collection. Even though it was kind of a greatest hits album, *Sladest* had such an incredible collection of singles on it, it must have been my most played of all. I certainly remember cherishing it while I waited for my own record player for Christmas 1973.'

'*Sladest* was a stopgap; the content on there that wasn't the singles all fitted in superbly well,' Ian Edmundson says. 'It drew people back to *Play It Loud* who hadn't got it. The songs were excellent quality. There's a lot of stuff that they could have put on from the early period, but Chas was disowning *Beginnings*, so that's why they didn't go back to that. *Sladest* is a lot of people's favourite album and there's a lot of sentimentality attached to it because of the presentation. It's just such a strong collection of songs.'

Sladest was released in Australia as well. 'Skweeze Me, Pleeze Me' had been released around October 1973 and was in the Top 40 for quite a while, 'unlike 'My Friend Stan' which only just scraped into the Top 40 for a couple of weeks before dropping out entirely,' Stephen Cross says. 'The *Sladest* compilation was released late in 1973 and I remember buying a copy prior to Christmas. The gatefold booklet was the absolute confirmation for me that Slade were in fact a glam rock band. It didn't bother me at all as I just loved that classic Slade sound that they'd perfected and never bettered on 'Mama'.'

* * *

What seemed extremely strange by today's standards was that 'Merry Xmas Everybody' remained at the top of the charts until mid-January when, finally, The New Seekers' 'You Won't Find Another Fool Like Me' took it off the top, and it didn't leave the Top 40 until mid-February. Holder and Lea's 'working-class British Christmas song' quietly began its afterlife. The future for it had only just begun.

On 4 January 1974, with 'Merry Xmas Everybody' firmly ensconced at the top of the hit parade, Don Powell attended the inquest of Angela Morris at Wolverhampton coroner's court, although he did not give evidence, as he couldn't recall the incident. Richard Brownson – the owner of the club – said that he had taken the car keys from Morris and given them to Powell, before they left the club. A witness had seen Morris at the driver's seat outside Dix, but could not testify who was at the wheel when the car drove off. Coroner Walter Forsyth said there was doubtful evidence as to who drove the car and the jury brought in an open verdict.

CHAPTER 18

From Bilston to Burbank

1973 had been nothing less than the metaphorical roller-coaster for the group. Through all of the considerable trauma of Powell's accident and the 'misfire' of 'My Friend Stan', Slade had three of their four singles enter the chart at number one. There had been nothing like it since The Beatles, and the feat would not be seen again until 1980, when The Jam did similar. Slade had also, for a 'singles band', two albums at the top of the LP charts. Also, in the three years ending on New Year's Eve '73, the group had performed just shy of 400 gigs.

'In 1973 it was The Sweet vs Slade and they won,' Andy Scott concedes. 'Their records hit a mark, but then it's not so bad being the runners-up, is it?' The two bands were great friends and both encapsulated a working-class outsiderdom that Bolan and Bowie didn't have. By coincidence, Scott had played in the Bahamas alongside Slade during hotel residencies in '68. It seems fitting for glam, a genre so opulent, that the training ground should be the Caribbean, not a German port.

'When we really took off, by 1973, I'd say nothing could touch us at that time,' Dave Hill told Chris Roberts. 'We were on top of the pile, everywhere. Glam is just colourful rock, a way of expressing yourself. People go: oh my God, some of those costumes you wore, were you ever embarrassed? Well I never was! I actually got off on it! It's vaudeville, it's entertainment.'

'I was a little more T. Rex, Bowie,' Duran Duran's John Taylor says. 'Slade were very accessible; they were on TV a lot. They were on the radio a lot. I didn't need to listen to them at home. They were just out-and-out pop, a bit like The Sweet really, just classic pop. My tastes were a little darker than that, a tad more introspective. I liked the more narcissistic stuff.'

Like the early stages of a chronic illness, no one knew at the time quite how malignant Slade's decline would be; that their time to be over was arriving, gently. Not that it was in any way apparent with the release of *Old New Borrowed and Blue*, released on 15 February 1974. Their fourth studio album shot to the UK number one album spot. It contained the previous September's 'My Friend Stan', and from the cover inward, it offered a more reflective view of the group; and a feeling that the album was stitched together in something of a rush. In a way, as Beatles comparisons continued to be made, this was Slade's *Beatles for Sale*, recorded on the run at the height of the mania. There was one A-side and two B-sides, a cover, and then two tracks taken for the next single, so for those buying, there was only effectively six new songs.

However, there was an abundance of classic Slade – the old Rosco Gordon number 'Just Want A Little Bit' blasts in. The band had been playing it at soundchecks and it positively swings – drop to Holder's whispered interlude with the lightest touch on Powell's snare offering a glimpse of the stagecraft the band possessed in spades. 'My Town' (which had been the B-side of 'My Friend Stan') and 'Good Time Gals' (the forthcoming B-side of 'Everyday', and an A-side in America) were both stompers. 'Find Yourself a Rainbow' is a classic crowd-dividing number, a showcase for West Midlands legend and Trumpet stalwart Tommy Burton, whose honky-tonk piano defines the track; it's like Paul McCartney spinning in 'Honey Pie' or 'When I'm 64' – not for everyone, but playing to a different audience, a parent lending an ear to a teenager's record and tapping their toes. 'I love 'Find Yourself a Rainbow',' Paul Cookson says. 'I think that is fantastic. Again, that song shows where they came from. You wouldn't get Bowie or Roxy doing that, put on an album as

a pub singalong.' Jim Lea's first solo vocal, 'When the Lights Are
Out' is the ultimate single-that-never-was, just pure pop, as was the
lovely 'Miles Out to Sea', which mentioned Holder's love for the
film *Cabaret* (complete with 'Hello Stranger' spoken in a German
accent). The country-influenced 'How Can It Be' is a little hidden-
in-plain-sight gem, with a tremendous guitar solo.

'It's the patchwork quilt of Slade albums, isn't it? says Ian
Edmundson,

> Because of Don's accident, they just pulled it together from
> bits they had. There's a couple of rejects on there and bits
> where Dave went away on honeymoon. To a degree, it was the start
> of Slade recording without Dave. There's things he doesn't play
> on like 'Everyday'. He played it on stage perfectly. It was partly
> the start of Jim coming to dominance in the studio, having more
> of a say because it was between him and Nod. Don did his parts
> and went and laid down again. It was a very difficult album, and
> I couldn't for the life of me see the point of 'Find Yourself a
> Rainbow'. I know it went back to Nod doing the singalongs in the
> pub when he was a kid. They couldn't keep putting out 'Take Me
> Bak 'Ome'. They wanted to change and spread out a bit, to show
> what they could do. Noddy didn't want to be a shouter although
> that's got some of his more shouty vocals on it.

Kevin 'Billy' Adams, the avid fan from Bridgnorth agrees:

> '*Old New Borrowed and Blue* was what lost me really. I wasn't a fan
> of the single 'My Friend Stan', and can remember being quite
> disappointed by the first listen after I'd rushed home to play my
> new album. I was a huge fan, but typically as a teenager – I was
> born in 1960, so during the seventies, I was 9 at the start and 19
> at the end – I'd shift allegiance from one band and sub-culture to
> another. I slowly became a huge soul and Northern soul fan and
> glam rock took a back seat.'

Old New Borrowed and Blue splits the crowd. Stu Rutter, defends it:
'Nod's voice never sounded better on *Old New Borrowed and Blue* and
there's a great variety in the tracks. You can really feel with hindsight

that they were expanding their repertoire based on their abilities and not just supply and demand.'

Gered Mankowitz took the album's reflective cover photograph. The session had been taken in Norway on the European tour in November. 'I guess it was more economic to bring me out to Norway than it was to bring the band back for twenty-four hours,' Mankowitz says. 'They took me out to Oslo to do this session. The big challenge for me was getting them that close to each other because you must be very, very close, much closer than it looks and getting them in the space and getting them sharp. That was quite technical. It's all one shot. I didn't do collages or montages in those days. It was shot specifically for the cover. I think the inside spread was the same day.'

By now, they all had a great, instinctive, working relationship: 'They called me Hillary because of *Hancock's Half Hour*,' Mankowitz recalls. 'In the episode 'The Publicity Photograph' [Series 5, Episode 5, 18 February 1958] Kenneth Williams plays a press photographer called Hillary St Claire. If I said anything remotely pretentious or precocious, they used to take the piss out of me and say, "Oh, he's doing a Hillary." He actually says, "I paint with light." The boys always took the piss, which I loved.'

To celebrate the album's success, Powell bought himself a Jaguar, and became quite the fixture on the Wolverhampton pub scene. As roadie Haden Donovan told Lise Lyng Falkenberg in *Look Wot I Dun*, 'People would go, "come on then, Don. Your round," and Don would pay and forget it afterwards. People caught onto that and had Don buying drinks all night, because he couldn't remember.'

On 2 March 1974, as *Old New Borrowed and Blue* went to the top of the UK album charts, Wolverhampton Wanderers won the League Cup (2–1) with a late goal from striker John Richards in the eighty-fifth minute against Manchester City at Wembley in front of 97,000 people. It was the club's first silverware for thirteen years when Stan Cullis's team won the FA Cup. Captained by Mike Bailey and featuring forward Derek Dougan ('the Doog'), Wolves were never a glamour club yet incredibly popular and successful. For a period, it was almost fashionable to come from such an unfashionable city.

*   *   *

The group's next single, 'Everyday', was already available on *Old New Borrowed and Blue*; it still reached the UK Top 3, but it was the most downbeat Slade single to date. 'It had a more wistful, rueful feel to it,' Dave Hill wrote in *So Here It Is*. It gave Slade an enormous call-and-response moment for future stage shows, with the song becoming an massive fan favourite.

Lea's wife Louise came up with the initial melody and words for the tune at an evening with friends around Lea's house where everyone had a go at improvising a song, for which she failed to receive a credit, something was finally revised in the early 2020s. Hill suggested the wistful nature of the song was partially responsible for the melancholia that was to pervade the preliminary stage of the planning for their forthcoming film.

'When I heard 'Everyday',' writer Dave Ling says, 'I remember wondering whether this was the same band that was responsible for the unapologetically Neanderthal 'Look Wot You Dun'.' Its simplicity is its key: 'I have no equity in any of the stuff,' Alan O'Duffy says. 'I'm making these records and if I may be so arrogant to tell you, I'm the one experimenting with the sound. I'm the one making the suggestions about small stuff, not big time, working collaboratively and making sort of suggestions. There's a harmony thing at the end of 'Everyday' which I was going to sing and I couldn't do it. Tony Burrows came in and did it. It was sort of my idea, we were working together.' The sense of collaboration is strong.

However, Lea felt that 'When the Lights Are Out' would have made a more appropriate choice as single, given especially as Britain was in the three-day week at this point. The jaunty Lea-sung number would have continued the jollity of 'Merry Xmas Everybody', almost sitting as a perfect partner, and then releasing 'Everyday' after. In later years, Lea would state that Chas Chandler blocked it, because if people had realised that 'the quiet one' had so much talent, he would leave or be poached. *NME* wrote about 'Everyday' retrospectively in 1991, ''Everyday' – Slade's Leo Sayer period – a full six months before Leo Sayer's Leo Sayer period.'

'I started to think about how groups were put together,' John Taylor says. 'I started to appreciate what made Slade great. An incredibly subtle rhythm section. Don is a really underestimated drummer, everything swung really beautifully with him. Jim is an extraordinary musician. They weren't unlike The Beatles in some ways, Jim and Noddy particularly had that Paul and John thing. Noddy really was, I think, probably the closest singer in spirit to Lennon. His energy and how the energy of the band moved around him, but he was this very stable centre.'

Slade's touring machine went on. The second tour of Australia in 1974 saw the band playing much smaller venues than in 1973, like the Hordern Pavilion in Sydney and Melbourne's Festival Hall, both of which had a capacity of around 5,000, which was a far cry from the 25,000-strong crowd who had paid to see the band in Melbourne only one year earlier. 'This is only my own theory,' Australian fan Stephen Cross says:

'Slade's initial market in Australia was predominantly young men who were drawn to the heavy, melodic rock of the *Slade Alive!* and *Slayed?* albums. Hit singles, 'Take Me Bak 'Ome', 'Mama' and 'Cum On Feel the Noize' probably added to that. After the 'My Friend Stan' and 'Everyday' singles – possibly even earlier – I think a lot of the male fanbase lost interest in the band and that only hardcore fans like me continued buying their records along with an element of young girl fans.'

It was non-stop. 'Chas worked us to death, touring, touring, touring,' Holder told Mark Blake. 'Look at our date sheets, so many gigs. We never stopped all around the world. We'd go mad at Chas, to give us a break, we got to write and record an album, constant, never stop – Chas, slow us down – it was getting too much. He'd reply, "Boys, it's not the work that's knackering you out, it's the fucking partying" – and he was probably right.'

From Australia, the group went on to Japan for two nights. For Holder, visiting places such as this – especially at a time where travel was still a luxury rather than the mass-consumption thing it was to become in the eighties and nineties – offered validation for his decision not to continue in education back in the sixties.

* * *

178

Pop music, of course, was evolving all the time – on 6 April 1974, ABBA became the new phenomenon on the block when they won the Eurovision Song Contest, with 'Waterloo', a record that was to alter the direction of the contest and make them long-lasting superstars.

It was time for home crowds to witness that drive again. In mid-April, Slade went on their first tour in Britain since the shows that had culminated in Earls Court the previous July. Billed as Slade's Crazee Nite, the twenty-four-date tour took in twenty-two towns in England, Scotland and Wales. Supported by Newcastle band Beckett, the circus was indeed coming to town – each night there was a competition, as advertised on the tour poster:

> Wear your latest Slade gear and win a star prize
>
> The winner will also meet the boys in person
>
> Prize for runner up
>
> A winner at every Slade's Crazee Nite

As a result, although perhaps there wasn't quite the euphoria of the June 1973 tour, the audience was full of Holder and Hill-alikes, adding to the atmosphere of the carnival coming to town. The tour was a huge success, and a performance at the Kursaal in Southend-on-Sea, which can be heard in its entirety online, highlights just how much power the band brought.

The tour convinced Chas Chandler that they should now concentrate on the US: 'We had a tour of England, which had been massive, but there hadn't been the same dramatic rush to the box office,' Chandler said in 1984. 'We knew we had to conquer a new market. If we'd stayed in England, the market was going soft on them. It just felt there was no alternative but to go to America and try and do something there. It had reached its limits of growth, really, in the United Kingdom.' Slade's success coincided with some of the highest rates of personal income tax in Britain – 83 per cent on earned income. So, although Slade generated a great deal of cash, they, like many other pop and film stars, suffered with tax rates; indeed, it was a factor in their move to the States.

On top of this, the band were learning to deal with Don Powell post his crash; much to the rest of the group's chagrin, he would ask what time the bus would be leaving in the morning. They would tell him to write the details in his diary. Half an hour later, he would ask again what time the bus was arriving. 'It wasn't his fault. Now he can remember the detail of stuff from ten years ago but not half an hour before,' Holder said in 2019. That wasn't all: 'Quite often I'd find him wandering the hotel corridors at night, stark bollock naked,' Holder continued. 'He'd gone to bed, got up to use the bog and opened the wrong door and it shut behind him. Wandering the corridors and walked bollock naked to reception to get a key with the Do Not Disturb sign hanging from his dick. It was funny but it was a nightmare when doing it every day. So that was a hurdle we had to get over.'

Chas Chandler watched it all close at hand. He said that Powell's 'courage to continue through was just astonishing to me. The loyalty of the other three guys through that period was something I've never seen before.'

The group had a name for Powell: Mr Memory Man.

Slade's next single, 'The Bangin' Man', was released in July 1974. It continued the life-on-the-road trope that had started with 'Everyday', and was to continue on through their attempt to break America. As well, of course, as the enormous double entendre of the title, it was either inspired by road manager Graham Swinnerton, who would wake them up in hotel rooms every morning to get them to their next show, or Australian chamber maids on their second tour down under. The melancholic 'She Did It to Me' is the next in the line from 'My Friend Stan' through 'Everyday'. The wistfulness and alienation that was coming into their work was a sign for sections of their audience to depart. The song remains one of Lea's favourites.

John Peel, reviewing the singles in *Sounds* that week, was crystal clear in his appreciation of 'The Bangin' Man' in the 22 June issue: 'Slade are getting very good at getting the details right these days. All the playing is excellent; strong direct drumming, forceful bass and some lead guitar that would knock spots off some of our vaunted guitar heroes and their ego-centric buggering about.' Peel's championing of the group – and of pop in general – astounded his hardcore hippie fanbase who couldn't believe that he could condone anything away from his pervasive leftfield taste. In his column on 20 July that year, he addressed the issue:

There was a letter or two from disgruntled readers hinting that my enthusiasm for the current Slade single indicated that I was suffering from senile decay, hardening of the arteries, halitosis, and spots. How, they wanted to know, could I enjoy Slade, but not ELP, Yes and Focus and still call myself a member, albeit in poor standing, of the human race?

Peel suggests that his hatred for ELP is 'not so much a loathing of what they do, are, stand for; but rather frustration that so much attention is focused on them to the exclusion of bands, musicians, performers who are, in my view worthy of a portion of that attention.' The dilemma of Slade at Lincoln reared its head again – almost a case of how dare you begin to be seen as an intelligent grown-up rock band.

'Their most amazing period was slightly beyond the loud songs that they had in '72/'73, when they went a lot more Lennon and McCartney. Things like 'Far Far Away', 'How Does It Feel' and 'In for a Penny'. Sublime, beautifully crafted tracks. And then they came out with 'The Bangin' Man', which just completely blows your socks off. That's the one that always stays on my jukebox,' music industry grandee Tim Fraser-Harding says.

On the home front, Holder started seeing Leandra Russell. 'Noddy's girlfriend worked at Olympic Studios and knew her as Thin Lizzy recorded *Fighting* there; she was a working-class girl,' Chris O'Donnell recalls. Dave Hill upgraded his Jensen for a Rolls-Royce, retaining his YOB 1 number plate, complete with a Steve and Barbara Megson colour scheme.

In Keith Altham's pinnacle-of-the-moment interview with Dave Hill in February 1973, he asked Hill if he thought Slade would suffer from overexposure. 'Can you have too much of a good thing?' Hill replied. 'I mean, so long as people think it's still good. I really don't think we could afford to throw a moody and play hard to get, because while we were taking a six-month break someone would nip in and steal our audience.' In the next few years, Slade would do both – the music and film they would make would get moodier and their frequent enforced absences chasing the US dream meant that people did indeed nip in and take their audience.

*   *   *

It was now time for Slade to properly 'take America'. George Tremlett's iconic 1975 quickie paperback *The Slade Story*, for all of its 40p, was a very insightful read, exposing the workings of a band, captured right at their zenith. 'By now, by the end of 1973, Slade were clearly one of the world's top groups – with only the United States left to conquer'. The route map seemed to be so clear; after all, The Beatles had boarded that plane ten years earlier and the world fell at their feet. No mistakes could be made – and the Megsons had designed around eighteen new outfits for them.

'Chas had an American partner called Peter Kauff with whom he shared the management there,' Chris Charlesworth recalls. 'I met him a few times, tall bloke with dark hair, very smooth, and even went out to dinner in New York with him and Chas once. They signed Slade to Warners which they thought, probably correctly, was a better bet than Polydor.'

In his early 30s, Kauff was Vice President of Premier Talent, the biggest rock booking agency, where he worked with Frank Barsalona. Again, all the right parts were in place. With its label boasting its avenue of palm trees, and the legend 'Burbank, Home of Warner Brothers', Warners had a much greater understanding of the US market than Polydor. Founded as an offshoot of the film company in 1958, and initially specialising in soundtracks, comedy and spoken word recordings, their roster at this point included some very mellow turns indeed: Van Morrison, James Taylor, Carly Simon. Soon Fleetwood Mac, who had been somewhat ailing since 1970, would enjoy the most enormous revival on the label. In short, Warner was a very safe pair of hands. *Old New Borrowed and Blue* was retitled *Stomp Your Hands, Clap Your Feet* under the new Warner deal. The new association saw the album chart ninety-nine places lower than its predecessor.

Bob Geldof was a young reporter over in Canada when Slade were making their assault on the continent. 'When I was in Vancouver working on the *Georgia Straight* magazine in the seventies, I said Slade were one of the best things coming out of Britain, and I meant it. They were all having none of it. North America was never going to get them because it was all check shirts and denim. Although you could see the influence of Dave Hill's hair on Dee Dee Ramone.'

With Slade away so often, the Megsons had a little time on their hands: 'Chas Chandler wanted me to do more. I met Eric Burdon who was very famous by then, but not really doing very much. Chas was trying to line me up with other work, but Dave got very jealous, and he said, "No, you only work for me, I give you a living," and all this kind of stuff. I did some waistcoats for David Essex. I'm not blaming Dave at all because I can understand his feelings. Noddy was fine. He said I could go and work for anybody I liked. He wasn't bothered.'

Slade's sound was so unique there were hardly any cover versions made of their songs – the most interesting was a reggae treatment of 'Mama Weer All Crazee Now' by Denzil Dennis, which was released on PAMA in 1973. When the generation gap was much wider in the seventies, parents would often console themselves by listening to records by artists such as James Last or Max Bygraves. James Last was a German bandleader, who as well as being a gifted composer and arranger, released many popular easy-listening recordings, in a variety of series – his *Classics Up To Date*, or *Trumpet and Hammond A-Go Go*. Most popular of all were his *Non Stop Dancing* releases, where his orchestra and chorus would tackle the current hits of the day. The series ran for around thirty albums between 1965 to 2002. Four of Slade's songs graced the collections: 'Mama Weer All Crazee Now' on *Non Stop Dancing 1973*; 'Cum On Feel the Noize' on *Non Stop Dancing 1973 Volume 2* and 'Skweeze Me, Pleeze Me' and 'My Friend Stan' on *Non Stop Dancing 1974*. In late September 1974, actor, singer and comedian Max Bygraves released an album, *You Make Me Feel Like Singing a Song*. Bygraves was enjoying huge success with his *SingalongaMax* format, very much a barrow boy version of what James Last was up to. As bold as brass, opening the second side, is none other than his take on 'Find Yourself a Rainbow'. Later that year, Bygraves' Christmas album came out. It had a medley of 'Merry Xmas Everybody' with 'I Wish It Could Be Christmas Everyday'.

Slade hunkered down in Olympic with Chandler and Alan O'Duffy to record the soundtrack for their next project. 'When we first started working with Slade, no one gave a toss,' O'Duffy says. 'Gradually, you'd have fans showing up outside the studio, which for suburban Barnes was unusual, a tiny bit extraordinary in fact. Even the Stones didn't have that, but Slade did.' 'We'd bundle the band into a Transit at the back of Olympic,' assistant engineer Jon Astley says, 'while pretending they were about to leave at the front, to avoid the fans. Fun days.'

To close the year, the group embarked on a European tour. In mid-November, an emergency call was made back to Birmingham. 'I had to go over to Copenhagen because one of Dave Hill's suits had split the night before,' Steve Megson says. 'They called me, so I took my little travelling Frister & Rossmann. I stayed in a hotel opposite the Tivoli Gardens and then I went on the rest of the tour. I remember going up to Hamburg and ABBA had just done 'Waterloo' or maybe their second song and we met them on the same TV show. We all have this big meal and I can remember dancing with the blonde one of ABBA.'

'I remember one of the male singers, Björn Ulvaeus I'm sure, standing in front of us in the studio, watching us do our thing,' Don Powell says. 'I think/am almost sure, he'd had one too many glasses of the "falling-down water".'

ABBA certainly were watching – although surely coincidental, Frank Lea has a theory that the head shots of Slade facing each other on the cover of *Old New Borrowed and Blue* could have been influential to the Swedish pop titans. 'I find it interesting that ABBA years later used that pose many times to very good effect,' he laughs.

So, although 1974 hadn't quite scaled the giddy heights of the previous year, there was still huge fan support, the UK album charts had been conquered, their singles had performed respectably, and their work was even infiltrating the bastions of parental record collections; and it was even possible they may make it in America. Surely the feature film they had been working on would truly seal the deal.

CHAPTER 19

No Bloody Fish Finger – Slade in Flame Pt 1

'This is a first-class compartment, you know.'
'We are first class people.'
'Perhaps you'll try and behave like it.'

'The events in this film are purely fictitious and any similarity to
persons living or dead is purely co-incidental.'

Chas Chandler was very aware of the impact of the pop motion picture. During their time in The Animals, he and John Steel had performed 'The House of the Rising Sun' in the pop-doc *Pop Gear* (or as known in the US *Go Go Mania*). They had also appeared in MGM's *Get Yourself a College Girl* (also known as *Watusi A-Go-Go* and as *The Swinging Set* in the UK) in 1964. Alongside performances from The Dave Clark Five, The Standells, Stan Getz and Jimmy Smith, The Animals played 'Blue Feeling' and 'Around and Around' while former Miss America Mary Ann Mobley, Chad Everett and Nancy Sinatra searched for a plot in this quintessential US teen movie, which was often shown on a double bill with the bleaker German juvenile delinquent film *Teenage Wolfpack*. As one US exhibitor was to note about *Get Yourself a College Girl*, 'Here is a picture your teenage patrons will really enjoy. A good picture, nice colour, and clean fun.' Chandler was canny enough to realise that the world had turned, and he needed to put together something a little more substantial for his charges than *Watusi A-Go-Go*.

The well-documented original suggestion for the film project, *The Quiteamess Experiment*, was intended as a parody of the much-loved 1953 BBC TV series, *The Quatermass Experiment*. John Steel brought in the idea of a light-hearted sci-fi spoof (Chandler was a huge reader of sci-fi), with Holder as a Dr Quatermass figure. 'I still have the original draft,' John Steel laughs. 'I only wrote it as a tongue-in-cheek idea and Chas wisely left it at that. I seem to remember Chas and I did quite a lot of waccy baccy back then. Don't take it too seriously, nobody else did, least of all me.' The first treatment, dated erroneously 28/5/75 (a year out), has, in pen under the title, 'Copyright John Steel (Just in case Hollywood beckons)'. Steel wrote a synopsis:

> This treatment is the bare bones of an idea, the finished script can be as black and bizarre as we want it or lightweight depending on which certificate we decide to go for.
>
> It is obviously intended as an updated spoof on the sci-fi thriller movies of the 50s: *Quatermass*, *Them* etc. They all had a reporter who gets on the story first who plays the romantic lead.
>
> The Professor who is an expert on whatever the phenomenon is. He always has a glamourous daughter or assistant who falls for the reporter. The detective/cop/soldier who plays the tough hairy hero. He usually gets killed in the final confrontation with the monster (that again depends on what certificate we go for).
>
> And of course, the monster, who usually means no harm and only kills when he is threatened or frightened. (*King Kong* etc)
>
> We can pad the whole thing out with gags. For example, all the way through the script, Mark and Glenda are trying to make it

to bed with each other, but Mark always manages to cock it up somehow e.g. Mark: 'Will you marry me?'

Glenda: 'What and become Glenda Bender?'

One of the reasons given for the project's fall by the wayside was that Dave Hill objected to being eaten by the monster early into the film, but the script shows that Hill would have been present throughout, albeit in different roles.

Steel typed out the cast list:

```
PROF. QUITEAMESS  . . . . . . . . . . . . . . . . . . . . . NODDY HOLDER
MARK BENDER . . . . . . . . . . . . . . . . . . . . . . . . . . . . . . .JIMMY LEA
JEFF HUMPER . . . . . . . . . . . . . . . . . . . . . . . . . . . . .DON POWELL
TANKER DRIVER. . . . . . . . . . . . . . . . . . . . . . . . . . . DAVE HILL
THE MONSTER . . . . . . . . . . . . . . . . . . . . . . . . . . . . . DAVE HILL
```

The film is set at the mysterious Blackmoor Toxic Waste Disposal site, where livestock in surrounding fields have been poisoned. The pre-title sequence sees Hill's truck driver – who would be the first member of Slade seen – heading to the site, radio playing, being waved through the gates, which are being picketed by what today would be called Extinction Rebellion activists. Steel writes: 'Tanker pulls up, then reverses towards vast pit of bubbling waste. Stops close to edge. Driver clambers out of cab pulling on gas mask, but in doing so, knocks handbrake off with outrageous platform boots. He walks to rear of tanker and unscrews discharge valve. As chemical waste begins to gush out, tanker rolls backwards, and knocks driver off balance, his boots slipping on chemical mud. He falls into bubbling mess. Thunder crashes, and lightning strikes the spot where he falls… Loud chord and main title.' This early departure gave rise to the 'eaten by a triffid' line, and indeed would have been too much to bear for a man who deserved the limelight as much as Dave Hill. Yet Hill was also to play the monster who appears from the middle of the film, with plenty of screen time for him.

Noddy Holder would play the obsessed-with-his-work scientist – the youngest ever winner of the Nobel Prize for Chemistry and youngest ever Cambridge don – called in to investigate the plant.

Lea would play the reporter, the romantic lead, and Powell was to play detective Jeff Humper, brought into probe the strange goings on. The film ends with Glenda being taken by the monster, and with the other three members of Slade in pursuit, the monster bursts into a concert – as written by Steel: 'a very stoned rock playing. Repetitive rhythmic riff, audience grooving and clapping.' As the monster is being chased through the theatre's corridors, he makes it out onto the stage, and, after dropping Glenda by an amp, stops at the centre microphone. As Steel continues, 'The band keep playing, looking at each other, stoned. Saying things like "far out"' – the monster begins singing and the audience go absolutely crazy.

Humper, the detective, asks Quiteamess if he should use his ray gun to shoot the monster, and Quiteamess replies, 'Are you nuts? Look at that audience, that thing's worth a fortune, we sign him up and solve the toxic waste problem at the same time.' The film would close with Bender, Humper and Quiteamess laughing and shaking hands while 'over their shoulders we can see the monster freaking out.' A happy ending, then, for what would have been quite the caper. The film also has parodies of *Top of the Pops*, radio shows and music agents, and indeed some of the premises and language of the treatment do rather underline that considerable amounts of 'waccy baccy' had been taken.

While the *Carry On*-meets-Benny Hill-and-*The Goodies* style of *The Quiteamess Experiment* may have fitted the previous decade's 'good picture, nice colour, and clean fun,' maxim, the film that Slade made ultimately may have been a good picture, but it certainly didn't involve nice colour or clean fun.

) *   *   *

Since the release of *Performance* in 1971, what was expected from a rock film had travelled a long way from *Get Yourself a College Girl*. The genre was split between capturing huge concerts (*Woodstock, The Concert for Bangladesh, Wattstax*) or something narrative-driven (the two vehicles for David Essex, *That'll Be the Day* and *Stardust*); indeed, the last attempt at something zanier, T. Rex's *Born to Boogie*, had, in many respects, fallen flat on its arse, and was seen as the ego-trip it was for Marc Bolan. *Performance* and the David Essex films were clearly seen as important, as Sanford 'Sandy' Lieberson, the producer of *Performance*, both Essex films and the curio *The Pied Piper* which cast Donovan in the lead role, was consulted.

Originally entitled *The Performers*, *Performance*, directed by Donald Cammell and Nicholas Roeg, subverted the very notion of the rock vehicle. Commissioned by Warner Brothers, who thought they were getting a jolly Rolling Stones film, *Performance* was filmed in 1968, but remained unreleased in the UK until January 1971. It featured Mick Jagger at his satanic peak as rock star Turner, in a blur of gender and personality, with James Fox as the gangster Chas Devlin. Devlin, a member of Harry Flowers' (Johnny Shannon) gang, is on the run and holes up at Turner's tawdry bohemian Notting Hill mansion flat. Pervasive rumours around the film's initial screening suggest that the wife of one of Warner Brothers' executives had to leave the screening to vomit, and another came up with the notorious line 'even the bath water is dirty'.

Continuing Chandler's emulation of The Beatles blueprint, Slade had done their 10,000 hours, changed their name twice (as did The Beatles – The Quarrymen, The Silver Beetles) they had broken the UK, they had had records that went straight into the number one spot, while America was being put on the front ring, the other great feat was indeed to make the film.

Lieberson had founded Goodtimes Enterprises, in which he partnered with affable businessman and director David Puttnam, who brought structure to his endeavours.

'Chas came to us with a proposal to produce *Slade in Flame*,' Lieberson says. 'He put up the money and we organised the production. Gavrik became the actual producer and we supervised.' Son of film director Joseph, Gavrik Losey was a fascinating character, who knew Experience drummer Mitch Mitchell from their teenage school years. 'We picked up on Slade with a very tough film,' Losey says. 'They and that whole period of music, the glam rock piece, was actually coming to an end.'

'It was a combination of *Performance* and *That'll Be the Day* and *Stardust*,' Lieberson says. 'We were making films where music was at the centre. Chas recognised that and approached us. I'd met him kind of casually at different events. I knew who he was and respected his ability as a manager. He had some great acts and knew what to do with them. Although I'd never met them, I knew who Slade were.' Not everyone was enthused. 'Our backers at that point were Rothschilds Bank, Sotheby's and WHSmith, who didn't understand what the fuck we were doing with Slade,' Lieberson adds. 'They thought it was going downmarket. I argued that it was a continuation of our looking at film, music and contemporary pop. The guy from WHSmith was wonderful, though. He would turn out for meetings on a Vespa with a bowler hat and a pinstripe suit.'

Richard Loncraine was selected to direct the film, after he'd been asked by Puttnam and Lieberson to direct a film about BBC Radio One called *Radio Wonderful*, as a support feature to *That'll Be the Day*. Loncraine, who was 28 at the time, did not have enormous experience as a director, but was an intensively creative spirit. He had been around the advertising and film business; he made props and toys (he was one of the team responsible for inventing the seventies office desk essential, the Newton's Cradle) and his art was exhibited at the ICA with Yoko Ono. A proper bohemian, he'd lived in Powys Terrace with Marsha Hunt and Caroline Coon. 'Paul Smith used to bring T-shirts and jackets round door to door and sell them to us at art school,' Loncraine marvels. 'It was another era as they say.' He'd worked at the BBC directing the *Tomorrow's World* programme: 'Raymond Baxter had an amazing capacity for assimilating information. You could tell him the background on something, and he'd then talk to the television audience as if he studied it for twenty years.'

Radio Wonderful, never available commercially since its initial screening, is worth seeking out. 'I basically let the disc jockeys hang themselves,' Loncraine says. 'David thought if he made a documentary about them, and it was showing with *That'll Be the Day*, they'll all go on Radio One and say that you must see me at your local cinema. Unfortunately, they really hated it because it made some of them look like arseholes.'

To add to this illustriously free-thinking production team, Andrew Birkin was assigned as scriptwriter. 'I'd known Andrew and I knew his sister Jane in the early sixties,' Gavrik Losey, who'd worked with him on *Magical Mystery Tour*, says. 'It all kind of connects in an odd sort of way. Everyone hung out in the Portobello Road, then everyone went their own separate ways. Then Puttnam came in and pulled the whole thing together. He was a catalyst that caused it to happen. Puttnam also brought in the Rank Organisation for the film's distribution,' Losey says. 'They were a little bit chary about the content because they wanted a joyful, family picture. *Flame* was not a family film in that context.'

'I wanted to make a film about the dirty end of the rock'n'roll business,' Loncraine adds. 'I wanted to show the shitty little clubs that these bands have to play. Slade were very on board with this, even Chandler. He certainly would have said if he didn't like something.'

'I'd been working on a different project, which was about as different from Slade as you could get,' Andrew Birkin says. 'I was working with Albert Speer, Hitler's Minister of Armaments, on and off for about a year writing *Inside the Third Reich* based on his book. For various reasons, we never made it. Like most projects, it didn't die a sudden death and Puttnam said, "While we're waiting on the Speer thing, would you like to do this Slade movie?"'

Birkin travelled to Wolverhampton to meet Jim Lea. 'I liked him a lot,' says Birkin. 'He was the most approachable. Rather than talk about himself, he talked about this great new band called Queen, he was very taken with them. The next person I met was Chas Chandler who I really loved. I liked all the grungy stuff from Wolverhampton. I wanted to get the opposite of what we'd seen in *A Hard Day's Night*. Although I love that film, I had no interest in repeating it. Richard and I were very much on the same wavelength, we wanted to make something that was real."

Like Alun Owen had done with The Beatles in 1964 to inspire his *A Hard Day's Night* script, Chandler suggested Loncraine and Birkin went on tour with Slade to see how the band worked: 'We went along on their North American tour. We spent about three weeks, hitting Detroit, and quite hard places like Pittsburgh.'

'I remember going to America and bumming around with Andrew and seeing all these pretty sordid sights,' Richard Loncraine says. 'It was eye-opening. At the Hilton Hotel in Chicago, I remember coming up in the elevator and there were two women wearing fur coats and high-heeled shoes. They were talking about their kids and how the dishwasher had jammed, a completely banal conversation about suburban life. Then one of them turned to me and said, "You want to see my body?" and she was wearing suspenders underneath and nothing else. That's what the whole tour felt like. Pretty tacky and down-at-heel hotels. So that influenced the writing of the film.'

There was a little class tourism going on from the director. 'I remember Richard kept maintaining that he'd been to a secondary modern school. I knew he went to a public school because I could tell from the accent, there were a lot of giveaways and I went to one,' Andrew Birkin laughs. 'I was sent there by my dad and left as soon as I could, but you can usually tell if someone else had the same background, whereas Slade of course, completely different. But I don't know that that was a bad thing.'

'One got to know them quite well,' Birkin continues:

Therefore, it was a matter of keeping the characters as they were in real life. I used to carry around a briefcase full of cassette tapes with classical music and a lot of *Hancock's Half Hour*. When Noddy had these booze-ups after the gig which I found quite boring, I'd be sitting listening to Hancock. When Noddy heard, he said, 'Oh, I love Hancock', and we spent the rest of the tour listening to about thirty of those radio half-hours. I liked all of them, but especially Don, because his accident gave him a certain characteristic above and beyond his own character that we used in the film.

'We really didn't want to make *A Hard Day's Night*,' Don Powell says. 'When Richard and Andrew came on our American tour to hear stories – all the scenes in the film are actual stories, not all particularly us, but from all around the bands at that time. I'm glad we did what we did. It would have been easy to do a run-around, jump-around film, but I don't think we'd have got any respect for it. It's a heavy film.' Heavy it most certainly is. The decision was made to map the fortunes of a sixties act, Flame, as they rise to success.

'Chas was very supportive and when he read the script, as far as I can remember, he didn't bat an eyelid over the fact that clearly

192

some people would think that this was the real story and that he was therefore the unscrupulous manager. We put as much humour into it as we could,' says Andrew Birkin.

With a first draft finished, Loncraine brought in Dave Humphries to edit and polish the script: 'A very funny man,' Loncraine says. He sadly later died of a brain tumour. 'He was in hospital and my ex-wife saw him and he said, "I hope I haven't lost my sense of tumour."'

'I never really met Dave Humphries; clearly, I'm not from Wolverhampton and I don't know that dialect,' adds Birkin. 'I think he just threw in some dialogue. I've subsequently written scripts where the director has wangled his name on to it as a co-writer and has had a great deal less to do with the script than Richard did. He never tried to put his name on it as a co-writer. It would be more like the storyline, the two of us used to meet up and chew over the direction of the script.'

CHAPTER 20

Stay with Your Dog Pictures, Your Jukeboxes and Your Thugs – Slade in Flame Pt 2

Filming took place between July and September 1974. Things were shot mostly on location: the band moved between London, Sheffield, Tenterden, the Thames Estuary, Nottingham and Brighton. The live concert footage was captured at The Rainbow and Hammersmith Palais. 'Live, they were very magical,' Richard Loncraine says.

In Sheffield, 'We were all saying what a great shot it was and a resident came past and said, "You wouldn't want to live here." It was definitely a bit grim,' John Steel recalls. 'The terrace was empty, and I remember it was going to be pulled down to make way for these bloody awful high-rise flats. All these places needed was a little bit of money spent on them and far better living in there than up there.'

The Kelvin Flats were constructed in 1965 on Infirmary Road, so, would have been recently built at the time of the film's setting. The two blocks contained 948 flats linked by wide walkways, which became known as streets in the sky. The flats were demolished by 1996, demonstrating that the future was not meant to last forever.

Chas Chandler would visit the set. 'I would call him a rough diamond,' Gavrik Losey says. 'He knew his business and he knew the music business and, as an old Geordie, when it came to his boys, nobody messed with them. But on the other hand, he was very affable and fun to have a drink with. His world was different to mine.'

'Chas was extremely generous,' Andrew Birkin says. 'And very non-interfering, at least from my point of view, I don't know whether Richard would agree with that. But he let us get on with it.'

Loncraine would not agree with that: 'Chas Chandler was a monster. He was an animal, he lived up to his name, pretty unpleasant. We were filming at night in a garage. I was getting a shot of the petrol station and I was holding the Panaflex, which was quarter of a million quid's worth of brand-new camera. I was lining a shot up and suddenly it was grabbed out of my hands and Chas said, "I want more close-ups of my boys, you cunt," and threw it in a puddle. I'm not accustomed to people being quite that rude.' In this instance, it was the very essence of Chandler's sixties approach in the middle of the seventies, and in one sense could be applauded. These were his boys, nothing else mattered.

As a result, Loncraine dealt predominantly with John Steel. 'I spent a lot of time with them,' Steel remembers.

> The experience was fascinating for me, because I'd always been a movie fan. It was great to be on the other side of the camera. The crew were all good guys as well. They always used to say when Chas and I appeared: 'Here comes the money!' I often had to stop people from doing things by saying, 'Look, that's not the way it happens.' Chas and me were agreed on keeping it close to reality. There were lots of little details, such as Harding's two heavies: they were going to cast some great big geezers and I said, 'The hardest guy in Newcastle is Dave Findlay. He's about five foot four and moves like a dancer. Don't go getting some big cauliflower-eared lug heads.' The really dangerous guys in this world are like 'Mad' Frankie Fraser.

Steve Megson was around also: 'I was on the film set for the whole time that *Slade in Flame* was made. It was fascinating. Maybe I'm biased because I worked for Slade, but it was a well-made, well-crafted film. It had a blackness, a dark side to it. Richard kept a working-class realism to it.'

'David Puttnam was the go-to guy,' John Steel recalls. 'He put himself in a sort of executive producer role. He wasn't so much hands-on but he put everything else together. I met him a couple of times, went for a couple of meals. Gavrik was the actual hands-on producer.'

'John Steel looked after them and I looked after the whole thing,' Losey says. 'I had one major falling out with Richard. We were doing a dance sequence and he was churning through the footage for something that was going to be three minutes in the whole film. I finally had to step in and say, "Look, you can't go on any longer because you'll just destroy the film stock budget and there won't be enough to finish what you want to do." We had a slanging match on the set, but we got over it.'

'I met Richard a few times and he talked to me about the overall concept,' Steve Megson says.

Chas wanted me to do the costumes; he didn't want to bring anyone else in as I'd been doing it for years. As it was set in the sixties, the clothes are purposely made to be a little kitsch with the red-and-yellow satin things. The suits were like Beatles suits. We had to make a lot of clothes in a very short space of time. We used a material called 3M, strips of two-inch tape. The suits were a lightweight cotton, and we literally just taped tape all over them. So, when the actual flames were projected onto them, you could see them moving on the suits. It was difficult to do because the sewing machine kept sticking to the glue on the back of the adhesive. A bit of trial and error before we got it right.

One of the film's more notable scenes comes when the band go out to the pirate radio station set at the Maunsell Forts in the Thames Estuary. 'I'd shot those in *Radio Wonderful*,' Loncraine says. 'We climbed up those ladders and Dave Hill was shitting himself because they were probably 150 feet, a long way up. Health and safety didn't exist then; probably about thirty of us. We all climbed out, we put a rope around Dave and I went behind him and someone went in front. I have to say, it was quite brave of him to get up there. Some of these stories you forget how much is true and how much is what you've made up for the pubs. But that certainly is true, getting up there.'

John Steel was on the boat, too. 'Dave Hill was shitting himself trying to get up that ladder, somebody from the crew had to go behind him and keep hold of his bum so he didn't fall off.'

* * *

The opening sequence of *Slade in Flame* sets the tone: a guest at a wedding party taking a piss while drinking a half-pint out of a dimpled jug in a suburban toilet. It is one long tracking shot, going from upstairs to downstairs at a house in Pinner. The story is centred on the trials and tribulations of the group Flame, formed, just like the real-life Slade who played them, out of two bands, both initially with frontmen – Jack Daniels (Alan Lake) and The DTs with guitarist Barry Jenkins (Dave Hill) and bassist Paul Harris (Jim Lea). After the group's original drummer (a delightful cameo by John Steel) injures himself as he falls off the stage at a wedding punch-up, a replacement is sought. In comes Charlie Spencer (Don Powell) with a good kit and the right attitude. The other outfit is Roy Priest (Michael Coles) and The Undertakers, which features guitarist and vocalist Laurence Stoker (Noddy Holder).

As the groups merge with a new name, Iron Rod, they are managed by Ron Harding (Johnny Shannon), an archetypal small-town big shot with connections to the underworld ('an amalgamation of a lot of wise guy managers who were around in the early days,' Holder said). As Lise Lyng Falkenberg noted, Harding is more consumed with his 'greyhounds, fruit machines and thugs than the band'. The band and he fall out, and they effectively leave him. Harding: 'You can piss off any time you want. You're a good live act, and that's it... that crap you served up tonight that wasn't music... You're just second-rate comics working on a third-rate audience...' Stoker replies, 'With a fourth-rate agent copping ten per cent...' Harding proceeds to grab Stoker's hair, something he did for real to Holder, repeatedly during retakes. 'You just lost six weeks work and an agent, from now on you're all on your bloody own.'

The same night Devlin (Ken Colley) is in the club watching the band. He works for the Seymour Trust, headed by merchant banker Robert Seymour (Tom Conti) looking to branch out into the music scene. Devlin delivers a letter to Stoker's house, in one of the condemned rows of houses being torn down for the high-rises. Conducting the conversation through the letter box with Stoker's gran, Devlin has to repeat that he's not from the council but the Seymour Trust.

Paul thinks it's a 'knockout' that they have been headhunted by Seymour, and persuades the reticent Stoker to consider. As the band travel by train to meet Seymour, class and generation gaps are addressed. We see Seymour dealing with prospective clients – he drives a hard bargain, yet in the middle takes a call from his wife and enquires of his daughter's well-being. The initial meeting in the office between band a new management is one of the film's key scenes: 'Do you actually like what we do?' Paul asks of Seymour. He replies, 'My personal preference really doesn't come into it. Let me put it this way… I don't smoke cigarettes, but I manage to sell a few.'

Devlin expands the theme. 'You see, it's all a matter of packaging, Paul… promotion.' 'I'm no bloody fish finger,' Paul retorts. 'Yes,' Devlin replies, 'but that's part of the problem – they are a well-known commodity, you are unknown and there's thousands to choose from… we're just going to make you stand out a little.' The Chairman of the Board tells Seymour that the 'board are not too keen on the idea… and frankly, neither am I. It isn't the sort of thing we want to get tied up in – aside from the initial capital, of course… In no way should our name be associated with the venture… otherwise we'll all look bloody silly.'

Changing their name from Iron Rod to Flame, the band sail out to Radio City on the Maunsell Forts in the Thames Estuary. As they are promoting their single to DJ Ricky Storm (Tommy Vance), they are fired at while on air – which is clearly a publicity stunt. It was based on a real shooting that Chas Chandler had been aware of. As Storm speaks, panicked on air, Devlin shouts that he must 'Mention the bloody group.'

Flame go to Seymour's house where the realise the shooting has been a stunt. 'This is a cause for celebration,' Seymour says. 'What, us nearly getting killed?' Russell (Anthony Allen), the road manager replies. 'No, the fact that we've probably sold another 20,000 records.' However, it gets them on *News at Ten*. As a joke, Stoker says that they should be filmed at a fire station. The next thing we see is that they are.

At a gig, Charlie's parents turn up but as the band come off stage they are all at each other's throats. At Barry's 21st birthday party, Ron Harding reappears and talks to Seymour about 'his boys' being under contract, still having Charlie, Barry and Paul on the old DTs paperwork. Jack Daniels introduces himself to Seymour. Seymour asks Daniels to break into Harding's office and steal their contract. Seymour goes to Harding's office. Harding offers to be their agent on a 50/50 split and Seymour agrees, providing he sees the contract; the contract is missing – when Harding realises this, he sends his heavies, Ron (Barrie Houghton) and Lenny (John Dicks), to deal with Daniels. The heavies greet Daniels in his van where he's taking mucky snaps on his polaroid, and take pictures on the camera ('Watch the birdie, Jack') as they chop his toes off.

The scene is offset by the comedy of the car showroom, where Barry looks to buy a Rolls-Royce. 'Ange'll like this,' says Charlie as he bounces on the car seat, 'I think Stoker's already given her a demonstration.' As Barry gets more famous, he bosses roadie Russell around, and when Harding's heavies get to him, and give him the Polaroids of Daniels roughed up to the point that he leaves, Seymour gives one of the film's key speeches:

> The tin pot little dog trainer conned a contract out of your friends and wrapped that up for good, as far as this business is concerned. Now he's seen how good they are he wants to kick them about like one of his fruit machines until some money falls out. If he had any real claim on that talent, do you really think he would try something like this? If Harding takes this to court with me then your friends had better go back to the button factory, because not one of them would ever make a record or even pick up a guitar in

public, until a legal decision is made, by which time their adoring fans will have forgotten what they look like.

Harding comes to Seymour's office and sees him off the premises: 'With your fruit machines and a couple of psychopaths you can think you can worm your scummy little way up on my back – you stay with your dog pictures, your jukeboxes and your thugs.'

The group finally play a concert. Emperor Rosko introduces the *pièce de résistance* – three numbers: 'OK Yesterday Was Yesterday', 'Summer Song (Wishing You Were Here)' and 'Far Far Away' in their suits with flames projected on to them. As Flame make it, they fall apart. Stoker takes umbrage at Paul tuning up while he's making an onstage announcement, the sort of trifling thing that masks the bigger issue.

Both Seymour and Flame head back to their natural environments: home for Seymour, an after-show party for Flame. However, both are traumatic. After Flame head back to the party, Paul and Stoker stand uncomfortably in the lift with a well-heeled lady between them. 'What we going to do then?' Stoker asks. 'Are we going on, the group?' 'What group?' Paul replies. 'You know I didn't mean it,' Stoker says. 'Well, I did,' Paul replies. Paul packs his suitcases and goes home. Even more traumatic, Seymour's house has been broken into by Harding's thugs, and his daughter's bedroom has been vandalised, covered in red paint with the words 'rock a bye-baby' graffitied onto the wall. The party goes on, full of bit-part players and pals attracted when fame strikes and free booze is offered. As Harding returns to claim his prize, he tells Stoker that Seymour had had enough. Stoker, picking up his case with Ange, now his girlfriend, says, 'I'll tell you what Ron, we've all had enough.' As the film fades to black and white and a reprise of 'How Does It Feel', the frame freezes on the empty bottles the day after a party in a random hotel. The rock'n'roll dream ends right there.

* * *

Aside from the group, the cast were all accomplished actors. It was Tom Conti's debut film performance, after being in stage and television work, most notably appearing in the long-running TV series *Z Cars*. Described as 'saturnine' by *Halliwell's Who's Who in The Movies*, Conti's steely presence gives the film a gravitas, and, within four years, he would win an Emmy on Broadway. Slade were not paired with comic actors now out of work, appearing only in sex comedies. Even the nearest actor to this, Alan Lake, had some good form – when he wasn't intent on self-destruction.

Lake was something of a handful, his screen persona the closest to real life. The ebullient yet troubled actor was married to British siren Diana Dors, who by the mid-seventies had moved away from glamour roles into character acting.

There are contrasting views of how Alan Lake was nearly sacked from the film. 'The Jacaranda club was the first scene shot in the movie. It's actually The Burlesque off Berekley Square,' John Steel says.

> The manager was a man called Mr Toye. This was the scene where they did the coffin. Alan Lake went out with the crew at lunchtime and came back completely arseholed. We were sitting in this dressing room, talking to Mr Toye, and Alan came up behind him and got him in an armlock. The guy was seriously nervous because he wasn't holding back. Alan had to be pulled off. Richard gave him a severe dressing down and said he was going to be off the film if anything like that ever happened again. From that day, Alan never took a drink until the end of the shoot.

Or

'If it wasn't for Diana, he wouldn't have been on the film – he got fired the first day,' Don Powell says.

> We were doing the club scene in the Sherwood Rooms, where we were singing 'In the Midnight Hour'. The club owner said that we could all have free drinks, the bar is open. It was a bad move. Alan had a few too many. The owner said that Alan was taking the piss, said it was closing, and Alan grabbed him. Richard and Gavrik wanted to fire him. Diana came down and pleaded with them, saying that she was going to ensure that he wouldn't have another drink. He never drank again on the film after that. He was nice company; he had us laughing quite often.

202

Or

'I remember Alan because he was a serious alcoholic and we'd done a scene in the morning, very early on in the first week, and he'd gone to sleep because he'd been drinking already,' Richard Loncraine remembers. 'He woke up and the manager of that club was someone that he hated and he got a bottle of beer and smashed it over the back of the manager's head and we were all thrown out of the club. The police arrived. Diana promised that she would keep him dry for the rest of the shoot and she kind of did. But it was a pretty traumatic first few days.'

It was a club, it was a bottle... whatever the exact detail, Lake was as good as gold for the rest of the shoot. Johnny Shannon reprises his Harry Flowers role from *Performance* as Ron Harding, the epitome of the small-town big shot, all bluster and barely contained menace. 'Johnny was a really nice guy,' Powell recalls. 'He was a big softy, but he was perfect for the role.'

John Steel agrees: 'Johnny was the real deal. He didn't have to act much. We thought he's exactly the guy we need for a hardcase cockney manager. You wouldn't want to get on the wrong side of him.' 'Johnny certainly couldn't act but he was nice man. Very gentle. I used him in two or three movies,' Richard Loncraine says. 'A lovely man off set. He was absolutely fantastic to work with and very happy to do it.'

Of the group, Don Powell came out best, but all were convincing. 'Don was a sweetheart,' Loncraine adds. 'I'd have to remind him who he was, not only what part he was playing, but some mornings, he didn't know quite who he was because of the brain damage.'

John Steel says, 'Noddy was a natural for that. Jimmy was quite reticent and Don's very affable. Dave's an extrovert, but he's not the greatest actor in the world. He had a tendency to overdo things.'

Slade in Flame was to be premiered at the start of 1975. However, the soundtrack, recorded in late 1974, was released to give Slade fans something for Christmas.

CHAPTER 21

Attempting, Experimenting

The soundtrack to *Slade in Flame*, aside from *Play It Loud*, is possibly Slade's most consistent album. Released on 29 November 1974, it gave fans both a Christmas gift and the opportunity for familiarity with the songs before seeing the film early the following year. '*Flame* is an all-encompassing package, isn't it? It is to a degree, the masterwork. It was meant to be set in the sixties,' Ian Edmundson says. 'The guitars they used were a bit of a clue, but they didn't really give you an indication of when it was.'

'The early bubblegum hits became a part of our everyday lives, of course,' Dave Ling says, 'but were you to put a gun to my head and demand I chose two favourites I'd go with a pair from the *Slade in Flame* soundtrack – 'Far Far Away' and 'How Does It Feel'. Even as a youngster I was struck by the wistful maturity of both, particularly 'Far Far Away'.' Like watching the film, it makes the listener think that they are actually listening to the work of a constructed band – this is Slade performing the songs that they think Flame themselves would be playing. If one wanted to ride The Beatles comparisons even further, are they writing their *Sgt. Pepper*?

The short answer, of course, is no, but… If one wants to understand the absolute locked-in synergy of Slade, listen to 'Far Far Away', as it encapsulates the very best of the group. Holder's travelogue of a touring band in many ways is a mid-seventies update of Sammy Cahn and Jimmy Van Heusen's 'It's Nice to Go Trav'ling' immortalised by Frank Sinatra on *Come Fly With Me*. Although it is debatable that Ol' Blue Eyes would have sung about a 'red light off the wrist'.

The song is such a poignant capture of being removed from your loved ones – and moves from continent to continent with a stately aplomb. The listener is taken from Memphis, to Paris, to Alaska to hearing of 'arigato smiles' of Japan. The song has its genesis when Holder and Chandler were on a balcony of a hotel room in Memphis, and Holder – feeling a mixture of homesickness and incredulity at how a boy from the Beechdale Estate could be doing all this – commented on the lights on a passing paddle steamer on the Mississippi. Chandler, always able to draw out the commerciality from an idea, told Holder to go his room and write lyrics based around that opening. Originally entitled 'Letting Loose Around the World', Holder wrote the verses and Lea the chorus.

'Far Far Away', understandably, was taken as the lead single for the project, and had an old-fashioned Slade-like crash into the charts at number three in October 1974, peaking at number two. Again, it was kept off the top spot by a wide-appeal, mainstream track that sold beyond the castle walls – the Trojan populist reggae of Ken Boothe's version of Bread's already well-loved 'Everything I Own'. But still, a number two single wasn't bad at all for a group who had been less visible that year.

John Steel asked the band to come up with a theme for the film, and Lea recalled the number he had in reserve since he'd been 13. 'How Does It Feel' is one of the greatest songs Slade recorded – from Lea's piano to the sound of the horn section adding to the song's overall heft. ''Merry Xmas Everybody' may, as Holder has said, have represented how Everyman feels at Christmas, but it's 'How Does It Feel' that best encapsulates how Everyman felt for the other 364 days of the year,' Rob Chapman was to write. It was one of the very first melodies that Lea ever wrote as a young teenager, in 1964. Brother Frank recalls hearing it, playing the piano with keys like 'broken teeth'. David Puttnam liked it immediately.

The horn players inspired the group, as it was (aside from Tommy Burton) one of the first times they had properly worked with outside performers. The eight-piece horn section had first made contact with Chas Chandler in the sixties – all had been around the London scene – now they were playing in the wholly dependable UK soul outfit, Gonzalez, who would later enjoy chart success with the disco classic 'Haven't Stopped Dancin' Yet'.

Between the eight – Chris Smith (trombone), Bud Beadle (spelled as 'Byd on the sleeve) (baritone sax), Malcolm Griffiths (bass trombone), Mick Eve, Steve Gregory (tenor saxes), Chris Mercer (tenor and baritone sax), Eddie Quansah and Ron Carthy (trumpet) – they had played with artists such as Tubby Hayes, Benny Goodman, Otis Spann, John Surman, John Dankworth, Ginger Baker's Airforce, Wynder K. Frog, and Toots and the Maytals. Mick Eve, who arranged the session, was the sax player on Georgie Fame and the Blue Flames' *Rhythm and Blues at the Flamingo*, back in 1964 – the same LP John Gunnell had introduced and written the notes for. In short, Slade had little option but to raise their game with players of this calibre involved. 'Steve Gregory, Buddy Beadle – they were the go-to sax players that I would always use,' Andy Fairweather Low says. 'Steve was a lovely man and a beautiful sax player.'

The lyrical sentiment of 'How Does It Feel' simultaneously induces pathos, despair, poignancy and hope. Many people, Noddy Holder, Jim Lea and Noel Gallagher included, now regard it as Slade's best record. Despite the retrospective plaudits, at the time, 'How Does It Feel' reached number fifteen in the UK charts, which for Slade meant barely scraping into them, spending just seven weeks in the Top 30 in February 1975 – the group's lowest placing since 1970, ending an unbroken run of a dozen Top 10 hits. It had been available on the album for some time, and now *Slade in Flame* was on release, the track seemed to epitomise the mordant nature of the film, from its use over the opening scenes in the foundry, to the tension when the band record it near the film's climax, to the freeze-frame and black-and-white playout over the end credits.

"How Does It Feel' is a lovely song,' Alan O'Duffy says, recalling the engineering and recording process. 'There wasn't a pint of anything or any drugs or anything that was rolled up in a silver foil paper. They were very straight, very organised, very collected, especially Jimmy Lea, who knew what he was doing big time. Very, very serious.'

'It was an old song that I'd written, and Nod put some great lyrics to it,' Lea told Chris Charlesworth in 1984. 'Tommy Vance said that it was good but that we were in for a hard time. But it didn't matter to me whether it was number one or number fifteen… to me it was a much better record than we'd made before and that was all I cared about.' When the flute – played by tenor sax man Steve Gregory – goes down toward the end, it is one of the greatest moments in popular music, full stop. 'The flute part fits perfect,' Powell says. 'We couldn't believe it when we were in the control room when he "adlibbed" it.'

'That was a very long time ago,' Steve Gregory says. 'It was me; Mick and Chris didn't play flutes. We were at Olympic. Mick would have fixed it. It was a big section.' Again, it shows the quality of the company that Slade kept. Within a decade, Steve Gregory would play one of the most well-known sax parts in popular music – the mournful refrain on George Michael's 'Careless Whisper'.

'Some of the brass on that is absolutely fucking epic,' ex-Beta Band leader and Slade fan Steve Mason says. 'I was talking to Ed Simons from The Chemical Brothers one day, and I mentioned that and he said he'd never heard it so I sent it to him and he couldn't fucking believe what he was hearing. It starts off almost like a Faces or Who track. It does remind me of *Quadrophenia* – the way he's doing the high stuff on the bass.'

Jon Astley was a young assistant engineer when Slade were recording *Slade in Flame* at Olympic. Jim Lea needed some assistance playing the piano part on 'How Does It Feel', Astley suggested he could assist, but Chandler was having none of it. 'Chas was funny,' Astley says. 'He said, "No one else is playing on a Slade record." Jim could only play the right-hand part, as it was complicated, so I volunteered to play the left, which Jim was all for. So, we had to do it while Chas went for a "pony" as he put it, where he would take the newspaper for a while. So, I did it, and he never knew. If you can imagine "pony" in his Geordie accent, it's even funnier.'

* * *

The key thing that the listener has to understand is that the *Slade in Flame* album is framed as if it is made by a band in the sixties.

'Standin' on the Corner' and 'Them Kinda Monkeys Can't Swing' were big, fat Slade via Flame rockers, something to inject life into the film's narrative. *Rolling Stone* went as far as to say that 'Standin' on the Corner' was, 'joyous rock'n'roll with added brass which couldn't be bettered by anyone else, pub-rockers, the Faces, or whoever'.

'So Far So Good' (which was to be the B-side of 'How Does It Feel') is truly good-time Slade at their very best, as is 'Summer Song (Wishing You Were Here)', which makes its play to be a sunny counterpart to the snow of 'Merry Xmas Everybody'. 'This Girl', so effective in the film as Roy Priest and The Undertakers' *pièce de résistance* is incredible, if somewhat jarringly out of context. There is also the optimism of 'OK Yesterday Was Yesterday', used strikingly in the film when the band rise up through the floor of the Rainbow stage, and first heard as the B-side to 'Far Far Away', with all the verve and bite of the early Slade stompers. 'Lay It Down' has got a great swing and tricksy wordplay, with subtle showcasing of the players – Holder gives an impassioned vocal performance, while each of the players have great, if fleeting, solos as they are introduced: Powell's drum intro after 'A beat on the drum', Hill's tone bend on 'a note on the bend', and finally Lea's cascading part on 'a chance on the bass'. Hill's guitar solo here is one of his finest, demonstrating how proficient he was. The brass charge in to finish the song, one of the group's most sweetly successful numbers. Hill's guitar effect at the end is not dissimilar to the 'long lunar note' of Zoot Horn Rollo of Captain Beefheart's Magic Band on 'Big Eyed Beans from Venus'. The sunny, sixties-tinged 'Heaven Knows' is one of Slade's hidden classics, a view of where the fictional and real group were at that time: 'caught up in a happy masquerade'. It is also one of the few songs to describe vomit as a 'technicolour yawn'. The talk is of a 'twinkle of hope', but, of course, heaven knows what will happen.

The album had another striking sleeve, captured, of course, by Gered Mankowitz. 'They always loved my sessions, and we'd become friends,' he recalls.

If they were in London, they'd always come to my Christmas party at the studio. They'd devour the turkey before anybody else arrived. Their roadies were friends of mine and I always felt part of their gang. It was always a pleasure to work with them and it was always creative. They worked hard in the studio, they worked hard to make it work. I can't remember once any hint of moodiness or difficulty or anything like that.

For *Slade in Flame*, Mankowitz wanted to utilise Steve and Barbara Megson's ground-breaking outfits from the film on the cover: 'The idea was to project flames on them. I'd just discovered something called front projection, where you have a strobe-powered projector aligned through a prism with your camera and a special screen behind your subject that's made out of this material that 3M produced. It was basically the same material that's used on road signs and things like that. It's incredibly reflective and from the right angle it reflects 100 per cent back at you.'

'That kind of material now is much more sophisticated,' Steve Megson adds. 'I don't think anyone had ever used it in that way before, it had only been used for things like taping for emergency lights. It was meant for that kind of thing, not for making clothes at all.'

Mankowitz projected flames on the outfits. This picture ended on the rear of the sleeve, while the front was shot with Mankowitz using Calgel. That actually is a flame behind them. Mankowitz says:

Calgel was a petroleum adhesive that graphic artists used, but it burned beautifully. It made black smoke, which was a bit of a bore, but it gave off a beautiful orange flame. We had Polaroid by that time, so they could see it and they just made these marvellous shapes. I was very into smoke filters by this time that were designed for movies. They fitted my Hasselblad and gave a slight glow, where the light is sort of flared out. They are flames and that's a flame going up. In a way the flames inspired the technological approach to the shoot. Obviously, everybody agreed that the white glow was far more impactful and if you look at the Slade picture, you can see the creases in the fabric.

The images for *Slade in Flame* were everywhere, and the scale of film marketing meant they were seen far and wide: 'I remember being very pleased that the images played out on buses and things. A fan pointed out it was several years before the same effect was used in *Superman*. It was the same material and I pointed out to the person who wrote it that I did know Richard Donner a bit, so maybe,' Mankowitz continues.

'To look at the outfits in the cold light of day they were a dirty grey colour,' Don Powell says. 'Only when it had bright light shone on it, it became luminous.' That could be a metaphor for the group themselves.

'Personally, I think *Slade in Flame* is probably our most complete album,' Holder said in 2019. 'Although it was stuff written for the movie, we had songs already in place that fitted the movie.' The album reached number six in the UK charts, five places lower than their previous three albums, and the first time outside the Top 5 since 1972. They would never chart as highly again.

Simon Frith wrote presciently in *Let It Rock*:

Slade have reached the career time when the traumas start – break a successful formula or not? They must, to save them and us from boredom. But few groups survive such changes, and later the original style becomes the vision of the golden past – why did we fiddle with it? All Slade can do is the thoughtful. I think they can grow and prosper but only if they begin to challenge themselves as musicians, go back to learning and worrying about their skills. Their next new venture (in between churning out the hits, guaranteed for a year or two more) should be an album with a new producer. Chas Chandler has exploited to the limits what Slade have got; they need someone now to demand things from them they didn't know they had.

Kevin 'Billy' Adams encapsulates the views of the committed, yet casual fan: 'They were pretty much off my radar by the time *Slade in Flame* was released. There was a deliberate attempt to break America, and although it was only around a year, that seemed like an eternity to me back then. By the time the film was out, they'd vanished, and I'd lost interest in them.'

CHAPTER 22

Scorching Off Pop's Glamorous Skin – Slade in Flame Pt 3

The pull-out quote that adorned the adverts for the film from the *Sunday Express* was absolutely spot-on: 'Scorches the glamorous skin off the pop world like a blow torch.' The press release and synopsis for the film stated: 'Filmed In Panavision And Color, with an original score by Slade, *Flame* will engender the audience with a feeling of having participated in what might have been a slice of a pop band's own life.' 'A FILM AN ALBUM A BOOK', as the third part of this multi-media onslaught was John Pidgeon's novelisation of the film script, which, selling for 40p, was what a lot of people who couldn't get to the movie lapped up. One thing was for sure, at the start of 1975, few would not have known Slade had a film out. Whether they would wish to see it was another matter.

Among the most powerful images in *Slade in Flame* is that of the opening credits at Doncaster's steelworks in Sheffield. The symbolism of the steel being hammered and the opening of the furnace for the titles, reflects exactly a curtain being lifted on the tale. It is a film of muted palettes and broken fruit machines, with the band played as colourful peacocks as part of a wider game. Everything and everyone seem to be at loggerheads in the film – north vs south; upper vs working class; rich vs poor; musicians vs businessmen; art vs marketing; old money vs new money; old vs new.

A strong sense of nostalgia courses through it. Pop is old enough now to have a past. The action is set in spring/summer 1967, as big business was beginning to realise the potency of the music industry as an investment. If this is the Summer of Love, there's precious little of it in the film. Toleration at best. The managers don't like the band, the band don't like the managers, or indeed each other; the only thing that seems to be cared for are the birds in Stoker's loft.

At the start, we hear the radio informing us of the Torrey Canyon disaster of March 1967, which sets the context perfectly. As the band progress, the Arab–Israeli Six-Day War (5–10 June) is mentioned, and then the sleeve of *Sgt. Pepper's Lonely Hearts Club Band*, released on 1 June, is seen on the console at Radio City. That year's 'New York Mining Disaster 1941' by The Bee Gees (April) and Cream's 'Strange Brew' (June) are heard. Pirate radio was outlawed in the UK on 14 August of that year, with the Marine Broadcasting Offences Act.

There is also a strong feeling that the hope of the sixties has truly evaporated. It is a film about the recent British past being written through the lens of an American present: at the height of Watergate and the collective American disgust at Vietnam, *Slade in Flame* acts as a parable for the fact that, in a handful of years, the big dreams of the previous decade had unravelled at a rate of knots.

The blueprint for the modern rock film, *A Hard Day's Night*, is both referenced and rubbished. Indeed, *Slade in Flame* is the anti-*A Hard Day's Night*: it uses a lot of the 1964 film's set pieces (train journeys, encounters with marketing gurus, live performance, visiting a police station) and tarnishes them, as if to suggest, to put it somewhat uncouthly, your popular music experiment has all turned to shit. In *Slade in Flame*, the band are actually locked up – Powell and Alan Lake sit eating baked beans next to a toilet in a cell; they have been fundamentally reduced to eating and excreting, the most basic instincts of man.

Tom Conti's performance as Robert Seymour caught the coldness of the movie perfectly: Seymour is the extension of Kenneth Haigh's Simon Marshall character in *A Hard Day's Night* who corners George Harrison ('It's rather touching, really. Here's this kid, giving me his utterly valueless opinion.'). The worst suspicions of how the hierarchy of the music machine treat bands was, after all, ALL TRUE. Although Marshall was a TV man, the lack of real interest in the product they were selling was picked up by Conti's character.

Slade in Flame also showed clearly the British north/south divide. According to popular mythology everyone was floating around in a kaftan, when in reality, they were looking at turds floating in a canal. Powell's Charlie walks with Harold (Patrick Connor), his old boss, and he gets a reality check on his newfound superstardom. Harold talks about playing here in the war, but now the waterway is home to 'more turds in here than fish, coming down here like bloody coal barges'. Powell's Charlie says, 'You make a few records – that's all right. The rest is just bleedin' gangsters in dinner jackets.' That sense of ennui, of inertia, or travelling to somewhere you are not going to find an end result, let alone happiness, is rife throughout the film. Everyone is a turd in their own canal.

The first scene of Sheffield's back-to-back terraces, which could be any UK inner city in the seventies, is one of clearance and renewal – mirroring what pop music was doing – and the generation slightly older who had seen the war or conscription was now wondering where it was all going. We see a motorbike and sidecar, already feeling like a relic in the seventies and a comedy staple from *On the Buses* to *George and Mildred*, being driven up High House Street, Hillsborough; and we see the estates cleared to reveal the controversial Kelvin Flats, where Powell's character lives – climbing endless stairs to find the little box in which his family is located.

The class divide is highlighted too. The disconnect between the educated ideals of the PR man, Sommers, and the reality of the group is highlighted when he shows the group a microphone from which shoots flame. 'Come on Stoker – think of the effect: flames, power, sexual symbolism,' he says. 'He'll look a real prat with his eyebrows on fire,' Charlie replies. When Seymour declines sugar, Harding's off-screen reply of 'oh' makes it clear that only upper classes do such faddish healthy things as not take sugar in their tea. When Angie (Sara Clee) asks for a rum and black – the ultimate aspirational working-class drink – at Seymour's house there is horror on all of Seymour's friends' and family's faces. When Stoker and Paul are in the lift, they are separated by a well-heeled genteel lady who looks clearly upper class. The way she suspiciously eyes Stoker suggests that money does not buy class.

The compartmentalisation of Seymour – loving father, cultural aesthete, ruthless businessman – is all played with a dispassionate sangfroid. Also the fact he worked for the Seymour Trust – the implication is that the band can trust him. After all, he has the breeding. As Stoker says, 'Seymour Trust, Ron Harding Trust, they are all the same. It's just that he's got better notepaper, that's all.' 'Trust?' Stoker's gran shouts though the letterbox at Devlin (Ken Colley), 'I wouldn't trust you further than I could spit.'

There is so much artifice – the front of house in the Sherwood Rooms in Greyfriar Gate, Nottingham, has the comparative glitter of the bingo and the mythical stage, while behind it is clutter, detritus everywhere. We see the clutter too in the yard where road manager Russell works; we see it piled up on the stairs to Harding's office. The band are simply bit-part players in other people's success. The music clearly doesn't matter – here is a commodity that could be marketed. The pressure is on – once started, more is wanted. That leads to bickering, jealousies, egos going astray.

Birds are seen throughout the film: we first see a caged budgie at Charlie's parent's flat; we then see Paul and Stoker in Stoker's pigeon loft. When Paul delivers his big speech for the band's grab for stardom, he is framed through the bars of the loft – it's clear that even from this early stage of the film, he is going nowhere. The use of pigeons is telling; they are beautiful birds, yet they are in a coop. Like people, the birds will return to the cage – given the opportunity, people will choose to return to their cage and not set themselves free. It is also telling that immediately as Paul concludes his play for freedom, Stoker is shat on by a pigeon.

When Seymour and Devlin have their discussion about the band after their first meeting, they walk through a leafy conservatory in a building in West London. We only hear the birdsong, we do not actually see the birds. In fact, the class divide returns as the birds are flying freely, but they too are caged, just with a far higher glass ceiling – giving the look of their freedom, where in reality they have none. In fact, where working-class people ensnare birds and look after them, upper class people shoot them.

216

The final bird we see is a duck on the wallpaper of Paul and Julie's home, as they are reluctantly moving to somewhere bigger, the trappings that are attached to making it within the music business. Stoker does his utmost to ensure they are buying into the dream. If taken symbolically, as the band are starting to come apart, the duck represents 'zero' as it does in cricket, a metaphor reinforced as Seymour refers to cricket when he talks to others of his class: they cannot play his game; nor can he theirs.

The portrayal of women, the other 'birds' in this film, is problematic, but not out of keeping with the era. We see Charlie, Barry and Stoker all chasing women, yet Paul is more comfortable with the feathered variety. The panty-sniffing of Stoker when the band are on stage is distasteful through a 21st-century lens, yet it was not out of keeping with the rain of underwear that used to come to the stage for pop performers of the day. 'You could have pulled her,' Stoker tells the road manager Russ, 'you could have had one of them.' He then repeatedly pulls the mic stand up and down as if wanking it.

Powell and Hill's characters are captured as lighter than Holder and Lea's. The pair are seen in a London car showroom flaunting their new-found wealth; the disgruntled salesman has to curtail his dealings with a Middle Eastern customer (the stereotype of the wealthy Arab in London was commonplace in the seventies) to deal with them. This too explodes the assumption that working-class males are going to be poor. As this was the first real era of seeing sheikhs in their headdresses in London, as we see behind the glamour of the music business, the naughty boys in the car play with the electrics and erect the aerial up and remove the customer's headdress, removing any Arabic mystique and making him look like another balding ageing man, of which the film has many.

It was the disconnect between the public image of Slade as good-time glam-rockers and what was portrayed on screen that was so dark. 'That's an Andrew Birkin thing,' Gavrik Losey says. 'He wrote the film *The Pied Piper*, which was the bleakest children's story you ever wanted to see. So the bleakness comes out of Andrew Birkin's mind.'

'Richard did a really good job,' Sandy Lieberson says. 'We had seen bits and pieces of it as they were shooting. So it wasn't as if we weren't aware of what was happening, but seeing it all together in the first cut, I thought that he had done a really good job directing it and getting them integrated into the story so it wasn't just a performance film, but it actually had some form of story to it as well.'

* * *

Slade in Flame opened on 12 January 1975 at the Pavilion Theatre in Newcastle. It had its London premiere at the Metropole Theatre in Victoria on 13 February and simultaneously at the Rialto in Coventry Street. The band turned up to the premiere at the Metropole on – of course – an antique fire engine; Chas Chandler ordered searchlights to scud the sky. Aside from the cast and crew, those also there were Rosko, Lynsey de Paul, Pilot, Mud, Sweet, Suzi Quatro, Bill Oddie, Kiki Dee, Alan Price, Lulu, Steve and Barbara Megson, Gary Glitter and Roy Wood. Chandler's new signings, Bunny, were also in attendance. 'Diana Dors was put out at the premiere because Alan had full dinner suit on, she had evening dress, and we were all in casual wear,' Powell recalls. 'She berated us for not being in dinner suits – that would be the Hollywood in her.'

'At the premiere, it was the invited audience upstairs and the kids downstairs,' Don Powell continues. 'There was a different reaction from them than from the balcony. The people within the business would get certain things while the kids would be laughing at the obvious things.'

'We were all on a high, really, because it was just, it was true to life,' Bunny drummer Terry McCusker says. 'I thought it was more than a documentary really than anything else. You know, if you're gonna go in a band, go and have a look at this and see what could happen. And a lot worse things can happen than that as well.'

It's pretty harrowing, and amazing that it actually was passed into cinemas with just an A certificate. An original edit with swearing was a straight X. The plot-climax reveal of the bedroom suggesting a kidnapped/killed child is a true shocker, even in this millennial age. The final scenes of the comedown in Brighton hardly leave an audience full of hope.

There were still things for younger fans to enjoy – the band's live performances are spot on, there are car crashes, violence, swearing at a time when the word 'piss' was seen as fairly inciendary, and toilets, something that you rarely saw on screen. It is easy, too, to get blown away by the elegance and audacity of the clothing designs of the Megsons. 'I remember sitting at the end, watching the film and they said I'd get a credit,' Steve Megson says. 'It said 'thanks to Steve and Barbara Megson' on screen. It was a real funny feeling. When I go to the movies now, I will always see people get up and walk out. I always sit and watch the credits and I always look for people, just to see who's done certain things in the movie.'

'We were pretty proud of what we'd done,' John Steel says. 'But I never personally thought it was a really important movie. I thought it was a nice try for a first time. I wasn't too disappointed when it didn't do as well as you might have hoped. I thought "fair comment".'

'It's probably a better movie than I remember it in a way,' Richard Loncraine says. 'It died a death of course. It was too raw.'

*   *   *

Just what BBC *Top of the Pops* producer Robin Nash exactly said that night to Slade at the premiere for *Slade in Flame* is – although unclear in the precise detail, its thrust is the same – a sort of 'What the fuck do you think you are playing at?' Hill recalled that he said, 'Do you think you've done the right thing? Sometimes you're showing things that we're all trying to hide.' Powell wrote that Nash had said, 'I really admire what you have done. You've done the right thing, but do you really think the kids want to see that? That side of the business?' Whatever Nash actually said, it was hugely appropriate – the kids didn't want to see it.

A decade after its release Chris Charlesworth wrote in *Feel the Noize!*: 'Confrontations between the various members and their changing managements were realistically treated, and the overall impression created by the film is that behind the scenes there is much unpleasantness in the lives of successful pop musicians. This, of course, is an accurate observation but whether the public need – or even want – to be told about it is another matter.'

Simon Frith wrote in *Let It Rock* at the time of the film's release: 'Slade's latest attempt to cope is *Flame*, a movie which casts them (inevitably) as a pop group but sets them down (interestingly) in the 1960s and in a context of brutal disillusion.'

Slade were the first band that John Maher – who within eighteen months would be the drummer for Buzzcocks – saw live at King's Hall, Belle Vue, Manchester. 'It was my 14th birthday. I was deaf in one ear for three days afterwards,' he says. He was smitten. 'In February 1975, I was one of four schoolkids to win a *Manchester Evening News* competition to meet the band. The organisers sent a taxi to collect me from school and took me to Manchester Odeon to meet my heroes.'

As part of a promotion for *Slade in Flame*, Maher met them at the New Oxford Manchester Odeon on 36 Oxford Street. After posing for pictures, 'We were each given a signed copy of the soundtrack album and two tickets to see the film. We were supposed to get a copy of the *Slade in Flame* book as well, but someone decided the content was too racy for schoolkids, so they gave us an extra pair of film tickets instead.' Indeed, John Pidgeon's cash-in paperback book of the film was much spicier than the film, with more swearing, violence and sex. Ideal for a 14-year-old Manchester schoolboy. 'Being a true fan, I bought the book the following Saturday from Paperchase, in St Anne's Square.' Another future popstar wasn't so lucky – Nick Heyward: 'I couldn't get in to see *Slade in Flame*. It was sold out at Streatham Odeon.'

Holder said in 2005:

We didn't go in and make a knockabout comedy movie, which everybody thought we would. We came out with a solid, credible rock film about what went on behind the scenes in the rock business. There were some laughs in it, but a lot of people came out of the cinema shocked. If you ask Dave, he'll probably say the biggest mistake of our career was *Slade in Flame.* He thinks we should've have done a comedy spoof. But I fought tooth and nail at the time not to do that.

Will Hodgkinson wrote in his book *In Perfect Harmony: Singalong Pop in '70s Britain* that *Slade in Flame* was 'a commercial bomb, it was critically lacerated and by depicting their seedy reality rather than their fun, escapist image, it is even credited with destroying Slade's career.'

Nevertheless, the film has gone on to be well loved. '*Slade in Flame* is brilliant, it's so un-glam rock,' comedian and artist Jim Moir says. 'It's like a Ken Loach film. I've seen it thrice, which is unusual for me. I remember the last time I watched it I saw a new angle. At the time, I was probably put off by the T. Rex film, I think I saw it a bit late as I presumed it would be another one of those. It's probably the best rock film, ever.'

'It wasn't the success we thought it might be because of the content. It was very dark and shot dark and behind the scenes stuff in, but is stuff that does happen to bands,' Holder told Mark Blake. 'We weren't cheeky-chap-happy-go-lucky Slade. It was the reality of the rock'n'roll band, especially as based in the sixties. Now in retrospect looking back at it now and it's a bloody great movie. Mark Kermode rates it as his favourite rock'n'roll movie and I take his critique as a good milestone.'

Kermode has called *Slade in Flame* the '*Citizen Kane* of British pop movies.' 'It is, to some extent, in the tradition of *Performance*,' the respected film critic added on BBC Four. '*Performance* is a much more adult film, a much more experimental film, it's film dealing with real issues – it's not a film about rock and roll, it's a film about violence; well, *Slade in Flame* is not really a film about rock and roll, it's a film about people falling apart whilst on tour.'

'So many bands get the film thing wrong, but *Slade in Flame* is so right,' singer-songwriter Steve Mason says. 'It's such a great film and they're brilliant in it. As actors, they don't look out of place. They just look like what they are, a bunch of guys in a band from the Black Country. I love that film. It took me a long, long time for a mate of mine to persuade me to watch it because you always get *Give My Regards to Broad Street*. It's like, "I don't give a fuck about your fucking tape. Just leave it in the bin or wherever it is, fucking nobody cares." But then *Slade in Flame*, it's brilliant.'

It's the sort of film that couldn't fail to win over retrospective praise; had Led Zeppelin or indeed Black Sabbath made it, it would have fitted in perfectly with their lofty profiles and would have been seen very much as an act who treated their audience with the intelligence and respect they deserved. And here again was the disconnect – a good chunk of Slade's fans were just moving into their teenage years, and the sixties that were depicted in the film seemed so far far away. And the three years from 1974 were fascinating – glam had tarnished, Big Rock had got bigger, pub was becoming punk. Whereas fifties nostalgia was the thing – *American Graffiti* had been released in the UK on 28 March 1974, paving the way for the *Happy Days* series and the filmed version of the hit stage musical, *Grease* – there just wasn't enough dust on the sixties to make the film relevant to its young audience. And Slade were far too lightweight to attract the serious music fans; so, sadly, but inevitably, *Slade in Flame* fell down the cracks. The movie was 'too real', in a world which still believed that, despite all their differences, The Beatles still all lived together in knocked-through terrace houses in the same street, and The Monkees co-habited beneath a spiral staircase.

Holder has suggested more than once that an idea was mooted for Slade to star in a film with British comic actors Ronnie Barker and Ronnie Corbett – known professionally as The Two Ronnies – a spy caper, but the group couldn't afford to take the time. Dave Hill mentions it in a 1986 interview and Holder in his autobiography. There could well have been; no one else can recall these discussions.

However, Andrew Birkin revealed that he had discussions with Chas Chandler about making a follow-up to the film, and it featuring Flame again. 'Chas wanted to make a second one, where the fans would have more fun,' Birkin says. 'I had them as a band, also down on their luck, playing on a cross-Channel ferry, going to and from Sweden. Then the ship hits an iceberg or something and they're floating around on top of the piano. I can't remember the rest of it. But the idea was it was a spoof Titanic, with the band playing on.' Birkin wrote a treatment, but not a script. It had a provisional title of *Down in Flames*.

One of the most interesting by-products of *Slade in Flame*, was that Richard Loncraine was part of a team (with Laurie Frost and Peter Hannah) who won a Scientific and Engineering Oscar for inventing the Hot-Head, a remote camera at the head of a crane arm. At the time of the film, there was similar technology, but it needed to be operated by a cameraperson. When the car crash sequence occurred in *Slade in Flame*, it narrowly missed the operator. Says Loncraine, 'Some weeks later, another cameraman was killed. We started a company called Kaleidoscope with Sting's money to produce a remote camera head which has really changed the way films are made. I was always interested in keeping cameras moving.'

Slade turned up to the film's premier in Scotland in March in a horse-drawn hearse, complete with driver Jimmy McDonald in full funereal garb. It seemed a bizarre stunt, not unlike one Flame would have been made to perform themselves in the film. It looked as if it was not only sounding a death knell for the group, but the era itself. Once again, The 'NBetweens were in between.

CHAPTER 23

Just Another Band

On 2 March 1975, 'How Does It Feel' reached its peak number fifteen position in the UK singles charts. It was clear that the Slade shilling from younger listeners had moved across to the Bay City Rollers. The ultimately tragic Scottish teenybop phenomenon, whose new single, a reworking of The Four Seasons' 1965 North American hit, 'Bye Bye Baby', was that week's highest new entry at number eight. It must also be noted that the week that 'How Does It Feel' reached its peak, two other retrospectively acknowledged career zenith singles, 'Young Americans' by David Bowie and '#9 Dream' by John Lennon, also hit their highest positions, number eighteen and number twenty-three, respectively. The pop world was turning, and 1975 proved that Slade were no longer the chart shoo-in that they had once been. Couple that with a focus on America, and it was clear that UK listeners would find newer pastures.

Slade's first and only tour of the UK of 1975 began on Friday 18 April. They would be supported by Chas Chandler's protégés, Liverpool-based Bunny, led by former Lord Sutch singer Linda Millington, and featuring Terry McCusker and Dave Dover who'd been in Colonel Bagshot's Incredible Bucket Band. Bagshot had supported Slade on their European tour at the end of 1973, and with the addition of Millington, Bunny had come to the attention of Henri Henroid, the agent who had first recommended The Animals to Mickie Most back in the early sixties. Bunny's sole single, 'Baby, You're Getting to Me', was released by Polydor in 1975.

Produced by Chas Chandler, it was said that he was so impressed when he heard the band that he would record them in the studio himself. Bunny was a marriage of inconvenience. 'Linda Millington was a bloody nuisance,' Terry McCusker says. 'We were much, much heavier than the single (a very mid-seventies Smokie-style affair), a real hard rock group. And she was brilliant. But she liked the wilder side of things, which none of us did. Well, we all drank our height in ale a day. But apart from that, we didn't do anything else.' Bunny were bestowed the accolade of having the Megsons design for them: 'I did a whole series of outfits for them and Dave was OK about that because they weren't well known,' Steve Megson says.

The thirteen dates were ostensibly to showcase the *Slade in Flame* album, which had just ended its eighteen-week run in the charts, and to promote the group's latest single (and their first new material since the film) 'Thanks for the Memory (Wham Bam Thank You Mam)'. The concerts were somewhat hastily arranged when the group realised that due to their US commitments, they wouldn't be able to tour again in the UK until 1977.

The tour began in Bournemouth and ended on Monday 5 May at the Liverpool Empire. The London concert on 25 April at the New Victoria was reviewed in *MM* by Ray Coleman: 'Slade are happy pop at its best, no lyrics of deep philosophy, no harmonising, not even a good voice. Instead Noddy's "football vocals" and everybody determined to have a good night out. Shout your heads off, clap yer' hands, and do as Noddy says.' The concert was a joyous run-through of old and new played by a band finely tuned and in lockstep. Holder was at his cheeky, showman best – Coleman continued in his review, '"The manager of the hall," yells Noddy, "Is a bit frightened in case he gets his seats broken…" A mocking roar of laughter from the crowd, and later, "We'd better get quiet now, there's a bloke from the council here who reckons we're exceeding the noise limit." More laughter.'

Stuart Grundy and a BBC team joined the group for a BBC Radio One documentary about the group on tour, for a new series called

Insight. The two-part show, *Six Days on the Road*, was broadcast that summer, and provided a fascinating investigation of a band on the road, with audio recordings from inside the band car. The recording followed the band from the Civic Hall show on 27 April and then ended in Liverpool.

As writer Chris Ingham notes, 'Noddy Holder found himself reassuring younger fans on the post-*Flame* 1975 tour that he wasn't Stoker, Jim wasn't Paul, they hadn't really fallen out and Slade weren't splitting up.' Steve Peacock followed the tour for *Sounds* and spoke with promoter Mel Bush, who said this of Holder:

> Have you ever looked out from the back of the stage while Noddy's talking to the audience? It's something I only ever see with this group, and that's that every pair of eyes is turned towards Nod. Not 90 per cent, but every one. The communication Nod has with those kids is... unique. The kids identify with him – he's not the most good-looking guy in the world, he's not the ugliest, it's like there's one of them up there and he's talking their language. He's not talking down to them, he's talking to them.

The Liverpool show would be the last live concert performance of the group in the UK until May 1977.

Over the next period the band, bar Hill, took residence (or a second home) in London: 'I moved down here was because I'd got a girlfriend who couldn't settle in Wolverhampton. She was Japanese, from Tokyo,' Powell says. 'I enjoyed it at the time. Don't get me wrong, it was exciting. But that was the only reason I moved down here.' Powell's relationship with Mari Tachikawa – a model with a German father and Japanese mother – was not to last long.

Another relationship that wasn't to last long was that of Bunny: 'It all came to an end when we were booked to support Duane Eddy,' Terry McCusker says. 'The first night was in Colston Hall in Bristol. We went on, waiting for Linda to come on. She didn't appear until about halfway through. We were going down well as a trio. We'd been playing together for ten years by that time, you know, so we could handle anything. And then she came on, absolutely out of the game, literally falling over. That was that was the end of the Duane

Eddy tour, and that was the end of Bunny as well. I haven't seen her since that night.'

'Slade's star in Australia had waned by the middle of 1974,' Stephen Cross notes. 'I don't believe 'The Bangin' Man' even made Top 40 and it was not until 'Far Far Away' was released in late 1974 that I heard Slade on my local radio station for the first time. They even cracked an appearance on the ABC's new Sunday evening music show *Countdown* in early 1975 with the film clip of 'Far Far Away' featuring the band in their white suits from *Slade in Flame.*'

Despite the exposure, 'Far Far Away' only made Top 20, while the *Slade in Flame* album stalled in the Top 30. The film had a cinema release in Sydney and Melbourne. 'The *Slade in Flame* album was virtually the end of Slade in Australia,' adds Cross. *JUKE* magazine captured the Australian view of the band with their review of the soundtrack to *Slade in Flame*: 'S'funny thing about Slade. They started out as a revolution and ended up as just another band. A good one, sure, but their days as a phenomenon seems to be past. Their blast furnace intensity, once upon a time a good eight hundred degrees hotter than anything else available seems to have cooled.' *RAM (Rock Australia Magazine)* reported reported that *Slade in Flame* closed after a solitary week in Sydney. 'The flick wasn't that bad, really. The main problem,' bemoans Richard Cahill for the film's distributors, 'is that there don't seem to be any Slade fans anymore.'

* * *

The Bay City Rollers would appear again shortly in Slade's career. Noddy Holder was a guest at a BBC Radio One fun day at Mallory Park race circuit, near Leicester, on 18 May 1975. There to plug 'Thanks for the Memory (Wham Bam Thank You Mam)', Holder was in attendance, joining the DJs broadcasting on an island adjacent to the race track. Various pop stars of the moment, including the Rollers – a group that, like Slade, had taken several years to become an overnight success – were there. 'We're all huddled into a tiny room here; there are the Rollers, Desmond Dekker, The Three Degrees, and in one little corner, with me is Noddy Holder from Slade,' DJ David 'Diddy' Hamilton broadcast. Holder said he was getting worried about crowd control, and adds that he would have liked a race, but he'd been 'a little bit drunk' the night before. He talked about the challenge of the forthcoming US tour, and that the other three were in London 'laying down tracks' for him to come and join later in the evening.

Bolstered by BBC hospitality whiskey and choosing his favourite Four Tops song 'Reach Out, I'll Be There', the cheerful professionalism in his tone seemed to belie the fact that this was the point when Noddy Holder, kept waiting by the mayhem following the Rollers, realised that Slade's teenybop days were far, far behind them. John Peel, the venerated UK DJ, was begrudgingly present as part of the fun day. He noted in his autobiography, *Margrave of the Marshes*, that he and fellow Radio One DJ Johnnie Walker recognised the significant moment 'albeit one almost lost in the turmoil', noting that Holder crossed the bridge to the island and 'strode unnoticed through the Rollers fans'. Peel concluded, 'He must have thought "well, that's the end of that, then."'

'Thanks for the Memory (Wham Bam Thank You Mam)' became Slade's last Top 10 single for six years. Hitting the charts on 17 May, it almost had the funk, with Jim Lea playing a boogie clavinet, and the double-tracked twin guitars at the end offering a glimpse of what Thin Lizzy were soon about to do. It also seemed to acknowledge that their glory days were over, and a new chapter was beginning. They appeared on *Shang-A-Lang*, the Bay City Rollers' teatime TV pop programme, recorded at Granada Studios in Manchester on 2 June, with the Rollers singer Les McKeown introducing the band, somewhat uncomfortably, 'And now, the star of our show today, the unforgettable Slade.'

The B-side, 'Raining in My Champagne', a playful rewrite of 'La Bamba', showed what the group were truly capable of – a lovely soulful shuffle, impeccably played – proving that absolutely nothing was wasted from their experience back in the Bahamas. In the live version, captured officially on the release of the New Victoria Theatre show from the *Slade in Flame* tour, Holder suddenly breaks into the Jamaican traditional 'The Banana Boat Song (Day-O)', popularised by Harry Belafonte. Ten years later, Freddie Mercury would do similar playing with Queen at Live Aid.

'I've had a word with the Committee, and we're really going to let it go tonight,' Holder says at the New Victoria Theatre. Holder's reference to 'the Committee' was a nod to Colin Crompton's Chairman character on the ITV programme *The Wheeltappers and Shunters Social Club*, a variety show based in a northern working man's club, which had begun broadcasting in April 1974. Slade had played many of these establishments in their early days around the West Midlands, and indeed Holder had begun his career in Walsall Labour Working Men's Club. Little did they suspect at this point that within thirty-six months, they would be playing similar again.

CHAPTER 24

From Burbank to Bilston

'As everyone knows, the Slades went off on the Queen Mary one
day when they should have stayed in Birmingham.'
James Parade, *Record Mirror*, 1979

A common trope throughout the seventies was that of emigration,
people leaving their home country to begin a new life. Chas
Chandler would not let America rest. He knew the power of his
band; he knew the power of their brand – and he felt that they could
still make it through, putting in the hard yards, just as they had done
in all the clubs in the Black Country. So, leaving behind the question
mark that was *Slade in Flame*, the group relocated to New York City.
'Some say that moving to the States killed us off, and maybe it did,
but there was no choice,' Holder said. 'We'd been over several times
before for short periods of time and the only way to crack the place
was by staying there. By 1975 we decided to have a go at the golden
goose.'

Graham Swinnerton went with them, moving into an apartment
on the Upper East Side, not far from Jim Lea and Dave Hill, while
Noddy Holder became a permanent resident at the Mayflower Hotel
and Don Powell lived downtown. Swinnerton would pick them up
and drove them to gigs, this time over an area bigger than the Black

Country. Someone who didn't make the journey was Steve Megson: 'I worked with them right up until they went to the States in '75. I used the money that I earned from them to pay for my PGCE teaching qualification, not really expecting to be a teacher, but my mother-in-law at the time said, "Steve, you want to get a proper job," my eldest son was on the way, so she was quite right. Obviously, I don't regret it, it's been a good career teaching, but when I started teaching, I left all that stuff behind.'

All the stops were pulled out for Slade's return to the US. In July, the group played the Wollman Memorial Skating Rink in Central Park. The adverts blared, 'On July 21, New York becomes Slade City: Slade is back after more than a year of films and concerts around the world.' The group stayed at the legendary art deco Essex House Hotel at 160 Central Park South, famed for its red neon sign high above its roof, and were able to walk to and from the show at the rink, which became an event space across the summer. Playing as part of the annual Schaefer Beer Festival at the 6,000-capacity venue with Brownsville Station, the show was billed as 'Slade Under The Stars'. It showed that Slade had lost none of their live magic – yet Brownsville Station proved that the US already had their own version of Slade. And of course, one of the reasons that Brownsville Station never made it in the UK was because it had its own Slade. David McGee reviewed the show in *Rolling Stone*, 'Slade's is shoot first – ask questions later rock; rather than wash over you, their sound pulverises you. You respond by sheer animal instinct.'

In August, Slade shared some bills with their old friends Status Quo, who were similarly struggling to get a foothold in the US market: 'We were sitting in a coffee shop having lunch before we went to the gig,' Francis Rossi recalls. 'They were higher on the bill than us. It was one of those five-band bills; they had a lot of those in America. I learned something from them that day. We were chummy, great mates as far as I was concerned. They took longer in their soundcheck and were cutting it fine for us. That's when I learned, there was no animosity to it, but they made sure they did their fucking soundcheck. Fuck their mates coming after them! Whether they were cognitively aware that they were doing that or not, but it was a learning curve for me.'

In September, Leandra Russell, Jan Hill and Lou Lea all came to join their partners in New York. Mari Tachikawa came over as well for a while, but stayed in LA. Almost as soon as the three New York partners arrived, they were caught up in a bank robbery, where the protagonist was shot by police. Jan Hill had young Jade with her in the pram. This did not augur well.

Andrew Reschke reviewed Slade in the *Syracuse Journal*, a support slot with ZZ Top at the Onondaga War Memorial Auditorium in the city on 25 September 1975:

> Although its popularity seems to be on the wane since it was here last, headlining its own concert, the quartet was determined the audience have a good time. Such numbers as 'Them Kinda Monkeys Can't Swing', 'Gudbuy T'Jane', 'Thanks for the Memory', 'How Does It Feel', 'Let the Good Times Roll' and 'A Little Bit' were proof of talent, but there seems to be something lacking here. Perhaps if Slade concentrated more on its own style and less on being glitter type imitations of Led Zeppelin, that void might be filled.

Someone who did bump into Slade in the US was none other than Kim Fowley, who had spotted them all those years ago at Tiles in Oxford Street. 'We saw him later in LA after we'd become successful in the UK, we told him that he always said that we would make it. He said, "I told you, I told you,"' Powell laughs. 'People like that, you'll never forget.'

Chris Charlesworth, too, had moved from LA to New York, to continue his role as *Melody Maker*'s US correspondent. 'I went to a party at the flat where Jim and Dave lived on the Upper East Side,' he says. 'Swin rolled a joint that was as big as a Cuban cigar. Chas came to NY once or twice when I was there for *MM*, and he'd call me and we'd go out for a drink or three. He smoked like a chimney and loved to smoke grass too.'

Slade in Flame had a limited release in America, opening in their heartland of St Louis on Friday 12 September 1975 in the French renaissance-styled Ambassador Theatre on 411 N. 7th Street, where the group had played in February the previous year and had endured a power cut. Few could make any sense of the Black Country brogue, and the film had to show with subtitles in the rest of America. 'It was such a great experience,' Holder told Dave Ling.

> I had some of the most brilliant moments of my life. Things like going into a bar in New Orleans and seeing ZZ Top during their blues era. There's no way I could ever regret that. When we had Thin Lizzy playing with us, if I hadn't pulled, me and Brian Robertson would go out after the show to find a bar band to play with. One night we did half an hour with a Mariachi band, him playing bluesy licks over their Mexican music. That would never have happened in Britain, I was just too famous.

'When Thin Lizzy were touring America, we did some gigs with Slade and hung out with them at the hotel,' Chris O'Donnell says. 'That's when you thought, "*Why are you here?*" There was no way on God's earth that America was going to get Slade. They had to lose that whole thing that had made them Slade and just be a band again. They were a great band, but certainly, they didn't get 'Coz I Luv You'... Noddy... any of that. None of that translated in America except they were a pretty good band. They were back to being Ambrose Slade or The 'Nbetweens. They certainly weren't going anywhere. They were slogging around America. I don't know why Chas thought that was important, well I do, it was the holy grail.'

They weren't alone in not clicking: Roxy Music and Cockney Rebel, two further groups whose Europeanness was at their very core, also failed to replicate the success they enjoyed in the UK. David Bowie's Ziggy era positioned him as an art-rock delicacy until the mid-seventies when he appealed directly to the US market with his *Young Americans* LP and number one single 'Fame' in 1975. Thereafter he played arenas.

If anything, what makes the group's lack of success even more surprising is Chas Chandler's unerring belief that they would, indeed, succeed. He'd been right in bringing Jimi Hendrix to Britain to make it, and he had been absolutely correct in his belief that Slade would make it in the UK. They had most definitely put in the legwork – few bands were able to bring on side the most questioning of souls. But it just wasn't to be. In the four years Slade tried hardest to crack America, it was a case of the country simply not being ready for them. It was said that post-Watergate, there was a collective moment during which America wanted to turn inward, just as it had done after the Second World War. Graham Swinnerton said that America wanted 'to feel sorry for itself… it was not looking for a good time.'

'At that time in the seventies it was jeans and T-shirts over there,' Don Powell says, 'and we come on looking like we'd come out the bar in *Star Wars*. They just didn't get it.'

'Just because it didn't work out the way we had planned, well… I don't recall anyone complaining at the time,' Holder said in 2022. 'And when we came back to the UK, musically speaking, we were a band revitalised. We were playing shit-hot.'

'It wasted our time. I can't blame anybody,' Powell continues.

We didn't really have a record company. We didn't really have anything that was warm to American radio either. Too heavy for AM or not hip enough for FM. The only time we got radio play a lot of the time in the seventies was when local radio stations co-promoted the gigs. Plus, the fact that we were billed as 'The New Beatles' and Americans just didn't want to hear that. It was never really gonna work. You know, we had a few good tours there. ZZ Top, that was good. We had a month in Canada, in the mid-seventies on our own and that was pretty good. We had a couple of areas in the States which were good for us, but not enough. St Louis was great for us. San Francisco was not bad.

'I saw them twice in St Louis which was the one city where they could guarantee to sell out the local arena,' Chris Charlesworth says. 'I think a DJ there had played their records a lot. It was slightly freaky how they were big in this one city. In New York they played the Felt Forum, which held 6,000 and was part of the Madison Square Garden complex.'

However, Powell noted that people were watching. 'Kiss became mates,' he says. 'Gene Simmons and Paul Stanley were always in the audience in New York and said, we're gonna take that show and make it bigger. They always acknowledge it.'

'We modelled our all-out attacking style on Slade,' Simmons said. 'They were our greatest influence, not only in the crafting of rock songs but also as performers. They fired on all four pistons and are an inspiration to young bands.'

'I went back to New York in 1995,' Don Powell told me. 'Bob Meyrowitz [creator of the *King Biscuit Flower Hour*] told me that Bill Graham had wanted to manage us, but it never went any further as Chas was still with us then. Bill felt we'd been handled totally wrong in the States. We went top of the bill far too early. We were with Premier Talent; Chas knew them personally through Hendrix. We forced our promoters' hands – "you can have The Eagles, but you've got to have Slade" – and they didn't want us.'

* * *

In December 1975, a new Slade album hit the racks. For a very short period. *Beginnings of Slade* was released by Contour, the budget label. Except it wasn't a new release, it was 1969's long unavailable *Beginnings* repackaged with a new running order. Contour was part of Musical Rendezvous, the low-price label set up by Polydor and Philips in 1971. The labels were following Decca, who had joined forces with EMI three years earlier to establish the Record Merchandisers rack-jobbing company, to ensure that Decca and EMI product would be prominently displayed by non-specialist retailers. EMI had started the trend in the UK by setting up Music for Pleasure (MFP) in 1965, itself emulating the US Pickwick label. It was a joint venture with publisher Paul Hamlyn, and it sought to get EMI's repertoire into outlets such as UK high-street retailer WHSmith and the then-new phenomenon, supermarkets. For a generation growing up, before grocers effectively became their own record shops in the 1990s, the white-wire spinner rack full of budget LPs typified a supermarket's music offering, and this is exactly where *Beginnings of Slade* was aimed.

The ruse of the album was simple: retailing around half a full-price album's cost, these records were to be sold in volume, and the sleight of hand was straightforward – take early or obscure recordings from a well-known artist's career and repackage with a current or classic photograph of them, entirely out of era with the original. For example, Decca's *The World of David Bowie*, first released in 1970, captured him as a bubble-permed experimental folk/Anthony Newley type. When it was reissued in 1973, there he was in Ziggy Stardust pose.

Although Slade were on a different label, *Beginnings of Slade* had a shot of the band from late 1972 on its cover, with Holder in full coachman's hat pose, and Hill disguising his recently broken ankle. Of course, to the person in the street, it looked exactly like a brand-new album. It had a new running order frontloaded with the most recognisable tracks ('Born to Be Wild', 'Genesis', 'Martha My Dear' – although possibly the hoodwink extended its web so people thought that the group Genesis might be on there, too) and gone were Peter Jones's cosmic 'heavy collection of strictly good vibes' notes, replaced by Roger St Pierre's summary of the album. His notes made no attempt to disguise the fact customers were buying something that was six years old. 'Today, Slade are an acknowledged teen phenomenon with a string of hit singles, the successful movie *Slade in Flame* behind them, and a fan following of fanatical intensity. Back in 1969 they were Ambrose Slade, one of the many emergent young rock groups, not sure which direction to take in both music and image.'

St Pierre also suggested that the group were now moving on to cater 'for a slightly more mature audience, their rule as king teenybopper group having been usurped by the Bay City Rollers'. Although part of the Polydor empire, Contour would have been given the all-clear legally to release this album without management consent, yet, understandably, when Chas Chandler found out, he demanded the album was withdrawn from the racks, which in some ways was a shame as it would have shown how the group had matured in the past half-decade; this was no hippie whimsy, this was the then set-list of a working band. Many copies were returned, yet many had already sold or were simply kept by stores. It made for an instant collector's item. While an original Fontana copy of *Beginnings* could cost you over £1,000, the cut-price, no-frills *Beginnings of Slade* itself sells over a £100.

* * *

It was time for a 'real' new album. Released in November, the first taster for it was the single 'In for a Penny', their first since May's 'Thanks for the Memory'. It was a step back to Slade in Roma folk song mode, evoking 'Coz I Luv You'. Bathed in harmonium and strummed guitar, it probably wasn't what audiences were expecting from the group at that point. Dave Hill's guitar solos are striking, and the second is introduced by Holder with the phrase 'ee, they got a band,' similar to his mentioning of 'the Committee' in live shows. It meant that, no matter where in the world you may be, you couldn't ever take the boy out of Beechdale, as he seemed to esoterically reference UK TV. 'Ee, they got a band' came from a Birds Eye beefburger commercial from 1970 that was shown often on British telly. Commissioned by the leading Collett Dickenson Pearce agency, it featured American-British actress Sandra Dickinson, famed for her ditzy blonde roles. Set in the US during the gangster era, Dickinson and her beau are at a table in a restaurant when the mob move in, all brandishing violin cases, the universal disguise for carrying machine guns. As she orders her Birds Eye burgers from the menu to the chagrin of her lover, she looks at the hoodlums saying, 'Ee, they got a band.' It is these fabulous parochial details that seem to ground the band so heavily in their time. Again, it can be seen as a John Lennon-ism, who refers to the Freddie Frinton-Thora Hird comedy *Meet the Wife* in 'Good Morning, Good Morning'.

'In for a Penny' was backed with its *Slade in Flame*-processing 'Can You Just Imagine', another in Slade's run of classic B-sides. 'If you want the story of Slade, you get much more autobiographical stuff on the B-sides,' Paul Cookson says. "I'm Mee, I'm Now An' That's Orl' is almost like punk rock and 'Don't Blame Me' might seem throwaway, but there were the lines about the gold discs being polished by Noddy's mama, and when they had no money. So, there's much more in terms of autobiography. 'Can You Just Imagine' is about filming *Flame*, isn't it? The B-sides provide some really interesting insights into where they were.'

'In for a Penny' entered the UK charts at number twenty-seven, the week before Queen went to number one with 'Bohemian Rhapsody'. By the middle of December, it left its peak position of number eleven, and early January 1976, it had left the Top 40.

The Top 10 was no longer Slade's domain, a fact borne out by the performance of their next single, the second track to be taken off their new album. The jaunty, thumbs-in-braces knees-up of 'Let's Call It Quits', released at the end of January, also stalled at number eleven. At the end of February 1976, the single reached its peak, behind 'Squeeze Box' by The Who. It was said that the track owed a debt to 'Brickyard Blues' by Allen Toussaint, which had been covered by Maria Muldaur and Frankie Miller. Three Dog Night had taken it into the US Top 40 under the name 'Play Something Sweet' in 1974. It was written that Toussaint sued for the song – something that Lea was later to refute. Its B-side, 'When the Chips Are Down', started life as the theme song to the BBC Radio One documentary about the group, *Six Days on the Road* that had been broadcast in July 1975. The original verité lyrics of getting 'fish and chips for dinner' had been transplanted to the wild west and a gang riding into town. The high-powered pub-shuffle showed that Slade were this bunch of desperados as they turned up at their next US venue.

All of this acted as a trailer for the main feature, *Nobody's Fools*, the result of their American sojourn and, arguably, their most 'produced' record. *Nobody's Fools* toyed with their standard instrumentation, adding female vocals into the mix and actually looking at tempos and variations in the Slade palette. It is another of Slade's most consistent albums, with Holder and Lea's writing reaching a level of intensity and three-dimension. Recorded again at the Record Plant in mid-1975, with 'Merry Xmas Everybody' engineer Dennis Ferrante working with Chas Chandler, the album had a clean, bright sound, with less noise and reverb than their previous work. In short, it was being tailored for the US market. The band hit it off with Ferrante, known as 'the fly' – a true product of the New York studio system, talkative, wisecracking, experienced. The list of people he had and went on to work with was a veritable who's who of popular music, but the association for which he was best known was working as part of the engineering team on John Lennon's US-made solo albums.

After getting the taste with the horn section for *Slade in Flame*, again a small selection of outside musicians were employed to supplement the band, adding some depth and range to the sound. Tasha Thomas, who had sung with singers ranging from Carly

Simon to Stevie Wonder and would release her sole album, *Midnight Rendezvous* in 1979, offered backing vocals and Paul Prestopino (listed as Paul Prestotino), who'd played sessions with artists ranging from John Denver to Alice Cooper, on Dobro. Journalist Michael Wale wrote a track-by-track critique of the album for the collection of sheet music of *Nobody's Fools* – then an important format for a new album's marketing: 'First I should say that for me, this is the best album that Slade have made so far, and I say that not just because I am writing for Slade admirers but because musically this is the breakthrough, I have been hoping they were going to make.'

'It was a different way of recording and the songs were lighter,' Powell told Mark Blake. 'I enjoyed making that. Different outlook, Dennis was great. Brand new approach for us and like making a real record. Girl singers on it as well. Fun time and a fun album.'

Opening with piano, the almost title track, 'Nobody's Fool', is sweet and cheery, double-tracked guitar, with Holder not appearing until nearly a minute in, perfect for DJs to speak over the intro. It's infectious, nimble yet still punchy – the most striking difference is the presence of Thomas's vocals, the first female voice on a Slade recording.

Led by the very of-the-moment cry of 'BOOGIE!', 'Do the Dirty' has a fine urban funk to it, taking inspiration from Led Zeppelin's 'Trampled Under Foot', and the overall influence of Stevie Wonder. 'Pack Up Your Troubles' must have further confused US radio programmers, with its country rock feel complete with pedal steel guitar.

'Get On Up' updates the classic Slade swayer; Michael Wale wrote that it was, 'The most traditional Slade number on the whole album, right from the opening raunchy guitar sound to Noddy's rendering of the typical Slade chorus.' It was to become a rabble-rousing crowd-pleaser that was to soon become the sole representative of the album in the group's live set. 'L.A. Jinx' is, given is subject material, arguably the most US-influenced track on the album, talking about how the group are overcoming the misfortunes that hampered them in the city.

'Did Ya Mama Ever Tell Ya' seeks out the double entendres from nursery rhymes over a reggae rhythm with Tasha Thomas's banked backing vocals. This goes on for over three minutes. It is not one of Slade's finest moments. 'Not too rude,' Michael Wale wrote, 'as they used to say in the days of variety: Naughty but nice.' The reggae tinge returns for 'I'm a Talker', which, as Wale notes, is 'another song reflecting California with its love of star signs'. The album closes with 'All the World Is a Stage', a track that has the dubious distinction of being noted by Chris Ingham as 'one of the very few genuinely pretentious Slade tracks in their history'. With lyrics such as 'you are the eyes of the reader, and I am the hand of the writer', Holder celebrates the relationship between artist and performer. The album ends with the sound of a Lachsack, the novelty yellow bag that contained a device playing pre-recorded laughter. Invented in 1968, it became an all-the-rage novelty must-have in the seventies, along with the wind-up chattering teeth and the whoopee cushion. The processed laughter ending the album seems to suggest the band were aware of their own pretentiousness, a very un-Sladelike quality. Although Stu Rutter, one of Slade's oldest fans, disagrees: "'All the World Is a Stage' should have been the single off the album rather than 'Nobody's Fool'. So different for them, the synth effect, the lyrics but still the powerful guitar make it stand out.'

Gered Mankowitz shot the sleeve for *Nobody's Fools*, and it was all very much business as usual. 'I remember it very well, because I was terribly disappointed in the cover, as I didn't want it to look like that at all,' he recalls.

> I'd shot it in black and white and I coloured in the noses. I showed it to Chas and I said that I felt that doing it like that caught the essence. They objected. The problem was that it's on a white background, and it needs to be clean. I knew that Polydor's printing, the shitty board they used, that it would never ever have the impact. The other thing was, in those days, if you said to a printer, the noses have got to be really red, everything else would have a pink tinge to it because they upped the red. They did 'Slade' in the same red. Anyway, I was terribly upset but Polydor didn't have the taste or the style to see that a black-and-white cover would have been really good. It looks like the noses have been stuck on, so I've always been a bit disappointed.

241

However, as always with Mankowitz and Chandler's 'lads', the session was great fun. 'I loved it,' Mankowitz continues. 'Slade looked marvellous, their outfits, their clothes, the look, Noddy in the New York policeman's hat and the braces and everything, they were looking great. It was only the noses. It was just the noses and I just thought it was so funny. They wore the noses for the whole afternoon. Don came up to me and went, "I don't want to look silly," and I said, "Don't worry, none of you look silly." It was a really enjoyable session as ever. They were a great joy to work with and funny.'

Nobody's Fools was released at the start of March 1976, and peaked and number fourteen, leaving the charts after four weeks. Reviews were mixed, but not unfavourable, although Tony Stewart, writing in *RAM* in Australia, said: 'Though superficially the music is of a reasonable standard, there's not a lot of depth... the only feature which cuts through with any effect is Holder's vulgarity expressed on 'In for a Penny' and 'Did Ya Mama Ever Tell Ya'.'

The almost title track, 'Nobody's Fool', was released as a single in April, a month after the album's release. Peaking at number fifty-three, it became the first Slade single to miss the Top 40 since 'Know Who You Are' in September 1970.

* * *

The band returned to the US for their final full-length tour in April 1976; paired on several shows with fellow brit Peter Frampton, who, since leaving The Herd and then Humble Pie (and lending his guitar to Hill for 'Look Wot You Dun'), had been greeted with, at best, indifference in his home country. It couldn't have been further from the truth in the US, where Frampton's hard work, poster-boy looks, and good tunes had propelled him to the kind of superstar status that Chas Chandler so craved for his charges. Like Slade, he had broken through with an album captured in concert, unlike Slade the album had global appeal, which had started in the US.

When the group supported him in April 1976, *Frampton Comes Alive!* was beginning its ten non-consecutive-week run at the top of the US charts. On the other hand, *Nobody's Fools* had not managed even a ripple in the *Billboard* Top 200. *Frampton Comes Alive!* like a certain other album nearly five years old, made use of the word 'alive' and an exclamation mark to underline the vibrancy of Frampton's performance. And like *Slade Alive!*, the album was full of songs that a listener felt almost guilty for not having heard and felt compelled to enjoy to the level that the crowd on the record, who seemed to hang on every word, were.

The pairings on the tour seemed far more appropriate for Slade than the mismatches of the previous years: Montrose, Thin Lizzy, Aerosmith, Golden Earring; only Santana and Be-Bop Deluxe seemed somewhat out of kilter. 'American bands are not like English bands who come in the dressing room and you're mixing,' Powell says. 'I remember the one time we were on with Aerosmith, they asked for this particular spring water from the springs of Colorado, and it was just spring water, and they weren't gonna play. The promoter came and grabbed the singer by the neck and said, "On that stage!!"'

Sadly, one of the most intriguing bills didn't happen – or if it did, no one remembers it: on 7 and 8 May 1976, Slade were supporting Blue Öyster Cult at the Capitol Theater, New Jersey, and at the bottom of the bill, tantalisingly credited, are Dr Feelgood. 'I have discussed these gigs with Sparko at length and the conclusion is we do not remember appearing with Slade, ever,' Dr Feelgood drummer, John 'The Big Figure' Martin says. 'Noddy Holder's colossal voice was their unmistakeable hallmark. They made a great noise on record. I remember eating at greasy cafés on the road full of hope for what we did being blasted out of our seats by Noddy's tonsils as if to say "No, do it like this!" Slade, unforgettable especially at Christmas, would like to have met them.'

A band with whom they did share a bill, however, was Be-Bop Deluxe. 'It was a long time ago and I only have vague memories of it,' Bill Nelson says. 'Not sure if we did more than one show with them, but certainly we did at least one. I didn't actually see them perform as I was backstage in our dressing room, but after the show Robbie Wilson, Be-Bop's crew boss who had worked with Slade, introduced me to Noddy Holder. Noddy seemed to be a very jolly, nice guy but, I have to admit, seemed rather "worse for wear" at the time, probably as a result of the copious amounts of booze provided by the show's promoter! In some respects, Be-Bop and Slade were an unusual pairing as Slade were far more of a pop band than Be-Bop Deluxe were, but perhaps that didn't matter at the time, particularly in America. They were certainly more compatible than Ted Nugent though, who we also did a couple of shows with.'

'The best shows were with ZZ Top – but this was before beards, when they were just a down-home Texas boogie band,' Holder recalled. '*Tres Hombres, Fandango, Rio Grande Mud*, they were such great albums. It was a fantastic time to be on the road with ZZ Top.'

On 28 June, when the group were playing the Commodore Ballroom in Vancouver, their pal from the Great Western Festival, Stanley Baker, passed away of lung cancer at the tragically early age of 48. As the US were celebrating their independence bicentennial, the group were in Canada.

On 31 July 1976, Slade played their final gig in America at The Showplace, Dover, New Jersey. Two days later, the band left the US. Powell wrote in his diary, 'Our last ever tour of the U.S. ... AND it still remained un-conquered.' Although they would return for isolated shows and promotion in the later eighties, the great four-year US experiment had reached its conclusion.

'In my opinion, Slade were only suited to a European, primarily British, market,' John Halsall reiterates. 'Having them slog it round the USA was a huge mistake and their long absences, over there, badly impacted on their popularity here. In fact, it more or less finished their run. The Les Perrin move was pure snobbery on Chas's part; but there was no telling Chas, he knew it all. I got a huge amount of sympathy from music business icons who concurred with these opinions.'

'They were too British,' John Steel says. 'I mean, there's none more British than The Beatles, but Slade didn't click with the USA, and me among several people around thought Chas was flogging a dead horse by having them persistently work in America and they just weren't cracking it. I always thought that was a bit of a blind side that Chas had. He was determined that they were going to make it in the States, and if you're not big in the States, you're not big anywhere.'

From Burbank to Bilston

Fontana talent scout Irving Martin offers:

I've worked all over the place, and I'll tell you something, if Slade
would have stayed with me, they would have been an international
band that would have had American hits. I knew all the producers
in the States: some of them I trained already, who would have
been better than the guys they had. They saw Wolverhampton
and the UK with the few American hits they had as the end of
the world for them. If they were with me, they would have been a
much bigger band. I may not have produced them, I may not have
managed them, but I would have opened doors for them that they
could never have opened themselves and that the management
they had would never have even been aware of.

'Why didn't they make it in America? Probably the same reason I
couldn't,' Emperor Rosko offers. 'Still to this day I'm not doing as
well as I'd like to in the USA; what is it – coals to Newcastle? Slade
were a rock band. They were another rock band in America. They
had great songs and they charted a little bit, but it just wasn't the
same thing. Had Slade come along instead of The Beatles at that
time, when the accent was everything, they might have had a much
better chance. That's certainly not anything to take away from them.
They are first rate.'

Status Quo suffered a similar fate to Slade: 'staying with our
managers,' Francis Rossi offers.

Chas was never going to give it to somebody else at the time, nor
was our manager. As soon as we left the States, it was dead, the
same with Slade. There was no one working it, no money invested
in it. Whereas if you had a manager over there, they would push
the record company and we'd have started to make ground. Slade
and us were so English. I remember walking into the Travelodge
in Sunset La Brea, which was seen as a shithole but it had double
beds, twenty-four-hour television and a shower. You didn't get that
in England and this was the bottom chain. We took a view, I'm not
sure whether they did the same, that if we lose it in a few years'
time, which it looked like you were going to, most acts did one way

or another, and you've wasted all your dosh trying to chase that Yankee dollar. There was a certain intimidation by the American confidence in their accent. I married an American subsequently and she always thought the English sound like they're educated when to me, the Americans sounded confident. And I think those things affected both the bands.

'I remember Chas saying that they hadn't cracked it, although the band had been fantastic in concert,' Gered Mankowitz says. 'They'd blown lots of other American acts away. People thought they were absolutely fantastic, but they didn't crack it and I think that was a real sadness to them.'

'It was true of quite a few acts like T. Rex, and Hot Chocolate, who were pretty big at the time,' lyricist and chart historian Tim Rice says. 'And there was no logical reason why they wouldn't have a lot of success in the States. I mean, they had some but some of their latest stuff did better. But I thought they were very good.'

'Trouble was they fell between two stools,' Chris Charlesworth surmises.

Were they a pop band (like a far more competent Bay City Rollers) or a rock band (like the Stones) but who dressed like a novelty/ glitter act? There wasn't a category for them, and Americans liked to categorise acts into AM (pop) or FM (rock), as per radio play. Maybe if they'd dressed in jeans like The Eagles and appeared more serious they'd have made it. Then again, Elton dressed like a novelty act and it didn't hurt him. He managed to bridge the gap but Slade didn't.

However, although it may not have translated into sales at that point, in terms of influence, it was there, and it would be felt in the coming years: 'I spent most of the early seventies listening to *Slade Alive!* thinking to myself, "Wow – this is what I want to do. I want to make that kind of intensity for myself." A couple of years later I found myself at CBGBs doing my best Noddy Holder,' Joey Ramone was later to say.

Slade were also to provide the inspiration for the name of one of the US's most loved art-pop bands. When friends Tom Petersson,

Rick Nielsen and Bun E. Carlos saw Slade live at the Spectrum in Philadelphia in May 1973, Petersson commented that they used 'every cheap trick in the book' during their performance; Rick Nielsen suggested that that was perfect for their group's name. Many years later, Cheap Trick underlined their love for Slade by the inclusion of their version of 'When the Lights Are Out' on their 2009 album *The Latest*. The version had actually been recorded in 1976 and was retrieved from the vaults by their producer Julian Raymond.

'The reason it didn't work in America, apart from the parochialism of Slade, is that they exist in a place where Americans feel really uncomfortable,' Alexis Petridis says, 'which is on the cusp of rock and pop and in America the twain very seldom meets. America has that sort of stick up its arse about "serious rock music" and even the way Elton is seen in America, you go to see him in the States, which I've done a few times, and it's very different from going to see him in Britain, the audience are the kind of people that will also go and see Crosby, Stills & Nash and it's not what it's like when you go and see Elton in England at all.'

Slade's disappearance to the US had cost them in the UK. Ian Edmundson captures it well: 'The thing about Slade being absent was we knew *why* they were absent. It wasn't so much that they hadn't toured because if a band doesn't tour in a year, it's not the end of the world.'

Certainly, at this point, bands like Pink Floyd and Led Zeppelin were increasingly rationing their touring yet, by telling everyone they were going to take the US and then not doing so, for the first time, Slade appeared beleaguered.

*　*　*

Returning from the US, Holder married Leandra Russell in August in Lichfield, with Swin as his best man. The Holders set up a second residence overlooking the Thames at Chelsea, a long way from Gurney Road. 'For a working-class boy, he lived in a very nice flat on Chelsea Embankment,' Chris O'Donnell recalls. 'His neighbours were, of course, Mick and Keith, two lovely boys from Dartford.

I went round there a couple of times. That was a slightly different take on being from the Black Country. We're talking Cheyne Walk.'

The Holders' first daughter, Charisse, was born on 27 December 1976, at Queen Charlotte's Hospital on London's Goldhawk Road. It seemed appropriate she was born in the heart of the festive season. Dave Hill's mother Dorothy was to pass away in her early sixties in 1976, after battling mental illness, leaving Jack, ten years older, a widower. Powell's relationship with Mari Tachikawa ended, and he lived for a while with an air hostess. Thus, would continue a spell of shifting relationships for the drummer – in direct contrast with the other three members of Slade. Jim and Louise Lea retreated to the Staffordshire countryside.

Chas Chandler had founded Barn Records in 1976, as the next logical step from Barn Productions and Barn Publishing. It was named thus after the studio he built in the old barn adjacent to his house in Lingfield. 'Chas made plenty of money but spent it freely,' Chris Charlesworth says.

He wasn't one of those people who accumulated it and kept it, a miser, but he was a bit of a gambler businesswise. It was a gamble for him to send Slade to the US to live in 1975, and it was a gamble he (and they) lost. But they wouldn't have gone unless Chas suggested it. Then again, Chas always told them not to fritter their money away on pointless luxuries – hence their staying in the cheapo Edward Hotel in Paddington when Bolan & co were at the Hilton, and driving around the UK in an old Vauxhall when Bolan & co had a Roller. Chas was like that with studio time too. He made sure they knew a song back to front before going in the studio. There was no wasting studio time rehearsing. He probably learned that from Mickie Most who produced The Animals. 'The House of the Rising Sun' was done in two takes. Then half an hour for the B-side!

Barn Records was launched with the album *Love on My Mind*, and single of the same name by former Parrish & Gurvitz and Badger vocalist and guitarist Brian Parrish. Originally in beat group The Londoners and then The Knack, Parrish had a wealth of experience:

'We were expected to back Brian Parrish,' Terry McCusker says. 'I didn't rate him at all. Chas asked me what I thought of him after our first rehearsal. I said, to be honest, I wouldn't have him in a band in Liverpool. He told me that he'd just spent £12,000 on him. I was out of the band then.' Medicine Head were also signings to the label.

From 1977 to 1979, although still being distributed by Polydor, all Slade releases would be on the Barn imprint.

CHAPTER 25

"Back to The Trumpet for a Drink as If Nothing Had Happened"

The two years since Slade had played live in the UK, punk rock had arrived. While Slade showed a clear lineage in the UK to music that was now emanating from city centres, Dave Hill, Noddy Holder, Jim Lea and Don Powell seemed as old and as remote as the progressive rock bands that were the punks' clearest targets. Had Slade been around Wolverhampton or London in 1976, they could have taken the opportunity to be adopted by punks like their original *TOTP* running mate, Marc Bolan, had been. Bolan toured with The Damned and made himself available to be feted as a forefather by the kids who were early teens when he broke through.

'I don't understand why Slade did not reap the benefits of punk at all,' Alexis Petridis says.

Marc completely gloms onto it, and you cannot be a punk band without Bolan suddenly appearing in the background of the photograph. If you listen to a record like 'Garageland' by The Clash, that song basically sounds like Slade. The drums on it, it's got the descending chords, it's got all these things. All these people in punk were people who had grown up in front of *Top of the Pops* in the early seventies and in many ways, Slade sort of had more to do with it sonically and in terms of attitude than Roxy or Marc does. It just doesn't seem to impact on them at all as a band. It's another aspect of their career I just don't really understand.

Steve Jones's overdriven and multi-tracked guitar in The Sex Pistols singles offered a clear debt of gratitude to Slade's golden run; in fact, Jones was later to say, 'Slade never compromised. We always had the feeling that they were on our side. I don't know but I think we were right.' It could even be said that Johnny Rotten's voice was initially as unconventional as Holder's.

But Slade were somewhere else, doing something else: they had been busy trying to out-top ZZ Top. Recorded in August 1976 at Advision Studios, the group's new album would bring to bear everything that they had learned on the road. As Bob Stanley notes in *Yeah Yeah Yeah*, 'By the time they got home, the scene was greyer, their profile wizened and they called their 1977 album, *Whatever Happened to Slade*. It seemed that nobody knew.'

'By the time they came back, their place had been taken by the Bay City Rollers,' John Steel says. 'They were suddenly the flavour of the month for the kids. Then punk, so they were over the hill.'

* * *

The first new material heard from Slade in nine months came at the end of January 1977.

'Gypsy Roadhog' was a curious choice for a lead single. It typifies the nudge-nudge, wink-wink attitude to drugs prevalent in the music industry in the seventies. A bit naughty, a bit immature. To hear Slade reeling off a list of US cities would have been akin to hear the Allman Brothers singing about Walsall, Leicester and Southampton.

Released as a single on Barn, it scraped into the Top 50, and was featured – bizarrely – on long-running BBC children's television institution, *Blue Peter*. The song's lyrics, mainly about cocaine use were tidied up for the BBC performance at the rumoured request of show editor Biddy Baxter, which was superbly surreal. Introduced by show presenter Lesley Judd, the band mimed the single with

Holder, wearing his *Nobody's Fools* red shirt, army cap and braces look, behind the wheel of a prop car. Lea and Hill stood up on the back seat, while Powell and his drums were on a trailer. Behind them is a moving projection of US landscape. Then, in almost a Brechtian manner to showcase the artifice, the images were turned off and Judd comes out for a talk with them against an enormous green screen. Judd questioned them about their American sojourn and asks if they were all glad to be back in the UK. 'Yes,' Holder replies, 'we got very homesick.' 'We wanted our bacon sandwiches,' Hill pipes up. 'I know the feeling – I like bacon sandwiches as well,' Judd affirms.

It would be difficult to imagine Led Zeppelin having this exchange. They performed the single on *Top of the Pops* as well: 'There's that clip of them on *Top of the Pops*,' Alexis Petridis says. 'Why would anybody want to listen to Slade singing about doing coke in America?'

Its flipside showed the group's American influence clearly – 'Forest Full of Needles' sways hard, and gainfully blasts away for its three and a half minutes, with a strong organ outro. Sadly, there were fewer people bothering to snuffle out these truffles. And when the controversy surrounding its subject matter came to light, it was removed from BBC radio altogether. *NME* stated that the single made 'all the right sounds and even has a toe tapping beat, but it isn't a patch on the rude, offensive and entirely wonderful noise these boys made some four or more years ago. Its careful use of American place name and general blandness could give them that desperately needed American hit, but as far as these isles are concerned, it's just the latest step in their continuing irrelevance.' With punk swamping the cooler end of the media, now was not the time to sound American.

Whatever Happened to Slade was the right album, wrong title and wrong time. The unity and musicianship of the group is at a peak – four players who had been out on the road extensively in the US and learned how to play in lockstep again. Firstly, the title. Chas Chandler allegedly saw it written as graffiti on a wall, and it mirrored what people had been saying to the band in the flesh. Already, it would put the wider audience on the backfoot, because having been titled thus, it would need to do something remarkable to change opinion. Jim Lea, ever the realist, was against the title.

Secondly, the cover. *Whatever Happened to Slade* showed their skinhead selves on billboards, while the older, wiser band looked at their younger images with a degree of amusement; underlining quite how they were there first, and how far they had travelled in six years. Punk? Pah! Gered Mankowitz's photoshoot was straightforward and superb. However, the selection of the skinhead Slade, never a popular commercial choice, as the main image on the sleeve added to the confusion surrounding the record – never was there a time when Slade needed to look like Slade to reinforce their image and underline quite how central they had been. And although the sleeve was clever, the modern-day Slade looking at their younger selves didn't particularly look like Slade. In short, as you browsed through your local record shop, it looked like a cobbled-together collection of early material, just like the Contour compilation of Ambrose Slade in recent years. It all simply served to underline the question posed by its question mark-less title.

'I remember the photo session well,' Gered Mankowitz says. 'The skinhead pictures were added in post-production. Chas had found Rock Street and we did the session there. I did the funny pictures on the back cover. The skinhead pictures aren't mine on the cover. It's amazing now, because they'd only gone away for a year. It felt like forever. And obviously in that time, punk started to break through all those things. So, people were asking whatever happened to Slade, and it was one of those almost self-fulfilling prophecies.' The album's accompanying blurb laid it straight: 'All the songs were written in America, and some of them standout as being obviously inspired by the place and the people. Yet, they've managed to combine acute, detailed observations with a vintage Slade "feel" that has survived ever since 'Get Down and Get With It' days.'

Whatever Happened to Slade is a exceptional album – if you heard it blind it would take a while to appreciate that you were listening to Slade. It had a sheen and unity than makes it among the most consistent of all the Slade albums. With its overlapping guitar parts, and sloppily tight chorus vocals, 'Be' is possibly one of Slade's greatest songs, and 'Big Apple Blues' had a swing to it – that could have easily been better single choices than 'Gypsy Roadhog'. 'My favourite lyric on there is 'Big Apple Blues',' Paul Cookson says. 'I think that's a superb lyric. Things like 'Dogs of Vengeance', I quite like 'Dead Men Tell No Tales', there's a good narrative to that and 'Be' with its tongue-twister, I think that's fantastic.'

Whatever Happened to Slade drifted out on 21 March 1977, the same month as *Trans-Europe Express* by Kraftwerk and *The Idiot* by Iggy Pop. David Bowie had proved his ability to shape-shift with the left turn of his album *Low*, released that January. The world had seemed to turn, and Slade were no longer a part of it. It is ironic that in September 1977, The Stranglers, a band with a mean average age higher than Slade (due in large part to their drummer, Jet Black, being in his late 30s), had an enormous hit with 'No More Heroes', which had the repeated question in its lyrics 'Whatever happened to...'? – a subconscious Nod, perhaps? Of all, Jim Lea was not enamoured by the new kids on the block.

'The trouble is we'd gone cold by *Nobody's Fools* in the UK,' Holder told Mark Blake.

In Europe we hadn't, but we spent so much time in America in that period, we gone cold in the UK so it never got the recognition that it deserved. With the following album, *Whatever Happened to Slade*, we thought we were still coming up with good songs but we weren't fashionable anymore. The punk explosion had taken place and we were considered old farts. When you get to that point, do you knock it on the head or carry on and start again? And we decided to start again. Started in the UK playing smaller theatres and build up a new following because we still had confidence in what we were putting out.

When Slade returned from the USA, their career as a major concern was effectively finished. Not downscaling their touring programme, they began to downsize their venues.

To launch the tour, and to reposition Slade in the UK media, Polydor flew seven selected journalists from the UK rock press over to watch Slade play a show and interview the band at Falkoner Teatret in Copenhagen on 25 April. Tony Stewart from *NME* was one of the writers, and, despite Nick Kent's championing of the band several years earlier, *NME* were now standard bearers for the punk movement, and Stewart's article emphasised the band in decline. 'In a situation like this, the Copenhagen press-relations gig is obviously very important,' Stewart wrote. 'Meaning, it's up to Slade to perform well. Sadly they don't.' Their performance skills that night remained a moot point. It was as if they were targets, whatever was going to happen.

'We had an absolute disaster of a gig in Copenhagen,' Chas Chandler said. 'The band played great but a lot of press had come out and they absolutely nailed them to the floor. They absolutely just tore them to shreds. Literally ruined them overnight in one review.'

As 'Gypsy Roadhog' reached its number forty-eight apex in the singles charts, and their confidence knocked by their press reception, the band embarked on their first full-length tour of the UK since the *Slade in Flame* supporting shows in February 1975. Supported by the group Liar (complete with ex-members of Edison Lighthouse and Egg), who had just released their album *Straight from the Hip* on Decca, the shows – which began on 1 May in Bristol – were as stunning as usual, yet the tour, taking in such stalwart venues as Newcastle City Hall was not completely sold out. The tour also introduced a new look for Dave Hill – as a possible concession to punk or indeed popular TV detective series *Kojak*, he shaved all his hair off and took to wearing huge hoop earrings.

Miles Hunt of The Wonder Stuff, whose uncle Bill was in Wizzard and would go on to write and record with Dave Hill, was taken, as a 10-year-old, to see Slade at Birmingham Hippodrome. The life-changing experience was lovingly written up in his book *The Wonder Stuff Diaries 1986–1989*. On 7 May, Ian Edmundson saw them at Manchester Free Trade Hall. 'They went a bit prog again, although they'd call it American riff rock which influenced them. They went back to showing what they could do. When I saw them at the *Whatever Happened to Slade* tour, I couldn't believe it. They opened with 'Hear Me Calling', but 'Be' was the second song. They were firing on all cylinders and tighter than they'd ever been.

'It was a shock to the system; the visual impact and everything,' Edmundson continues 'The place wasn't full, but they played a great show and that's what counted for me. There was still the crush at the front. I'd seen Thin Lizzy there on the *Jailbreak* tour, I'd seen Queen there on the *Opera* tour. At Slade, there wasn't quite the buzz and you looked behind and you could see the back of the hall wasn't populated, but it was still an incredible night. They put on a killer show.'

'So,' the press release for the album concluded, 'whatever DID happen to Slade? They went, they saw, they came back and now they are going to conquer with this album, which is the most confident, the most musically mature and the Sladest thing they've ever done.'

Slade kept on chasing the elusive hit. The polished AOR of 'Burning in the Heat of Love', and its B-side 'Ready Steady Kids', had been recorded at Advision in March, and was released on 15 April just ahead of the tour. Non-album singles were still common in the later seventies, but it felt as if they were already drawing a line under the album they were supposed to be promoting. And listening to the single, the B-side 'Ready Steady Kids' would have chimed far more with contemporary themes, having a sparky new-wave edge, sounding as if it was the theme song to an edgy ITV punk-inspired tea-time kids show.

For the first time since *Play It Loud* and 'Know Who You Are', *Whatever Happened to Slade* and 'Burning in the Heat of Love' BOTH failed to chart. Although there are many other markers of success, the pop chart in Britain was seen as the only real test of popularity. Because the group's playground had been strictly the Top 5 for so many years, even if it wasn't a bitter pill to swallow, the assumption was that Slade had had their day; especially as groups that had supported them in the past were now enjoying something of an imperial phase in the charts – Status Quo and Thin Lizzy were regulars – Lizzy went as far as being somewhat adopted by punks.

Perhaps it was a case that only a few groups could be allowed in – once again, Slade were on the outside. Of course, the group and Chandler were having absolutely none of it. It was another moment with the backs against the wall to continue doing what they did – the war of attrition was back. One foot soldier who wouldn't be with them was John Steel: 'To be honest, I felt like Chas was losing his way looking for the next thing. Like he almost lost his mojo. I was tiring of big city life and Anne [Steel's wife] and me decided to get out and live a quietly somewhere.' Steel would intermittently reunite with The Animals – in fact that year the group reunited in its original line-up for *Before We Were So Rudely Interrupted*. Later, he has led various incarnations of his group.

A blackly ironic comment on the public standing of Slade was made by some petty thieves on the night of the Queen's Silver Jubilee Bank Holiday, Monday 7 June 1977. Don Powell had gone to see Queen, who the band used to see flogging their wares in Kensington Market in the early days, headline Earls Court. While he was enjoying the show, Powell's car was broken into. He wrote in his diary that night: 'They stole the alarm system and the 8-track player. There were eight tracks in the rack, including two Slade ones. They took eight, and left the Slade ones – talk about a kick in the teeth!'

* * *

Late summer 1977 saw the passing of two artists who had had direct and indirect influence on Slade. On 16 August, Elvis Presley died of a cardiac arrest in Graceland, his home in Memphis that Slade had visited on tour and commemorated in song in 'Far Far Away'. Exactly a month later, Marc Bolan was killed instantly when the Mini his partner Gloria Jones was driving struck a fence post on Barnes Common, south-west London. It was a reverse situation to what had happened to Powell four years earlier. Although Bolan and Slade's relationship had been distant, their ascendancy had ended his superstar phase, just as the Bay City Rollers were to do to Slade, just as The Sex Pistols had done to the Bay City Rollers; and just, of course, as The Beatles had done to Presley.

On 14 October, Slade released a medley of Arthur Crudup's 'My Baby Left Me' and 'That's Alright Mama', the latter Presley's debut single on Sun Records in 1954, as a tribute. Recorded at Advision more or less immediately after his passing, it was a highly effective, high-powered version of two tracks from Presley's pre-RCA era. It seemed strange to hear the group singing a cover again, something that had once been a staple of their act, that had, over time, reduced to just 'Get Down and Get With It'. It was exactly the back-to-basics sound they needed at this juncture, and importantly, it sounded like the group were actually having fun, especially when Holder introduces Hill's guitar solo with the line 'take it, big boy' as a reference to writer Crudup's nickname. What is fascinating, is quite how the sound emulates Dr Feelgood (who had, of course, *not* supported them a couple of times in America) with Lea's churning rhythm playing sounding like Feelgood's influential founder, Wilko Johnson.

The single's flipside, 'OHMS' was an attack on the tax system, which was starting to bite further as revenues began to decrease. It was said that the group owed £350,000 to the government. If 'Taxman' by The Beatles was caustic, this was savage: Holder sings of being bled dry, miles of tax exiles and money files and how rock'n'roll was a prime money-maker for the Inland Revenue. It had all the aggression of punk – and the breakdown suggests an awareness of The Stranglers as the semi-spoken asides are similar in spirit to 'Peaches', which The Stranglers had released that May. The subject matter was not one that would trouble many street urchins, although it was possibly one of the first songs to mention 'dole queue', beating Sham 69's debut single 'I Don't Wanna' by a matter of weeks.

What was also striking about the release was Gered Mankowitz's sleeve photograph – the band are pictured standing against the back wall of Mankowitz's studio in North London, unveiling Dave Hill's completely bald head to the wider world. 'I love that session. That was very consciously influenced by The Beatles in Hamburg,' Mankowitz says. 'You'd see it if you knew it. Putting instruments in the picture was always considered terribly uncool. In the sixties, it was something that everybody wanted to try and get away from. So, we were very much going back. You remember that picture of The Beatles on the cover of Bill Harry's *Mersey Beat* turned into a piece of artwork? Well, that was my influence.'

Mankowitz found their spirit strong: 'That's one of the reasons why I found them so incredibly appealing and attractive. The fact that they never ever lost, or wanted to escape their roots. They loved being Black Country boys and going to The Trumpet. It made no difference to the other people in the pub or to them. I think that was a very appealing aspect of them.'

Whatever Happened to Slade?

Reaching number thirty-two, 'My Baby Left Me'/'That's Alright Mama' returned Slade to the UK Top 40 for the first time since February of the preceding year. It finished Slade's seventies singles chart arc that began six years earlier with 'Get Down and Get With It'. Ironically, seventeen largely glorious Top 40 singles were bookended with rock'n'roll cover versions.

* * *

At the end of October, the group most identified with the UK punk movement, The Sex Pistols, released their first and only original album, *Never Mind the Bollocks, Here's The Sex Pistols.* Its effect was incendiary. Although the original UK punk movement, an arty underground conglomerate of London and Manchester aesthetes that had offered the Pistols, The Clash, and Buzzcocks (whose drummer, John Maher, just over two years earlier had won tickets to see *Slade in Flame*) had either petered out or were going overground, a new strain of groups, loud and rampaging were coming through. Slade's influence could be heard distinctly in this rougher end, that was to become known as the Oi! movement.

Yet Slade were left high and dry; although not the prog-rock dinosaurs the punks despised, just out of step. Popular taste was now consumed with disco, and the rise of soft rock, headed by Fleetwood Mac, another group who were on the scene in the late sixties and early seventies with Slade. Fleetwood Mac had, like Slade, relocated to America to seek their fortune. Unlike Slade, they co-opted two Americans and with their 1977 album, *Rumours,* became one of the very biggest bands in the world. Chas Chandler's ex-partner Robert Stigwood's charges, The Bee Gees, too, had had an enormous wind of change and reinvented themselves as southern soul gentlemen with their *Main Course* album, and were now on their way to writing their era-defining disco hits for the *Saturday Night Fever* soundtrack.

There's a fascinating full stop to Slade's peak period, with Dave Hill returning to *ATV Today* on 15 December 1977, interviewed during the final days of living at his house in Solihull. Lynda Berry talks about how one can achieve 'the good things in life' quickly – suggesting that a bank could be robbed, win the pools or, 'become

260

a successful member of the music industry... which is just how Dave Hill of Slade rock group, managed to attain a large house, Rolls-Royce, and all that goes with it.' Hill said that with success, 'you buy things' and at 'the end of the day, you find you have to keep on working to keep them, because the tax is so heavy.' Berry suggests that Slade were one of the first 'really raw' groups, and they had been described as 'soiled angels'. 'We've always been a boozy band, and never tried to be nicey nicey,' said Hill.

Footage of him and Jan at a local restaurant is priceless.

'What's good tonight?' asks Hill.

The burgundy-jacketed moustached waiter says, 'I can't tell you what you want – you have to choose yourself.'

'What do they call this?' Hill asks, with a smile breaking across his face, demonstrating he'd been an exceptionally good boy. 'Beef bourguignon?' He breaks into a fit of giggles. Jan orders a fillet steak, and Hill adds 'and we'll have a bottle of a la plonk,' again finding it hugely amusing.

'Have a bottle of champagne, then,' the somewhat exasperated waiter replies.

'Ooh arr,' is heard off screen.

The interview with Jan Hill alone, with toddler Jade, is telling. 'He'll be here for a few days, then he goes away for a few weeks, and this is how it goes on... it's very lonely... it's not what it seems.'

'For me, stage is the most important thing – in front of an audience, sweating and raving it up, it's an exciting feeling,' Hill says.

* * *

In *Feel the Noize!*, Chris Charlesworth wrote saliently, 'The two years that followed are remembered with heavy hearts by all but Jim Lea. All maintained a fighting spirit, but it was the youngest member of Slade who appeared to float quite happily through the unrelenting torrent of misfortune.'

Unlike his three comrades, Jim Lea looked on success and its by-product, fame, as inconsequential and relished the challenge of starting again. He told Charlesworth: 'It was a hiatus, but I was never despondent. We were still the same band. We had never disappeared into the ionosphere of stardom. We always had our feet on the ground and life goes on. We just went back to The Trumpet for a drink as if nothing had happened.'

But something had happened – they were no longer making the money they had, and Lea and Holder had to subsidise the band with their songwriting royalties.

Given that this was a low ebb, Dave Kemp came into their orbit. Without his dedication, the group might have completely called it quits at that juncture. Kemp was 17 at the time: 'I bumped into Don in my corner shop on one of their trips back from the States. I happened to be in the corner shop, in the queue and heard this Wolverhampton accent in front of me,' Kemp says. 'It was like – what are you doing here? Don told me that he'd just bought a flat up the road in Hampstead. I lived in West Hampstead, he lived across the Finchley Road near me. I was of the age where I'd started going to pubs and I began to socialise with him. I wasn't just a fan. I was a friend; he had a circle of friends, and I was in it – I didn't want more than just being a friend.' Powell confirms how they met: 'He was in the supermarket and he said, "What are you doing here?" I told him I'd just moved here and that's how we really became friends.'

Intrigued by the fact that he now had a ringside seat to his favourite band, Kemp and his friends were surprised and amazed that they could find out so little about what the group they loved was up to:

> They came back from the States; it was around 1978, when they were playing anywhere and everywhere. The group of fans I knew had no idea where they were playing because the music press wasn't writing about them. I was still at school doing A-levels and Chas Chandler's office was literally opposite my school. I used to know his secretary and she would give me all their dates. I kept telling Chas he needed to reopen their fan club, which had shut a year before. Because there was no money to be made out of it, they weren't big enough to have a professionally organised club any longer. Chas told me that if I wanted a fan club, I should run it myself, and would grant me

the approval. He didn't want the money – not that I was going to make any, I was doing it for the love of running it.

And so, in 1978, the Slade Fan Club rose from the ashes. 'I suddenly got all this information and I'd put it out in newsletters,' Kemp recalled. 'The fans loved it – they could find out where the band were playing and organise going to the shows. I found it quite easy, and I liked it because it cemented me more in with the band.'

Don Powell said in 2017 that Dave Kemp was 'just a really lovely friend. Almost like a brother and it's nice.'

*   *   *

In late January 1978, with the wind in at least three of their hair, Slade returned to Advision to record their next attempt at cracking the singles chart. As most of their big songs were akin to football terrace anthems, so, it was time for them to write their own football terrace anthem. Football and pop were a long way removed from each other at this point, an ongoing marriage which truly began when England teamed up with the ultra-hip New Order in 1990 and recorded 'World in Motion'. Football songs at this point were novelties like 'World Cup Willie' by Lonnie Donegan; emotion-tugging easy-listening singalongs like the England World Cup Squad's 'Back Home' in 1970; or Cockerel Chorus's jokey 'Nice One Cyril', released for the 1973 League Cup adapting Tottenham Hotspur's fan chant (taken from a Wonderloaf TV commercial) for their legendary left-back Cyril Knowles.

Football had made scant impact on 'serious' rock either, although Pink Floyd had used a field recording of the Kop singing 'You'll Never Walk Alone' at the end of their track 'Fearless' in 1971, and in May 1977, Genesis had released the *Spot the Pigeon* EP, with the lead track 'Match of the Day', with the most un-Genesis line in its chorus, 'kick you to death, Ref.'

Slade recognised a gap in the market, like they had with the Christmas song. Aside from Lea, who was an occasional visitor to Wolverhampton Wanderers (unlike season ticket-holder brother Frank), the others were not especially football supporters. Still, that shouldn't stand in the way of making a good record. The first version was recorded at Advision, but the band returned to Olympic to get some of that old 'drums in the corridor' magic. 'Give Us a Goal' is a record destined to split opinion. 'I wrote this tune and Nod said "Let's do one about football because we've always had this football following," I was never really convinced about doing a football song, nevertheless the video was fun,' Lea said in 1991.

The video is not only fun, but also a fascinating snapshot of Britain in the late seventies, with Slade playing at Brighton & Hove Albion's old Goldstone Ground. On 11 February, half an hour before kick-off at the home game against Burnley FC, thanks to Chas Chandler fixing it with his nearest major football club, Slade played the single to the home crowd on a platform in front of the North Stand. Brighton, then in the old Second Division, had had a strong season after being promoted from the Third Division the previous year under their manager, ex-England, Spurs and Fulham player, Alan Mullery.

However, the video demonstrates that the money that began to flood the game after the 1990 World Cup and the formation of the Premier League is nowhere to be seen. Slade's boisterous performance is intercut with footage of the band playing football with Brighton filmed some days previously. The corrugated-iron roof and stanchions of the stand seem so far away from what top tier clubs are used to these days in the wake of the Taylor Report after the Hillsborough tragedy of 1989. The football goers, bald men in car coats and children in wool hats, fill the stand. Being a mile or so in from the English Channel and facing the Downs, it was a very cold wind that was blowing on the group as they recorded the footage; snow is on the ground. Hill, with his shorn head, wore a bobble-hat throughout.

To promote the single, Slade appeared on *Get It Together* with Roy North on 17 March and, a month later, on the second edition of a new series, *Cheggers Plays Pop*. It was produced by Peter Ridsdale-Scott, who booked Slade back in 1969, finally seeing through the *Plays Pop* idea that he'd originally intended for *Monster Music Mash*. Slade were most definitely not the skinheads they'd been, but, if anything, Dave Hill with his bald head and his leathers looked far more menacing. Sadly, the single did not make the Top 50. However, with a theme like that, as the crossover of pop and soccer developed, the record keeps being rediscovered. Whenever there are football TV shows, it is never too long before producers reach for this redoubtable terrace anthem, which has the benefit, unlike 'Merry Xmas Everybody', of being under the radar.

Slade's crisis of confidence is spelled out in these single releases. After the AOR of 'Burning in the Heat of Love', they had veered to the Dr Feelgood rockabilly of 'That's All Right', then the yobbo stomp of 'Give Us a Goal'. The joyous schizophrenia of the flipsides can be heard at this point. If fish weren't biting on the As, it was time to experiment, like with the whoppingly dippy rock of 'Ready Steady Kids', complete with the naughtiness of Slade talking about weed, grass and cigs, dancing jigs, offering another tale of the mythical America they left behind. If 'OHMS' was the group sizing up punk, then 'Daddio', the reverse of 'Give Us a Goal' is overdriven fuzz rockabilly. The band sound like they are having the time of their life combining Mud, Showaddywaddy and Darts, the new rock'n'roll pop chart phenomenon, with John Dummer on drums.

'People had this vision of them being like The Beatles in *A Hard Day's Night* or *Help!* or whichever film was on,' Ian Edmundson says. 'People think that pop stars for some reason aren't ordinary working people. People have this vision of Slade as being this big thing on the telly and they weren't, they were ordinary people. The first time I saw Slade in 1978, they were outside Wigan Casino. They were all sat in the Bentley and Nod's sat in the back picking his nose. They could just about get this Bentley up the narrow alley at the side of the casino and they could hardly open the doors. They managed to open the back door so it opened inside the stage door and got in.'

In July 1978, Chas Chandler bought the IBC Studios at 35 Portland Place in the shadow of the BBC and renamed it Portland Recording Studios. The studios had an illustrious history – it was here that Lonnie Donegan made 'My Old Man's a Dustman', and The Kinks recorded 'You Really Got Me'. Chandler was going through a period of major turbulence. After a dalliance with Lynsey de Paul, he had divorced Lotte and had been living with – and was soon to marry – Miss UK, Madeline Stringer. His belief in Slade was

265

unerring, and enough for the singles to keep coming, but tensions were growing between him and Jim Lea, mainly because Lea now wanted to produce the group himself. Don Powell wrote in his diary on 15 June, the group had a meeting, and after their next single, Chandler would no longer produce any Slade records. It was time to return to the drawing board.

* * *

None of this stopped Chandler from being the talent scout and Svengali. He got himself a bright, new artist for Barn. 'The music business is about fairy tales. I was very young and I had a job, working in an operating theatre at Queen Victoria Hospital in East Grinstead,' singer-songwriter Nick Van Eede says. 'Every Thursday night I'd play The Guinea Pig, the pub next to hospital. I'd play a few covers, and a few of my own. This towering guy in a camel hair coat walks up at the end of the set and gave me his card. He told me to call him Monday morning. I gasped because everybody knew Chas lived in the area. He was visiting his son who was having a minor operation. About three weeks later, I was up at Barn, Chas signed me for management, publishing and recording and I was in Poland on that fourth week with my acoustic guitar supporting Slade in front of about 20,000 people.'

Van Eede had a baptism of fire in going to Bilston for his first rehearsal. 'Swin got in touch with me and told me to get to Birmingham, get a taxi and ask for "The Cunt and Trumpet". I was like, "I know I am a bit innocent, but are you winding me up?" He assured me he wasn't. So, I got into a cab and I just said, "I need to go to Bilston to the Cunt and Trumpet," and the driver said, "Alright, I'll take you there."'

Breathing space was offered to Slade with a lucrative twenty-date tour of Poland. At this time, this was a big step: western bands had played isolated shows in major cities in the satellite states of the Soviet Union, but here, the band were going deep into the country, playing towns such as Bydgoszcz, Sopot and Katowice. There was a spirit of change in the air in the country. The Polish football team had acquitted itself admirably in that year's World Cup in Argentina, and although not progressing beyond the group stage, they had not been humiliated, like Peru, against the other two members of the group, Brazil and the host nation, who would go on to win. More importantly, in 1976 there had been anti-government protests in the country, which united workers and intellectuals for the first time. Lech Wałęsa, who at this time was under government surveillance, sought change through his role in establishing Trade Unions in the Gdańsk shipyards. Although Solidarność was still a few years off, there was an eager youth hungry for change. And Slade came to entertain them. And entertain they did – these were audiences hungry for Western rock. And so just over a month since hospital orderly Nick Van Eede was singing in his local pub, he was now onstage at the 5,000-capacity Opera Leśna in the Polish holiday resort of Sopot, opening for Slade.

'I had no idea, you think you're prepared for anything, of course you're not,' Van Eede recalls. 'I was just a kid and I remember that tour more than anything because it was the first in my life and it was astonishing. Chas had obviously said to the road crew, and to Slade themselves: "Roast him. He needs to grow up a bit within the rock'n'roll world, but maybe don't kill him. Just shy of kill him." The stuff they threw at me. All with a loving Wolverhampton kiss, of course. I used to sit on a stool with my Ovation guitar and my pretty shirt. On the first night, they'd sawn all the legs off. All they wanted was for me to put my arse on it. So I fell, holding my guitar in the air and smashed my bum.'

Mickey Legge was assigned to look after Van Eede. 'He had my back. Mickey was the guitar tuning guy. He would have a room with about four WEM amplifiers all lined up. He'd get hold of Nod's SG and play a big G chord and he would tune the guitar by oscillation. It was all about the strings reverberating against each other. I remember Swin being bemused by me. He was like, "*who the fuck has Chas signed now?*" But never ever hung out to dry. They were always there for you. I saw up close the real hard end of hairy-arsed roadies who had been with Slade probably since they were formed.'

Another night Van Eede got a mild shock from the microphone, and saw JJ there giggling at the side of the stage. 'I knew it was initiation and if I had a strop, then I'll get more. I used to play a ballad. I got lights and everything, the full production. One night I remember playing it, and everybody was crying with laughter in the audience. I looked to the side, I looked down, but what I didn't do is look up. They had these toilet rolls being lowered from the lighting, not two, not four, there must have been over 100. The effort they'd put into that. I think even Jimmy and Nod were on the side, laughing.'

Van Eede was intrigued by the personalities on display: 'Jim was the hardest to get to know, almost my favourite because of that, because when he did open up, he wanted to tell me a bit about writing. Nod was always kind, always supportive, but always busy being the main guy. Dave was the star. Let's just put it like that. None of them ever gave me any shit, not once. Don was the one that I'd sit with for hours and we became friends. I went to his wedding. He told me stuff about the diary that he wrote and about the awful tragedy. So, he let me in, and I'll always thank him for that. I'll always remember buying him a vodka tonic. Of course, he has no sense of taste or smell and then I bought him a tonic once and he said, "Where's the vodka?"'

However, the tour was not all fun and games. On 11 August, the group visited Auschwitz. At this point, with Poland deep behind the Iron Curtain, the camp was far less accessible than it is today. For a band and a crew brought up in the immediate aftermath of war, it was a completely sobering perspective. Powell wrote in his diary: 'George, our interpreter got so drunk, so he wouldn't have to go round. We found out later he lost his family there.'

Not hitting the Top 50 in the UK seemed as trivial as it really is in comparison. 'All of that rock'n'roll bollocks went out the window just like that, that levelled us all and I'll never forget that day,' Van Eede says.

Of course, Western reprobates such as these needed an eye keeping on them: 'There really was a man that was allotted to follow us around and he really did have a newspaper with holes in it,' says Van Eede. 'Nod would go over and say, "Y'alright?" and pull the newspaper down.' Also, because he had more time after his support, Van Eede could watch the band, audience and backstage activity: 'One of their trucks that had all the gear in was being loaded with all this mechanism. I asked the guy what was happening, and he told me that "We can't pay them money, so we give them parts for tractors to sell in Germany on the way home." Because the Polish zloty was a such a weak currency, Massey Ferguson or something paid for Slade.' Sadly, there was also issues of police oppression. As Slade were playing amphitheatres, 'I remember one night there were fountains in front of the stage and if the kids ran down the front, the police would get their nightsticks out and smack them around. That night, the audience got their own back on the police. They put washing-up liquid in the fountains. It was chaos.'

* * *

Returning from Poland, where Slade felt adulation on the scale they hadn't since their spring UK tour of 1974, it was back to five dates they had committed to, a tour of seaside resorts around the August Bank Holiday. Nick Van Eede, having more than passed the test, was asked to support Slade as they hit the road in the UK. The tour opened in Withernsea on 26 August, before moving on to West Runton, Porthcawl and then two nights in Cleethorpes. At Withernsea, Nick Van Eede was hit by a flying bottle aimed squarely at his head.

The show at Porthcawl turned out not quite as they were expecting. The band were playing the Stoneleigh Nightclub on South Road; the converted cinema was a popular nitespot, hosting acts such as Lulu and Bob Monkhouse. The bank holiday audience were ready to party; the bouncers were creating a bad atmosphere by using force to control the crowd. Holder over the mic, said to one, Des Brothers, 'You must be a big boy taking on people half your size.' Brothers replied, 'Call me what you like – I'll see you later.'

Slade had been in many scrapes before, but South Walian security staff at that time could be a force of nature, and Porthcawl, the Valleys equivalent of Blackpool, had seen its fair share of action. After the show, Brothers introduced himself as 'the big boy' before smacking Holder square on the nose, knocking him to the floor. 'I was immediately backstage when Noddy came off. Swin gave me

Noddy's SG and said he couldn't hold it,' Nick Van Eede says. 'I saw the blood. It must have been at the point where he'd literally been whacked by this bouncer. It wasn't just a punch on the nose. He fucking ripped his nose off. It was horrible and it was all very dramatic and upsetting.'

Holder was taken to Bridgend hospital, before being discharged with a broken nose and two black eyes. 'It shook us up a bit,' Van Eede says. 'There are a lot of bands that stoke up that shit and there's a lot of bands that thrive off that, but if there was ever a band that was all about love and singing along, have a few beers. They weren't pretending to be Chekhov or anything. It was all about community.'

In true show-must-go-on fashion, Slade were back on stage at Bunny's in Cleethorpes the following night. Holder with his nose in a splint. The band gave statements at Cleethorpes police station on Wednesday 30. 'By the end of that tour, I even got encores some nights,' Nick Van Eede says, 'not because they thought I was the greatest thing ever. But because Slade fans can be hard – there was a leftover of skins down the front and a lot of gobbing on you – but they had a kind of awkward or maybe grudging respect for me, shall we say?'

On a happier note, 8 September, Holder became a father for the second time, when Leandra gave birth to Jessica, a sister for Charisse. On 14 October, Chas Chandler married Madeline Stringer in Newcastle. 'I remember going to Chas's wedding up in a posh part just north of Newcastle,' Van Eede says. 'I saw Slade out of their stage garb. They were exactly the same. You know, Dave holding court in the corner with twenty people. Jimmy avoiding people; Don chatty.'

* * *

Originally titled 'I've Been Rejected', 'Rock'n'Roll Bolero' – recorded in June at Advision and released in October 1978 – is possibly one of Slade's greatest capers. Professional and expensive-sounding, it is a splendid record, offering a glimpse of a parallel universe where it was Slade not the Electric Light Orchestra (ELO) who were pop's darlings at that current moment. In fact, one of the greatest surprises of the later seventies was just how successful ELO had become. Jeff Lynne from Erdington, fifteen miles south-east of Bilston, had taken his particular journey at the same time as Slade: moving from the much-loved but hitless Idle Race to the later line-up of The Move, and then, with Roy Wood, breaking away to form ELO, a marriage of pop and string-driven classical. By 1977, four years after Wood had left to form Wizzard, Lynne's group had managed to pull off the feat of being popular with both album and singles audiences. The smooth pop-disco-lite of their double album *Out of the Blue* seemed to create hit after hit. It would be easy to see how Jim Lea would have reacted to this – he was playing stringed instruments long before ELO dabbled; perhaps this could be the direction Slade could take. Powell and Lea had both been to see the group that summer in their residency at the Empire Pool in Wembley. Lea was reported as being somewhat underwhelmed.

With its subtle syndrums and lilting disco rhythm, 'Rock'n'Roll Bolero' could have so easily been a hit. It wasn't a simple case of Slade 'going disco' as so many of their peers attempted to do in the late seventies, it was a slick pop/dance crossover, underscored with Lea's fine electric fiddle playing, and its warm homage to both Ravel's 'Bolero' and Dean Parrish's northern soul stomper 'I'm On My Way'. Holder's lyrics about Comancheros heading for a rock'n'roll bolero are the very daftness on which pop has its foundations, a nod to ZZ Top as well as a cheeky 'roll over Bizet'. Jim Lea acknowledged that it was different for the group, but, as he told Dave Kemp, 'Ordinary compared to everything else that was going around at the time... I really dig the record myself.'

The flipside, 'It's Alright Buy Me', while ostensibly another attempt to process the group's American sojourn, is also an affectionate homage to music. Anchored on Lea's 'Friday on My Mind' bassline, it demonstrates that both Slade's playing and writing standards had not dropped. The additional 'u' in the world 'by', pays homage to the old days of misspelt titles as well as underlining the fact that the group would rather people were purchasing more of their output at this point. 'I hated 'Rock'n'Roll Bolero',' Frank Lea says. 'James goes mad when I say it's a crap song. I don't like the production and everything although he was involved in it. I popped by the studio, with my band Slack Alice, and they played that track, and I didn't like it at all. Then they played another track, that was going to be the B-side that was really good, that was more like Slade.'

Sounds were prescient in their review: 'The position that Slade occupy these days in the sad netherworld of pop's wasteland has a reservation or ten already booked for the current TOTPunks in a few years' time.' How true they were. The record might have fared better if it hadn't been released two weeks ahead of *Slade Alive Vol Two*, the release of which seemed to send out a mixed message – while trying to move into the future with their singles, they seemed mired in the past with the live album. As a result, people didn't seem to be drawn to either, and neither made the chart.

The irony was that Slade were ahead of their time with 'Rock'n'Roll Bolero'. In early 1980, the previous year's US smash-hit comedy, *10*, was released in the UK. Starring Dudley Moore, Bo Derek and Julie Andrews, it became a box-office sensation – and the film's use of Ravel's 'Bolero', as mid-life crisis man George Webber (Moore) is seduced by the much younger Jenny Hanley (Derek), introduced many to the sultry orchestral piece. So much so that it was said that Ravel was the top earning composer of 1980, despite his death forty years previously. 'Bolero' fever continued into the mid-eighties, when the music was later adopted by UK ice-dancing darlings Torvill and Dean for their record-breaking 1984 Winter Olympics performance. It seemed to conform to a pattern of the group being too early or too late.

Long-term Slade fan Stu Rutter says it's his 'second favourite single': 'I mentioned that to Jim in a relatively recent chat and he felt the same, he was disappointed it didn't do better. But without the clout of Polydor it would never have happened. Very fond memories of hearing it at several gigs at the time.' David Graham agrees: 'I actually really liked it at the time, and still do now, it was a departure from where they were and, in many ways, a strange single to push out. I saw it performed live a couple of times at the chicken-in-a-basket clubs and at the Music Machine, but it was quickly dropped from the live set, which was a pity. I also like the B-side, 'It's Alright

Buy Me', I thought with both tracks that their writing was back on track.' Nick Van Eede watched it all from close quarters. 'Because I was signed to Barn, I'd get given all their latest stuff. Nothing really changed as far as I'm concerned in their quality. But when you're over, you're over.'

'More Alive Than You'd Believe' the advert led with. It is easy to see the rationale behind releasing *Slade Alive Vol Two*. If it had worked in 1972, showing the world what an amazing live act they were, it could happen again and rescue them from the pop wilderness in which they now found themselves. Released on 27 October 1978, the ten-track album was recorded on the American tour in 1976 and the rescheduled Ipswich Gaumont show from 28 May 1977. Rumours persist that some of the album was recorded in the studio with crowd noise, yet Jim Lea has gone on the record to say that it was all captured in concert. Certainly, with the relative obscurity of most of the tracks on the group's first live album, there was no duplication, and this was the first place you could get many of Slade's biggest numbers, live.

Whether it was overdubbed or not, *Slade Alive Vol Two* packs a fierce punch, and if it had been released after *Slade in Flame* it would have done well in the UK charts. There is certainly evidence that some of the tracks must have been recorded live in the studio with some crowd overdubbing, namely 'My Baby Left Me', the single of which had not been recorded until after the tours had finished that make up the album. However, it's a great vital version, with Holder replacing the 'big boy' introduction of Hill's guitar solo that was on the single with the amusing 'take it, Grasshopper,' a reference to Hill's shaven head being like that of David Carradine's character in the US TV series *Kung Fu*, which had been something of a small-screen sensation throughout the seventies. The version of 'Be' from *Whatever Happened to Slade* is an absolute belter, especially the eight-second extended vocal interplay which shows quite how drilled the group were. Elsewhere, everything is amped up as if to meet the amphetamine charged pace of punk rock. The version of 'Everyday' is quite beautiful, however, capturing Holder in full flow as the crowd's MC, leading the choir. The audience on other tracks is all rather uniform, and the disproportionate cheers to recent album tracks may suggest that there was a degree of post-production. *Slade Alive Vol Two* is not without its charms. It was the final Slade album to be distributed via Polydor. The deal had ended, and Chandler shopped Slade and the Barn catalogue around. Few were interested.

CHAPTER 26

Daydream to Has-Been

For Slade, the autumn 1978 tour really encapsulated the downturn – there was hardly anything that resembled a date sheet of old. Or rather it did – akin to something The 'NBetweens would have played in 1966. A country club in Loxton near Axbridge ('Former Millionaire's Home Now The Night Spot Of The West' as its adverts ran), a leisure centre near Warrington, clubs and polytechnics. Nick Van Eede was their ever-reliable support, even though his releases on Barn – singles 'Rock'n'Roll Fool' and the soon-to-be-released 'I Only Want to Be Number One' – had yet to shift the required units or pre-orders.

'I met John Steel when I made 'Rock'n'Roll Fool'. Chas got Johnny in to play the drums, because he was doing a bit of decorating at that point,' Nick Van Eede says. 'John is the nicest man on the planet and Mike Hugg from Manfred Mann produced. Chas basically recorded about seven or eight songs and they released three singles. Andy Miller looked after me when I was making my records with Chas. He told me that Chas would light the biggest spliff this side of Kingston and begin to mix. It would be more bass drum, more… and then it would get to the top and he'd go "Oh fuck" and they'd give him a ruler and he'd pull all the faders down and start again.'

Van Eede could sense all maybe wasn't as well as it once was:

Chas's empire was beginning to wane because it was such a huge empire. If you ever went into Portland Place, for a 'nobody' like me to be signed, not just to a very famous manager, have a record deal and a publishing deal for the first time, but to go into this four-storey building just off Regent Street, where they had their own cutting room with George 'Porky Prime Cuts' Peckham in the basement. We had the management and the beautiful studio. That's the one area I did get the vibe from was the band. I would be invited up maybe just to sit in when Slade were making a record, just because I was Nick and I was not a VIP and they're not going to kick me out. I could see that Jim was in charge, very much to the fore. In the production of the records, it didn't feel the same any more.

If times were that low, between the four members of Slade it was very much business as usual. Dave Kemp recalls: 'They weren't confiding in me, but you could just tell – they didn't want to mention it, but they always thought the next single would do better, but I think they knew in their heart of hearts that the skids were on.' According to Kemp, it was at this time Noddy Holder christened the Slade hardcore the 'magic 500'.

'It didn't matter where Slade played, either pubs, small clubs or universities – it always seemed that 500 people always turned up,' Dave Kemp says. The crew were still very much in effect: Swin would drive them to their cabaret shows. 'Nod and Don didn't mind the cabaret shows but Jim and Dave hated them, and they travelled separately, the former pair in what became known as the Happy Car, the latter two in the Hospital Car. Swin insisted on driving the Happy Car,' recalls Chris Charlesworth.

'We were still drawing,' Holder told Charlesworth. 'We used to pull 500 people in clubs… We'd sell out 1,000 tickets in two hours at universities as soon as our name was announced. That kept us afloat. It was the only way we could keep going.'

'If people liked the stuff, we still had a shot,' Hill said in 1986. 'We lived on the merit of the performance.' The 500 would instruct the newcomers how to behave at a Slade show. Nick Van Eede saw a band in good spirits with a challenge on their hands: 'They still had that massive sound, they still did exactly the same show. I was lucky enough to be able to sit in the dressing room with them some nights, so I would have spotted if they were not a happy bunch. But yeah, it was all right.'

It really was like the old days. Slade went back to Keith Altham, where a young press officer, Chris Carr, was getting his first significant break. 'They were good times, fun times, hard times,' he says. 'They had come back from America and punk was three-quarters full swing... So, it's at a period when they were pretty exhausted and just did not know where to go next. Don was still in recovery. It was like scraping the barrel. They were putting out things through Barn and they were in the studio just off Regent Street and I think there was desperation that Chas hadn't really moved on.'

Given this enormous reversal in fortunes, Dave Kemp struggled to see any fissures within the band. 'They were watertight. They had four different personalities, and they didn't necessarily socialise with each other – in the late seventies you had Jim and Dave who still lived in Wolverhampton; and you had Don and Nod in London. Don and Nod would meet up, but they didn't really socialise together. It was still that mentality that was forged all the way back in the Bahamas.'

Slade played the Music Machine in Camden at the end of October 1978, watched by many on the punk scene – members of The Damned and Generation X were in the crowd. So, too, was comedian and writer Bob Mills, who went under some duress, and remembers it as one of the best shows he ever attended. 'Slade already make Sham 69 look extremely silly,' Harry George wrote in *Melody Maker*. 'With a hit single and album they'd leave most mainstream rockers so far down the field you'd have to pump air into 'em.'

There was interest in Slade. In a way, they had moved underground again, and were for the first time since Ambrose Slade, a cult. At the end of 1978, The Runaways, the controversial US all-girl rockers that had been championed by Kim Fowley in 1976, released their final album *And Now... The Runaways*. One of its standout tracks was a cover of 'Mama Weer All Crazee Now', with Joan Jett in full throat. There were also the students to play to – who had been junior noizefeelers when Slade were in their pomp. 'University gigs worked, actually, because it was scruffy and divey. It was loud, kids, fun, beer in hand. It kind of came back to that thing which would have been like them playing The Robin,' Nick Van Eede recalls.

There was one show that stood out, and sent out a calling card that suggested they should not be written off. Mel Bush booked them onto the Great British Music Experience, an indoor festival at Wembley Arena, as the old Empire Pool had recently been re-christened. Slade found themselves on a bill with The Jam and Generation X. Again, like they had done before and would do again, the group had to go out and prove themselves. It provoked contrasting views. Frank Lea said: 'There were all these punky types on, and then, there was Slade. It was a strange thing. I could see they were working hard. It was good down the front, but the crowd were restless towards the middle and I nearly got into a fight, as people weren't into it. That's what they were up against'. The band shared their surprise and displeasure with Mel Bush in the dressing room afterwards for their brave but mismatched addition to the bill. 'Paul Weller told me later he hated that gig, too,' Frank Lea continues. 'It was a good idea that didn't quite come off the way it should have done.'

Yet punky type Gary Crowley, now making his way as a DJ, was in the audience: 'I thought they were fantastic. Me and my pals at the time were all punks and mods. We all would have been about 10 or 11 when Slade first exploded, so we all knew and loved the songs. They went down fantastically well. They really did 'mack schau!' as the Germans used to demand. They had it down pat; they'd been doing it for years and really knew how to get the crowd going. Even though they were out of step with the crowd, they were still cutting through, they were still resonating.'

'I saw them at Christmas parties, I'd met them,' Chris Carr says. 'You got that sense of a fractured thing; Don was still on his way back to health. They were recording and at the recording sessions I saw, it was all intense, but there was this, like, dislocation, "Where do we fit in with all this?"'

1979 began with Don Powell being banned from driving for a year and fined £120 for a drink driving offence at Hampstead magistrates' court. 'I tried to use the fact I can't smell or taste, and someone had

Even though posed on the set of *Slade In Flame* in summer 1974, it is impossible to think of another band at such a level of superstardom that would be pictured by a pigeon loft. MIRRORPIX

The US going crazee. To a point. Like Alun Owen had done a decade before with The Beatles, writer Andrew Birkin went on tour with Slade in order to inform his script for *Slade In Flame*. This photograph captures the rapture the group experienced. ANDREW BIRKIN

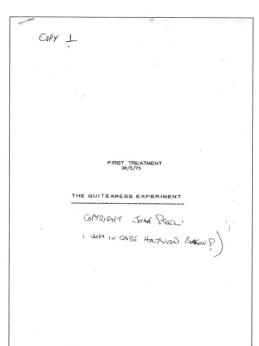

COPY 1

FIRST TREATMENT
28/5/75

THE QUITEAMESS EXPERIMENT

COPYRIGHT JOHN STEEL.
(JUST IN CASE HOLLYWOOD BECKONS)

The title page of John Steel's fabled *The Quiteamess Experiment*, briefly considered for Slade's feature film. 'Chas and I did quite a lot of waccy baccy back then. Don't take it too seriously, nobody else did, least of all me,' Steel says today. JOHN STEEL

With driver Jimmy McDonald, the group arrive on a horse-drawn hearse at the Glasgow premiere for *Slade In Flame*, 10 March 1975. It seemed a bizarre stunt, not unlike one the fictional Flame would have been made to perform themselves. MIRRORPIX

Sailing into New York – the group's home for a year – on Independence Day, 1975, as the group began their year based in the US, their final, most concentrated effort to 'break the states'. MIRRORPIX

1977: As glam and glitter receded, and punk exploded, Dave Hill responded by shaving his head, leading to Holder's *Kojak* and *Kung Fu* gags. The hits may have dried up, but the spirit certainly hadn't. ALAMY

'The magic 500' are roistering as Slade play a homecoming gig at Wolverhampton Civic in October 1979. The joy of performing live couldn't be made clearer than by Hill's expression. IAN EDMUNDSON

Slade at the Reading Festival, Sunday 24 August 1980. A week prior, the group were considering calling it a day. The mood went 'from apathy . . . to mild astonishment,' writer Dave Ling recalls. 'By the halfway mark, euphoria had set in.' BARRY PLUMMER

The comeback kings leave the stage. The element of surprise and the intensity of the entertainment had the Reading audience in Slade's thrall within minutes. BARRY PLUMMER

Acceptable in the 80s: The group receive a 'singing telegram' at the launch of *Rogues Gallery* at The Trumpet in March 1985. Liz Lenten worked for the Songbird Agency: 'I went on my own – before mobile phones and the internet, you'd just be given an address, a time to be there and whatever costume – and off I went.' MIRRORPIX/GETTY

For some, *Crackers* will always be hard to swallow, but it is a fine example of a seasoned act having fun. Bagpipe player Victor Herman appeared on the album and was guest of honour at its launch party in 1985. BARRY PLUMMER

Slade with Betty Edwards, the tea lady and receptionist at Wessex Sound Studios, who said, 'You boys make big noise', which was Slade-ified for the title of the group's final studio album. Edwards was also part of the team who stomped and clapped on Queen's 'We Will Rock You' a decade earlier. BARRY PLUMMER

On stage, April 1991 at Walsall Town Hall. The group's performance of 'Johnny B. Goode' was the last song the original group played live together. 'Nod had been made to do something that he didn't want to do, using unfamiliar gear and the sound was awful,' Ian Edmundson, who took the photo, recalls. IAN EDMUNDSON

The sincerest form of flattery. Slady, captured backstage at Punk on the Peninsula, Dunoon, May 2023. L-R Jem Lea (Wendy Solomon), Davina Hill (Dawn Firth-Godbehere), Donna Powell (Jess Dann) and Gobby Holder (Danie Cox). ALAN DOYLE

Rhythm section reunited. Don Powell and Jim Lea with the author, August 2022, Wolverhampton Art Gallery. WOLVERHAMPTON ART GALLERY

been "topping" my glass up,' Powell wrote in his diary. 'IT DIDN'T WORK... So, I spent the day in the Prince of Wales pub (in West Hampstead) as I didn't have the driving problem anymore. Don't know what time I got home.' Powell's drinking was going off the scale. Obviously, a coping mechanism for dealing with his accident, he would drink heavily, and the group was worried.

'The thing is, I had that discipline. I never drank when I went on stage but as soon as I'd come off I'd go for it,' Powell says. What is worse was that he wouldn't get a hangover. 'It got to the point where no one would drink with me because they couldn't keep up or they felt like shit the following morning and I was OK.'

* * *

Slade hadn't quite descended to the working men's clubs that Holder referenced on stage at the New Victoria Theatre in 1975, but the Bailey's Nightclub chain, the Rank Organisation's cabaret venue wing, came close. In late 1978, the group played three week-long residences at the Bailey's in Blackburn, Watford and Leicester, where a ticket could be bought, inclusive of meal. 'All I could see was these little purple lamps and people eating chicken in a basket,' support Van Eede says.

Again, it was another challenge for the band; here was an audience who would visit out of loyalty to the nitespot, as much to watch the act. It was an audience just waiting to be won over. As Jim Lea said, 'We're not trying to be The Three Degrees.' That they weren't. Van Eede witnessed it all: 'It was almost surreal to watch them ripping through their songs again at a billion decibels because back then I don't think they had limiters on sounds. Just people's faces pinned back.' Of course, complaints came in the form of the noise and suitability of the band to such a venue, but for many this would be the first time they had witnessed rock music. The novelty was so great that Bailey's rebooked the group in early 1979.

'We were offered to come back to do these Bailey's clubs,' Lea told Dave Kemp in 1979. 'We didn't want to do them in the first place, but we've returned and drawn twice as many people than the first time we appeared here. Playing here for a week, in Watford alone, means we are going to play to 14,000 people. Whereas if we did a one-nighter at the college we would only play to 1,000 even if it was sold out.'

In 1979, the group seemed resigned to their fate, yet not once did they consider throwing in the towel. The year began with three further weeks at Bailey's. Steve Clarke at *NME* saw the group playing at the Watford club in March 1979 and wrote: 'The Bailey's audience wasn't exactly bristling with life, but for all the band seemed to care, they could have been bill-topping at Earls Court.' Earls Court was not yet six years in the rear-view mirror. On 15 February, the group began a residency at the Cavendish nitespot in Blackburn, Lancashire. 'We played the difficult gigs, the gigs where people have chicken in a basket and then go on the dancefloor,' Hill recalled in 2021. 'People might say: "Oh dear, that's a big decline," but we had an armoury of fantastic songs so nobody was going to argue with us. We managed to survive that.'

Keith Altham was cooking up idea for them. The one music paper that remained somewhat onside was the poppier *Record Mirror*. A competition was hatched to meet the group, with editor Alf Martin in tow. A couple from Scotland, Mike McKillop and Linda McIvor, keen Slade fans, who were going to get married, were chosen. The furthest that Altham and *Record Mirror* could afford was to bring them to Bradford, where Slade were playing the university. So, on 7 March, Martin and Chris Carr travelled up there.

'We met at this motel that everybody was staying at, the band included,' Chris Carr says. 'Because they were going to get married, they were in separate rooms. We go to the bar and then, to the gig, and everything and meet the band beforehand. Then afterwards, we go to a Bradford curry house and they all want curry, but with chips not rice and tomato sauce. They have to send sent a waiter out to go and get tomato sauce. By the time we get back to the hotel, an argument had broken out and the wedding was over. Having to put a band that you have a certain amount of respect for into a situation like that was funny.'

Bob Geldof encountered the group on their German tour of March 1979. 'I met Slade when they hadn't had a hit for a while,' he says.

We were just reaching our peak in The Boomtown Rats and were playing the big arena, and they were in a small club and we were all in the same hotel. I was genuinely intrigued by how a band of that size could be playing a venue like that, as if to get some tips of what could happen to me in the future. I certainly wasn't being snitty. We had a great talk – it was a case of, well, we could go back to Wolverhampton and get a job on the buses, and take home £40, or pack out a club over here, get £2,000 and as much beer as we want, transport and people cheering for you. There was no contest, really.

The meeting resonated with Lea and Holder who knew it was wholly possible that the Rats could well experience similar.

On 2 May, Graham Swinnerton, the group's much-loved road manager, married Debbie in Wolverhampton. All of the band were in attendance and Holder was best man.

* * *

Chas Chandler was struggling to keep Barn and Portland Studios afloat. 'When Chas had his own record label, he was out of his depth, he didn't understand the workings of it,' Frank Lea says. 'I used to call it Bomb Records. I don't think he had any radio play.'

Don Powell's diary provided insight to the life of the band. For example, on 17 May 1979, Powell went to see the cult John Landis comedy *Kentucky Fried Movie*, then 'had a meeting at Nod's place in Chelsea – BARN HAD GONE BUST !!!' Chas Chandler's dream was simply not to be. Lea and Holder bought out his stake in Slade's catalogue, and formed Whild John Music Ltd. The Barn imprint continued for a while longer, and Chandler continued to work out of Portland Place.

'I met Chas Chandler once,' Gary Crowley recalls. 'Barn used to be in the same building as IBC voiceover studios. I would do the voiceovers for these cool punky TV compilations. Chas came in and said hello to me, which I was absolutely thrilled about.'

Later in May, the first fruits of the next set of recordings were heard. Released at the end of the month and trying out the current and collectible fad of coloured vinyl, 'Ginny Ginny' was the latest Lea and Holder offering that the group were optimistic about, and the first to be handled by Pinnacle distribution, effectively making Slade an 'indie band'. Quietly, after *Slade Alive Vol Two*, the Philips/Polydor deal had lapsed. This in some ways meant that the record would not be as easily distributed as when the group were on a major label; not necessarily an issue with the speed on the distribution, it was a matter that record shops would be on the phone to the major labels more often, while 'indies' would require a minimum order, which may have meant they may only be spoken to weekly, or less. Availability seemed to be an issue, which led to Barn's director, Mike Hales, contacting Dave Kemp at the fan club with a message to print:

> A number of you have contacted me about difficulty in obtaining 'Ginny Ginny' (Barn 002) from record shops. The record is readily available from our distribution company Pinnacle in Orpington, Kent, so if you have a problem obtaining the single please insist that the dealer orders it from Pinnacle on 0689-73141. Don't call that number yourself because it is a number for record dealers only, and you might block the lines and stop a dealer getting through. You can help us tremendously by writing to radio stations and seeking a request. Why not write to Radio One and your local commercial station today? As I write 'Ginny Ginny' has entered the 200 Best Sellers Chart, so I hope that as you read this that the single is much higher, where Slade belong.

'Ginny Ginny' at least it sounded like a Slade record, with an anthemic pop chorus. 'It's very catchy, and we're going to make it, yeah. Our writing is returning to a more concise format,' Lea told the fan club. The flipside 'Dizzy Mama' was an utter return to base – stomping rock, somewhere on an axis between heavy metal and punk, a large nod toward the group's rock'n'roll heroes, with Holder going the full Robert Plant/Elvis Presley in the break. It's little wonder it went on to open the group's live set, as it is undoubtedly the most exciting the group had sounded on record since 1973. However, despite the group's pleas, and with some support from

Radio One, the record failed to chart. *Melody Maker* told it as it was: 'Slade's record comes on piss yellow vinyl: the drive's still there, but not the sense of direction.'

'Dizzy Mama' could have fitted in easily with another style of music that was arriving, from the white working-class areas of East London such as Canning Town. Slade's DNA was all over this rougher, tougher no-holds-barred music where the violence and allegiance to football was real, not theatrical. Oi!, a termed coined by journalist Garry Bushell, was headed by the Cockney Rejects, whose music began where the rowdier end of Slade's music ended.

\ * * *

One thing that did go in Slade's favour in the dog days of 1979 was at the court hearing for the incident at the Stoneleigh Nightclub in Porthcawl the previous August. At Cardiff Crown Court on 1 July 1979, bouncer Des Brothers was charged with inflicting grievous bodily harm on Noddy Holder and served three months in prison. Handing down the verdict, Judge Michael Gibbon said: 'No doubt you have your good qualities, but you have your bad ones too.' After his release, Brothers returned to work at the club, and would soon find himself the inspiration for a future Slade song.

Slade had spent eleven days in the studio in 1979, the result of which, *Return to Base*, became Slade's eighth album. Released in October on Barn through Pinnacle, it is not without its moments. 'Sign of the Times' – the album's de facto title track – is an exceptionally powerful ballad, again showing again that Slade could have been ELO. With a contemporary referencing lyric (computers, space travel, and one of the few songs to mention both UK magazines, the *TV* and *Radio Times*), it manages to encompass many styles and tempos, and, in doing so, arguably invented Oasis. It was released as a single on Barn just ahead of the album in October 1979, backed with the jaunty 'Not Tonight Josephine'.

'I'm a Rocker' highlights this schizophrenia – in case you were worried we'd gone too far away from our core sound, here's a dirty obvious cover. But then, that said, like 'Get Down and Get With It' from almost a decade earlier, Holder had to do some research to

283

find the original, which seems so thoroughly strange in this current Spotify and YouTube world. The original was a later-period Chuck Berry track from his 1970 album, *Back Home*. 'There's nothing wrong with *Return to Base*,' Ian Edmundson says. 'It was Slade trying a number of new things, writing with different approaches, like 'Chakeeta', where did that come from? That's not like a Slade song is it?'

'Wheels Ain't Coming Down' is strident, pulsing rock – not a million miles remove from the commercial turn Ritchie Blackmore's Rainbow had taken. 'Lemme Love Into Ya' is, however, quite astonishing, and hearing it for the first time, its introduction is akin to stumbling across a Siouxsie and the Banshees track or something by The Cure. Dave Hill's overdriven guitar and Lea's thick, double-tracked, echoing bass make it sound like a strange Roma folk ballad. Lea wouldn't let this song lie, adapting it later as 'Poland', and releasing under the pseudonym Greenfields of Tong.

'They were trying all this different stuff and they were a band who didn't know who they were any more,' Edmundson continues. 'They didn't know what was going to work. It's a band who's floundering, but they're coming up with great stuff. But they can't get radio to take them, the press hate them. The press really hated Slade at that time.'

That was largely true; there was a sense of desperation over at the PR company: 'Keith Altham just said at one point, "For fuck's sake Chris, call up London Zoo and see if you can hire two armadillos with collars and take them down for a photo opportunity for Slade in Bond Street,"' junior PR Chris Carr says.

> I was like, 'What are you talking about Keith?' and he said, 'You know, we've got to get them something. This is PR, this is the way Les Perrin would have done it.' I was like, 'Who's gonna be interested?' I think it was to make sure they continued to pay the invoices, but it was also part of the media circus at the time, so all sorts of plots were hatched. Keith was out of kilter. The *NME* was at its peak, *Smash Hits* was only just started. I just looked at him and thought, 'You're fucking mad. I'm not going to do that to them and I'm not going to do it to you.' I did what I could.

Nevertheless, the gigs just kept coming, the 1979 tour sheet was as packed as one would expect and to the outside world there were no signs that the band were feeling the pressure. 'They've got a showbiz attitude,' Ian Edmundson says. 'If you listen to a Dave Hill interview, he's very showbiz, positive and there's no cracks, the wheels aren't falling off the bus. Basically, they always had a united front, that was the great thing about them. You never knew that they thought they'd gone down the pan and that they were disappointed that the new record hadn't charted.'

Kevin 'Billy' Adams, two years off joining Dexys Midnight Runners, said 'I didn't catch them live until 1979. A few of us went along to see them at Barbarella's in Birmingham including at least a couple of the guys from Dexys. Kevin [Rowland] and [Big] Jimmy [Paterson] were there. I finally got to see them live. People were yelling for 'Merry Xmas Everybody' through the set and Noddy kind of made a joke of it, then relented and they played it anyway, even though it was October.'

Chandler suggested that Holder and Lea should consider going it alone, but they resisted. It was – as it had been for the past decade and a half – all or nothing. The very suggestion shocked Holder, the band were more important than their manager, no matter how important he was. Though the relationship was tested somewhat over the release of their next single. In time for Christmas 1979, the group released their most contentious single: a rocked-up version of the party standard, 'Hokey Cokey' (spelt 'Okey Cokey'). It was something of a nadir for the band. It was one thing trying different styles to regain a toehold in the chart, but a song seemingly as vulgar as this, no matter how well it may go down live, will never do wonders for credibility.

'I don't know what it must have been like to have that ability that Noddy and Jim had for years, when everything you write is just "Wow!", it's gonna hit,' Alexis Petridis says. 'And then, suddenly you don't even know what the fuck you're doing. It's like somebody banging the top of the telly trying to get the picture back and it's not working.'

'"Okey Cokey'?' Stu Rutter says, 'there's just no excuse for it no matter how desperate they were. Embarrassing for the fans who were left by then. Thankfully the gigs of the time were still brilliant.' However, there was a deeper reason for the record: Noddy Holder told Selby and Edmundson that the original intention was that it would be an extra track on a Polydor re-release of 'Merry Xmas Everybody' but as there was a delay in recording, when it was finally captured at Portland Place it was too late for inclusion. Chas Chandler heard it and thought it would make a perfect festive counterpart to 'Merry Xmas Everybody'.

There was some talk of the single being released through RSO, Robert Stigwood's label, which was now one of the most successful labels in the world thanks to The Bee Gees, *Saturday Night Fever* and *Grease*. Some copies were pressed, but the single came out at the start of December on Barn. The record itself? It's exactly like Slade doing a version of the 'Hokey Cokey'. Where it *was* reviewed, *Record Mirror* wrote the most amusingly: 'Yes, it's that one. Don't laugh; one day The Clash may be old men, singing beer drinking songs on MFP. Let's hope not.' That Christmas, The Clash were at their pinnacle of being the critics' darlings with the release of their *London Calling* album.

* * *

As a way of dealing with the downturn, the ever-inventive Jim and Frank Lea formed Cheapskate Records in an attempt to see whether they could achieve more airplay than they did as Slade. 'I did it on Mum and Dad's lounge floor,' Frank Lea says. 'Because I was on the dole, I was waiting for James to come back because I had all these ideas.'

Forming the mysterious, studio-based The Dummies, the brothers' aim was to make a series of records which chimed in a post-punky/ light-metal manner. It had been a long-planned venture, but the opportunity to record hadn't been there. 'My brother was blagging me into it,' Jim Lea says. 'He's still got tapes of me and him playing. Sounded like three bands at once. We had two singles on Radio Luxembourg and Record of the Week on Radio One. The next one was Simon Bates's Record of the Week.'

Their first release was a cover of Slade's 'When the Lights Are Out', the hit single his parent group never had. It sounded not unlike that year's new-wave breakthrough act, Squeeze, and though it had plenty of airplay with its chirpy, upbeat take on the *Old New Borrowed and Blue* track, The Dummies couldn't chart either. Cheapskate would also provide a home for various Slade releases over the coming years when the group were in-between labels.

Cutting engineer Phil Kinrade, a lifelong fan, was in hospital in December 1979 at St Barts in London's Smithfield. Recovering from an operation, lying in bed, he kept thinking he could hear Slade playing in the distance. Worried, perhaps, that he may be hallucinating, Kinrade asked a nurse if he could hear Slade. It transpired the band were playing the hospital's Christmas party.

* * *

1980 was to prove as pivotal for Slade as any year from the group's high period. Few could have foreseen how Slade would finish the year. At the start of it, it really was beginning to look as if they were washed up. Slade had undoubtedly influenced punk and post-punk, but were outcasts. It is impossible to hear the bravura riffs of Steve Jones on The Sex Pistols hits and not be reminded of Dave Hill. Later, Skids (and later still, Big Country) were enormous, stomping versions of the Slade brand. But the group themselves simply could not get arrested. Without a significant record deal, Slade were effectively an indie band, and on 2 May, they formed their own company Perseverance Ltd, taking the name off the shelf (Top Knot Limited was also available), which would be cheaper than creating your own. ('The company costs about £250, and we're not paying £250 for anything,' Lea said in 1986.) Hill, Holder, Lea and Powell were listed as directors. They felt that it was a most appropriate name for the group, especially given the previous three years.

Record Mirror's Mike Gardiner wrote in October 1979, that it was 'time for a re-evaluation of Slade and it might as well start with you. I advise you to come on and feel the noise soon.' But that was not shared with the mainstream. Worse still, it seemed as if the band were being written out of history. Even their old record label, Polydor, were experiencing collective amnesia as the new decade got underway. In March 1980, 'Going Underground'/'Dreams of

Children' by The Jam, the Woking-based power-trio who had been forged in punk's crucible, yet owed a far bigger debt to the sixties, went straight into the charts at number one. It was the first time anyone had achieved that since 'Merry Xmas Everybody' in 1973.

'It really pissed the band off when The Jam came out and 'Going Underground' went straight in at number one on the singles charts,' Dave Kemp recalled. 'Polydor were saying that it was the first time it had happened since The Beatles. Slade were on the same label and actually did it three times in a year; it's now seven years later and they just didn't know.'

Raucous Australian group AC/DC lost Bon Scott, their singer in February 1980. It has been said over the years that Noddy Holder was suggested as a frontrunner for his replacement, something Holder was asked in 2000 by Andrew Darlington: 'Yes. It is true. I was approached. AC/DC did offer me the job, and I turned it down – so they went and got the guy from the band Geordie, Brian Johnson, who sounded exactly like me anyway.' Geordie, who the *Liverpool Echo* once described as 'a poor man's Slade', supported Slade at the Palladium show back in January 1973. 'I had the pleasure of meeting Noddy Holder, who couldn't have been friendlier,' Brian Johnson wrote in his autobiography, *The Lives of Brian*.

'That's a tough one because there's so many names that are bandied around,' Jerry Ewing, who has written two books on AC/DC, says. 'I've never heard anything official. I wouldn't be in the least bit surprised if it was true. It works in my head.'

'When AC/DC had Bon Scott, the twinkle in his eye suggested that "This is probably the best thing you'll ever see in your life," and it's so good,' ex-Beta Band frontman and huge Slade fan Steve Mason says. 'He was letting you know that he knew that this was really fucking special. Slade had that too. Noddy is an amazing soul singer. Britain doesn't produce too many white male guys that can sing like that. Obviously, Eric Burdon, Van Morrison, the ones that just pop into your head, but Noddy should definitely be up there and I don't know why he isn't.'

In May 1980, Slade released an EP, their first release since 'Okey Cokey' the previous December. Released on the short-lived Barn offshoot label Six of the Best (that also boasted Maidstone new wavers En Route and Poundland Ian Dury Arrogant Adams) the *Six of the Best* EP was available as a 12-inch single, six tracks for £1.49 – one side was the rock side, and one the 'back side'. Three tracks from *Return to Base* – 'I'm a Rocka' (*sic*), 'Don't Waste Your Time' and 'Wheels Ain't Coming Down', were supplemented by '9 to 5', 'When I'm Dancin' I Ain't Fightin'' and lead track, 'Night Starvation'. Long-term fan Stu Rutter suggests that here 'Nod's lyrics are like a rejected Benny Hill script.' It's certainly a long way away from 'Coz I Luv You'. The sleeve – an explosion in a Letraset factory – looked very indie, almost underground. The record came and went without a trace.

The prolonged lack of success was all taking its toll on Dave Hill. Without Don Powell's cheery optimism, and Noddy Holder and Jim Lea's publishing income stream, the guitarist had had enough. Hill had left the house in Solihull and moved to a farm in Albrighton in early 1978, but that didn't work out either. In 1980, he and Jan, with their young daughter Jade, left Albrighton and moved to Penn, much nearer Jan's family in Wolverhampton. Looking to make ends meet, Hill decided to put his most ostentatious purchase to tremendous use. He could use his Radford Convertible Rolls-Royce Silver Cloud with the YOB 1 number plate to start a business where he would be a wedding chauffeur – hire a rock star for the day.

For the first time since they had formed, as the June tour to support the *Six of the Best* EP concluded at the West Runton Pavilion, they had no further shows planned. As Selby and Edmundson note, 'At the end of the tour, they all went their separate ways and took a break from each other. No forward plans were made for Slade to re-group and work together again.' 'I think it finally dawned on them, they could have just gone "Look here, just stop,"' Nick Van Eede says. 'But… they had their renaissance.'

CHAPTER 27

Nostalgia Mixed with Power – The Reading Festival, August 1980

Established in 1971, the roots of the Reading Festival can be traced back to the Beaulieu Jazz Festival in the fifties. In the sixties it became the National Jazz & Blues Festival, first at Windsor, then at Plumpton near Lewes, and finally at Reading. After going through a prog phase and flirting with new wave, by the late seventies it had effectively become a heavy metal festival. In 1980, its headliners were David Coverdale's Whitesnake, UFO and Rory Gallagher. Heavy metal had received a new lease of life through NWOBHM (New Wave of British Heavy Metal), hard rock that adopted the punk do-it-yourself ethos of bands releasing singles on small labels and working their way up through clubs. Def Leppard and Iron Maiden represented the newcomers. Hotly tipped for the festival weekend was ex-Black Sabbath frontman Ozzy Osbourne – an old West Midlands running mate of Slade – introducing his new band Blizzard of Ozz. However, the news began to spread around the festival site that Osbourne was unwell, and that Slade were going to replace him. But not everyone was aware.

There very nearly wasn't a Slade at all. Dave Hill's wedding car business was taking off, and, although unannounced, it was wholly possibly that, effectively the band had split up. 'Dave's guitar was up for sale,' Duran Duran's John Taylor says. 'It was in the window of Musical Exchanges on Broad Street [Birmingham] for years, that Super Yob guitar. I remember and to this day I regret not buying, I don't know where it ended up.' It was said that Marco Pirroni, guitarist and co-founder of Adam and the Ants, is the proud owner of the original.

'We'd tried to get onto Reading for the previous few years, but we just weren't cool enough, and when the call came Dave's mind was made up – he didn't want to do it,' Holder told Dave Ling. 'Luckily, Chas was able to persuade him that this was a good place to finish the band: to go out with a bang.' Chas Chandler had lost none of his magic or charm, and he convinced Hill that playing the festival would be the right thing to do.

'We didn't have security passes, just parked in the public car park and walked in with our guitars,' Holder said in 2015. Haden Donovan drove the group car with Frank Lea also on board. 'I just loved that they almost didn't get in because they didn't have passes, but they knew who they were at the gate,' attendee Tim Fraser-Harding states.

Jim Lea painted a vivid picture to Chris Charlesworth in *Feel the Noize!*, 'We were carrying our own guitars. We didn't even have a roadie with us. It was hot and dusty, and we felt like gunslingers at high noon... we were strutting through this area in a line and holding up someone's roller behind us. I refused to move... why should I? I'd written more bloody hits than all that lot put together.'

And so, on Sunday 24 August 1980, Slade took to the stage at the Reading Festival. 'Everyone thought it was the last show,' Holder said. 'Then Tommy Vance from *The Friday Rock Show*, who was acting as compere, walked in and predicted we were going to go down a storm. We weren't so sure. Reading had turned into a metal festival and that wasn't us, but Tommy was insistent.' Vance, of course, had history with the group, after playing the pirate radio station DJ Ricky Storm in *Slade in Flame*.

Slade were positioned between two NWOBHM acts; they took to the stage soon after six, just after Girl, the Jet Records-signed glam-metal act fronted by Phil Lewis, and before young Sheffield rockers Def Leppard, seen very much as the northern poster boys for the new movement. David Coverdale's Whitesnake, then at the end of the first phase of their hard-rocking pomp, were that night's headliners.

'When they announced it, everyone went mental because everyone who couldn't see them when they were young could see them now,' rock writer and industry expert Steve Hammonds says. 'They weren't past their sell-by date then either. They were still in their prime, good musicians so they could grind it out. They'd put in their 10,000 hours. The crowd reaction was like, unbelievable. If you could perfectly pitch something, that was it.'

Holder walked on stage and opened with, 'Everyone in Reading pissed tonight?' The vulgarity that was so lost in translation in the US was greeted with joy by a home crowd waiting to be won over. The set, an exhilarating balance of old and new, was almost identical to that from the June tour, with only 'Lemme Love Into Ya' and 'Night Starvation' dropped. After 'Dizzy Mama' and 'My Baby Left Me', the familiarity of 'Take Me Bak 'Ome' whipped the crowd up even further.

Again, it was Slade who emerged from out of town, more than capable of rising to the challenge, like they had done back in the Bahamas, at Studio 51 in 1969 in front of Chas Chandler, at Lincoln in 1972. The element of surprise and the intensity of the entertainment had the audience in their thrall within minutes.

The band knew it was going well as the show progressed: 'In front of the stage there was a pit for the media which was empty when we went on, but the noise of the crowd was so loud that it filled up right away,' Holder said. 'The audience was perfect for us – a lot of them were kids who had been too young to see us first time around.' Steve Hammonds assesses their success: 'There was so much excitement, and the fact that all the people who had been 10, 11, 12 when they were having their big hits were now all now 17, 18, 19. The right audience at the right time – it was just perfect timing.'

'Reading was my baptism of fire,' rock writer Dave Ling says. 'Truth told, by 1980, like so many, I had given up on them. I was caught up in the NWOBHM and diving back through the catalogues of Quo, Lizzy, Purple and Zeppelin. News that they had replaced

Ozzy on the bill would have been greeted by a raised eyebrow – or worse. I still remember it as though it were yesterday. The growing realisation of: "Wow, we are witnessing something special here."'

'We knew Ozzy Osbourne wasn't there, but nobody in the crowd knew who the band was going to be until they came on,' Tim Fraser-Harding said.

'As one hit followed another the mood developed from apathy and in some cases borderline ridicule to mild astonishment,' Dave Ling recalls. 'By the halfway mark, euphoria had set in.'

'They came on and they blew the place apart,' Fraser-Harding continues. 'When they did 'Get Down and Get With It', everybody was stamping on the ground. It hadn't rained for a few days. It was the biggest dust cloud I've ever seen. It was quite incredible. They just blew the place apart, a real moment. It still resonates forty years later. There was already nostalgia mixed into their power.'

'These were the songs of our childhood being performed by the very same heroes that had worn out the carpet in the corner of our living rooms... only now they were right in front of our eyes,' Ling adds. 'What an experience. Who cared that it was late August and that Noddy had no inclination to sing 'Merry Xmas Everybody', WE were gonna do it. And we did. Ozzy Osbourne had been quickly forgotten.'

'We thought we were boring old farts, but the audience went absolutely berserk,' Holder said in 2015. The response was tumultuous: 'They were chanting for 'Merry Xmas Everybody', in August! I said: "If you want it, you sing it!" and they did, so we joined in. The next week, we were on all the music paper covers and back on the radio.'

Slade didn't just conquer the festival-goers. Frank Lea remembers vividly the reception the band received as they went into the backstage marquee for a drink afterwards. 'In all my years with the group, I'd never seen anything quite like it; all the other acts were mobbing them, they were all over Slade. It was a very special day.'

Back on the main stage, Def Leppard were next. Singer Joe Elliott was to say, 'The worst thing of all for us was having to follow Slade. They were great. They put on an amazing show and went down a storm, played the hits. It was a classic case of "follow that". We did our best, but it didn't seem to go too well… I got half a tin of Tartan lager in my bollocks.'

'Not three months earlier the press had treated them as anthrax carriers; now they were front page news,' Chris Charlesworth was to write. Slade had returned.

This would be an amazing moment to freeze the frame in a Slade biopic. The last gunslingers ride into town, and jubilantly return to claim what is theirs. As the credits roll, a composite of the group's remaining years plays out.

PART THREE

WHATEVER HAPPENED
TO SLADE

CHAPTER 28

Bringing the House Down

After their appearance at Reading, Slade lasted into the nineties, offering the group a coda that provided greater closure than if they had fizzled out in 1980. Their showmanship and verve had won through. And, it was a similar time of social division as when they first tasted fame. As 'Merry Xmas Everybody' had calmed nerves during the union unrest and three-day weeks, it was now the era of Margaret Thatcher's high-period shenanigans. In the early part of the decade, mass unemployment, inner-city riots and a questionable war for British territory far away in the south Atlantic all led to a sense of unease. Slade did not have the platform they had a decade earlier, but importantly, the UK metal fraternity, one of the most close-knit, inclusive and thoroughly convivial of all the UK music tribes, welcomed Slade with open arms. In many respects, the group's early eighties mirrored their early seventies – the band showing just how their performing chops could blow younger, less experienced acts, not to mention older, more established, acts clean off the stage.

Slade were suddenly hot again. Sadly, Graham Swinnerton would not continue the journey with them – and it was down to a simple case of economics; as he told Chris Charlesworth, 'They weren't playing live as often as they used to, and I was actually working for Saxon whenever I could. I was working for Slade for £80 a week, and

Saxon offered me £250 to be their tour manager. I couldn't really resist.' Swin subsequently worked with Southside Johnny and the Asbury Jukes, Ian Matthews and The Damned, before relocating to America where he was employed by The Fugees, and then, after the group split, individually by Wyclef Jean and Lauryn Hill. 'Swin had that sixth sense about things, apart from Noddy getting punched,' Nick Van Eede says. 'He was always one step ahead.'

Haden Donovan, who had been with the group's road crew on and off since 1973, took over as tour manager, with his brother Dave – who was nearly the stand-in for Don back in 1973 – as their driver. Ian 'Charlie' Newnham remained in charge of sound. Keith 'Smokie' Abingdon looked after monitors, with Michael Fitzsimmons, Peter Merrix and Robin Lloyd looking after drums and guitars. On 30 August that year both Holder and Lea attended Newnham's wedding to Eileen Delahay in Birmingham. Holder was best man, and pictures show bride, groom and Lea all perched precariously on a vintage fire truck. Just like old times.

* * *

Ahead of the Reading Festival, Frank and Jim Lea had released their next instalment of The Dummies side project on Cheapskate. 'Didn't You Used to Be You' was written by Lea and Holder, again to see if they could garner airplay away from the name Slade. A supremely quirky piece of new wave, the single also featured Louise Lea on vocals, and got the band on *Multi-Coloured Swap Shop* on prime-time TV. Its success was not to be.

'We got it on the A-list at Radio One, and it started selling really well through RCA distribution, and then, the sales went down to ten and twenty a day, and we'd had telly,' Frank Lea explains. 'I phoned up the sales manager to ask what was happening, as it was heading for the Top 10. He said Chas Chandler phoned up, as he wanted it off the vans, as in a couple of weeks' time there was a new Slade single coming. And he never told me, by the time I found out we'd lost momentum. He didn't want it to be a hit. Because it was nothing to do with him.' Frank and Jim Lea had set up what was looking to be a potentially successful label, after Barn had not succeeded. Chandler, as Slade's manager, would soon be part of the Cheapskate set-up.

Jim (who was to become a father again in February 1981 when Louise gave birth to Kristian James) and Frank Lea concentrated on Cheapskate Records, which was to release a variety of interesting singles and albums. As well as offering the opportunity for further Dummies releases, there was the fantastic ska take on The Shadows' 'Apache' by the Ska-Dows (which featured ex-members of Animal Kwackers); some muscular new wave from Tich Turner's Escalators; the power pop of Top Secret. Roy Wood signed up with his Helicopters project.

Cheapskate even had a nibble at the Top 40 with the novelty record 'You've Gotta Be a Hustler If You Wanna Get On' by Sue Wilkinson, who had previously worked as an actress and model under the name of Sue England. It reached number twenty-five in the charts at the end of August 1980. Wilkinson appeared on *Top of the Pops* on 28 August, with Don Powell playing percussion.

* * *

Slade went back on tour on 25 September and did not stop until a short break at Christmas. Returning to Reading (at the university) and Runton (which could have been their final ever show back in July), the shows were high-powered fun – exactly the same as before, but now with added confidence and purpose. There was no time now for side projects like The Dummies as Slade were back in business. The new Slade single, rush-released for 3 October on Cheapskate, was the *Slade Alive at Reading* EP. Taking 'When I'm Dancin' I Ain't Fighting' and 'Born to Be Wild' for the A-side, and the rock'n'roll medley for its flip, it reached number forty-four in the charts – not brilliant, but a great deal better than the preceding six singles.

To promote *Slade Alive at Reading*, Slade headlined London's Lyceum on 19 October 1980, topping a bill which was opened by hardcore Stoke-on-Trent punk band, Discharge, and on the actual eve of the release of their debut album, *Boy*, U2. Slade archivist Mark Brennan, who later played bass in The Business, was there: 'I bought my first bass from Paul Gray from Eddie and the Hot Rods, and I

301

went to pick it up from him at the Lyceum that night. Because I'd gotten backstage, I could stay there.'

'Discharge were one of my favourite bands, and Cal [Kevin Morris], the singer, used to run round giving it large. I was watching him, and suddenly became aware that there was this little fellow standing beside me. Suddenly, Cal's gone sliding off the stage and bashed his head open; he carries on singing with blood pouring out as if nothing had happened. This bloke beside me pipes up, "Fucking hell!" It was Dave Hill. He's only tiny, especially when he hasn't got his boots on. You could see he was thinking "What the fuck is that?" It was an absolute racket to start with, and then the bloke fell off the stage. An hour or so later, Slade were absolutely fantastic.'

Polydor released a compilation album on the back of their resurrection. On their TV-advertised Polystar label, *Slade Smashes* was released on 1 November 1980, and it was the first compilation to contain all the group's biggest records for the label. Complete with Chris Charlesworth sleevenotes, it reached number twenty-one in the UK charts, selling around 200,000 copies. As Chris Selby and Ian Edmundson noted, 'Slade were back. All they had to do now was STAY back.'

In December, Slade were voted 'Comeback of the Year' in the *Record Mirror* poll. They ended the year with another curious release to capitalise on the comeback. The *Xmas Ear Bender* EP had 'Merry Xmas Everybody' – the crowd version from Reading – the live 'Get Down and Get With It' and the studio version of 'Okey Cokey'. Like the 'Okey Cokey', it briefly went in (number seventy for two weeks) and then out of the chart. The senseless murder of John Lennon, with whom they'd shared a harmonium in 1973, and to whom Holder had so often been compared, early that December, cast a very long shadow over that festive season.

* * *

It was one thing repackaging the Reading material, but it was time for something new from the group to sustain momentum. The Lea brothers acted quickly and decisively; some brand-new material was needed from the group. One wrote it, one packaged it. Inspired by a chant Jim Lea heard the audience doing while waiting for the group to return to the stage at one show, he took it, Holder added his magic and a rollicking new Slade song was born: 'We'll Bring the House Down'. Portland Studios engineer Andy Miller, who had joined them on *Return to Base*, says, 'The 'We'll Bring the House Down' single got them back on *TOTP* after many years, and I recorded a couple of albums with them.'

Miller's engineering did play a large part in the song, but the joy was in Slade's playing. 'We'll Bring the House Down' was a gold-standard single, riotous, rambunctious, all faders up, all guns blazing – not unlike 'Get Down and Get With It', a decade before, a calling card for the work they had put in over the past five years. It was messy like punk, and had all the precision of metal. It was as if Powell had been told the only way he could have his vodka would be to hit the drums as hard as humanly possible, and he did so in the toilets at Portland Place to get that classic Slade echo. Importantly, it sounded as if they were having fun. Released with louche rocker 'Hold on to Your Hats' from *Return to Base*, the single was released in a simple black bag with the Slade fist on 23 January 1981. It entered the charts at number thirty-one in early February, and by the 15th of the month, Slade stood within the UK Top 10 for the first time since 1975. The record helped shake people out of the post-Lennon shock, and seemed completely at home in a chart alongside Madness, Adam and the Ants and The Stray Cats.

'I remember seeing 'We'll Bring the House Down' on *Top of the Pops* for the first time and thinking that it was just the most exciting record,' Michael Hann, author of *Denim and Leather: The Rise and Fall of the New Wave of British Heavy Metal*, says. 'And also slightly confused. Weren't Slade from a different era? Slade were part of *The Friday Rock Show* firmament to me, a contemporary heavy group. *Kerrang!* treated them seriously. It wasn't some kind of "let's reappraise" thing, Slade were part of what we are.'

'The adrenaline rush I still get from listening to 'We'll Bring the House Down' has never gone away,' Jerry Ewing says. 'I find it absolutely exciting to listen to today. If you ever did a look through my Spotify stats, that'd be my most listened to Slade song by miles.'

'They knew they could deliver,' Ian Edmundson says. 'Once they got a foot in door, once they saw that crack of light, they said, "We'll go for that" – they were back.'

'"We'll Bring the House Down' brought a lot of the crowds back,' Frank Lea says. 'I said that we needed an album out, which they didn't have. We named it after the single, and it charted. It shows how fickle fans are. Sometimes you'd have one play of a record on the radio and people say – your record's on the radio all the time!' It was a shrewd compilation, gathering ten big old thumpers that were truly able to capitalise on Slade's newfound success. As nobody outside the magic 500 and fellow travellers had really heard *Return to Base*, the decision was taken to take the best tracks from it, pepper in some recent B-sides, some from *Six of the Best* and add both sides of the Top 10 single. Packaged in the simplest of sleeves for which Chas Chandler kept his name with a credit for the cover concept.

Designed by former Decca art director Laurie Richards, the use of old English fonts and a sword and shield emphasised the inherent Britishness of the band, yet the link with the more recent past was there by the Slade fist punching through the shield. Slade were back, punching through any armour. Deviations from formula were not included – there was no place for *Return to Base*'s 'I'm Mad', 'Chakeeta' or 'Sign of the Times' in this heady brew. However, amid all the 'Nuts Bolts and Screws' and 'Hold on to Your Hats', there was still time for the euro-goth gloom of 'Lemme Love Into Ya'. The album reached number twenty-five in the charts, the highest position for a 'new' album (even though, of course, it was a compilation) since *Nobody's Fools*' number fourteen ranking in March 1976.

A choice had to be made for the next single: 'I said, like *Tiswas*, we've got to give them what they want. I thought a remaster of 'When I'm Dancin' I Ain't Fightin'' from *Six of the Best* with its chant,' Frank Lea says. 'The band said that Chas said they had to release 'Wheels Ain't Coming Down', because the Americans liked it. I said it was wrong, as that was something from eighteen months ago. It was released, it went on Radio One's *Roundtable* – they said it was a good record, but they were expecting something a bit more raucous from them. Didn't matter what I said, if Chas said it, that was it.' 'Wheels Ain't Coming Down', now in its third release, was the follow-up single. One of the standout songs from *Return to Base*, and again, on the *Six of the Best* EP, here, the strident rock number, released on 27 March 1981, simply wasn't enough to sustain the momentum, stalling at number sixty.

Chas Chandler negotiated a deal to have Slade's releases on Cheapskate distributed by RCA. Tensions grew between him and label co-founder Frank Lea, and Lea left the partnership. Frank picks up the story: 'Chas had to come into Cheapskate because he was doing no good, and we were doing alright. Once Slade got to number ten with 'We'll Bring the House Down', Chas came into my office with his dark, mirrored glasses, a long silver cigarette holder with his fag,' Frank Lea says. 'He told me from now I had to have nothing to do with the band. He was the manager, and "You don't talk to any of them, and you don't talk to your brother. You just work here." I replied, "I don't just work here; I own half the fucking company." He said again, "I'm the manager. Nothing to do with you now." That was the beginning of the end.' Back from all his Barn side projects, Chandler wanted to be hands-on manager again.

Taken from the sessions for their forthcoming album, 'Knuckle Sandwich Nancy' was chosen by the band as their next single, released at the end of May. The release furthered the rift that was growing between the band and Chandler, as he didn't feel it should be a single. With Frank Lea departing, the group realised the scale of his contribution was. 'I did everything to the promotion, the pressing, sleeves, the marketing set-up,' Frank Lea said. 'Me and Chandler had the fallout, and then 'Knuckle Sandwich Nancy' was scheduled for a certain time. I phoned Nod, and I said, I don't think you'll see anything. He asked why not? I replied because it's not even mastered. It's not even gone to the pressing plant. There's no sleeve been done, nothing, and it's supposed to be out in a few days' time.'

The tale of a woman who used her fists first was based on another character from Slade's past, also with a nod to Holder's altercation with Des Brothers in Porthcawl in 1978. It was a hard rocking, if somewhat unremarkable, addition to the Slade canon that the group felt Chandler did not sufficiently promote.

* * *

305

Chas Chandler and Slade parted company in early summer 1981, but there was no major fight: as Chris Charlesworth wrote in *Feel the Noize!*, the relationship 'did not deteriorate into hostility as drift into indifference from both sides of the fence.' The parting was a long time coming. 'Noddy told me that they "worshipped" Chas,' Chris Charlesworth wrote elsewhere. 'They'd do anything he said. At least until the hits stopped and Jim decided they'd be better off without him.'

'In the eighties we sacked Chas Chandler and I was doing the day-to-day managing from a touring point of view,' Noddy Holder told Mark Blake. 'We had a business manager who is still my guy today, but I was looking after all the day-to-day. I never realised how hard a job it is. Democracy does not work in bands, where all four have an equal vote. At least Chas had the deciding vote as it were. We accepted that.'

In the summer of 1981, Chandler brokered a deal to sign Slade directly to RCA, who distributed Cheapskate, and sold his interest in Barn and Cheapskate. It was, according to Chandler, 'a very sweet contract'. It was his last act for Slade; he had stood down from producing, it was obvious that the next step would be relinquishing management. Holder went on behalf of the group to say his services were no longer required. Although, when Holder called a meeting, it was said that Chandler initially thought Holder was going to tell him he was about to go solo. Holder told Charlesworth in 1984: 'It was quite an amicable meeting. Chas realised it was coming. There was a lot of business problems that needed sorting out. Jim was not enamoured of Chas – not only from our situation, but from the Cheapskate angle too. There had been rucks going on with Chas and Jim's brother Frank.' Chandler told Charlesworth: 'They'd all grown up since I first met them, and the time had come to part company. There was an unstated agreement that we would stay together until they reached the chart again.'

Lea added, 'Nobody can take away what Chas did for us. He flew the flag and continued to do so during the duff period. But the time had come to leave home... we had come of age. It was like leaving our parents.'

The group managed themselves with specialist music industry accountant Colin Newman, ever-present in the background since 1970. 'It was exciting, it was almost like starting again,' Don Powell says. 'Like we did before the hits. You can feel something happening. It was like the same again. We went back to doing proper tours. Although, in the down years, we never reneged on the big show. We just kept on playing and I was actually enjoying it a lot more because in the smaller places there was a better atmosphere. I always like to do smaller places personally, that's me.'

* * *

Slade's role as forefathers of NWOBHM was brief but blazed; in the way that other survivors like Gillan and Motörhead were in step, doing what they had been doing for years. In 1981, their place within the rock community was sealed by their place on the bill at the second Monsters of Rock festival at Castle Donington, Derbyshire, almost a year to the day after they had played Reading. The festival was promoted by Paul Loasby, and none other than their very first manager, Maurice Jones, who had gone on to found MCP (Midland Concert Promotions) and become one of the most well-known promoters in the UK. Slade were on the bill with AC/DC, Blue Öyster Cult and Whitesnake.

'From memory – and I may be wrong – it was raining,' Dave Ling says. 'If it wasn't, the old grey cells inform me that it felt like it was. One cannot lose one's virginity twice. Reading had been a moment of joyous spontaneity, now it felt just a wee bit contrived.' The rain hammered down through Slade's mid-afternoon set, and the PA wasn't brilliant either. 'Still, Slade went against the odds,' Dave Kemp wrote in *The Slade Supporters Club* September/October 1981 newsletter: 'No lights, pouring rain and they still went down a storm (sorry, no pun intended). I doubt if many other bands could have done the same.'

On 4 September, the first of Slade's new material on RCA was released. Backed with another run out for 'Sign of the Times', 'Lock Up Your Daughters' had a fabulous AOR sheen that probably still sounds the most contemporaneous of all this era's releases. It took the band back to *Top of the Pops* and up to number twenty-nine on the listings.

Released on 13 November, *Till Deaf Do Us Part* was the first truly longform new material since the Reading triumph. Recorded at Portland Studios, it was the first album entirely self-produced by the band, with Andy Miller receiving an assistant producer and engineering credit. Miller recalls what it was like working with Slade in the studio. 'I liked Don a lot, he would stand over me when I was mixing wearing a "MORE DRUMS" T-shirt,' Miller says today. 'Jimmy was driven and made it feel like working in a factory. Once, in a break, he accused me of eating my sandwich too slowly. Dave Hill was rarely allowed to play on their records. Jimmy either played guitar parts, or taught them to Dave note by note. When Noddy opened his mouth to sing, it would blow the mic up. A basic Shure 57 is all he needed.'

'It's a proper whomping, stomping scene,' as Dave Hill told *Sounds*. 'This album is a thumper, and we want it loud. That's the direction we are heading for, like having a live show in the studio almost. It's got guts and melody. That is us really.' The white sleeve with its illustration of a nail in an ear, left little room for ambiguity. The rear of the sleeve features the incredible shot of Dave Hill leading the crowd from his platform at Reading. People stretch as far as the eye can see, with clouds of dust rising in several places. It is rock'n'roll rapture, right there.

'Rock and Roll Preacher (Hallelujah I'm on Fire)' is a superb opener, with Holder at full stretch, the minister of metal, the Pope of pomp, leading his flock. The call-and-response harks back to the 'Skweeze Me, Pleeze Me' era, and starts the album as it means to continue. 'It's Your Body Not Your Mind' is pure early eighties sexism, a girl wearing a school uniform, driving everyone insane, showing off her IQ to psyche you. Even Dave Hill writes a number – 'M'Hat M'Coat', a two-minute instrumental that reminds a listener that this was the same man who played 'Peace Pipe' with The Vendors back in 1964. 'That Was No Lady That Was My Wife' actually manages not to be as clichéd as its title, and is one of Holder's most powerful, soulful vocals. Jim Lea's bass solo is aggressive and mixed loud.

''Ruby Red' [is] a number that we've had around for a long time,'
Holder told Dave Kemp. 'Me and Jim wrote it maybe two or three
years ago. We tried to record it before, but we never managed to
get it down how we actually wanted it. We recorded it here first
when Chas was producing us. Then, recently, when we were looking
through the songs that we'd got for the album, we remembered that
we'd never been able to get 'Ruby Red' down on tape properly, but
that it was a good, strong, commercial sound. So, we added some
new riffs to it and got it down and it's a good commercial song.'
Released as a single in March 1982, 'Ruby Red' was a shiny, catchy
song, which although only reaching number fifty-one in the charts,
remained well-loved by fans. It was backed with the confident,
strutting, 'Funk, Punk and Junk', which had arrived during the
Portland Place sessions with Andy Miller.

Till Deaf Do Us Part is tremendous fun, the sound of a band
enjoying themselves, and stands up far better than other hard rock
albums of this vintage. Every scrap of their experience was brought
to bear. 'The reason I think those recordings from '80 and '81 are
so phenomenally exciting is that you can hear a band desperately
fighting for their lives, aware that they do still have something,'
Michael Hann says. 'The band is fully in control. That power is not
desperate, you know, feel a sense of – No, no, look at us. Look. Listen.
You can hear what the band is trying to do by not just churning out
a single because another single is due.'

* * *

After the demise of Cheapskate, the Leas founded Speed Records
at the very end of 1981. One of their early signings was True Life
Confessions, the project of ex-Darts drummer, John Dummer.
Dummer, of course, had been the leader of The John Dummer
Blues Band back in the seventies. 'I'd left Darts in the early eighties
and formed my own group, True Life Confessions, with my wife,
Helen April,' Dummer said. 'Helen and I had recorded a single as
a duo before this, 'Own Up If You're Over 25', which got a bit of
airplay.'

Frank was interested in recording the off-the-wall outfit. 'We went
back to Jimmy's London flat and had coffees after a gig,' Dummer

remembers. 'I had been a record plugger for various record companies before Darts and knew all the BBC producers and DJs so that helped. We also did a whistling and singing version of Irving Berlin's 'Blue Skies', as the duo John Dummer & Helen April which came out on Speed. We had a deal with A&M Records for TLC with a proviso for me and Helen as a duo if we came up with anything. We played 'Blue Skies' to A&M managing director Derek Green, but he couldn't see it, which left us free to punt it about, which was how we chanced on Frank who liked it.' Frank Lea always had an entrepreneurial spirit, and enjoyed working with characters, and those with long histories.

'True Life Confessions was a strange outfit,' Dummer recalls. 'Helen was out front as a sort of toaster, we had two Afro-French singers, sisters Any and Myriam Tocko-Salvetti, me and Esso from The Lurkers on drums, two guitarists, Robin Bibi and Mark Nevin who went on to write 'Perfect' for his group Fairground Attraction – and Harri Kakoulli, one-time bass player for Squeeze. It was a good laugh and quite successful in the London pubs and clubs. It was kind of veiled feminism, erotica and taking the piss out of men.'

Frank Lea signed the group. 'We got to know Slade and Frank took us along to some of their gigs and told us they wanted True Life Confessions on their next tour. We jumped at the chance (me and Helen loved Noddy and Jimmy and really rated the band) and were to support them at their opening gig at Hammersmith Odeon.' Dummer maintained his connection with Frank Lea: 'We put out a few more singles, none of which did as well as 'Blue Skies'. Later, Frank put out some reissues of early stuff recorded by the John Dummer Blues Band in the sixties.'

Other acts that were signed to Speed included Sue Scadding (who sang the Lea-Holder compositions 'Simple Love'/'Poland'), Three Phase, the group that featured Noddy Holder's schoolfriend Phil Burnell (Holder co-produced their extremely collectable single, 'All I Want To Do Is (Fall in Love With You)'), Wolfie Witcher & The Night Riders (London-based blues singer Stuart Witcher), Nick Gilder (in between recording for Casablanca and RCA) and Wizzard (Roy Wood's *Singles* album reached number thirty-seven). Most of these got on the Radio One playlist, but distribution hampered sales.

In 1982, it even reissued Slade's most contentious single, 'Okey Cokey'. And, in keeping with the times, issued it as a limited-edition picture disc, which at time of writing sells for sums in excess of £6.

Importantly, Speed also became the home of Jim Lea's pseudonymous releases – 'One Hit Wonder' by The China Dolls, and intriguingly, 'Poland' – a reworking of 'Lemme Love Into Ya' – by Greenfields of Tong, one of Lea's best aliases, named after a view of the landscape around the Shropshire village of the same name, six or so miles away from Lea's village of Brewood. 'Lemme Love Into Ya' had been turned into glacial futurist electronica. Lea was hoping that the pseudonym would see the record get airplay from those who wouldn't go anywhere near Slade. Sadly, few went near this.

CHAPTER 29

A High-Powered Metal/ Punk Pick'n'Mix

There was little question of Slade's ongoing popularity in 1982. While the charts were a playground for a more sophisticated pop that was replacing the new romantic experimentations and white-boy funk of the previous year, Slade's brand was in good shape as they continued down their metal path. This was borne out by their spring tour, back into decent-sized venues, a twelve-date sprint around the Gaumonts, Apollos and Assembly Rooms of the UK. It was clear to see the audience they were going for – tour support was split between two bands signed to RCA, Liverpool NWOBHM band Spider and Wakefield-based glam metallers, Vardis.

In summer, Slade travelled over to Finland to play the Kuusrock Festival in Oulu in July, on a bill with many Finnish rockers, a festival played by Iron Maiden in 1980 and Saxon in 1981. Saxon leader Biff Byford was later to tell *Classic Rock*: 'It was my first experience of twenty-four-hour daylight. I'd never seen people drink solidly for forty-eight hours before.' Slade suited that demographic well.

Slade began working on the follow-up to *Till Deaf Do Us Part* at Portland Studios; most of the follow-up album had been recorded, and in November, the first new material appeared; an anthemic single, '(And Now the Waltz) C'est La Vie', with a live version of

'Merry Xmas Everybody' on the flip. The waltz tempo and Holder's impassioned vocals, backed by choir-like voices, had a whiff of festivity to it, but as the last time the wider world had heard the group was in its hard rocking guise, people weren't ready for a Slade power ballad. Andy Miller was on hand as engineer: 'Unlike many of my clients, they made it feel like factory work. Don was nice. I had some nice times drinking with Noddy; and Jim was OK as a very bright, amazing musician. They were famously tight with money. I remember Dave asking the tape-op (my assistant) to get him a pint from the pub and gave him 50p.'

However, the album they had been working on failed to materialise. RCA felt more work needed doing to it, as it didn't have any big hits on it, borne out by '(And Now the Waltz) C'est La Vie''s number fifty chart placing. So, in the interim, if there was a way to keep Slade in the public eye, it was their old standby, the live album. But still, conversation was strong about Slade's live ability and how they had not only slain Reading, but now Donington as well. Like 'Rock'n'Roll Bolero' with *Slade Alive Vol Two*, '(And Now the Waltz) C'est La Vie' had little to do with the album that was being released more or less simultaneously.

John Taylor from Duran Duran recalls meeting the group around this time. 'I think it must have been in '82 when we were doing *Rio* and that was the first time, we connected with them as fellow Midlanders, so to speak. I don't know if the music businesses is like it today, but I always felt very welcomed by the elder statesmen and that was definitely the case with them. They clearly knew who we were, and I don't know whether it was pride, but they were like, "These are the new boys from Birmingham," they're just friendly guys.'

Released on 11 December 1982, *Slade on Stage* – the group's third and final live album – is a visceral attack on the senses, and admirably captures just how powerful the group still were live. It's an exhausting, exhilarating example of the relationship between group and audience. That the group are playing like a high-powered metal/punk pick'n'mix adds to the utter thrill of the set. It demonstrates just how amazingly tight the group were, and their training on the circuit meant that they could adapt to anything the audience demanded – the high-powered fiddle work, and the drop down to 'Sprit in the Sky' in 'A Night to Remember' underlined their slickness and professionalism.

'Even from way, way back Newcastle was always amazing for us – it was Chas's home town, remember – so we did the City Hall on every tour,' Holder told Dave Ling.

We had first appeared there in 1969 as the warm-up act for Amen Corner and Dave Dee, Dozy, Beaky, Mick & Tich. It was an audience of screaming girls, which we'd never seen before. From then on, our tours often opened at the City Hall. Not just for Slade, there's something magical about that place. When we had Thin Lizzy and Suzi Quatro open on a tour for us there, they couldn't believe the hullabaloo. So when we made a third album, Newcastle City Hall was one of the first names on the list.

Its cover marked the final time they worked with Gered Mankowitz:

I did that session with them under the motorway. It was a section of the M25 that hadn't yet opened yet. That was a nice session actually. There was some nice pictures from that session, quite moody pictures. In my mind the reason Slade lasted so long, the reason they were so good, the reason they were so continuously creative through that period was because they were an amazing unit. They worked together. I mean, they're all individual characters, which is very important in a band. They all have their roles to play, equally important. Dave was always off on a tangent, but they all understood that that was good. He was their Brian Jones; he was their Ringo. The eccentric one who's out on the edge somehow. Even in those early sessions, he was bossy. He was a bossy bloke full of ideas.

'It's always been on stage where Slade come alive most, and this sensational album goes some way towards demonstrating just why they're one of the best live rock bands in the world,' *Sounds* writer and Oi! architect, Garry Bushell wrote. 'Indeed, this is one of the livest albums you'll ever hear in your life, so raucously resplendent in rowdy crowd participation that it sounds like you've got the Kop in your bedroom. I only hope the noisy sods are on a royalty earner.'

Michael Hann remains an ardent admirer of the album: 'It has an intensity that's almost heartstopping – like Thin Lizzy's *Live and Dangerous* or UFO's *Strangers in the Night*, it's a live album that makes it feel like you really are at the show,' he wrote in his *The Quietus* essay, 'Bak 'Ome To The Top'.

A short Christmas tour reflected the fact that Slade's days of truly slogging the country were over. After two university warm-up shows at Loughborough and Keele, they played a ten-date tour taking in eight locations. Supporting them were Australian 'pub rockers' Cold Chisel, fronted by Jimmy Barnes, who, unlike AC/DC, resolutely hadn't succeeded in taking their Australian superstardom global. It did make for some interesting concerts, especially with the attendance of most of the West London ex-pat Australian community for the Hammersmith shows. Add that into the Slade massive and a Christmas party was truly had. Speed recording artists, True Life Confessions, opened the first Hammersmith show: TLC were quite of their time, somewhat eccentric and boundary-pushing. 'Mark Nevin came on naked playing guitar with the group as "nude Santa",' leader John Dummer recalls. 'In some ways TLC were a fairly outrageous group and sometimes some people were offended by us, although others loved us. The promoter took against TLC's act at Hammersmith and threw us off the Slade tour, so that was that.' The tour finished at Birmingham Odeon on 20 December, and there was a party thrown after by Maurice Jones.

And Christmas was, of course, Slade's time of year, and Christmas 1982 had an added extra. Firstly, the reissued version of 'Merry Xmas Everybody' from the previous year managed to get back in the Top 75 (although number sixty-seven was not as striking as the previous year's number thirty-two), but a cover version of it from one of the year's biggest groups was shown on prime-time TV. Granada TV's *Pop Goes Christmas* was a simple, effective idea: a line-up of then-current artists would perform their new hit single, and would then perform a Christmas classic. Shown on Christmas Sunday 26 December (Christmas and Boxing Day fell on the weekend that year so the holidays were the days after) at 4.45 p.m., David

Essex, Toyah Willcox, The Nolans, Mari Wilson, Wah!, Toto Coelo, Shakin' Stevens and illusionist Simon Drake all appeared. Fellow Wulfrunian Kevin Rowland, then at the peak of his band Dexys Midnight Runners' commercial success, performed, alongside the group's current single, 'Let's Get This Straight (From the Start)', a version of 'Merry Xmas Everybody', complete with new flourishes added by backing singers, The Brothers Just. It was like the passing of the baton from one generation to the next – Dexys' 'Come on Eileen', which had been released earlier that year, had taken the sort of place in the popular imagination as Slade's hit had done not yet a decade before; but culturally it seemed many years away.

'It was Kevin's idea and I suppose part of the appeal is that it would be quite unexpected,' Kevin 'Billy' Adams says. 'He even suggested loud guitars at the start, but the acoustic arrangement came together quite quickly, and the fiddles sounded amazing with that too, so the guitar idea was forgotten. Made me laugh at the time though.'

'I immediately thought we would do a carol,' Helen O'Hara says. 'And long story short, Kevin came up with 'Merry Xmas Everybody'. We did the arrangement between us so quickly, and I absolutely love it. We had The Brothers Just interacting with Kevin and having the violin was really nice, because of Jim. Yeah. And it just worked well. Because – mainly because it's such a brilliant song.'

Slade's tenacity was about to pay off. By the following Christmas, they too would be back in the UK Top 3 with a hit bigger than many of their seventies classics.

CHAPTER 30

Cocky Rock Boys

1983 brought unexpected success for Slade in the UK, and surprisingly, in America. On 27 August 1983, Quiet Riot released an identikit cover version of 'Cum On Feel the Noize'. The single spent two weeks at number five on the *Billboard* Hot 100 chart in November 1983 and made history as the first heavy metal song to ever crack the Hot 100. "Cum On Feel the Noize' by Quiet Riot opened the door in America,' Holder said to Mark Blake. 'All these American acts at that time were glam metal; they were kids who'd grown up seeing us in the seventies and took that image and they wanted to sound more like us. When we went to LA and NY and met these bands, they said wish we could get a sound like you do. It's weird how it goes around.'

Noddy Holder and Jim Lea did some outside production together. In May and August 1983, the pair worked at London's Roundhouse Studios on *Play Dirty*, the fourth album by London rock band Girlschool. The sessions were somewhat unfocused given the group's timekeeping and desire to pop over to The Belmont over the road for multiple drinks. *Play Dirty* has a terrific mid-eighties rock sheen, and of interest to Slade aficionados are their versions of 'High and Dry', a song recorded by Slade for their next album, as well as a truly splendid cover of 'Burning in the Heat of Love'. It is also the only album to feature both Lemmy and Marc 'Ilford'

Fox from Haircut 100. Girlschool drummer Denise Dufort cites it as her favourite of her group's fourteen albums and said to writer Joe Geesin that it 'sounds a bit like Def Leppard'.

For the first time since Chas Chandler became their producer as well as manager, Slade worked with an outside producer as well. John Punter had a fabulous pedigree: starting as an engineer at Decca's Broadhurst Gardens facility in the mid-sixties, working with Bill Price, before moving to George Martin's AIR studios. He had worked with a wide spectrum of acts, most recently producing refined art-poppers Japan, who were clearly inspired by Roxy Music, one of the groups with whom Punter was most associated from the previous decade. Importantly for Slade, he had a long association with Scottish rockers Nazareth and Manchester grown-up melodists Sad Café.

Lea and Holder had been working on a couple of new tracks, on which they enlisted Punter's expertise. Although their paths had never crossed, 'I'd grown up with Slade,' John Punter says. 'We're the same age. I'd always loved their music and their performance and to get the opportunity to work with them was just amazing. My over-the-top production and their over-the-top performance was going to be a perfect combination.' Punter immediately assessed what he was working with: 'Two very clever and talented songwriters, who had great chemistry and a knack for writing catchy, commercial songs and a bunch of guys who really knew their craft. And their live performance, which was never disappointing.'

Lea and Holder demoed the new tracks – something they had never before done, and played them to Punter. For the first time in Slade's career, the group were required to record their parts separately. Although vocals and overdubs may have previously been added, the essence was strictly and fundamentally live. 'We built everything up in the studio, because that's the way I worked and that's how I got my best results,' Punter adds. He also brought the LinnDrum into Slade's orbit: 'I used the Linn to take some of the pressure off Don, because of his short-memory problem. That way, he and I could work more closely together, to get the results we wanted.' And the results came in the form of two tracks, 'Run Runaway' and 'My Oh My'.

* * *

'My Oh My' seemed to drop out of the clear blue sky. "My Oh My' is very much in the vein of their big ballads from the seventies, like 'Everyday' and all that,' Jonathan 'Chas' Chandler (no relation), who was later to work on their catalogue, was to say. 'When you are not flavour of the month, you will also look to incorporate the sound of the day.'

Big rock was making a comeback; led by Stuart Adamson, Big Country were in the ascendency, and had started to make their mark on the charts, and U2 – who had become quite successful since supporting Slade at the Lyceum – were again popularising guitar-based rock. It was very clear who both bands had been listening to in their radio diet of the seventies. Slade knew exactly how to make popular guitar-based rock.

And 'My Oh My' became very big news indeed, reaching number two over Christmas 1983. A decade after their biggest success, Slade were back where they knew best. They were only kept from the top spot by the sort of novelty record that only UK audiences can take to their hearts. The Flying Pickets, a doo-wop group formed by unemployed left-wing actors, had recorded an a capella cover version of 'Only You', the electro-pop ballad performed by Yazoo – Alison Moyet and Vince Clarke – that had been a Top 3 hit in its own right the previous year. It was like 'My Ding-A-Ling', 'Eye Level' and 'Everything I Own' before it. With such a unique record at the top spot, it was as if Slade were the 'real' number one that Christmas.

'My Oh My' had that beguiling mix of nursery rhyme and anthem that proved irresistible, especially at that time of year. It was if no stone was to be left unturned, with a full choir to finish as the hard rockin' balladry gave way to 'Vienna' by Ultravox. It was a curious record. But, my heavens did it strike a chord. It certainly got played, and played. 'When you first heard 'My Oh My', you thought, wow, *this is brilliant*,' Jerry Ewing says. 'Six weeks later, I didn't ever want to hear that again.'

'I remember thinking it was one of the best records I'd ever heard,' adds Francis Rossi. 'Such a fabulous progression away because they'd got out of the misspelling of song titles and got out of the stomp thing. 'Mama Weer All Crazee Now' and all those fucking records were brilliant. But it suddenly becomes part of the last decade.'

The video for 'My Oh My', directed by Keith Coe, showed where Slade were at in late 1983: shorter hair than their heyday, flying jackets, Hill's voodoo-inspired top-hat, playing on the back of an articulated lorry, taking their music through the country lanes out to their fans. At the outset of the video, we see the lorry driver take to the cab, bewilderingly wearing a crash helmet. The lorry stops, and a full-blown scarf-waving concert ensues (filmed in London's Surrey Docks), with the oh-so-important backstory of the era – the driver gets down from the cab, takes off their crash helmet, and is revealed – with an exaggerated shake of long blonde hair – to be a woman. Her leathers are unzipped, not only is she a woman, but she is wearing a crop-top as well. And then we see the choir. It is a thoroughly splendid piece of eighties tomfoolery. And it underlined what had first been rekindled at Reading in summer 1980: Slade were back. 'There was nobody happier than me when 'My Oh My' was a smash,' ex-manager Chas Chandler said the following year. 'I was delighted. It was wonderful.'

* * *

Because of the scale and somewhat unexpected success of 'My Oh My', *The Amazing Kamikaze Syndrome*, which had been scheduled for a late January 1984 release, was rushed forward to early December. Released to accompany the single, it was an album of little shade – this was full-strength hard rock Slade. But people had the single, and it could easily have been allowed to run its course. Most of the album had been recorded in 1982, and, with the addition of the two John Punter-produced tracks – as well as '(And Now the Waltz) C'est La Vie' – made it a compelling proposition.

Over an ominous whirr of synthesiser, sounding not unlike the helicopters at the start of *Apocalypse Now*, a heavily reverbed Holder begins preaching 'Hey you! You out there, yeah you, CAN YOU HEAR ME? I said, I said CAN YOU HEAR ME? You better listen to me when I'm talking to you. If you're going to go for it, you've got to go for it good, AND THAT MEANS YOU AIN'T GONNA GET

AWAY FROM WHAT YOU'VE GOT COMING!' – as it crashes in to 'Slam the Hammer Down'. The album starts as it means to go on, rocking ferociously. Tracks like 'In the Doghouse' and the Powell-led onslaught of 'Cocky Rock Boys (Rule O.K.)' hit the 'We'll Bring the House Down' intensity; 'Cheap'n'Nasty Love' is in the 'Lock Up Your Daughters' vein. It was clear, though, that the two new tracks made the difference, giving the album two glorious peaks to enliven the rock of the rest.

Finally, Slade got round to an opus – their longest non-live track to date had been 'How Does It Feel' at just short of six minutes. Now, 'Ready to Explode' was a multi-parted eight-and-a-half-minute opus about motor-racing, with Grand Prix-like announcements from former pirate and Radio One DJ, Pete Drummond. It is virtually the template for The Darkness's entire career. Ian Edmundson calls the track 'Jim going into Jim land'. As Chris Ingham writes in the 2022 edition sleevenotes, the album is 'an impressive display of pumped-up, hi-tech rock-pop'.

A fifteen-date UK tour to support the album and single began at the King's Hall in Aberystwyth on Monday 28 November. The set was a crowd-pleasing mixture of old and new, opening with 'Rock and Roll Preacher' and concluding – obviously, given the time of year – with 'Merry Xmas Everybody'. The final show, at Liverpool's Royal Court Theatre on 18 December would be Slade's last ever full-length show in the UK, although nobody knew that at the time.

Christmas 1983 can be viewed as Slade's final peak in the UK, another place where the biopic could freeze-frame and end. Polydor, never backward in coming forward when there was some catalogue to exploit, reissued 'Merry Xmas Everybody', and this time it made number twenty, its highest position since 1973. Which meant, in Christmas week, the group had two records in the UK Top 20, a feat they hadn't even been able to manage in their heyday. Which meant two appearances in the studio on the Christmas *Top of the Pops*. At that time, Chris Selby and Ian Edmundson's plea regarding their return in 1980 that 'All they had to do now was STAY back', had happened. Of all their chart peers of the Christmas Top 5 from the decade earlier, Gary Glitter and Alvin Stardust were only having intermittent chart success, The New Seekers had long gone, as had

Wizzard. Slade proved that perseverance would indeed out. The Top 5 Slade found themselves among this time also included old rivals and friends, Status Quo with 'Marguerita Time'. There was still room for the old-timers.

An era ended in 1983 when Les and Ethel Megson retired from running The Trumpet to live in North Wales. 'My dad knew the boys very well,' Steve Megson, on the verge of an international teaching career, says. 'They loved my dad and gave my dad a couple of gold discs with his name engraved on them.' However, continuity was maintained when Tony Swinnerton, who'd worked with the Megsons since the early seventies, took over, keeping the décor exactly the same. Of course, Tony was Swin's brother.

* * *

Released at the start of February 1984, the third single from *The Amazing Kamikaze Syndrome* was 'Run Runaway', the second of the John Punter-produced tracks. It was an absolute hoot, with virtually everything but the kitchen sink thrown in. Lea got the idea for the folk-rock based jig while hearing Hill and Holder tuning up before a show. With plenty of mid-eighties production flourishes, it was another late flowering of the Lea-Holder writing team. Backed with the non-album 'Two Track Stereo One Track Mind', 'Run Runaway' began to strike a chord, especially, and gleefully in America, where the video began to get traction at MTV.

The video was directed by Tim Pope, then the *enfant terrible* of the burgeoning pop promo scene. Making his name with Soft Cell, he started a long-lasting association with The Cure in 1982, and Neil Young in 1983. He had recently directed the faux-*Monty Python and The Holy Grail* romp of 'The Safety Dance' by Men Without Hats, and that stylistically acts as a template for 'Run Runaway'. Slade went to Eastnor Castle in the Malvern Hills for the shoot, where they had – somewhat bizarrely – once played in 1969 at the wrap for the Jerry Lewis-directed Sammy Davis Jr film *One More Time*.

Keith Altham wrote with affection about shooting the 'Run Runaway' video on location, when the band and crew were all turfed out of their rooms due to a fire alarm. Because there was a Celtic theme to the video, Altham described that in reception that night there were a 'band of Scottish Highland Pipers in kilts… TV wrestling commentator Kent Walton, a giant caber tosser, two dwarves, 12 firemen with axes and yellow oxygen cylinders on their backs, plus the disgruntled TV presenter of *Mastermind*, Magnus Magnusson, who happened to be in the same hotel… we should have just shot that fiasco and forgot the video. Life was never dull around Slade'.

The video, all Eastnor battlements and tall hats, was perfectly eccentric enough to translate to the States, displaying another bunch of limeys up to something strange. 'The Yanks adored the video for that record and it was on heavy rotation on MTV,' Holder recalled. Powell says, 'they thought that's where we lived.'

After all those years chasing America and hardly getting anywhere, the US came to them. Warner had quietly dropped the group after *Nobody's Fools*, and none of their subsequent albums had been released domestically in the States. With the advent of MTV, Slade could now reach the parts of the continent that would appreciate them most, and, due to the Ozzy Osbourne connection, Sharon Osbourne came in to manage the group. As daughter of controversial manager Don Arden, whose unique way with an artist assisted the success of The Small Faces, The Move, Wizzard, Black Sabbath, Lynsey de Paul and most significantly, ELO, she had grown up around the business. Estranged from her father from the late seventies, she had entered into a relationship with Ozzy that has lasted to this day. Given that Slade and Osbourne went back a long way, it made perfect sense for them to join her roster.

A US tour was booked to build on the success of 'Run Runaway', supporting Ozzy, and with the pulling power of Osbourne at CBS, a deal was brokered with the company by Sharon in February 1984, with experienced A&R Tony Martell overseeing their work. Slade again were signed to one of the biggest companies in America. And this time, success followed. Partially thanks to all the bands that they had influenced the first time around, aside from Quiet Riot's very explicit tribute. Kiss were in their pomp, and newish acts like Twisted Sister, Dokken and W.A.S.P., were all gaining ground, and Van Halen were enjoying some of their biggest global hits. All had cartoon elements and a heavy rocking eccentricity, and the twenty-four-hour schedules of MTV meant promos were needed to showcase their work. Thanks to the brash silliness of Tim Pope's 'Run Runaway' video, it was perfect for heavy rotation. As a result, it reached number twenty in the US charts, forty-eight places higher than their previous US single success with 'Gudbuy T'Jane', which reached number sixty-eight in 1973. Slade had finally breached the US Top 20.

The Amazing Kamikaze Syndrome was repackaged for the US without its clever and, for most North American residents, deeply offensive album title. Taking its name from the B-side to 'My Oh My', *Keep Your Hands Off My Power Supply* was released on CBS in April with its bright cartoon sleeve of purple-varnished nails on the fretboard of a red guitar. On the rear sleeve, the cartoon showed the neck of the guitar with a big hairy hand with 'Slade' written on its knuckles. Showing again that Slade worked with some of the best in the business, the sleeve was only one of three designed throughout the career of esteemed American cartoonist Lou Brooks, whose work had appeared in virtually every major US publication. Known as 'the world's oldest kid', to illustrate Brooks's standing, the following year, he was approached by Parker Brothers to redesign the Monopoly artwork for the board game's 50th anniversary. *Keep Your Hands Off My Power Supply* had a different running order to *The Amazing Kamikaze Syndrome* as well – the title track and 'Can't Tame a Hurricane' (the 12-inch B-side to 'My Oh My') were added in place of 'Razzle Dazzle Man' and 'Cocky Rock Boys (Rule O.K.)'.

However, a Slade twist of fate was to intervene. Jim Lea contracted hepatitis, which forced the band to return to the UK. Their concert at Cow Palace on 28 March 1984 was to be the final full show the group played, although they did return to the US to do some promo that May, recording *American Bandstand* for transmission in June and, on 24 and 25 May, honouring commitments in Cleveland, Ohio, where they played *Party in the Park*, with Holder singing a live vocal to tape. 'It was like karaoke. What the hell are we doing... I got in the car and I said to the others, this is never going to happen with this band again, never.' Holder said on *It's Slade*. 'The end of us live was the end of the band, really,' Lea said. The irony that after a decade earlier when the group wanted America, but the country didn't want them, now it was reversed.

* * *

The band's disillusionment with playing live was unknown at the time to writer Chris Charlesworth who was putting the finishing touches to his illustrated biography of the group, *Feel the Noize!*, published in November 1984, ready for the Christmas market. By now Charlesworth had become managing editor of Omnibus Press, a sub-division of Music Sales, the print music publishers, which specialised in music biographies, so was able to publish it as well. 'I approached the band through Keith Altham,' he says. 'They were up for it but Chas Chandler said in order for the group to co-operate Omnibus had to cede copyright to them, which I agreed. Keith and I spent a couple of nights in Walsall where I interviewed Nod, Jim and Dave and also Swin. Don lived in London.'

Long known as 'the Slade bible' – *Feel the Noize!* was a 128-page large-format book that became recognised as the gold standard of Slade writing. 'Although the book was "authorised", the members of the group and others were remarkably candid about their lives and the ups and downs of Slade's career,' says Charlesworth. 'No one, not Chandler or the band, requested text approval.' Lea insisted that Charlesworth interview the band individually, Lea insisted that Charlesworth interview the band individually, and a result, the writer found a very different band than he thought he would. Certainly, four very individual characters appeared in the text. Perhaps it was all a little too bald. But brilliant it undoubtedly is, capturing a time when access to bands was easy, and press people worked for both the artist and writer. It was a wonderful time to publish, as the group were very much at the peak of their renewed game. 'It also sort of coincided with their 20th anniversary as group,' says Charlesworth, 'and we had a launch party for the book at the Spice of Life pub in Cambridge Circus which they all attended.'

The book was a comprehensive take on Slade from one who had so long championed them, right from 1970. Charlesworth had unparalleled access. 'By the beginning of 1984 Slade's star was as bright as ever. The resurgence of American interest generated by Quiet Riot's hit recording on 'Cum On Feel the Noize' became a tangible entity on 3 February when the massive CBS Records empire signed the group to their first US recording contract since Warner Brothers dropped them back in 1977' is how he opens the final chapter, 'Today'. Holder concludes by saying, 'Some people say we should give up because we've had our turn and we're getting old but why should we? I still love it,' a sharp contrast to how he really was feeling. Unwittingly, the book gave a false sense of hope that disguised the growing unease within the Slade camp.

'It didn't sell particularly well,' adds Charlesworth. 'We overprinted and had to pulp some stock. Nowadays it's become a sort of collector's item. I've seen it on sale on Amazon for over £50, but it seems to have settled around the £30 mark now. I feel very flattered that fans still refer to it as the Slade "bible".'

Another issue that was to stymie the group during this period was that Holder learned that his wife, Leandra, was filing for divorce. Holder, who believed in family to the core, was shaken by this, especially as the couple had two young daughters, Charisse and Jessica. His father had also fallen ill, and as an only child, his responsibilities were clear – Slade could no longer be the highest priority in his life. Holder's father, Jack, passed away in 1988, at the age of 77.

* * *

It was a simple question of how to follow up such late-flowering overnight success. The answer was straightforward for Jim Lea – return to the studio for a follow-up album to *The Amazing Kamikaze Syndrome*. John Punter, whose magic touch so enlivened their comeback, was again in the chair for some of the tracks. However, as before, it was a different scene to Chandler's smash-and-grab raids of the seventies. The painstaking layering was right up perfectionist Lea's street. 'Jim always knew what he wanted and he knew how to get it,' John Punter says. It was less so for the rest of the band, who had prided themselves on capturing the live feel in the studio.

'First rehearsal, four of us, we all slotted in and it was a magic we had… it set us aside from a lot of other bands,' Holder told Mark Blake:

But in the eighties it went the other way. Everything was dissected and rock'n'roll went to the wall. It was painting by numbers, but the musical version. Every band was doing it, especially the way production was in those days. It wasn't our forte, or how you got the best out of us. In the seventies we went in, get them down, spontaneity, rock'n'roll records and they sound great. In the eighties, it was get the drum sound for a week, two days on the bass drum, and you don't play as a band either. You build it in layers, everything on separately.

One of the earlier tracks recorded, 'All Join Hands', was selected as the lead single, picking up where 'My Oh My' had left off, an anthemic, flag-waving, arms-in-the-air number. Lea told *Record Mirror*, 'It's another anthem. I come up with these on my way down to the chip shop.' Loosely based on 'Auld Lang Syne', it's a full-on swayer. A video was shot, directed by Philip Davey, which continued the 'My Oh My' feel – a pianist (actually eccentric occasional hit-maker John Otway) is playing to a well-heeled private audience in evening attire, when Holder bursts through the door singing, and Lea appears and pulls Otway off his stool and takes over the piano. As the duo play (looking a little like a Roma Sparks) the audience, after their initial shock, begin to warm to the spectacle. Dave Hill appears out of nowhere to wield his axe on the piano lid, and presto, it's soon a Slade concert.

The record entered the chart at thirty-eight, and rose to number fifteen, and stayed in the Top 30 until the new year. Its B-side was 'Here's To… (the New Year)', which kept the full Hogmanay vibe of the A-side going. It was fundamentally a new year's version of 'Thanks for the Memory', but not without its charms – 'Big Ben's banging away.' It was The Stranglers' 'Golden Brown' meeting Newkie Brown with Lea's fretless bass in the forefront.

Although Slade, unlike their peers Status Quo, were not asked to appear on that year's Band Aid single, the general upturn in sales because of the single's success greatly benefitted Slade, and 'Merry Xmas Everybody' again rose inside the UK Top 50. With this clear mandate, recording for the next album – which had been made with John Punter at Angel, Portland, RAK and Utopia Studios across

London – was completed. Originally titled *Partners in Crime*, *Rogues Gallery* boasted ten new Holder-Lea tracks, all building on their eighties template – a touch of rock, a touch of metal, a touch of Celtic, with a lot of added synthesiser. Mid-eighties Queen and Van Halen are in the mix as well. Every song is packed so full of licks, wrapped in a professional sheen – the band's playing is remarkable throughout; every track could have been a single.

'What an intense album that was, both musically and personality-wise,' John Punter comments. 'I'm not sure we didn't overdo it. It's relentless. But it's fun. It was great to work on a full album with the guys, to really explore the songs and do the best job possible.' 'Harmony' is an incredible piece of yacht-rock meeting gospel; '7 Year Bitch' has all the infectious catchiness of a TV advert; 'I'll Be There' is very much in the 'Run Runaway' mode; 'Walking on Water, Running on Alcohol' was huge and anthemic. The downside was simply that everything was so hook-laden, so perfect, it was akin to eating a chocolate gateau – towards the end, it's just too rich. There's even mass whistling on 'Time to Rock'. 'All Join Hands' closes the album, as a beautiful coda, a moment to take stock and recover from the sensory bombardment of the rest of the album.

'I think that maybe too many of the songs on *Rogues Gallery* sounded like pop hits,' Dave Hill told *Percy* magazine. 'So, the album began to lean too much to being regarded as a sort of "poppy" album, and there is nothing worse than that for me.' It certainly was a hugely commercial sound – the sort of album The Who or ABBA could have made if they had remained together, and not a million miles from what Genesis were about to do on *Invisible Touch* the following year.

'My favourite tracks were 'All Join Hands', 'Walking on Water, Running on Alcohol', 'Hey Ho Wish You Well' and '7 Year Bitch',' John Punter says. 'I always thought that *Rogues Gallery* had the potential to be like ZZ Top's *Eliminator*.'

Paul Cookson adds, 'It might have been over-produced but there's some great songs on it. I still think that 'Time to Rock' could be a football song. I can just imagine a football crowd doing a whistling thing.'

The sleeve was fairly curious as well: four geezers sitting in a pub wearing a collection of hats. If people liked to theorise about the sleeve of The Beatles' *Abbey Road* album – George, the gravedigger; Paul, the deceased; Ringo, the undertaker; and John, the preacher – *Rogues Gallery* offers two landowners (Lea and Powell), a yokel (Holder) and a farmer (Hill). 'They looked like Age Concern was involved,' Ian Edmundson says. 'Was that the sleeve to bring out for an album that was trying to break them in America? That was not the sleeve they needed.'

Rogues Gallery was launched with a party at The Trumpet on 21 March. All the band appear on fine form, pictured around the piano, and, with it being the mid-eighties, being confronted by a kissogram, Liz Lenten from the Songbird Agency, dressed as a policewoman. Lenten remembers the evening with affection: 'That was a press call. I'd gone as policewoman to complain about the noise – there was always some ruse. The amount of people who'd fall for it! I used to think, how many policewomen turn up in fishnets, high black stilettos and red lipstick, really?'

Lenten had just moved to London and was singing professionally at the Sheraton Skyline Hotel in Heathrow, when she got her messenger side-line. 'I started working with Kara Noble, who ran the agency. We liked to call them "Singing Telegrams". I did some crazy ones for some really cool people – and one of the gigs was to go up to the *Rogues Gallery* launch. I stripped down to my corset and suspenders, sang the song and then stayed for the party. They got me a cab from London to Bilston and back, which was quite unheard of at the time. I went on my own – before mobile phones and the internet you'd just be given an address, a time to be there and whatever costume – and off I went.'

Lenten's party piece was to write and sing new words to 'My Favourite Things' with inside information on the targets, which she duly did for Slade and their new album. Although the band looked a little refreshed, Lenten recalls them fondly: 'They weren't inappropriate at all; they were dead funny. They were taking the mickey out of my lack of cleavage. I replied, you've either got the voice or the tits. I had the voice.'

Years later, Lenten – who at the time of writing, is a much-respected singer-songwriter, artist and label manager, and educator, and in 2022 was awarded a British Empire Medal for her services to music – was confronted by Mark Gustavina, the guitarist in her band, Auburn, a huge Slade fan, who'd found one of the pictures of her and Slade turned into a jigsaw online. 'He couldn't believe I hadn't told him. I didn't think about it afterwards, it was just another night.' Lenten recently sold the corset she wore that night and other telegram nights on Vinted. The Slade connection wasn't listed as a selling point.

* * *

Sadly, given the full promotion of RCA and the will of the band, none of the singles after 'All Join Hands' caught flame. Despite its big, daft *Alice in Wonderland*-meets-fairground Philip Davey-directed video, the title of '7 Year Bitch', and its lyrical content of 'a bit on the side' fell foul of radio programmers and the public. As a result, it only reached number sixty in the UK; the follow-up single 'Myzsterious Mizster Jones', with its bright synthesiser riff and daft video went ten places higher. Its ZZ Top-inspired B-side 'Mama Nature Is a Rocker' ('She'll get your head spinnin' in the spring') is an early eco-anthem.

'Little Sheila' was taken as a single in the US and Canada, and got to number eighty-six in the *Billboard* 100, and number thirteen in the Mainstream Rock Chart, thanks to the promo video directed by Nick Morris. If the clip for 'Myzsterious Mizster Jones' was daft, this was preposterous – broken into a five-act play, it has all the lighting and effects of the mid-eighties high-hair videos that MTV so favoured. One thing is for sure, although the process may have been long and arduous, and the stop-start nature of filming very much unlike the one-two of the earlier days, everyone looks like they are having the absolute time of their lives. As younger people in the 2020s say, strong recommend.

As glossy and mid-eighties as it sounded, *Rogues Gallery*, with its Brian Aris picture of the four rogues on its cover, was only to reach number sixty in the UK charts and 132 in the *Billboard* 200, which is a huge shame as it deserved more than this. One of the reasons the album wasn't a bigger success was that, for the first time in their career, Slade didn't undertake any touring to support it. A twenty-three-date string of shows was announced to support the album in late 1984, taking in all of March 1985 with a lot of favourite haunts included – three nights at Hammersmith Odeon, the Civic Hall in Wolverhampton, Ipswich's Gaumont, and ending with a trio of nights at Birmingham. The tour was announced without full approval of the band, and Holder vetoed the plans.

'Nobody knew it was over until the '85 tour was cancelled. I bought tickets to three shows on that,' Ian Edmundson says. 'To the question, "When are you going to tour again?", Noddy would say, "Personal reasons." I think he did the right thing, he put his life first.' Aside from one brief shambolic performance in 1991, Slade would never play live in the UK again.

CHAPTER 31

Uncool for Everything

While *Rogues Gallery* was puttering out and Holder was dealing with his personal problems, the Live Aid concert was staged at Wembley and Philadelphia. The brainchild of Bob Geldof, for people of a certain age it was as if the world stopped dead in its tracks on 13 July 1985. Aside from the wonder of its altruism, for the music industry the Live Aid concerts came just at the right time and acted as a worldwide shop-window for its recently developed innovation, the compact disc. Appalled by seeing the Ethiopian famine on television, Geldof marshalled as many rock star friends as possible along to Sarm Studios in Basing Street, London, in November 1984, when they recorded 'Do They Know It's Christmas?', which topped the UK charts and became the best-selling single in the UK of all time at that point.

Several months later, this impromptu spirit coalesced into something altogether grander: Live Aid, a concert split across two venues on either side of the Atlantic. With other events happening around the world, it was to be broadcast live globally with every artist waiving their fee – and all money raised going to aid the Ethiopian people. The logistics were simply bewildering, something that is almost too easily taken for granted today. From venue hire to television schedule clearances; from transport to hospitality – all of this had to be considered before the not too

335

trivial matter of assembling a world-class bill that would encourage people to attend, or to tune in, and most importantly, donate large sums of money to the cause. Winging it beyond belief, and frequently exceeding his own expectations, Geldof used his unique method of personability, aggression and savoir faire to assemble the greatest acts in the world at that moment. The intention was simple: it was, in Geldof's words, to be a day for 'unalloyed hits or classics, the global juke-box'.

With performers ranging from Queen – who stole the show and rebooted their career in the process – to The Who, David Bowie, U2 and, closing the show, Paul McCartney, the enterprise was a remarkable success. Given that Slade had been enjoying their '84/'85 renaissance, former tour-mates Status Quo and Holder's alleged Kensington Market hat-seller Freddie Mercury plus his band Queen were on the bill, it seemed unusual that Slade were not invited to take part – even just in the closing chorus. But it was not to be.

'We were never asked,' Holder told Chris Selby and Ian Edmundson in 2020. 'I think we were considered "uncool" for Live Aid. We should have been asked, but we were always considered uncool for everything.'

It was simply a case of overall record sales for the Global Jukebox and Slade hadn't racked up enough. 'Like Queen, Slade's music had become part of everyone's DNA,' fan Steve Mason says. 'But maybe you don't realise that until it gets awakened. With Queen, everyone suddenly realised, "Oh, fuck, we know all these songs." It's an interesting idea if Slade had got that slot. That would have been amazing, wouldn't it?'

Someone who was at Live Aid from Slade's diaspora was the first manager, Maurice Jones, who had looked after Bob Geldof when he was in The Boomtown Rats. With partner in MCP, Tim Parsons, Jones came on board with Harvey Goldsmith to make the concerts happen. Unlike Goldsmith, who became known around the globe after the concert, Jones and Parsons kept their anonymity. 'Interestingly, Harvey Goldsmith got all the plaudits for Live Aid, but as the promoter of the Rats, Mo was the actual promoter of the Wembley gig. A great guy,' Chris O'Donnell recalls.

Like many, Lea and Holder were in awe of Geldof's achievement. They wrote the song 'Do You Believe in Miracles' in dedication to him, recalling when they'd met in Germany when Slade were at a low, and RCA wanted it rushed out. With its huge anthemic introduction, the band stomped into a 'Run Runaway' mode, telling the story of their meeting and his achievement. Like the friend in a pub who ties up all the prevailing arguments and talks supreme sense, it was another example of Slade's ability to take the everyman's voice and show sincere appreciation for Geldof's achievement. In other hands it could have simply sounded mawkish. In Slade's hands, it just seemed so very natural. Although the record didn't chart highly (number fifty-four) it seemed to be everywhere that Christmas, especially when backed by the entertaining 'My Oh My (Swing Version)'. In fact, its performance was scuppered by its appearance on Slade's rather special next studio album.

* * *

As the Thatcherite revolution took hold in the UK, and among the upper working classes and beyond, disposable income became more readily available, partying was big news as the eighties progressed. Russ Abbot, who had been the drummer in The Black Abbots, a more northern version of the Wolverhampton scene's The Montanas, told his peak-time Saturday night TV audience how much he enjoyed parties with a 'happy atmosphere'. Black Lace were the undisputed rulers of this niche through their single 'Superman', and then, importantly, the ultra-mindless ultra-entertaining 'Agadoo'. How could Slade, the original party starters, fit in with all this? Very easily it transpired.

It is, even by the standards of the band, quite astonishing how the *Crackers: The Christmas Party Album* came about; however, it is actually one of their best studio albums of the eighties – the fun and energy levels are high, and the four are playing in the studio together as a band. In that sense, it is on a par – no, really – with the original *Slade Alive!*. The band were approached by Telstar Records, a company that specialised in TV-advertised albums, who had released, and seen enormous sales figures for Black Lace's *Party Party – 16 Great*

337

Party Icebreakers the previous festive season. Label owners Sean O'Brien and Neil Palmer knew that Slade had the ability to out-party them all, and licensing the group from RCA, with whom Telstar had associations, the deal was for a part-new, part-greatest hits album. Eight new or re-recorded hits, up against eight classics or recent numbers.

Crackers: The Christmas Party Album was recorded in the time it took John Punter to capture the snare sound he wanted. The album recalls the intensity of *Slade Alive!* but importantly, how exciting it must have been to see The 'NBetweens at Willenhall Baths. The album starts with Powell's feral drumming on the Chris Montez hit 'Let's Dance'; a fabulously rocky version of 'Santa Claus is Coming to Town' follows, and somehow, Slade manage to make 'Hi Ho Silver Lining' sound vital, updated without following Jeff Beck's notorious pop-psychedelic version. The original 'We'll Being the House Down' clatters in in its rambunctious manner before a re-recorded 'Cum On Feel the Noize'. A breather is needed, and after an arm-wave with 'All Join Hands', at last, 'Okey Cokey' makes sense. The side ends, an embarrassment of riches straight from the cash'n'carry with the original 'Merry Xmas Everybody'.

Side two blends in some more contemplation amid the stomping – after the new single 'Do You Believe in Miracles', the inclusion of which made the band wonder if it scuppered its chance on the singles charts; 'Let's Have a Party' removes any of the subtlety of Elvis Presley's original, while the re-recording of 'Get Down and Get With It' is rather poignant. Without any live shows to back it up, this was probably the last time the band ever played it, fourteen years on from the original. The vocals are broadly the same, but behind Slade are flaming even harder than on the original, with far looser production. 'My Oh My' and 'Run Runaway' follow, then 'Here's To... (the New Year)'. The final tracks offer an opportunity for reflection; a year after release, Slade became one of the first artists to cover 'Do They Know Its Christmas?', an anthem of the same spirit as 'Merry Xmas Everybody', but the home and domestic comfort of Slade's song is turned on its head: here the lyrics are graver, dealing with the devastating famine in Ethiopia. It's fascinating to hear the sombre nature of the original replaced with some cheery rocking.

The publishing royalty went to The Band Aid Trust, and the record royalty to UK Children in Need.

And, of course, a festive party couldn't conclude without 'Auld Lang Syne', and Slade perform it, rocking into 'You'll Never Walk Alone'. There was, being Slade, a great story attached – when they were recording the album at Portland Studios, just near Oxford Circus, Dave Hill chanced upon Victor Herman, a bagpipe-playing busker on Oxford Street, and felt he would be perfect to add a touch of authenticity to the track. Herman recorded his part, and as a gesture of thanks for his time and expertise, Slade gave him a wedge of cash. The next day, Herman returned the money to the studios saying the enjoyment he'd had was payment enough. The band invited him to the launch party and later presented him with a gold disc.

The sleeve for *Crackers: The Christmas Party Album* was not high art, nor was it ever intended to be: this was an album for piling high and selling competitively this festive season, amid Telstar's other baubles – Black Lace's *Party Party 2* album (the group in a can-can line with a family of all ages and balloons and streamers); and *The Love Album* (16 Classic Love Songs) (a couple about to kiss). The sleeve shows that Slade were everybody's fools after all. There is a huge picture of Noddy Holder blowing up a balloon, and then four snapshots which adorn the right-hand side of the cover – Dave Hill strewn with streamers; Holder again with a big yellow balloon; Jim Lea actually smiling – something that had only been seen twice before on a Slade album cover – with a miniature cracker; and, possibly to reflect his excessive nature at the time, Don Powell with both a party horn AND a sparkler. Art, it wasn't. Fun, it was. To the rear of the sleeve a note was written by the group, as if to nip their critics in the bud.

> Some things you do for love.
> Some things you do for money.
> Somethings you do for the fun.
> We had great fun making this album
> And hope you do listening to it.
> Ave-a-good'n
> Thanks to you all, and a Merry Christmas

At the time, beyond the Slade hardcore, the album was treated with a sense of derision, a nail in the coffin for any credibility the group may have had. That assessment is far far away from the mark. If it had had a superior sleeve and had not been on Telstar, it might have been better received. That said, Telstar had been discreetly raising its game, and collections by artists such as Elvis Costello and Marvin Gaye earlier that year were not 'bargain basement'.

Crackers: The Christmas Party Album reached number thirty-four in the chart, and remained on the listings across the festive season, earning Slade a gold disc. If anything, it was a shot in the arm for the group, clearly now listing thanks to Holder's resolute decision to give up touring, and the recording techniques favoured by producers that played directly to Lea's perfectionism.

'I enjoyed making the tracks for *Crackers* a lot more than those for *Rogues Gallery*,' Dave Hill said in 1986. 'The basic tracks for *Crackers* were done in Portland which is sort of a "beer and skittles" place – sort of "pint of beer and then record the next number". It is hardly the big scene, like AIR or the other places.'

Another link with the recent past was severed as Chas Chandler then sold Portland Studios to Don Arden, who also bought out Chandler's shares in RadioTracks, the company that Gary Crowley had recorded his voiceover for back in 1979 when he was in awe of meeting Chandler.

'*Crackers* is Slade playing in a room together,' Ian Edmundson says. 'On the whole, that album is joyous. *Rogues Gallery* wasn't joyous. *Kamikaze* wasn't joyous and the Americans got the better track listing. *Crackers* was joyous, that was the place where 'Okey Cokey' finds its home there.'

With hindsight, *Crackers: The Christmas Party Album* can be seen as the full stop to the group as they are known and loved. Perhaps it should have ended there.

CHAPTER 32

It's Hard Having Fun Nowadays

A side from its title, and frankly shocking cover, *Crackers: The Christmas Party Album* had been a great deal of fun and promoted a unity within the group. The same cannot be said for what was to become the final Slade album, *You Boyz Make Big Noize*, which was recorded throughout 1986 and early 1987 at Portland Place, AIR, Wessex, Music Works and Redan Recorders.

Before that, it had been reported in the fan club newsletter that Lea and Holder had been invited to write a song for a yet-unnamed movie about rival teenage marching bands in Northern Britain. The director was Ian Emes, who after years as an animator (he'd drawn a lot of Pink Floyd's live backdrops), had branched out into filmmaking with his much-admired short *Goodie-Two-Shoes*. The film, which became *Knights & Emeralds* starring Warren Mitchell and Nadim Sawalha, was released that October. Slade contributed two songs to the interesting and varied soundtrack album, 'We Won't Give In' and 'Wild Wild Party'. Both were fine, redoubtable Slade tracks that augured well for the group's forthcoming album: one a big old ballad, and the other a stormy rocker. The two seemed out of place on a soundtrack that included Maxi Priest, lover's rock star Carroll Thompson, The Joubert Singers, and, making one of his very earliest appearances, Rick Astley. The film ('A stand-up-and-cheer movie for everyone who reached for Fame and danced with *Flashdance*) tanked, but Slade acquitted themselves well.

An intriguing documentary was made at the time about the group – a forty-five-minute special for European Satellite TV channel Music Box, a forerunner of MTV Europe, which wasn't to start broadcasting until August 1987. Entitled *Perseverance*, it was presented and scripted by Gareth Jones, a DJ and presenter from North Wales, who went by his *Nom de TV* Gaz Top. The band were interviewed in pairs: Powell and Hill; Holder and Lea. Intercut with some of their biggest videos, it's a warm, touching and detailed tribute by lifetime fan Jones. Lea takes the lead and talks in his unguarded way. Holder sits beside him almost like a bit-part player. Jones gets Lea to reveal that he has played guitar throughout Slade's career, but Lea insists, 'The strength of the band is four members. What's the point of us standing up and saying he plays everything, but in the studio and when it comes to music, I'm sort of Amadeus you know, I'm on another planet. Everybody else is down the street somewhere. I get a bit frustrated at times.' Hill provides one of the most telling quotes in his attitude to the group and how it contrasted sharply with Lea's. Talking about the look he says: 'It's very much part-showbusiness – the Arthur Askeys of rock'n'roll.' It is easy to see how comments like this, Hill taking Lea's precious musical vision and comparing it to the diminutive Liverpudlian music hall legend, could lead to division. If Lea was 'Be', Hill was 'The Bee Song'.

Selected by RCA, 'Still the Same' was the lead single, released in February 1987, for *You Boyz Make Big Noize*. They'd discussed releasing it over the festive season, but there was a worry that it would further reinforce the naysayers' opinion that Slade existed only at Christmas time. Produced by John Punter, it's a great big ballad, which indeed sounds Christmassy. 'What a great track,' Punter emphasises. The world had turned, however, and, like their attempts to chart a decade earlier, the record was ignored in the main by Radio One DJs, who now had new rock bands such as Bon Jovi and Europe to play if they were to play rock at all. There is also a danger, for a long-running band with a definable sound to release a record called 'Still the Same' and attract cynicism. RCA brought their marketing might to the table for the release, offering the single in a 'Commemorative Double Pack' to celebrate Slade's 21st birthday, with the affirmation 'Slade – Twenty One Years And Still Making More Noize Than Anyone Else'. The extra tracks again showed the Slade flame was burning brighter on their Bs – 'Gotta Go Home' is a rocking romp, while 'Don't Talk To Me About Love' had great interaction between Lea (on the verses) and Holder on the choruses.

In April 1987, Slade's fourteenth studio album *You Boyz Make Big Noize* – its title coming from Betty Edwards, the tea lady at Wessex Studio, as she passed the studio – was released. It upped the ante from *Rogues Gallery*, and, as a result, it is bigger, beatier, louder, and somewhat one-dimensional. It also brought a new producer into the mix, aside from Jim Lea and John Punter: Roy Thomas Baker. Baker came with an enormous reputation – rising through the studio system like John Punter, Baker went to Trident where he formed a relationship with Queen, co-producing five of their albums with the group, including *A Night at the Opera* and its much-adored and revered single, 'Bohemian Rhapsody'. Recent works had included The Cars, Journey and Mötley Crüe. In short, this was big news.

'It was very expensive having Roy Baker on the last album, but I was pleased to let other producers do all the work, I didn't want the pressure,' Jim Lea told the *International Fan Club Magazine* in January 1990. 'The idea was to bring him in to update our sound somewhat. He did a perfectly fine job.'

Holder said in 2005: 'Jim liked working with him, but I didn't. Roy took three or four days to get the drum sound alone. It was like a jigsaw, the way Roy wanted to put our songs together. It wasn't the way I saw Slade. Slade were spontaneous. None of our classic singles was made that way. That was one of the reasons why I didn't want to carry on in the band.'

'I was in the studio for three days while he was doing different mics and all,' Don Powell told *Trouser Press* in 2023. 'I was getting to hate that guy because I was just there playing drums the whole time.'

In the end, due to time and expense, Roy Thomas Baker only produced two tracks on the album, but they were the first two: 'Love Is Like a Rock' had been a 1981 US hit for Donnie Iris and was ahead of its time in terms of it being an airheaded power-driven sing-song, not unlike J. Geils Band's 'Centerfold'. Baker dials up the excess and removes any trace of the original's funky guitar. It also was enough to impress Ozzy Osbourne, who, according to Jim Lea, went on to hire Baker on the strength of this for his next album.

Taken as the album's second single, 'That's What Friends Are For' is a standout track, a heartfelt paean to good pals who look out for each other in hard times; there is just enough syrup in it but it is not mawkish – a great late addition to a generally fabulous singles catalogue. Released a week ahead of the album, its B-side was 'Wild Wild Party', written for *Knights & Emeralds*, which is, as Slade writer Chris Ingham notes, 'an impressively decadent wall of noise'.

'Fools Go Crazy', all power guitar and block synthesiser chords, has an affectionate tribute to Aretha, one of Holder's favourites; 'She's Heavy' with its keyboard bass, is a tad problematic through the 21st-century lens, – it could be viewed as a roaring approval for a full-figured female, or at worst, fat shaming.

"Ooh La La in LA' should have been a hit,' John Punter says. It's difficult to assess really why it wasn't. It is a rather splendid piece of euro-flummery, big drums, high hair, the whole works, another of Holder's travelogue songs of the group's time in the City of Angels. It refers to Powell's dalliance with Bob Dylan's daughter and mentions BLTs ('but there ain't no sauce'). Holder was to write, and in many respects, this is the absolute key to the entire group: 'I was dreaming of a proper bacon sandwich, though, on a white bread bap, with brown sauce... ecstasy.' Echoing what he'd said about the sandwich in 1977 to Lesley Judd on *Blue Peter*, one wonders if there had been proper bacon sarnies in the US, the group would have cracked the country.

'Won't You Rock with Me' has a fabulous synth part; 'Me and The Boys' is an affectionate tribute to Queen's 'We Will Rock You'. Its sheer chutzpah is to be scrupulously applauded, its lyric so splendid, speaking squarely to the group's audience – a celebration of 'never being too old to gadabout'. This is a great example of the fears of the time of how rock was going to survive middle age; bear in mind that three of the group were then 41, with Lea at 38. At the time of writing, in the current grown-up youth club, those ages are positively junior. Only Slade could sing about sweating during eating a vindaloo convincingly. 'Sing Shout (Knock Yourself Out)' is as light and fluffy as its title. 'The Roaring Silence' is big and ambitious, sounding something at times like a hymn. The album closes with 'It's Hard Having Fun Nowadays', the irony of its title not lost on many commentators. Selby and Edmundson suggest that it was 'an ominous title. Were the band having much fun at all?'

You Boyz Make Big Noize was the final long-player from Slade. Some eighteen years after *Beginnings*, it is not without its appeal. 'It's good,' Ian Edmundson says. 'It had Slade on the label and we all thought it was a Slade record. It didn't become apparent how little Dave is involved in some things until much later on. As a result, it just didn't take off in the right places.'

'*You Boyz Make Big Noize* came out in 1987, the year hair metal ruled the world,' *Prog* editor Jerry Ewing says. 'They had half credibility. They were great when they were a glam band, and my god, weren't they were brilliant when they went really heavy, but it's not *quite* as good as it should have been, is it?'

'We could've captured that album a lot easier, a lot better, I feel,' Powell said in 2023. Despite the amount of money and time spent, *You Boyz Make Big Noize* had a solitary week in the UK album chart at number ninety-eight.

As a result, RCA allowed their contract to lapse and Slade were again releasing singles on the Cheapskate imprint, looking to see if, for another time, the house could be brought down. 'You Boyz Make Big Noize', the album's title track that wasn't on the album, was released as a 7-inch and 12-inch single on 31 July. It is an astonishing record, as Slade take on the rap/metal crossover that the Beastie Boys had brought to UK shores earlier that year with their breakthrough hit (and US number one) '(You Gotta) Fight for Your Right (To Party)'. It's entirely professional, accomplished and very funny – and, of course, the band play and Holder raps with the elan and professionalism you'd expect. Famed session singer Vicki Brown was passing by and was brought in to sing the female part. Whereas after a wall of guitar on the Beasties single, the rappers (Ad-Rock, MCA and Mike D) shout 'KICK IT' to kick it off, on the Cheapskate version, Holder shouts 'GET STUCK IN' – it is all executed OK, on one level it's impossible to find fault.

It's as if Slade have been possessed by The Grumbleweeds or similar doing a sketch of what they think it would be like if Slade made a rap record ('It's better than the nutter who nuts you in the nuts' is pretty special). That said, the group's defiant message is fully intact, and the song references 'Mama Weer All Crazee Now', and possibly even 'Wild Winds Are Blowing'.

When Slade lost their way, how they lost their way. It came down to relentless chasing a hit, a chart position – fully understandable, as that was the world they knew. They also knew the oldest adage of what goes around comes around, hence their glorious Top 10 success of 1983/84 – but this feels as removed as 'Rock'n'Roll Bolero' was to 'Cum On Feel the Noize'. The single, even with a performance on ITV programme *Get Fresh* (hosted by Gaz Top) failed to make the UK Top 100. 'It was different for them and I liked it,' Stu Rutter says. 'But they were still being pushed as a kid's band and were only getting slots on kids TV shows.'

The last release from *You Boyz Make Big Noize* was the single that the group had wanted to release first – the classy ballad 'We Won't Give In' that had been written for *Knights & Emeralds*. Released in November 1987, and backed with 'Ooh La La in LA', the single trickled out on Cheapskate. Despite a favourable review in *Kerrang!*, it failed to make the UK charts.

It seemed clear that the band were disintegrating. Noddy Holder was tiring of the machinations of the industry. 'This was the start of it becoming very corporate, I was going to record companies for meetings about album sleeves and promotion, which Chas always handled,' Holder said in 2019. 'Now it was me, and I would get some 25-year-old out of media school telling me what I should be doing with my career, but I had been in the business in my first pro band in 1962. It became a thing. Maybe that's how the business works today.'

If the real band's disintegration was kept on the downlow, UK audiences had the opportunity to watch their fictional group implode with the TV premiere of *Slade in Flame*, on Saturday 12 December 1987. The Jan-Feb-March 1988 edition of the *International Fan Club Newsletter* reported some fans held what would now be known as 'watch parties'. The write-ups in the papers at the time range from haughty indifference to critical appreciation – *The Guardian* said that it was a 'shrewdly discerning examination of the mid-sixties pop music scene using the rise and fall of a band played by Slade to comment sharply on media manipulation and the strain of snatched success'. *The Sun*, on the other hand, suggested, 'Remember sideburns, flares and awful rock music? Slade do – and the seventies rock group decided to base a whole film around them.'

'With the benefit of hindsight, the music of Slade's eighties chapter generated mixed feelings, being completely truthful,' Dave Ling says. 'At the time it was all good. We were simply glad to have them back. The songs 'We'll Bring the House Down', 'When I'm Dancin' I Ain't Fightin'', 'Rock and Roll Preacher (Halleuljah, I'm On Fire)' and 'Lock Up Your Daughters' connected with the prevailing musical vibe of the NWOBHM, and later on I can still find much pleasure in 'My Oh My' and 'Run Runaway', but those diamonds were surrounded by a fair degree of filler.'

* * *

At this time, Slade's influence could be seen in the UK in bands like Mama's Boys, Little Angels and The Quireboys, all hair and populist riffs, while in the States 'hair metal' had become a huge thing. Poison, Bon Jovi, Guns N' Roses could all be said to have some Slade in their DNA. Yet Slade were not in a position to capitalise on this. The group were still together in name but were all doing other things. A decision was taken to take an eighteen-month break. In fact, it is generally accepted that around this time Holder told the others of his intention to leave the group.

'I wasn't content in the band at that period,' Holder told Mark Blake. 'When you start you're all on the same page, heading for the same goal, all happy and working together. In our second wind, we were having a certain amount of success and still touring and broke America with a couple of records, and the equilibrium had changed. It happens in every band, but I never thought it would happen in Slade, where outside forces happened.' However, mindful of the power of the brand, his thoughts were kept only within the band at this time.

Holder embarked on what was to become a highly successful broadcasting career, presenting shows in Birmingham and

Manchester. Holder broadcast a Slade special on Piccadilly Radio, and then was asked to do a six-week series on the seventies, which then grew into a weekly slot. In 1988, Holder recorded 'Pepsi Anthem (Tear Into the Weekend)' for a Canadian Pepsi-Cola commercial. Recorded at Redwood Studios in London's Camden Town over a backing track, with Abbey Road engineer Brian Fifield, Holder told the fan club, 'It had already been written and they asked me to put the vocal to it. It is a rock'n'roll type tune in the 'Mama Weer All Crazee Now' mould. I got a phone call out of the blue, they sent me the lyric and offered me some nice money, so I couldn't refuse.' With Holder screaming 'The weekend starts here', it is a much sought-after piece of Slade-associated ephemera. 'Give me a Pepsi because I'm taking flight,' he sings, proving the adage that certain singers could sing the phone book and still make it sound convincing. Redwood owner André Jacquemin – who oversaw all Monty Python's recordings – recalls 'he was, as usual, really good and very "Noddy Holder".'

On 16 June 1988, another tie with the past was severed when Dave Hill sold his 1962 Radford Convertible Rolls-Royce Silver Cloud with the YOB 1 number plate that he'd transferred from his Jensen in 1974. It sold for £29,000. Looking to find musical interests beyond Slade, Hill formed Blessings In Disguise featuring former ELO and Wizzard keyboard player, Bill Hunt, bassist Craig Fenney and drummer Bob Lamb. Holder sang vocals on their 1989 Everly Brothers' cover, 'Crying in the Rain'. It was backed by a Hill and Hunt song, 'Wild Nights'.

Central News featured the single and an interview with Hill and Holder in The Bottle and Glass Inn at Dudley's relatively recently opened Black Country Museum. As the camera hovered over Holder, Hill implored throughout the interview that it was his project, and that he was hoping to get a different vocalist for each track. The clip ends with Hill and Holder miming to 'Wild Nights' ('a thank you to all the fans for the great nights we've had on tour') as they leave the pub and dance off down the street. It's a perfect capture of two very old friends. The group – with Hill and a different line-up – released a follow-up, 'Chance to Be', in 1991.

* * *

Slade collapsed as the eighties closed. 'I told the others I'd had enough,' Holder wrote in his first autobiography. 'I said I wanted to try other things. They weren't very happy. Don wasn't interested in touring either, but Dave and Jim wanted to carry on. I couldn't believe it. They were the two who moaned the most whenever we were on the road.'

'There was a dearth of song consistency,' Dave Ling comments. 'The fact that bad luck prevented them from finally breaking America just as it seemed they might have done so. The record label deciding not to renew the contract when it expired. And from what I understand, as realisation grew that the golden goose was not theirs for the taking, little niggles began to set in. A couple of years ago, Noddy told me: "We hadn't been getting on for a while."'

'They ran out of steam in a way, but that that's not their fault, because everybody does, of course,' said Tim Rice.

Slade appeared on a number one record in December 1989, when current phenomenon (and Telstar signing) Jive Bunny and the Mastermixers (in reality Doncaster DJ Les Hemstock, and father and son John and Andy Pickles) issued their third single, 'Let's Party'. It was a megamix of Christmas hits, in which – amid 'March of the Mods' and a Chubby Checker impersonator – a heavily pitched-up 'Merry Xmas Everybody' was featured, alongside Wizzard's 'I Wish It Could Be Christmas Everyday'.

Noddy Holder appeared on *Sky By Day*, a magazine show with Tony Blackburn and Jenny Hanley, on Friday 5 January 1990 to celebrate the record's success and to promote Blessings In Disguise. Hanley asked if Jive Bunny needed permission to release it. 'Yes,' Holder replied. 'And then we agree a price – that's the first concern!' He was questioned on the future of Slade. Asked why the group had been together so long, Holder said it was because the group didn't socialise, keeping it fresh for when they got together. He also announced that the group had indeed taken an eighteen-month break, and that he was looking forward to the band's releases appearing on compact disc. Misspelling was spoken about, the five-year cycle of pop music. He talked about he and Jim Lea stockpiling songs, and the 'Gypsy Roadhog' controversy.

Asked if he had any ambitions left, Holder said to get a US number one single, but he also made it clear that the band were to record again. Later in 1990, Holder and Lea produced a version of 'Merry Xmas Everybody' by The Metal Gurus, with the group's members, Slink, Rick Spangle, Hipster Loony and Lucky Mick. With all artist royalties going to the charity Childline, it was goth-rockers The Mission in full-glam disguise, highlighting the influence of Slade on artists like Mission leader Wayne Hussey, who would have been 15 when the original was released.

* * *

In April 1991, a chaotic event at Walsall Town Hall marked closure for the group as a live act. A twenty-five-year celebratory Slade exhibition had been planned by Slade fan Mark Richards at the Town Hall where the group had played their first ever gig in 1966. Items were sourced from throughout their career – the 4-track acetate of the first Vendors single from Powell, while Lea arrived with some of his stage clothes for the retrospective. On 6 April, the four members of Slade came together to celebrate the moment, in front of fan club members.

A shambolic onstage performance of Chuck Berry's 'Johnny B. Goode' ensued. Berry, of course, was the act that the four members of the group stood and watched after they had opened for him at the Lanchester Arts Festival in Coventry nineteen years earlier.

Ian Edmundson was playing guitar and witnessed this final performance: 'I was playing guitar at the back of Jim,' he says. 'Noddy played my red Tokai Stratocaster. I saw the whole thing, was backstage when there were discussions about going on. I was backstage afterwards; I was on stage at the side when it was going on.'

Edmundson stood and watched Slade's final appearance unfold. 'They turned up and they walked on stage and looked at this big stage rig, all the Marshall amps, the drum kit and the PA and you could just see them going, "we've been got", because they didn't know this was happening. They knew there was a band playing, but a support band doesn't have that kind of rig. Jim turned his amp up to 11 and scared Nod who really wasn't very pleased with the volume.'

Trevor Slaughter ran the *Slade fan club* at that time with Malcolm Skellington and had arranged with Marshall to lend them amplifiers. 'Malcolm asked Nod if he would play something for the fans. Suggestions went around of what they should play, and Nod said no to all of them. He said, "We'll do 'Johnny B. Goode' and that's that." You can't screw that up. When they came off, Nod had a face like fizz. The other three were all buzzing, they loved it. Nod had been made to do something that he didn't want to do, using unfamiliar gear and the sound was awful. I imagine Nod was mortified. When I spoke to him about whether he'd been tricked into doing it, he agreed. But at least he did it. Then he went off stage, the place went nuts and they beat it down the road to another hotel.' The video of the performance shows that, for a band for whom performance was everything, it was distinctly below par.

Slade would never play live together as a four-piece again.

CHAPTER 33

A New Era for the Group

The final release from Slade came via their old label, Polydor. Polydor had been interested in the release of the Blessings In Disguise version of 'Crying in the Rain', and had suggested Slade might re-record it. Although that fell through, Slade were asked to employ the then current marketing fad of adding one or two new tracks to a new greatest hits CD collection, as an incentive to buy the same old hits again. With Holder resigned to departure, Jim Lea stepped up as usual. The two new songs, 'Radio Wall of Sound' (which had actually been a Dummies track) and 'Universe' fortunately offer a positive full stop to the original Slade.

Getting its first public play at the Donington festival in August, a decade after the group had performed there, 'Radio Wall of Sound' gives a thrilling, fleeting glimpse into what may have been had Slade continued. With Lea taking a lead vocal, and Holder on the bridge and chorus, it sounded like an incredible start to the nineties. Radio One DJ Mike Read added some smooth mid-Atlantic patter to the track's intro and throughout, almost a calling card to other DJs on the station to play them. It's an affectionate homage to radio, and 'Telegram Sam' from their old rival Marc Bolan gets a mention as well. Directed by William Clark, the video captured their black, frockcoat and behatted look, set on the roof of the fictional radio station of the song. It is pure theatre, when Holder appears from behind Lea and Hill in his shades and hat to sing his bridge, it is at once exciting and reassuring – the group are back, all together, how fans would recall them. Complete with a 'Bohemian Rhapsody'-style set-piece at the end, it underlined that 'Radio Wall of Sound' was a credible return to form.

Twenty years almost to the date of 'Coz I Luv You', 'Radio Wall of Sound' was issued on 7 October and backed up with a *Top of the Pops* performance, recorded on the 16th.

Broadcast the following day, complete with pyrotechnics, it opened the show – quite literally – with a bang. Dave Hill stood on one leg showing off his heels, Holder prowled the stage wearing spectacles giving him a striking appearance and Lea took his responsibilities as band leader seriously. Powell was hardly seen, but certainly heard. Backed with the Dave Hill/Bill Hunt 'Lay Your Love on the Line', the single reached number twenty-one in the chart, returning the group to the UK Top 30 for the first time since 1984, and giving them the very billable fact that they had now enjoyed a Top 30 hit in three decades.

"Radio Wall of Sound' is a Jim song with Nod's voice added, so it's not really a Slade track,' Ian Edmundson says. 'But we saw the video of them playing the songs. It said Slade on the label and that's what matters really. To see them on *TOTP* doing that was great. It was a vindication, and it was a relief after years when nothing happened.'

'I love 'Radio Wall of Sound'," *Prog* editor Jerry Ewing adds. 'I was really hoping that might be a springboard, but it all fell apart. It was too little too late, but it just showed you that Slade still had something. They had enough for me to be really upset that that was probably going to be it.'

Released to coincide with the 20th anniversary of their first number one, *Wall of Hits* was their first compilation to truly embrace the CD age. Chris Charlesworth, the band's go-to journalist, was no longer part of the music press, but they still asked him to provide sleevenotes, which he was happy to do. 'Rock historians have been less than charitable to Slade,' he wrote. 'Their happy-go-lucky, good humoured personalities, their complete lack of pretension or political motivation and their generally irreverent attitude towards the art of rock were never likely to appeal to serious rock critics and there seems to have been a post-Slade conspiracy to place them in the file marked "trivial"; little more than an amusing footnote in the story of glam rock.' And so, it came, hit after hit, after hit – a twenty-track CD and eighteen-track LP with virtually all of the bangers in chronological order, apart from, of course, 'Merry Xmas Everybody' placed at the end, giving all the opportunity to skip it if played out of season. To coincide with the release, Slade's Polydor albums were made available on CD, in the scantest of packaging.

Hill and Holder took to the promo trail, and *NME*, always a supporter of their work, ran a two-page feature 'Holder But Wiser', where David Quantick and Terry Staunton (written David Kwantick and Terry Stortnton in the full spirit of '71–'73) interviewed them, followed by a Slade Top 10. It was a time when political correctness, the necessary forerunner of today's so-called 'woke' culture, had begun to rear its head. The butterfly effect of wings flapped in the mid-eighties by alternative comedians about sexism had manifested itself in some of the older TV programmes not being recommissioned for television, and certain comics effectively blacklisted. Holder, discussing 'Merry Xmas Everybody', was having none of it: 'It's like Benny Hill being taken off TV, which to me is feminism taken to its silliest extremes, because Benny Hill is British like seaside postcards, that's all it is. It's as British as music hall, and 'Merry Xmas Everybody' is in that bag to me.'

Sadly, Slade weren't to fit in a Christmas singles bag that year. Released at the start of December, the final piece of the original Slade jigsaw was 'Universe' – backed with Dave Hill and Bill Hunt's 'Red Hot' – the last release of the four-piece Slade. 'Universe' was a big anthemic ballad, which, had 'Radio Wall of Sound' caught more of the imagination, would have been a shoo-in for festive success – after all, it was their time of year. Its video, again directed by William Clark, was suitably grandiose, windswept and epic. Shot in a studio in Shepherd's Bush, with – in pre-CGI days – film shot through a small piece of painted glass, while the group emoted. It made the group look as if they were playing in a stunning, wind-blown landscape, like something out of *Dune*. The group promoted the single – and continued to do so in Europe until early 1992. Sadly, the single missed the UK chart altogether. *Wall of Hits* reached number thirty-four – exactly the same position as *Crackers: The Christmas Party Album* had done six years earlier.

Polydor had mooted that if the singles were both hits, the label would consider signing the group for a brand-new album, their first in five years. At the end of his notes for *Wall of Hits*, Chris Charlesworth noted that 'Radio Wall of Sound' and 'Universe' were 'both written by Jim Lea alone, which could herald a new era for the group.' The new era for the group was not one that Charlesworth was anticipating: the four players spending the rest of their career apart. As 'Universe' failed to make the chart, Polydor's plan was shelved. Lea had long harboured an idea to update 'We'll Bring the House Down' in a dance style. In 1990, he talked to Dave Kemp about it, recasting it as 'a house number in the style of metal/house fusion with the chorus in metal and the verse in a house sampled type sound.' The four of them entered the studio to work on this still-to-be-released epic. It was the last time all four of them were inside a recording studio together.

The final performance Slade made on TV was in February 1992 on the German show *Wetten, Dass..?* on RTL, hosted by Thomas Gottschalk. Playing 'Universe', the band looked superb, especially Holder in his black suit with frilly shirt, his hair longer and parted just off-centre. It was befitting that for this ending, the last time he had looked this was way back on *Beginnings*.

* * *

With European promotional commitments for 'Universe' out of the way, on 23 March 1992, Holder and Hill had a meeting at Colin Newman's office; effectively Slade were over. 'There was often tension and friction between some of the guys and I think things just got to the point where some of the members had had enough,' John Punter assessed. Holder lost, as Keith Altham says, his 'enthusiasm for the road'. And that 'disagreements had destroyed the heart and camaraderie in the band'. Not only had Holder 'left' the group, but Jim Lea had as well. 'Firstly, I have to say that Slade never broke up,' Lea told the *Birmingham Post* in 2000. 'There was no "that's it then"; we just sort of stopped working and Nod went off doing his own stuff.' It had been a cumulative effect of things that had been building since 1984; or possibly even 1974.

'I got into a rock'n'roll band to play music with guys. We were a shit-hot band and didn't want to see it going down the pan,' Holder told Mark Blake. 'When I left the band, I was amazed that Jim left at the same time.'

As a result, Hill and Powell, after discussions over use of the name with Holder, Lea and Colin Newman, formed Slade II. 'They didn't ask… just went off and did it,' Jim Lea told Mark Blake. 'In the end, I thought hang on, they've got to make a living. Nod and I had the writing and publishing. So, I said to Nod, let it go, I was very angry at first but then philosophical.'

'Going out without Nod was hard,' Hill said in 2019. 'Like the Stones if Jagger left. In time, fans appreciated I kept it alive.'

Slade II released an album, *Keep On Rockin'* in 1994 on the Play That Beat! label, featuring nine songs written by Dave Hill and Bill Hunt, and 'Hot Luv' by Don Powell and writer Paul Despiegelaere, known as Paul Mellow, the leader of Belgian eighties pop act The Machines. The album was recorded with Despiegelaere over three days at Impuls Studios in Herent near Leuven, Belgium. Perhaps the greatest surprise was 'Do You Want Me', a revisit of 1971's 'Get Down and Get With It' B-side. Largely ignored at the time, and regarded as a poor relation of the group's main catalogue, *Keep On Rockin'* is actually a better album than many would have thought, let down by a) not being Slade, and b) the fact that when it was recorded, it was de rigueur to have synthesised horn parts on a lot of the material.

Aside from some fairly standard rocking fayre, 'Dirty Foot Lane' is only Hill's second solo write across the breadth of the Slade catalogue (after 'M'Hat M'Coat' from *Till Deaf Do Us Part*), and is a sweet acoustic ballad about Hill's youth. Slade II also introduced their own Christmas song, 'Merry Xmas Now!' which, had it been released by the main group, would have been compiled widely. Sadly, the whole project was doomed to failure by comparison.

The sleevenotes said: 'Slade music is rock music, Slade music is fun music. Slade are the good time band. The world is ready for a Slade revival which certainly is the antidote for the nineties depression! The world will keep on rockin'!'

Soon, with the advent of Britpop, the world was rockin' again, to the sound of groups that had grown up with Slade's music.

CHAPTER 34

Cup-a-Souperstars

One of the greatest tributes to Slade in the nineties came from comedians Jim Moir (aka Vic Reeves) and Bob Mortimer; *Slade in Residence* became cult viewing as part of their *The Smell of Reeves and Mortimer* show on BBC2. Airing from September 1993, the show portrayed the four members of Slade living in a shared house on a street in the Black Country. Roy Wood, Ozzy Osbourne and Duran Duran were all neighbours. Moir portrayed Holder as the father figure, while Bob Mortimer played Dave Hill as the long-suffering matriarch. Don (Mark Williams) and Jim (Paul Whitehouse) were warring children. Often, Hill would serve his family Cup-a-Soups (the powdered soup introduced by Batchelors in 1972) for their dinner. It seemed to be clearly influenced by the 1973 *ATV Today* report of Dave Hill at home in Brueton Avenue, Solihull.

Holder said in *The Guardian*, 'It shows how much we meant to people, for them to remember that stuff and satire it... All that stuff about cutting Dave's hair with a Fray Bentos tin around his head was pretty near the mark. We used to take the mick out of Dave, mainly about his clothes. You've got to remember that at the height of our fame, Dave bought a house right next to a girls' school! So they were camping on his lawn, screaming every time he left the house. He's always been on Planet Dave: naive, childlike. I've probably never met a nicer bloke.'

It would have been churlish for the group not to have accepted the joke, although often depicted as buffoons, you were laughing with them, certainly when up against Simon Le Bon from Duran Duran, who was played by Charlie Higson as a Little Lord Fauntleroy character. Reportedly Le Bon was not thrilled by his portrayal. 'It summed up the cartoon element of Slade,' Ian Edmundson says. 'It captured that perfectly. It captured the non-serious, fun, silliness of the group. It wasn't nasty or malicious.'

Slade's old designer, Steve Megson, saw it: 'It was perfect. He really exaggerated the Black Country accent. It overemphasised all of the kind of clichéd comments. Noddy was a sensible, smart bloke.'

The mercurial Moir and Mortimer got to know Holder a little and invited him to be a panellist on their surreal gameshow *Shooting Stars*, broadcast on BBC2 in November 1995. Holder was on the panel with Chris Rea on the team captained by Ulrika Jonsson. 'When we did *Shooting Stars*,' Jim Moir recalls, 'we toured it round the country, and he joined the panel a few times. We were in Manchester at the Britannia Hotel. I was standing at the bar with Noddy. Suddenly, there was a banging on the ceiling and then two legs came through. This bloke fell about twelve feet. He then walked to the bar and was grabbed my security and chucked out. It turned out it was a stag do and he'd been locked in a bedroom cupboard, he could hear the bar beneath. He saw his only route to escape was to kick the floor in. Noddy and I stood there with our mouths open.'

Slade's currency grew further with the advent of Britpop. In the same way the stomping had been a reaction against the excesses of flower power and progressive rock, the simplicity of Britpop offered a more traditional route than some of the existentialism of grunge. Alongside Britpop there was also something of a glam-stomp revival with Lawrence turning Felt into Denim, and noise terrors Earl Brutus. When Earl Brutus got underway in the early nineties the only rule bandied around at the time was to 'come out stomping'.

'We'd talk up any idea we had and play a few tunes before the recording,' Brutus co-leader Jim Fry says. 'I remember 'Gudbuy T'Jane' getting aired to fire us all up along with some Thin Lizzy and the music of Mike Leander. Not unlike Slade, loud echoey drums and distorted guitars and a raft of shouting was the Brutus way. Nick [Sanderson, Earl Brutus drummer and co-leader] had to unlearn his drumming skills to play 'like an old bloke called Len in a worky' to emphasise our 'truckers beat'. That sound is buried in the DNA of anyone who went to a youth club in the UK in the early seventies; it's the soundtrack for being chased to the bus stop to avoid getting your head kicked in, and will always be the very heartbeat of Earl Brutus.' Running to the bus stop to avoid getting your head kicked in espouses one strand of Slade's sound perfectly.

However, while Brutus were beloved yet marginal at best, the greatest endorsement Slade could have had at this point was Oasis. Arguably the group who had taken Slade's position in relation to the music scene of the day, Oasis were not slow in sharing their love for the group, which was sealed by them covering 'Cum On Feel the Noize' as an encore at their victorious homecoming shows at Manchester City's Maine Road in 1995. Noel Gallagher told Keith Altham: 'I never went to college nor had a lot of words, but I always felt they spoke to me as a kid through their music, energy and drive – and we recorded 'Cum On Feel the Noize' because it suited Liam's voice so perfectly.'

* * *

On 17 July 1996, Chas Chandler died of an aortic aneurysm at Newcastle General Hospital. He had moved back to the north-east after leaving Slade and had been helping local bands. 'In 1994, Keith Altham set up a meeting with me and him,' recalls Chris Charlesworth.

> Chas said he wanted to write his life story and Keith figured it would be good for Omnibus. The three of us met at Champneys, the posh gym/pool on Piccadilly. Chas had been ill, and he looked like a shadow of his former self, much thinner, gaunt, careworn. The booze and fags had caught up with him. I told him I wouldn't give him an advance until I saw some sample text, about 10,000 words. Fair enough, he said. He was up for it but it never happened.

In his final weeks, 'Noddy and I went to see him, and he was great,' Don Powell says, 'but then a few days later Nod called me and said, "He's gone."'

In his final years, Chandler's absolute passion was to build an arena in Newcastle that could bring major artists to the city, as Tynesiders had to travel to either Glasgow or Sheffield to see bands beyond the 2,000 capacity of Newcastle City Hall. With architect (and one-time John Mayall saxophonist) Nigel Stanger, and long-time associate Henry Henroid, Chandler established Park Arena Ltd, which developed the 10,500-seater Newcastle Arena which opened on 18 November 1995. David Bowie was the first major rock act to play there that December.

'I met Chas Chandler a couple of times; he was an amazing character,' Mark Knopfler's manager Paul Crockford says. 'To think, he did The Animals, then Hendrix, then Slade and then the Newcastle Arena, now that's a great story.'

On Monday 22 July, 400 mourners gathered in the imposing 19th-century French Gothic-style St George's Church in Cullercoats to celebrate the storied life of Chandler. Stanger, Keith Altham, Holder and Chandler's eldest son Steffan spoke to a packed congregation. Attendee Chris Charlesworth recalls, 'Noddy told a story about how they stayed at the Miyako Hotel in San Francisco which was Japanese and had paper walls. Chas and others walked through them (as did loads of people apparently) and Noddy saw his outline in the paper wall. "It was the biggest of them all," he said. "That's what Chas was – the biggest."'

All of Slade were present, as was Swin; Noel Redding from The Jimi Hendrix Experience; Jimmy Nail; Nick Van Eede; Hilton Valentine and John Steel from The Animals; and 78-year-old Al Hendricks, Hendrix's father, with his daughter Janie. Understandably, his widow Madeleine cut a lonely figure, with the two young children she had with Chas. Slade biographer Chris Charlesworth travelled up by train to the funeral with Altham, producer/manager Larry Page and Andy Paley from Warner Brothers, Hendrix's US label. 'Norman Greenbaum's 'Spirit in the Sky' was played as the coffin left the church at the end of the service,' recalls Charlesworth, 'Nice touch… "When I lay me down to die, Goin' up to the spirit in the sky."'

'Chas was a lot of fun,' John Steel says. 'It was a terrible shock when he died. I was on the road with my band in Sweden when I got the call at the hotel. Keith was there obviously and Johnny Gunnell was very funny guy in a deadpan way.'

Charlesworth was later to write, that Chandler was 'immensely proud of his Geordie roots, a plain-speaking, honest and hard-working man, and he could cut through bullshit like a hot knife through soft butter. His legacy will linger on in the music of The Animals, in the extraordinary records he made with Jimi Hendrix, and in the cheers that will ring out as future generations of rock stars appear on stage at the Newcastle Arena.'

The week after Chandler's funeral Charlesworth was invited to lunch with Janey Hendricks and her dad in London: 'Music Sales was doing a deal with her to publish Jimi's printed sheet music and I was invited along simply because I'd known Chas (and could keep the conversation going). At the end of the lunch, I took Janey on one side and told her that in my view Chas always had Jimi's best interests at heart, unlike certain others who were involved with his career, and that if there was any extra cash swishing around no one deserved it more than Madeleine. What a knight in shining armour I was!'

'He really, really believed in it, meant well, he never cut corners,' Chandler's protégé, Nick Van Eede, says. 'That was maybe one of his weaknesses... that he always believed right to the end that the next song was going to be a big hit. That's really beautiful. It's a bit old school, the old music mogul, but that's what was sensational about Chas.'

Chandler was right to have believed in Van Eede. It could be said that after Hendrix and Slade, Van Eede was his third great discovery. His band, Cutting Crew, had a global hit with his song '(I Just) Died in Your Arms'. Nine years after Chandler discovered him, Van Eede scored a US number one single with that record, a feat that neither Hendrix or Slade were to achieve. He'd come a long way since the legs had been sawn off his stool in Poland.

* * *

Love for Slade blossomed as the 20th century came to a close. Released at the summit of the popularity of CD in January 1997, to capitalise on their recent elevation by Oasis as godfathers of Britpop, an updated hits collection was prepared by Polydor, complete with dedication to Chas Chandler. Again with notes by Chris Charlesworth, *Greatest Hits (Feel the Noize)* saw Slade back inside the UK Top 20. Charlesworth updated his populist essay: 'Eventually, their career spanned three decades, two rock generations and several leaps of fashion. Nowhere is this more evident than in Oasis' 1996 note-for-note cover of one of Slade's biggest hits, 'Cum On Feel the Noize'.'

In 1998, Radio Two broadcast a documentary called *The Boyz From The Black Country*, narrated by Toyah Willcox. Using the then currency of the world's latest pop phenomenon, The Spice Girls, the group were described as Leather Lungs Slade (Holder), Glitter Slade (Hill), Baby Slade (Lea) and Crash Bang Wallop Slade (Powell). *Slade in Flame* began to gain weight as well – a screening at the National Film Theatre in 1998 was accompanied by Noddy Holder giving a talk afterwards. 'You'll have to give me a few minutes to collect my thoughts,' he said after watching the film. 'It is twenty years since I've seen the film and I'd forgotten how heavy it was.' The audience kept Holder talking for way over the allotted twenty minutes for the Q&A.

In 1999, in keeping with the then current froth of seventies nostalgia, the BBC commissioned a programme entitled *It's Slade*. Directed by former journalist Len Brown, the film was an affectionate homage to the group. Brown had been a fan at school in the seventies. 'At one point I had Slade painted on my school haversack and a Fruit of the Loom Slade T-shirt,' Brown says. Although, like so many, it was a phase he quickly passed through. 'By 1975, I'd gone a bit prog and then full-on Santana until punk happened.'

All four members were filmed separately, and *It's Slade* had guest talking heads such as Keith Altham, Noel Gallagher, Suzi Quatro, Toyah Willcox, Ozzy Osbourne and PR man and fan Dylan White. 'I'd made a documentary about The Animals for Channel Four and I got to know all the guys,' Brown continues.

Most of all, I got on with Chas Chandler. The Animals documentary also put me in contact with Colin Newman who was a good contact, too. Keith Altham was also in The Animals documentary, so it started to make sense to explore a Slade one. Unfortunately, Channel Four weren't interested. We ended up making Marc Bolan *Dandy in the Underworld* instead in 1997. When I moved to the BBC the following year, I tried the Slade idea again and thankfully, got it commissioned. The saddest thing about the delay in it being commissioned was that Chas had died. I really regret not interviewing him about Slade (and Jimi) before he passed. I spoke to him a couple of times when he was working on Newcastle Arena. He was a fantastic and funny guy, proper legend in the north-east.

Time and budget constraints meant that, as in all cases of programmes such as this, economies had to be made. 'We weren't able to travel to the States to pick up interviews and we were limited in buying in archive,' Brown says. 'Also, it was too short – it should have been an hour at least. So many stories on the cutting room floor. There should have been more of Chris Charlesworth and especially Swin, the roadie. So disappointing to have to drop him.'

The documentary has all the millennial patina of 'weren't the seventies brilliant' that seemed to pervade all culture at this point – everything seemed to be either a mirror ball or a platform boot, but it is a fine testament to the group, in their older-yet-still-young appearance.

In the early 21st century, the Digital Versatile Disc (DVD) was introduced and became another way for companies to repackage films that had been made available on video the decade earlier. In 2003, Union Square Music licenced the rights to *Slade in Flame*, and had it digitally restored by the team at London's Vanderquest Studios. As a result, it was released that year to a flurry of critical acclaim. The sleeve proclaimed, 'as scripted rock and roll films go, this is destined to join the hallowed ranks of *A Hard Day's Night*, *The Girl Can't Help It* and The Monkees' *Head* at the top of the list.' DJ Gary Crowley, who idolised Slade as a 10-year-old, and in the late seventies did voiceovers at IBC studios, interviewed Holder for a fifty-minute extra for the DVD. It is one of the best recorded interviews with Holder, relaxed and expansive on a subject clearly close to his heart. 'I remember him being on good form that afternoon and very candid,' Gary Crowley says. 'And, really, really enjoying it.'

'I thought the film was great at the time,' John Maher, Buzzcocks drummer and now professional photographer says, remembering his competition win in 1975. 'I saw it a few years ago, thinking it might not have stood the test of time that well, but I was pleasantly surprised. I think it still stands as one of the best rock'n'roll films. It's actually a quite dark and cynical take on the music biz – probably not what most people were expecting from a Slade at their peak.'

'*Slade in Flame* just seemed to find a life of its own,' John Steel says, 'Over the years, it's become quite the underground hit.'

This was soon followed by yet another hits collection on Polydor. *The Very Best of Slade* was just that, a juicy two-CD set with almost unreadable notes by Chris Charlesworth – the white text on a silver background was barely legible. 'I was furious,' says Charlesworth. 'I tried to do something different this time and interviewed Nod who was staying in London at the Landmark Hotel on Marylebone Road. We had dinner there, a few drinks and talked for ages. It was lovely to catch up with him. Then when it came out and I saw the design I sent a snotty fax to the marketing guy at Polydor saying they should sack the designer. That was the last time I was asked to write any Slade sleevenotes.'

The package was accompanied by a DVD of their hit singles, a mixture of TV performances and promos. Of great interest was the inclusion of 1971's Granada TV programme *Set of Six*, which is one of the best showcases of Slade live at this point in their career.

As the internet blossomed so did Slade sites, manned by forensic aficionados wanting nothing more than to shine a light on the group. David Graham began the *Slade In England* site, locating and enhancing rare performances of the group globally. 'I spent decades tracking down this stuff in the wild west days of the internet where a posted envelope with the universal currency of dollars would get me things,' Graham recalls. 'I started cleaning up the audio bootlegs first and digitising them into the new MP3 format and offering them for download on the *Slade In England* site when we all had 14k modems and they took ages. Then, I turned my attention to the video footage on tapes, all of them skewed or crinkled in placcs but I was able to cut and paste the good bits into a pristine edit of whatever they were miming.' It was this growing presence that attracted curious fans wishing to look behind the public image.

While Polydor retained the compilation rights to Slade's work for the time being, Slade's album catalogue, so relatively ignored over the years, had also been licenced from Lea and Holder's Whild John Music company to Union Square Records. In 2006, Salvo Records, an imprint of Union Square, began reissuing their albums under the collective name of *Slade Remastered.* Jim Lea oversaw the remastering. The early jewel in the catalogue came with the release of *The Slade Box.* With its seventy-two-page booklet, designed by Tony Lyons with photographs supplied by Andrew Birkin, Barry Plummer and Gered Mankowitz, it was a job executed properly, overseen by Colin Newman. The audio was remastered by one-time EMI signed member of The Car Thieves, Tim Turan, and the compilation by Mark Brennan, who stood next to Dave Hill in the wings of the Lyceum watching Discharge in 1980. Keith Altham was the natural choice for the comprehensive essay (*Let's Bring the House Down... Again*) – with involvement from all four of the band. Altham called it clearly: in his opening paragraph, he states that Slade 'were the most astonishingly underestimated rock band of all time'.

'It wasn't until my later years that I dived into the album catalogue,' Dave Ling confesses, and he, like many others, found much to enjoy.

Ironically, the releases were meticulously curated by journalist, DJ and A&R manager Jonathan Chandler, who is known by the nickname Chas, which did not go unnoticed in the Slade camp. 'The odd thing was when I first met the band I was introduced as Jonathan, a name that only my family use, possibly because my boss thought it might be weird for the band. But they didn't bat an eyelid about it. Some of their associates, people like Keith Altham, who knew Chas very well, were a bit taken aback. One of them said, in jest I think, "Just don't yell at me like he used to." But everyone spoke very, very highly of him. And the band especially because he did really bust a gut for them, because he believed in them.'

Chandler, like so many in the band's orbit, had a story to tell:

I was born in 1971 so I was only a toddler when they were having their first flush of success. At that point I was living in Wolverhampton, as my dad was a teacher at Regis school in Tettenhall. Slade were, of course, local heroes, you couldn't get away from them back then, even as a very little kid as it turned out. Not long after I was three, I was very ill in playgroup. My mum was out shopping, and this was, of course, pre-mobile phone. The playgroup had an emergency number for our neighbours, the Joneses, who had several daughters. Mrs Jones came and picked me up, and took me back to her house and put me in one of the girl's beds. Their bedroom was absolutely covered with posters of Slade. Being ill, with these toby jug faces staring down at me from all angles, made quite an impression. It's pretty much my very first memory.

Chandler is one of the diligent, music-loving, knowledgeable professionals who quietly releases quality product, proving wrong the lie that record companies are full of uncaring hacks. 'I quickly realised looking around at what had been done before by Polydor in the first flush of CDs: press them up, get them out and charge £15. So, I thought this was a brilliant opportunity. Slade were probably the biggest UK band never to have had expanded reissues or a comprehensive remastering programme, partly because they owned their own catalogue and partly because they slipped through the net, regarded as a pop band rather than a band of substance.'

The *Slade Remastered* releases and their promotion received the prestigious *Music Week* Catalogue Marketing Campaign award 2007, the first time the award had been won by an indie operator. The releases continued with the individual albums and then two well-received packages, *B-Sides* in 2007, which brought together their flipsides, many appearing for the first time on CD, from 1969's 'One Way Hotel' (the reverse of 'Wild Winds Are Blowing') to 1991's 'Red Hot' (Dave Hill and Bill Hunt's flip to 'Universe'). This was followed by the genuinely eagerly awaited *Live at the BBC* collection, which brought together most of their sessions and jingles recorded for the corporation between 1969 and 1972, from the first Dave Cash session in October 1969 to John Peel in May 1972. It also contained their August 1972 Paris Theatre concert.

For the first time in years, outside of bootlegs, fans could hear their covers of The Beatles' 'Getting Better', Traffic's 'Coloured Rain', The Moody Blues's 'Nights in White Satin', and somewhat bizarrely, to show quite how eclectic their palette was, 'It's Alright Ma, It's Only Witchcraft', the Ashley Hutchings/Richard Thompson track from the first Fairport Convention album. 'It was a revelation to me – I'd never heard the bootlegs – because a lot of it was recorded before they were writing their own material. And their covers were brilliantly judged. Like 'Nights in White Satin', the ultimate violin pop tune, and they killed it. The releases were the first time Slade had been taken to the media as a serious rock proposition,' Chandler says. 'This is a band who'd been almost discounted because of their enormous pop success and Christmas single. They are very strong albums; it was not all about the singles. Great musicians, very good songwriters and an extremely interesting story.'

Even America, so resistant to the group's charms, affectionately looked back on two CDs on The Shout! Factory label. *Get Yer Boots On: The Best of Slade* was released in 2004, a straightforward soup to nuts of Slade's obvious anthems. Of greatest interest to the hardcore was 2007's *In for a Penny: Raves & Faves*, which curated lesser A-sides and album tracks, offering for once an off-the-beaten track collection. Both CDs were compiled by *Rolling Stone* journalist Dan Epstein, clearly an admirer of the group.

There was also some good fortune for one of their most divisive tracks of old – for the 2009 edition of Electronic Arts' much-loved award-winning football computer game series, *Fifa*, 'Give Us a Goal' was used in its TV advert. Even one of the group's most sizeable flops proved a revenue stream. On 10 March 2010, the C4 nightclub in Wolverhampton changed its name to The Slade Rooms, in honour of the town's most famous rock'n'roll sons. Don Powell and Dave Hill were on hand to cut the ribbon.

CHAPTER 35

Whatever Happened to Slade?

i. A Clever Little Cookie: Whatever Happened to Noddy Holder?

As the public face of the group, it was obvious that Noddy Holder would go on to occupy British national treasure status. As John Punter assesses, Holder is 'one of the great voices in rock'n'roll and a great songwriter.' Slade laureate Paul Cookson ventures, 'I think there's two Noddys. There's the rock'n'roll Noddy, 'Cum On Feel the Noize', and there is the autobiographical, thoughtful Noddy with things like 'Far Far Away' and 'How Does It Feel'.'

Diversifying from playing music, Holder had begun broadcasting during the eighties, and in the nineties became a popular regular presenter on Manchester's Piccadilly Radio. In 1990, Holder started dating Suzan Price, a researcher on the show *Central Weekend Live*. In January 1995, she gave birth to their son, Django. By the mid-nineties, thanks in part to Britpop and the 'new lad' movement, the seventies seemed again to become ultra-fashionable, especially with the patronage of Oasis, and in November 1996, Holder was the target of Michael Aspel's *This Is Your Life* – the big red book was brandished at him. The ruse was that he was in Granada Television Centre to appear with Mrs Merton, writer and comedian Caroline Aherne's alter-ego, on her talk show; instead, he was called to celebrate his life. 'I've never been speechless, but tonight, definitely,' Holder said after being surprised. His mother Leah was there, partner Suzan, as were daughters Charisse and Jessica.

In the thoroughly urbane manner that had endeared him to millions, after a compilation of Slade hits had shown, Aspel said: 'They were great days for you, and they were great days for the rest of Slade – Jim Lea, Don Powell, and Dave Hill!' The other three members of Slade duly came on to play tribute, furthering the feeling that the group were simply resting as opposed to being ripped asunder.

Dave Hill recounted a well-told-yet-still-incredulous Bahamian tale: 'We were put in an expensive hotel and all our food way paid for, and we just run up bills and everything; the manager, Dan Darrow, comes along and says, "where's me money?"… we owed all this money and we had to stay there to pay this debt off.' As Hill recounted the tale, Powell looked at his watch, to suggest Hill was going on a bit. 'But it was an amazing experience,' Hill continued – 'we all lived together in a one-room place – we all learned to put up with each other, and not share a room together again!'

'Stranded in the Bahamas!' Aspel concluded.

The others all laughed and nodded and moved over to the front row of the seats opposite, with only Hill showing real affection to Holder. Phil Burnell appeared; and then Powell spoke of the fateful cross-Channel ferry meeting, and of Holder's exploits in a toilet in Torquay.

Gary Glitter appeared and recounted their 1966 residency in Kiel. Steffan Chandler represented his father, who had died that July, saying how Holder taught him how to swear when he was younger. Keith Altham recounted the skinhead tale; DJ Alan Freeman came on and gave a suitably gushing eulogy, commenting that although he thought 'Get Down and Get With It' sounded vulgar, he loved it and that they were a huge part of the 'glam-metal syndrome', making it sound something like the military-industrial complex. 'Their music has never been in; it's never been out but it's always been there, and as long as there is pop music and rock music, it will be part of us, and Noddy, you're a clever little cookie, alright?'

After Suzi Quatro, Brian May recounted how Freddie Mercury was telling Slade what they should do with their live act, and May

372

was waiting for Holder to explode, yet replied 'You guys, probably have a point, which I thought was very forbearing of you.' Jim Lea told the Reading arrival story, and Vic Reeves and Bob Mortimer acknowledged their Slade skits. Keith Chegwin and Toyah Willcox talked of the *Roll With It* programme. Samantha Janus talked of the work they had done on the forthcoming TV show, *The Grimleys*.

Most touching of all was the appearance of many from Slade's old road crew, and finally, Swin, Graham Swinnerton, who had gone on to become one of the most respected tour managers in the business. He had flown in from America where he was working with The Fugees, at that point one of the biggest acts in the world. In his very affectionate tribute, he remarked that Holder was one of the regular guys, one of the crew. The climax of the show was the then two-year-old Django 'performing' 'Coz I Luv You' on stage at The Trumpet. After Django appeared, there was the standard walk to the front of the stage with everyone gathered around. Lea bounded out to be by Holder's side.

Chris Charlesworth was there as well. 'They didn't require me to tell an anecdote, just appear on stage with all the rest,' he recalls. 'I was all set to talk about staying in the 13 Balkans in Amsterdam. There was a hospitality room with free booze at the Granada Centre in Manchester, then a party there afterwards, and then another in the bar at the hotel where everyone was staying. It went on very late and everyone got massively sloshed.'

* * *

In 1997, Noddy Holder's acceleration to national treasure status came with his role in a one-off pilot for Granada called *The Grimleys*, conceived and written by Jed Mercurio, who would later create *Line of Duty*. Billed as 'Neville' Holder, he played a music teacher, Mr Holder, in a comedy-drama set in 1975 on the fictional Jericho housing estate in Dudley. It centred on the Grimley family, the son of which, Gordon (James Bradshaw), is infatuated with teacher Miss Titley (Samantha Janus) at Aston Manor School in Birmingham. Doug 'Dynamo' Digby (Jack Dee) is an archetypal bullying games teacher who also has eyes for Miss Titley.

The pilot was successful enough for three series to follow between 1999 and 2001, with Amanda Holden taking the Miss Titley role, and Brian Conley becoming Doug Digby. The series was richly observed, painstakingly in-era, and crammed with knowing in-jokes, such as original *University Challenge* host, Bamber Gascoigne, playing the school's headmaster, or Alvin Stardust as a publican, who serves Mr Holder a pint: 'Look at us now, who'd a thought it, you're a music teacher, and I'm a successful publican,' Stardust says. Mr Holder replies, 'Thank our lucky stars we packed in those daft ideas of trying to start a pop group.' Lots of oblique references are made throughout to the actor playing Mr Holder's old career, and at the end of the episode *The Road Not Taken*, Holder sits in the school hall, singing an acoustic version of 'Cum On Feel the Noize'. By the third series, things had moved forward to the punk rock era.

On the back of the show's success and his elevated public profile, Holder became the first of Slade to write their own book. *Who's Crazee Now: My Autobiography* – written with Lisa Verrico – was published by Ebury in 1999. It was an instant success, written in Holder's affable, colloquial style, ever the showman but also deeply sincere when it came to family and relationships. Holder, schooled by Chandler, Altham, Halsall, Perrin et al. knew he had to put in the legwork to promote it and put in plenty of promotional and in-store appearances.

'When Nod's book came out, he was doing a signing at Books Etc, near Tottenham Court Road tube,' recalls Chris Charlesworth. 'I happened to walk by and see the sign saying he was there. So, I went in and joined the queue. When I got to the front Nod said: "'Ello Chris, are you going to buy my book?" "No," I replied. "Why not?" he asked. "Well, would you buy my CD?" To his credit he burst out laughing. "Good answer," he said.'

Holder was truly becoming part of the fabric of popular culture. As a 'local icon', he recorded the announcements for the lifts for the New Art Gallery in Walsall. As a 'national icon', Holder was awarded the MBE for services to showbusiness. He, Price and Django went to the award ceremony, where he was invested by Prince Charles, who commented on Holder's frock coat, saying that he was 'the best-dressed chap here today'. He was, as Holder said, as 'sound as a pound'. Don Powell sent him a note congratulating him on the MEB – short for Midlands Electricity Board. Jim Lea sent him a note with 'Dear Nod, there may be an existential problem with becoming a member of an empire that no longer exists. Nevertheless, it'll look really good on the CV.'

In 2000, Holder guested in a live 40th anniversary edition of *Coronation Street*, and was also on *Have I Got News for You*, *The Wright Stuff* and a Christmas edition of *Would I Lie to You?*, which is regularly repeated. He also became a chat show regular, appearing on Jonathan Ross and Frank Skinner's shows, Peter Kay and Paddy McGuinness's *Max and Paddy's Road to Nowhere*, and even voiced a puppet, Banger, on children's TV favourite *Bob the Builder*.

On Christmas Eve 2002, Holder's mother, Leah died. He later wrote about it very vividly and emotionally in his second book, *The World According to Noddy: Life Lessons Learned In and Out of Rock and Roll*, which was published in 2014. Holder and Price married in 2004, with Graham Swinnerton as best man, the only member of the Slade family present. Holder and Lynsey de Paul introduced a Marc Bolan tribute show at Shepherd's Bush Empire in 2012. Holder is frequently asked to partake in reality TV shows, such as *I'm A Celebrity... Get Me Out of Here* and *Big Brother*. He declined, aside from taking part in *All Star Mr and Mrs*, which he did with Suzan in January 2010, on a show with *Coronation Street*'s Beverley Callard and Boyzone's Mikey Graham. Together, he and Suzan won the £30,000 jackpot for the NSPCC.

Also in 2010, Holder presented the BRIT Award at Earls Court for the Best Album of the Past 30 Years. Live on ITV, comedian Peter Kay introduced Holder by saying that he was recording the theme for the next James Bond film. Oasis won the award for *(What's The Story) Morning Glory?*, and Liam Gallagher accepted it from Holder, pointedly thanked everyone in Oasis, aside from his brother Noel, said 'fuck' and then threw his microphone into the crowd, and gave his award away. Holder, now the wise older statesman, looked on the verge of saying something, but instead gathered his papers, brought Gallagher near, shook his hand, and Gallagher put his arm around Holder.

Noddy Holder has remained in heavy demand, a safe pair of hands to front a marketing campaign or voiceover. Immediately recognisable, hardworking, affable, but most importantly, professional, and reliable, all characteristic traits that had been enhanced by Chas Chandler. Holder became the voice for Australian peanut brand Nobby's Nuts, which launched in 2005, with its invitation to 'nibble Nobby's nuts'. Like with all his voiceover work, Holder carried it off with considerable elan. If peanuts were one thing, the great British sausage was another – in 2011, Holder was the face of British Sausage Week (31 October–6 November, in case you were wondering). A booklet, designed like a 7-inch single, was issued, featuring six new takes on sausage recipes, with Holder proudly on the front, the tines of his fork plunged deep into a big old Cumberland. The text written by, or at least approved by him, is superb: 'My Oh My,' it begins, 'When the Love Pork people told me they wanted a "British legend" to help them spread the word about British sausages, well, I'm nobody's fool – I just said "when can I start"?' Wearing a top hat with a badge on it advertising British Sausage Week, Holder holds a whopping plate of Desperate Dan-style bangers and mash. It's a long way from the bowler and upside-down 'Pope smokes dope' badge that drew *Clockwork Orange* comparisons at the Bardney Festival twenty-nine years previously.

Holder embarked on a speaking tour, *An Audience with Noddy Holder*, in spring 2013, with his friend, DJ and author, Mark Radcliffe as the host. From that, his second book, *The World According to Noddy: Life Lessons Learned In and Out of Rock and Roll*, arrived the following year with Holder using the first chapter to underline in no uncertain terms why he will never reform the group. Admitting that the question he is most asked is whether he would return to Slade, he writes: 'I left the band twenty-three years ago and yet people are still curious. So once and for all, here's my answer: will I ever get back with Slade? ... No!' In 2015, Holder received the Freedom of Walsall. 'Apparently this entitles me to lead sheep through the town, carry a rifle as long as it's got a bayonet fixed and demand a free drink in any pub in town. There's a lot of pubs in Walsall,' he told *The Guardian* in 2015.

'I'm slightly surprised that Noddy, as the driving force, hasn't done more, but in a way, perhaps he is highly sensible, thinking, well, I had a great moment,' Tim Rice says. 'He's still a lovely character and has done a bit of acting but hasn't made any records.'

It is fascinating that for such a prolific writer, Holder hasn't experimented at all, but exceptionally creditable that he hasn't. With such a full life, Holder wanted to ensure he didn't miss Django growing up and his older daughters, Suzan and Leandra all get on. Suzan has written two well-reviewed novels, *Shake It Up Beverley* and *Rock'n'Rose*. Django is now a respected audio engineer and manager at his own studios, Feel The Noize. That is worth more than putting the band back together.

'I still get a text message every Christmas from Noddy,' Gered Mankowitz says, 'and when I used to show up in Manchester, Noddy came to a couple of my openings there. He's always incredibly lovely and supportive and affectionate, funny.'

Holder returned to the studio in late 2022 to add his voice to The Evamore Project for the Cancer Awareness Trust. He added 'merry Christmas, everyone' to the end of 'This Christmas Time', a track that featured, among others, Ozzy Osbourne, Nick Mason, Andy Taylor, Samantha Womack, Nick Lloyd Webber. It was overseen by Brian Eno, who, with Roxy Music, was another participant on the bill at the 1972 Great Western Festival.

An illustration of just how firmly Holder was embedded in the popular psyche came from his immortalisation in sponge and icing on British TV institution, *The Great British Bake Off* on 16 April 2023. Businesswoman and *Dragon's Den* TV personality Deborah Meaden made Holder in cake for the Channel Four Stand Up To Cancer edition of the show. On Twitter, Suzan Holder posted: 'My husband has been knitted, sculpted, built out of Lego, woven in tapestry and painted on @SkyArts and now thanks to @DeborahMeaden #NoddyHolder is created in CAKE!'

One of the nicest surprises in 2023, was Holder's return to the stage, with accomplished jazz pianist Tom Seals, in Seals' revue series *Tom Seals Presents...* The sold-out shows, in Walsall and Salford in early July were a mixture of stories, Q and A, and songs. With support act, Holder's daughter-in-law to be, comedian Beth Fox, the nights were warm and emotional. Holder shared the fact that he had been treated for oesophageal cancer five years previously. He also sang 'Johnny B. Goode' and 'Just Want A Little Bit' with Seals and his band. Many of the Slade faithful were out to witness the performance. 'I saw him "bak 'ome" at the Walsall Arena in Bloxwich,' Chris Selby says. 'Noddy regaled us with some tales of rock and roll debauchery, being mistaken for various celebrities and poignantly, revealing his recovery from cancer. A splendid time was had by all.'

In October 2023, Suzan Holder shared with the wider world the news of her husband's recovery from cancer, and that in 2018, he had been given six months to live. 'We kept it incredibly quiet, even amongst our own friends and family, and we did that because it was such a shocking thing for us,' Suzan told the BBC in March 2024. 'We didn't see it coming, we didn't know what was going to happen.' The outpouring of love and support from every major media outlet in the UK underlined the esteem in which Holder is held.

'Slade did everything it set out to do,' Holder told Geoff Barton in December 2005. 'I didn't want to carry on touring, doing 'Cum On Feel the Noize' night after night. Now I'm doing something different every day – a bit of acting, I've got my own radio shows, television work, voiceover work. I did thirty episodes of *The Grimleys* on TV. It's good, I feel like I'm stretching myself again.' Holder is readily available with an assessment of Slade and is understandably thrilled with their legacy: 'We wrote and recorded, happy, catchy, uplifting songs, which are the hardest to do. We did do some cracking ballads but generally we were "party central".'

ii. Something Very British from a Bygone Age: Whatever Happened to Dave Hill?

Already looking at side projects as the original Slade were in their death pangs, it was clear that Hill would still wish to crave the limelight. As John Punter says, Hill is 'The consummate showman and a great guitar player.'

And so, in 1992, Slade II came into being, and Powell and Hill continued to spread the name of Slade the world over, with a shifting line-up of players based around the two (until 2020, that is) constants. The first had Blessings In Disguise's Craig Fenney on bass and guitarist Steve Makin, who had played with Cozy Powell. There would be many changes around Hill and Powell, but the core was secure. In 1997, they quietly dropped the 'II' from their name without any legal ramifications. Their sole album, 1994's *Keep on Rockin'* has been repackaged several times. In 1999 it was rechristened *Wild Nites*; in 2002 as *Cum On! Let's Party* and the following year's *Superyob*.

Hill has never been backward in coming forward. Mick Gallagher recalls: 'In the early 2000s, I toured Russia on a package tour with Slade and partook in an hilarious interview with the Russian music press when Dave expounded his theory that Slade invented heavy metal to the complete bewilderment of the rest of his band. Don was particularly animated and kept dropping in hilarious side remarks questioning Dave's sanity.'

On 30 June 2010, while Slade were playing live at the Moessingen Rockt! outdoor concert in Germany on a bill with Mud II, Sweet, The Rattles, and Smokie, Hill had a stroke while on stage. 'I woke up in hospital all wired up,' he later said. 'I was tearful because I felt I'd let the band down. I thought, is this it after all these years?' There was a possibility that he may never again play the guitar. However, with the tenacity and star quality that he displayed long before he was a star, he soldiered on to ensure he could master it again, and

379

not let his audience down. By October of the same year, his Slade were back on tour.

There is something deeply reassuring about Dave Hill. More so than the other three, he is always 'on'. Whether known all his life, or on a one-off meeting, what you see is what you get. British stand-up comic and 2023 *Britain's Got Talent* finalist Markus Birdman is a fellow stroke survivor, and, like Hill, is involved with the Stroke Association, often presenting at their annual awards in London. Birdman recalls the pleasure of meeting Hill at the ceremony at the Dorchester in November 2017: 'He seemed almost Dickensian, something very British from a bygone age,' Birdman says. 'Which perhaps he is – that old rocker in a paisley shirt, superb leather boots and jacket. He seemed very friendly and extremely happy that he was still being fussed over by the photographers. There was almost a childish, never-grown-up vibe to him. He knew which camera to aim at.'

Birdman's assessment is not that far from John Taylor's appraisal of seeing Hill in that Solihull Berni Inn when he was an 11-year-old in 1973, 'Suddenly, here was this guy with this extraordinary haircut. He was full-on rock star at that moment.' It could be listed as Hill's occupation on his passport: full-on rock star.

Although, Hill said in 1986 that that isn't always the case:

> I could be changing the baby's nappy one day or doing the washing-up, and then I could be putting my hat on and being me. I have a bizarre life like that. I have a life of extremes… one thing goes to another. I do like being Dave Hill, but I have to control the ego – apart from when I walk on stage, and I know what I'm doing. I try not to have any ego whatsoever when I'm out with people. I try to make people feel at home with me. I like to go down to the pub occasionally and have a drink without being hassled.

Hill's autobiography, *So Here It Is*, was crowd-funded and well liked. And, like Holder's and Powell's collaboration with Lise Lyng Falkenberg, it was a warm telling of the story from one so central to the group's success; Hill talked openly and freely of his stroke and the depression he suffers with. The book was deeply affecting. Jan Hill became a Jehovah's Witness and Hill is an ally: 'I celebrate Christmas, but my wife doesn't,' he told *The Daily Star* in 2020. 'She's religious. I'm religious too. But Christmas is for kids, so we have an arrangement. We have got a big family. All the grandkids come round. It's lovely.'

Hill has appeared in the celebrity edition of the BBC TV quiz show *Pointless*, but the stage will always be where it's at for him: 'I may be with a different set of blokes, but the actual experience is the same,' Hill told *The Guardian*. 'It's the moment of the connection with an audience. What better way could I feel?'

Nowadays, Hill is unencumbered by heavy touring schedules, artistic differences, endless promotion – he is right back playing to a crowd who clearly adore him. 'I've seen Dave, because they played down in Truro a few years ago and I contacted them,' Gered Mankowitz says. 'I went and had tea with Dave and Don. So funny. It was lovely. We had a lovely time and really enjoyed it.'

Don Powell departed from Slade at the start of 2020. The news was broken via Powell's website: 'It is with great sadness and regret that Don needs to inform his fans that he now is no longer a member of Dave Hill's Slade.' Dave Hill offered his own statement: 'I am sad to announce that Don and I will no longer be working together. Our parting of the ways has not come out of the blue and his announcement is not accurate. I wish Don every success in his future efforts. I will, of course, carry on and look forward to many future performances and meeting fans.'

Interviewed by *The Guardian* in 2022, Hill was reticent to discuss the matter further: 'I know the reasons, and it was painful. And I still have a love for Don, I really do. I don't really want to get into any discussions about it because it's personal... I'd rather say to you that I've moved on from that. I feel happy at the moment, and I'm looking forward to getting back with the band as it is now.'

For Hill, the show goes on. At the time of writing, the gig sheet for Slade – now Hill, Alex Bines on drums, Russell Keefe on keyboards, and 2002 veteran John Berry on bass and violin – stretches out for the rest of the year – festivals and shows in Sweden, Switzerland, the Czech Republic, Germany and Slovakia. They also have three shows at the lucrative Butlin's We Love The 70s weekends at Bognor Regis, Minehead and Skegness. Nostalgia, of course, has become big business, and few are more emblematic of the British seventies as Dave Hill. He spoke to *The Guardian* of the joy of playing the revival shows: 'There were 2,000 people, and everybody was dressed up. They've got top hats on, they've got funny hairstyles – some look like me, some like Bowie, some like Alice Cooper, and all they want you to do is walk on stage and hit them with the big ones.'

iii. Recognition for Our Music, Not Adulation: Whatever Happened to Jim Lea?

Although happy to revisit the past, Jim Lea has never particularly been one for nostalgia. After Slade's demise, Lea, as John Punter says, 'Super talented, brilliant musician and great songwriter,' seemed simply to vanish into thin air. Having neither Holder's all-encompassing personality, Hill's outfits or Powell's car crash, Lea has struggled to be the 'remembered' one within the group. That said, little should he worry – as co-writer of all the group's hits, he can afford to live in comfortable semi-retirement, appearing occasionally to ensure he is not written out entirely of the group's story. Married to his first girlfriend, Lou, he has had the same Staffordshire address for nearly fifty years, yet shrewd enough to move into property, and kept his London flat should he need to be near for business reasons. 'It's odd that somebody like Jimmy Lea should have been in the heart of a project like Slade,' writer David Stubbs says. Lea's reticent, almost academic persona, meant there was something for everyone in Slade.

'Jim had his place in London with his lovely wife,' Gered Mankowitz says. 'We were friends with them. They came to dinner with us a couple of times and we always got on well. Jim was already interested in psychology and psychotherapy. My mother had been a psychotherapist. We talked a bit about the psychology of taking photographs, because he always knew what I was doing, not that I was doing anything particularly Machiavellian, but he knew where I was going. Sometimes he looked at me and we'd just catch eyes.'

This writer, in a previous life, served Jim Lea on the Christmas counter at Our Price Wolverhampton in 1996. When he was recognised, he looked as thoroughly uncomfortable as he often looked in his heyday. 'I hated the fame,' Lea told Keith Altham in 2006. 'I used to be so shy I would even deny who I was when I was approached by an autograph hunter in the street at our peak. I used to pretend I couldn't remember old friends when I was reminded of them by strangers. I was someone in our band which thrived on publicity but who only wanted privacy. I wanted recognition for our music, not adulation, so I seldom did an interview if I could.' His twenty years of exploring psychotherapy made him a much more open person: 'I certainly am not like I was at all,' he said to Mark Blake in 2019. 'I am not sitting here being uptight about doing interviews any more.'

As the nineties progressed, Lea returned to making music, releasing one-off singles pseudonymously, and in 2000, under the name Whild, he released 'I'll Be John, You Be Yoko', which gained strong airplay because of its similarity to Oasis. It was even suggested Lea was copying the band he so influenced.

Lea began to be a little more visible on 16 November 2002, by making an appearance at The Robin 2 in Bilston, less than half a mile away from The Trumpet, a one-off live performance billed as Jim Jam. 'That was a strange thing,' Lea spoke of this Robin performance to the *Lancashire Post* in 2018, and his reappearance at the venue in 2017. 'I'd never done anything like that other than stand up and talk to the crowd sixteen years ago. At the end, I say, "I bet you've been wondering where I've been since Slade split. Well, it's to get away from you lot!" They laughed, and I said, "You think I'm joking?" This time I said, "Guess what? Here I am again, talking to you lot!" I was mobbed on the way in and out. More than in the band days.'

It was a cathartic evening, with Lea working with a rhythm section he barely knew – Dave Caitlin-Birch on bass and Michael Tongue on drums. Some of the old Slade backline was used, as it was being auctioned off that night for charity. As Mike Hamblett, the owner of The Robin 2, wrote, 'Jim stipulated that on the night I was to provide twice as much PA system as the club normally used because he felt it was too timid.' Hamblett protested saying many other artists had used it for years with no complaints – Lea replied that he wouldn't play unless it was that loud. As a result, Hamblett said it 'was the loudest gig I had ever heard in my life'.

Amid covers of 'Wild Thing', 'Pretty Vacant', 'I Am the Walrus' and 'Shakin' All Over' were 'Mama Weer All Crazy Now', 'Far Far

Away' and 'Cum On Feel the Noize'. The crowd, indeed, went wild, wild, wild. However, instead of further live shows, Lea set about making a solo record.

Lea released his album *Therapy* in 2007, full of melodic vignettes that if they had been released by Slade would have been viewed as a most remarkable reunion album. It included a retake on the final Slade single, 'Universe', as well as the anthemic 'The Smile of Elvis', the Oasis-flavoured 'Deadrock UK' and the sunshine pop of 'Valley of the Kings'. In 2009, a special edition was released with a recording of the Bilston gig, which received a hatful of 5 star reviews.

'Jim's solo album was fantastic,' Paul Cookson says. "The Smile of Elvis' was the best song that Noddy never sang.'

Throughout this period, Lea worked on *String Theory*, an orchestral album that has yet to see the light of day. 'I got my grandad's violin out and other ones I had, and in the end I had eight violins. My uncle Frank's viola was in the loft and then I bought another eight. Then I got a cello... *String Theory* grew out of that, it became an obsession. It's not rock'n'roll in the slightest.'

In 2014, Lea was diagnosed with prostate cancer, and underwent treatment. He was, as one would expect, intensely private about it and sanguine. 'If things go wrong, we've all got to get on the bus at some point. It's just a matter of when,' Lea told the *Shropshire Star*. 'I didn't really take a lot of notice of the cancer.'

In 2018, Lea released the well-reviewed six-track *Lost in Space* EP through Wienerworld, led by the hook-heavy title track, proving he'd lost nothing of his melodic gifts.

In summer 2019, Paul Weller – who in 1980, when he led The Jam, became the first artist since Slade and 'Merry Xmas Everybody' to enter the UK charts at number one – contacted Lea to see if he would play violin on a track on his forthcoming album. Again, it was the influential 'Coz I Luv You' that was the touchstone. Lea recorded the solo for the track 'Equanimity' on Weller's acclaimed *On Sunset* album, which was captured remotely at Mad Hat Studios at nearby Coven in the Staffordshire countryside. Weller told *Front View* that he had 'loved Slade's singles. They were a real lad's band – skinheads and suedeheads alike mainly listened to black music, but Slade were one of the few pop groups we loved.'

It was a pleasant surprise to see Lea back on a contemporary album. Lea also released a single, 'Am I The Greatest Now' in 2020, and saw it rise in the Heritage Chart, compiled from public vote, and broadcast in over eighty countries by old friend Mike Read. 'The Smile of Elvis' hit number one on the same chart also.

* * *

In early 2020, the Leas became grandparents for the fourth time, when Kristian and Zoe gave birth to a boy. Lea announced he was auctioning off a quantity of his stage clothes. By that October, £8,457.89 had been raised for Dementia UK – a charity close to Lea's heart after his father Frank suffered from the illness for years. A committed family man, Lea nursed Frank in his final days, then his elder brother Raymond and his mother, Edna, who finally passed away in 2022, after being looked after by Frank Jr and Jim. What Lea has succeeded in achieving, unlike his erstwhile bandmates, is actually creating demand. His baldness of statement and unvarnished honesty puts him in the realm of not wishing to leave everything rosy in the garden.

Chris Charlesworth says:

> Jim was definitely the quietest of the four during their heyday, and as a result I knew him the least. The other three were mad for it, as the Gallaghers used to say. Most rock stars love being famous but not Jim. Then, when it was over, I got to know him much better, and realised how different he was to them. He was a thinker. He was the most careful with his money. He owns a flat in a street near Marble Arch where he stays whenever he is in London and we'd meet from time to time, just for a chat and a drink. He liked to play me his new music and ask my opinion. He had such a low profile, but he liked it that way. He didn't want to be a pop star. He's lived in the same nice, detached house in a village near Stafford all his life, been married to Lou all that time. That's the way to hang on to your money.

'Last time I saw Jim he came to see me at Birmingham Town Hall,' Francis Rossi says. 'I said, "What you doing now?" and he said, "I'm doing proper music." There was a certain amount of disappointment, but now I'm thinking he might have been taking the piss. He and I have always been good at roasting each other. We used to say they were releasing too many singles. Chas was working the fuck out of them. Noddy kept saying, "He's got a point." Now when I think about it, they were really doing well. Jimmy always said, "Who's got the most money in the bank then, Chas?"'

iv. Open, Friendly & Exceptionally Amenable: Whatever Happened to Don Powell?

Don Powell is a truly fascinating fellow who has truly been through the mill, yet retains the sunniest exterior. Few people could be said to outdrink Ozzy Osbourne, but Powell, at his zenith, was one of them. In the later seventies, living in Cavendish Mansions in West Hampstead, Powell would frequent the nearby Spirals Wine Bar on the Finchley Road where landlord, *Candid Camera* actor, Arthur Atkins, and his wife Anita would supply off-sales for them to take the booze back to Osbourne's or Powell's nearby.

For an industry that encourages bad habits, heavy drinking in rock is positively part of the process, yet being an alcoholic is not – and that was clearly where Powell was heading. Chris Charlesworth even commemorated the fact in *Feel the Noize!*: 'Don still lives in his Hampstead flat and is often to be found consuming copious quantities of cheap white wine at the wine bar round the corner. He can't taste it of course. "It still affects me though," he says, and to prove the point, he'll stagger homewards in the early hours with a determined step and crooked smile.'

'It's quite frightening when I think back,' Don Powell says. 'The only time I didn't drink was when I was asleep. I'd get up in the morning, put the kettle on and think, "Oh sod it, I'll get the vodka out." I couldn't be bothered to wait for the kettle to boil. I mean, I'm not proud of it, but it's just what it was at the time.'

'I never drank beer,' Powell continues. 'It was wine and vodka or both at the same time. Sometimes I get embarrassed about it, but it's what it was. I've got no excuse for it. The worst thing was, especially with a credit card, I'd go into the wine bar with my card and place it behind the bar or Arthur would just run a tab. Then I got to the end of the week and he'd say, "You need more than that." It was great at the time. I'm not going to put it down.'

Chris Charlesworth elaborates in 2023:

Don was very obviously an alcoholic, but he didn't care. We spent a night at his local where he was a valued customer, and I went up there again two or three times as I got to know him better. He told me all about the lack of taste and smell he'd suffered as a result of the crash, how he had to be careful not to eat rotten meat (which he couldn't smell) and that he could eat the hottest curries without really tasting them. Also, that the cheapest wine and brandy was just the same as the most expensive.

Powell was very much on the scene in the early eighties. 'It's funny because our guitar tech spoke to me a couple of weeks ago and said, "I was just with Don Powell. He sends his love. He remembers going to your hotel room in the Parker Meridian in New York one night,"' says Duran Duran's John Taylor. 'For the life of me, I can't remember how that night came to be, like so many nights in the early eighties. We did have a partying night, which is code for getting fucked up together.'

Whereas the other members of the group found stability in their relationships early on, Powell was exactly the opposite, at least until the 21st century. There can be little doubt that his accident played a part in all of this. He'd left his long-term fiancée Pat Leighton for Angela Morris in 1973, and then began a relationship with Mari Tachikawa whom he brought back to Wolverhampton. In 1974 a Japanese national would be rare in London, let alone the Black Country. Their relationship facilitated Powell's move south but was not to last. After dating girls in New York, he had some long-term associations and spent four years with British Telecom worker Carol McPhee. In 1985, Powell moved into a basement flat in Harley House in Marylebone with antiques dealer, journalist and radio presenter Joan Komlosy, with Eric Clapton as an upstairs neighbour. They had met at a Live Aid party months earlier.

Komlosy had also contributed lyrics for records by The Bo Street Runners and the Northern beauty 'Love Feeling' by Val McKenna. Powell was truly smitten. The couple married at Marylebone Registry Office on 2 November 1985. Because the wedding was a quiet affair, on 13 November, Colin Newman arranged a party at Portland Studios. Noddy Holder and Graham Swinnerton attended, as did

Ozzy Osbourne, George Harrison and John Coghlan. Powell, sadly, was at the peak of his drinking days, so didn't notice the presence of a Beatle at his birthday do. The following year, Powell celebrated his 40th birthday there. Holder and Lea attended, as did Chris Charlesworth, and – essential for the era – a policewoman strip-o-gram was hired by Newman.

On 10 January 1986, Don Powell gave up drinking for good. 'When I stopped drinking, I was having more fun. At least I'm not waking up covered in bruises or not knowing where I am or anything like that. It was great when I stopped, I felt fantastic. I felt really good. More than anything I felt happy with myself.'

Powell sold his West Hampstead residence for Thorne Cottage in Bexhill-on-Sea, which the Powells used initially as a country retreat. However, the relationship was tempestuous, and often the couple would row and reunite publicly. By 1991, Powell had left Joan and set up with Diana Pepper, a hotel manager in Bexhill. After a prolonged divorce, he married Diana in Bexhill in 1997. As Slade II's popularity continued on the live circuit, Powell was rarely short for work, especially with the renewed interest in Slade due to Oasis's patronage. Sadly, Powell's mother, Dora, passed away on 6 October 1999, which facilitated a gathering of the clans back in Bilston.

When Powell wasn't touring, he would be working in the hotel in Bexhill, yet in April 2001, his life was to change: when Slade II were playing in Silkeborg in Denmark, Powell met Hanne Lumdy, a primary school teacher, who had seen Slade in concert when the group had played Vejlby-Risskov Hallen in Aarhus in November 1974. Lumdy was a single mother with three children. As his relationship with Diana petered out, Powell made many trips to Denmark, and, by 2004, he was living there. He proposed in 2007 and the two were married in 2010. Powell had finally found the stability he craved. While Slade II continued to gig around the world, Powell sat with Danish author Lise Lyng Falkenberg, to write his autobiography, *Look Wot I Dun: My Life in Slade.* Edited by Chris Charlesworth and published in 2013, it was free and frank, packed with interviews from those who were there. Powell promoted it at literary festivals and bookshops throughout Europe.

One of the greatest chapters in Powell's post-Slade career came when he united with two very old showbiz pals, Suzi Quatro and Andy Scott, to form glam supergroup QSP. In 2016, the QSP album was released: 'It was seeing the realisation of a dream ten years from conception to making it happen,' Quatro says. 'Our album, *Quatro, Scott and Powell* was an amazing piece of work that got to number sixteen in the Australian charts. It felt like Don and I had played together forever.'

'I saw Don a few years back again because he was in the band with Suzi and Andy. I did the cover for that. That was one of my few forays back into album sleeves in the last decade or so. It was so lovely to see him,' Gered Mankowitz says.

Don Powell is heading towards forty years of sobriety: 'I can keep drink in the house now,' he says. 'I could never do that before. Often people drink when they come round. My friends, everybody, was really helpful, they offered not to drink in my company, so I wasn't tempted. I said, "No, you don't have the problem. I've got to be able to do it with people around me drinking so I'm not tempted." As it happened, I wasn't.'

It would be difficult at times to see Don Powell as anything else than blighted. On 28 December 2018, while changing trains at Peterborough on the way to a gig at Wakefield, Powell's legs collapsed: both his tendons snapped. After a full recovery, on 29 February 2020, three weeks after his parting with Dave Hill, Powell suffered a stroke at home. Fortunately, his stepdaughter Emilie was a doctor so was able to deal with the situation straight away.

'The MRI and CT scan results shows two blood clots in the left frontal lobe, and he is now on medication,' Hanne wrote. 'There is a narrowing on his artery on his neck so we will know in a few days if he will need an operation. The scan results are sent to the cardiology surgeons to decide. Don is tired but in good spirits and he is happy that he can use/feel his right arm and leg again. So, we are all very relieved and thankful.'

Dave Kemp wrote, 'He's doing amazingly well. His stepdaughter who is a doctor was in the right place, with him, at the right time. He is so lucky! He is in good spirits but is far from well.' Again, Powell approached this with a cheery demeanour.

His withdrawal from Slade II gave him a new lease of life, recording his album with The Occasional Flames, The Don Powell Band and, at the age of 75, formed a new band, Don & the Dreamers.

'Don Powell is probably the nicest of the four and has always greeted me like an old mate,' John Halsall says.

Chris Charlesworth agrees. 'Don is the friendliest, most affable man in the world,' he says:

> but at the same time the most hard-wearing. He's like one of those kids' dolls on a round base that always comes back upright with a smile on its face when you knock it over. He went up to Manchester, to the *Louder Than Words* rock book event, to promote his book. He was only supposed to be there for one night but stayed the whole weekend because he was enjoying talking to everyone there and socialising so much. What impressed me was that all this socialising took place in the bar at the hotel late at night and he didn't touch a drop of alcohol.

Powell's gig with Don & the Dreamers at London's Water Rats on 22 March 2023 was well-attended and rapturously received. Given that the mean average age on stage was 72, the band played a sprightly series of cover versions. A gigging musician from the start, he will be a gigging musician to the very end. Don is a 'really good bloke and a great drummer,' John Punter adds. 'It is said that Don's memory was impaired by the car crash, but I always found him to have good recall,' Jonathan 'Chas' Chandler says. In May 2023, The Don Powell Band were joined by Jim Lea on a raucous cover version of 'My Sharona' by The Knack, which topped the Heritage Chart that July.

Lumdy also encouraged Powell to complete *The Adventures of Bibble Brick*, the children's book he'd begun writing in 1968; the story of a pebble who leaves the beach to live on the shore. Written again with Falkenberg, and illustrated by Mark Millicent, it's a sweet story, parts of which had been serialised in the Slade Fan Club magazine in the seventies. Don Powell is open, friendly, and exceptionally amenable; helpful from the off. His relocation to Denmark truly seemed to allow the peace he had been seeking to come through. It couldn't happen to a nicer bloke.

CHAPTER 36

Beer'n'Fags Hymns to the Proletariat

Slade were not a group to be dissected, overthought, theorised, yet they were certainly not one-dimensional. If Jim Lea and Noddy Holder had been writing for an earnest folk-rock outfit, their status as writers would be given greater gravitas, but frankly, they wouldn't be written about now. 'We were never arty buggers,' Dave Hill told Mark Blake. 'Nod's voice is a working-class man crying out.' Yet Nick Kent, the champion of many an arty bugger, wrote in 1973, 'If, as was stated before, The Beatles brought "art" back to the masses when such a project seemed impossible, then Slade have brought rock back to the people when it seemed to be going through its final death pangs.'

Slade remain separate, untouchable – a sum of their parts yet strangely unquantifiable, too rock to be pop, too full of melody to be straight-ahead rock. They are not even as their own ex-members present them: they are loved and revered, and their status secured with their fanbase. They do not represent nostalgia of sunlit uplands, but an exaggerated bonhomie of different days. A lot of this is down to the fact that not only were they not arty buggers, but also because they were complete outsiders. Provincial. Self-contained. They went Bak 'Ome. Even on their early records they didn't, like many bands, get top session players in. Discrete in music, in class, in location. It was fascinating how many times the word 'local' came up in various conversations – even when the group had the potential to go global, they stayed local. *Slade in Flame* is possibly one of the most *local* films that has ever been made.

And why *are* Slade written about now? Although they are far more than just that, it is *that* song that acts as a permanent calling card. In a 2007 poll for MSN Music, 'Merry Xmas Everybody' was voted the UK's most popular Christmas song, borne out by the fact that as soon as November arrives, in-store music systems blare it out throughout the UK. Although receiving challenges from The Pogues and Kirsty MacColl, Mariah Carey, and increasingly the 'also-ran' from the 1973 festive chart race, 'Step Into Christmas' by Elton John, 'Merry Xmas Everybody' rings out like a clarion call to signal the festive season has again arrived.

For the group, it is, as writer Chris Ingham notes, 'a diamond-encrusted straightjacket'. Holder told *NME* in 1991 that 'Merry Xmas Everybody' was not 'all about trendies. It's not about going off skiing for Christmas. It's about Christmas at home with yer mum and yer dad and yer wife and yer kids.' Hence its perennial popularity. Plays on streaming service, Spotify, offer a new metric for its popularity – whereas, at the end of May 2023, 'Cum On Feel the Noize' has been streamed 22,414,315 times, 'Merry Xmas Everybody' has been streamed 122,665,660 times.

* * *

Slade's influence runs deep in the UK psyche – thanks in the main to the signifiers such as the mirrored coachman's hat and the Super Yob guitar, which seem to feature in every cultural history of the seventies. On 21 December 2012, BBC Four screened a Slade night, which showed *Slade in Flame*, the 1999 *It's Slade* documentary, and the newly compiled *Slade at the BBC*, which brought together all their key performances between 1969 and 1991.

In 2014 a satirical news site, *The World Post Times*, offered the headline 'Royal Family Announces St. Edward's Crown To Be Replaced By Noddy Holder's Top Hat For All Future Coronation

Ceremonies.' It said that 'Prince Charles, heir apparent of Queen Elizabeth II, told BBC News that when the day comes to be crowned King of England, he'd much prefer to use Holder's top hat at the coronation ceremony. "To be honest, the crown means little to me. I've never seen it used for any meaningful purpose. On the other hand, I can remember seeing Noddy Holder's mirrored hat at a Slade concert in Earls Court when I was 24 years old, and that is a great memory."' The detail and the references in this parody suggests how deep Slade burrowed into the national psyche.

There are an increasing number of books and records to buy. As ever, Colin Newman oversees the business end of Slade ('Management – Recorded Works'), as he has done since the early seventies. Working with BMG (where the catalogue moved in the mid-2010s, when Union Square merged with the German recording label), a steady stream of reissues and repackages have been issued, product managed by Ian Randell and Andrew Rolland, still with Mark Brennan consulting. A meticulous attention to detail is offered.

The revamped series started in earnest with the enormous box set, *When Slade Rocked the World 1971–1975*, which embraced the bourgeoning vinyl revival by including their four biggest albums – *Slade Alive!*, *Slayed?*, *Old New Borrowed and Blue* and *Slade in Flame* on coloured vinyl, a double CD of the albums, four 7-inch singles that hoovered up the non-album sides, replicas of the *19* flexi-disc and George Tremlett's 1975 book, *The Slade Story*, alongside a fifty-two-page hardback memorabilia and cuttings book, complete with an essay by Mark Ellen, in the style of a seventies annual. This writer, reviewing in *Record Collector*, said that, 'To this young fan, their tunes – an uproarious update of Beatles rockers – were accessible in a way that, say, Bowie's were not.'

Meanwhile, the tributes kept on coming. Many fans were as imaginative as they were loyal, as evidenced by the *Sgt. Pepper*-style Slade collage created in 2015 by those behind the *Slade In England* Facebook page, most notably David Graham. The collage featured scores of characters with a link to Slade's past, musicians who'd influenced them, among them Little Richard and Al Jolson, and heroes like Stanley Baker, Terry-Thomas and Dave Kemp, as well as a few unlikely villains. Taking their cue from the famous Beatles

Pepper cover, the four members of Slade were featured centre stage in the white *Flame* suits, and to their left were the same quartet as fresh-faced young 'NBetweens.

Copies of the collage, measuring 58x58cm, were sent out to many of those in the picture, among them, of course, Hill, Holder, Lea, and Powell, with a request that they be photographed holding it. All four did so and a composite of them with the collage appeared on the *Slade In England* FB page soon after.

There are and have been many great Slade tribute acts over the years, such as Sladest and Slade UK, yet one of the most unusual and entirely heartfelt salutes to the group is the four-piece all-female act, Slady, who played their first show at Southend-on-Sea's fabled and much missed Railway Hotel on 24 November 2018. The group was the idea of 28-year-old Danie Cox, the lead singer and writer of the punk/glam group The Featherz. Recasting herself as 'Gobby Holder', she asked Southend-based bassist Wendy Solomon to join as 'Jem Lea'. Former Purson leader, guitarist Rosalie Cunningham, was a potential for the new line-up but commitments with her career meant although instrumental in the idea and naming of the band, she never played with them. The original drummer was Fi Dulake from the Tuppenny Bunters.

What began as a good wheeze started to gain ground. A visit to the annual Slade convention in Wolverhampton found the group gaining respect for Cox's uncanny performance as 'Gobby'. Dave Kemp encountered Slady, and acknowledging talent when he saw it, became the band's manager. It was an amazing full circle for Kemp, whose tenacity and love remained emblematic of what true fans of the band felt. 'I think they're the embodiment of Slade,' Paul Cookson says. 'At the fan club convention, I was standing at the back with Gaz Top and he said, "They've got the spirit. The spirit Slade had." Gobby's got real attitude and you wouldn't take her on in any way, shape, or form. They've got something there that's really original.'

In September 2020, *Cum On Feel the Hitz – The Best of Slade*, entered the UK charts at number eight, the group's highest album listings placing since *Slade in Flame* in late 1974. Released after the vinyl revival of the 2010s, the double album version – a slimmed-down dition of the expansive forty-three-track two CD – cut to the chase.

Its twenty-four tracks, arranged chronologically (with 'Merry Xmas Everybody' at the very end), still managed to burst through as a body of work. New listeners could marvel at the sheer audacity of the early sides; old fans could still hear how striking the gear-change was between 'Skweeze Me, Pleeze Me' and 'My Friend Stan'; all could hear the artistry of 'How Does It Feel'; and also, quite what a racket 'We'll Bring the House Down' remains. Around the same time, Slade's work finally went onto streaming services. As this was the first time many people had actually listened to the group's music through headphones, many heard the depth and richness of production behind all the wham-bam veneers.

*   *   *

The Trumpet remains in Bilston, still a mecca for jazz and Slade fans. 'Just wonderful music, top quality beer and intellyjunt konversayshun,' it says on its website, with a nod to its most famous sons. The connection remains strong – in June 2023, it hosted the launch for Darren Johnson's book, *Slade in the 70s* with Slade aficionados Pouk Hill Prophetz playing live. A tray is still passed around to pay for the entertainment the pub provides seven nights a week.

Of course, it was inevitable that members of the Slade family, near and distant, would pass. Chas Chandler, of course, left in 1996; Jack Baverstock has long gone; Tommy Burton went in 2000; Maurice Jones, after retiring from MCP in 1997, died in 2009 ('Absolutely wonderful chap,' says industry stalwart Paul Conroy); Roger Allen, who managed The 'NBetweens as they became Slade and took the group to Fontana, passed in 2017. Mickey Legge joined Slade's heavenly road crew in 2023; Roger Wake, Peter Kauff, Dennis Ferrante, Dave 'Cass' Jones, Reg Keirle and Les Megson have all gone. Even Des Brothers, who broke Holder's nose in Porthcawl, passed away.

But the departure that cut deepest was that of Graham Swinnerton who died in 2015. The tribute to Swin that Chris Charlesworth wrote for his blog *Just Backdated* was republished with his permission in the *Express and Star* and had a quote from Jim Lea that showed how the world had turned since Slade's heyday: 'He was amazed that when Lauryn Hill went over to do German TV she had an entourage of 27. When Slade did it, it was just us and him.'

'Of all the Slade-related posts on my blog that one about Swin has had the most hits,' says Charlesworth. 'And some of the most heartfelt comments from fans. One wrote anonymously: "Always thought of Slade as a five-piece. Swin was as much part of the band as the four on stage. It was an honour to know him."'

Dave Kemp, the kind and intelligent Slade flame-keeper, died on 1 December 2020, of Covid-19, due to a weakened immune system from issues with kidney health. The Slade community were understandably devastated, as Kemp had fought to keep the group's name alive in their late-seventies wilderness. Chris Selby and David Graham raised £4,150 for kidney research in tribute, double the appeal's target.

The irony is that, at the time of writing, while all four members are thankfully still with us, Slade themselves will never reunite. As the *Daily Mail* suggested in 2015, 'No other Christmas song in modern history has come close to emulating its success as the tune that brings the nation together in the festive season. How sad that for the four people who brought it to life, the end result has been the exact opposite.'

The schism between the four men is too great for them to ever resume activity. It would be one of the great purses in popular music should they wish to return, and they could easily fill a run at London's Eventim Apollo or even a night at the O2, if the four of them would get back together. Industry veteran Paul Crockford agrees: 'There's a band who would do really well if they were to do a UK tour. Noddy has absolutely 100 per cent refused.' This is an opinion shared by Jim Lea.

But it is about what there is, not what might be – four men in their 70s gave twenty-five years of their career to the band.

* * *

Powell and Holder meet intermittently at *Scribblers, Pluckers, Thumpers & Squawkers* lunches at The Bull's Head in Barnes, London, a twice-yearly event for old music business types, among them Chris

Charlesworth, that was inaugurated by Keith Altham in the early nineties. In February 2022, Suzan Holder posted a picture of Holder and Dave Hill together, with the comment 'Lunch TODAY. I will not be taking any further questions.'

'I went round to his house, and we mended our bridges – not that Dave and I really had bridges to fix,' Holder told Dave Ling. 'I accepted his eccentricity, and he accepted my own. There had been some business hassles, but we picked up the phone and discussed them. Dave's a funny bugger, still as daft as he was when I first met him in the mid-1960s.'

Don Powell's departure from Dave Hill's Slade rekindled the relationship of the other half of the band, Powell and Jim Lea, the group's rhythm section. Lea and Powell were photographed together in 2022 at the Black Country Beats exhibition at Wolverhampton Art Gallery. The show celebrated the area's music through beat to reggae to grime and beyond, and its first room was dedicated exclusively to Slade. Powell's drum kit, Lea's basses, outfits and ephemera were all on show.

On 6 August 2022, one of the hottest days of the year, Lea and Powell united in a joint Q&A, in front of an in-the-room audience (which sold out in less than two minutes) and a global livestream, hosted by this writer. It was an emotional day; there, in the front row of the audience, alongside Frank Lea, and Slade historian Chris Selby, sat Mick Marson and Johnny Howells, who, as both Vendors and 'NBetweens, were the original lighters of the Slade flame all those years ago. Gobby Holder from Slady played an acoustic set, complete with the somewhat bizarre spectacle of Jem Lea from the group wearing a horse's head while Gobby sang 'Dapple Rose'. Paul Cookson read poetry while Les Glover played.

Lea and Powell gassed on like the old pals they are, with Powell making asides and eyerolls to the audience while Lea talked of neural pathways, synapses, and other psychological learning.

Here, verbatim, is one of the most poignant moments, recounting their reunion:

Jim Lea: I hadn't seen him for decades, but it was here in the lobby and I didn't even recognise him. He came up to me and said, 'Jim I don't know what to do, hug you? Kiss you? I don't know what to do.' I didn't know what to do either.

Daryl Easlea: And what did you do?

Don Powell: I hugged him.

It was all tremendously good-natured. And, as was pointed out in the room, that afternoon, under the same roof there were 50 per cent of Slade, 50 per cent of Slady, 100 per cent of The Dummies, 100 per cent of Don Powell's Occasional Flames, and 75 per cent of The 'NBetweens. The Powell and Lea show sparked a reunion of The 'NBetweens in February 2023, with Marson and Howells joining Lea and Powell for a version of Johnny Burnette's 'The Train Kept A-Rollin'', recorded at Mad Hat Studios, near to Lea's home. Thanks to its global reach, 'The Train Kept A-Rollin'' reached number three in the Heritage Chart. Ian Edmundson and Chris Selby came together to produce a limited edition CD single of the track, with a percentage of the proceeds going to Compton Care, the palliative centre in Wolverhampton that looked after Edna, Lea's mother in her final days. The single sold out within its first week.

To promote 'The Train Kept A-Rollin'', Lea appeared on Boom Radio on 2 April 2023, on the *Still Busy Living* show with presenter Phil Riley. 'We just sort of floated away,' he said about the demise of Slade. The question, might we ever see Lea and Holder in a studio together, was speedily brushed away. 'No, no,' he replied, while remaining rather non-specific. 'I was always very quiet in the first part of the band and then I went to psychology college. And then I went into twenty years of psychotherapy. And I wouldn't be talking to you now if I hadn't have done that. Yeah, I sort of made friends with myself. It's weird, isn't it?'

* * *

The scale of Don Powell's crash could be seen as one of the truest unspoken factors in Slade's ultimate demise. At the time, the speed of events was astonishing, with his near death and the death of his girlfriend, his ongoing amnesia and lack of taste and smell. It's shocking enough when read about today from a distance, but for four friends in their mid-20s to have lived through that at such a peak of success, was doubly traumatic. It was just onward, there was no time to process or unpack the enormity of the issue. Someone died, and someone was critically injured, yet Powell was soon back in a recording studio. And then, back on tour, having to be lifted onto his drum stool, having to learn his parts again bit by bit. Then, to hear Holder calling him 'Mr Memory Man' on stage, or for him to be in a car accident in *Slade in Flame*, or that his first appearance in public afterwards was at Brands Hatch ('Britain's Best Loved Racing Circuit'), the home of the autocar, all seems rather unkind.

Had Frank Lea really known that Don was still in the club that night, Powell would have taken him a different route. Angela Morris would still be here today, Powell would have his memory; it might have been a very, very different story. But the pace of life and the pace of Slade then was immense. All these factors fed towards closure and into Noddy Holder's decision to effectively retire from the group, whereas Jim Lea dealt with it by throwing himself into the work; increasingly obsessed with sound, techniques and moving Slade forward. If Powell's accident had happened when they had more time on their hands and they'd been older, it may have been processed in a very different fashion.

* * *

There is something deep-rooted in the passion that people have for Slade. In interviews for this book, and on the record, there is so much love and goodwill for them, but also concern that their legacy is not as intact as others: 'For some reason they got turned into a comedy band and not taken very seriously,' life-long fan, songwriter Steve Mason says. 'You listen to a song like 'How Does It Feel' and you think *fucking hell that is just incredible.*'

'The *NME* preferred their rock stars to quote Rimbaud and name songs after Camus novels,' journalist Mick Middles wrote. 'You were never really going to get that with Slade. Difficult to unearth the hidden depths of 'Coz I Luv You'. This was sausage and chips music. Beer'n'fags hymns to the proletariat.'

'I loved them. They were so huge, there was never anything like their juggernaut of hits,' Nick Van Eede says. 'They changed my life in one huge way: they taught me that it's all about fun. It's all about having a laugh. I would watch Nod and it was such an incredible learning curve. You can be the biggest stars on this planet and there are some bands that have made a million out of staring at their shoes, but Slade never did, and I've carried that with me.'

'They were very, very grounded,' John Steel adds. 'Never changed from that, no matter how big they got, they were still the same guys. It doesn't always happen like that. They were always a better band than they got credit for. They did what they did very, very well. They knew exactly what they needed to do to get an audience going.'

'Slade were exciting,' Tim Rice says. 'They combined the music hall tradition with heavy rock'n'roll. I rather liked that. They weren't initially like The Beatles or Bowie or somebody who people at the time would take seriously and analyse. Then, they were unfairly lumped in with the Bay City Rollers. Slade had great punch and drive and good songs, and are underrated.'

'It isn't just affection I have for Slade, now, it's genuine respect,' David Stubbs says. 'I certainly rank them as superior to Oasis. There's a relevant comparison of a sort of group that arrived with a sense of football terrace culture manifesting itself in pop music; but it wasn't just the raucousness, the Dennis the Menace-ness, it was the craft actually, these songs were beautifully written. Their singles felt like a Christmas or birthday privilege.'

Ian Edmundson: 'They were a good-time band and that's why they're remembered with such affection. The people who know how good the music was and is and the people who saw them, that's what they're judged on. If people want to look at a picture of Dave Hill and his appalling Wonderbra outfit and say, "Well, that's what Slade were about," they've missed the point, haven't they? I liked them when they had the primary colour thing going on in '72 before the Bacofoil came out. If they'd stuck with that, they'd have been taken a lot more seriously.'

'I like Noddy being adamant that he's not going back. Noddy doesn't need it. Lucky bugger. I still need it obviously. I'm going out to 100 shows, I start next Thursday,' says Francis Rossi, laughing.

Gary Crowley: 'Those pop stars who get you early, you're always going to be excited to hear them, or meet them; the old hairs on the neck stand to attention.'

'Every band has its window,' Dave Ling concludes. 'Slade's was longer and more rewarding than the vast majority of their rivals. The hits still stand up wonderfully well, but over-familiarity can breed contempt, but even your great Aunt Gertrude knows 'Merry Xmas Everybody'... for better or worse it's become part of the wallpaper. Noddy is everyone's unofficial grandfather.'

Gered Mankowitz: 'I try and post slightly out of the ordinary or unexpected pictures on social media of people I've worked with. Slade always generate loads of responses. Slade fans are so enthusiastic. They're so loyal, and they love the band. People have short memories, don't they? I mean, the thing is, during their day, Slade were, if not the top, one of the top British bands for the whole of the seventies really. Outside of their fans, people and the music business generally talk about Slade; everyone has great memories, but the positivity has been eclipsed by the Christmas song and Noddy evolving into this sort of character actor. So, their importance to British popular music has probably not really been laid down in the way that it should have been.'

TV director Len Brown says, 'I think they're often regarded as comic glam-rock figures whereas everything musical about them is magic. I even loved their Reading comeback and I'm amazed they survived when so many of their contemporaries burnt out, died or went to prison. They're good, warm, friendly guys and the most down-to-earth British rock stars.'

John Taylor: 'The number of times with Duran we've tried to copy that foot stomp from 'Get Down and Get With It', it's just one of the greatest. We've sampled it, we've used it in beds of sound that we've then tried to replicate. It's a fantastic-sounding record. The fact that they were from the Midlands was meaningful to us. Their legacy is that outpouring of hit songs designed to be hit songs that we just took for granted. To do it as a group, we now know is considerably harder than it is to do it as an individual who can change the co-writers, can change the producers, can change the band. That kind of versatility is so rare now, it's almost non-existent. The time that they put in really showed. It just feels entirely real; you don't really feel the production – it just felt like a band playing live; no bells and whistles. But beautiful nonetheless:

there was just something very real about their sound. Very easy, easily relatable.'

Keith Altham wrote: 'Of all the bands I represented, Slade were one of the best to be with, drunk or sober… There was something particularly English about Slade. They were roast beef, black pud and saucy seaside postcard rock and roll. Your sheer Englishness may have been the reason that you never broke America, but you were hot as hell in the UK during the glam-rock seventies.'

'Mantas from Venom said Slade were his first favourite ever band. Joe Elliott talks about Slade a lot and the whole yob end of glam was a really big thing for all NWOBHM bands,' says Michael Hann. 'They are a very easy group to hold affection for as their biggest hit is about Christmas. And all but the most curmudgeonly love Christmas. Second, they're completely unthreatening. Every TV clip you see, Noddy Holder especially radiates a sort of Dickensian bonhomie. And the fact that they were so obviously provincial, there's nothing snooty about them at all. They seem like a very democratic sort of group, very democratic in aspiration.'

'Now those of us who were slightly embarrassed to say that they like Slade are recognising how good they were,' Helen O'Hara adds. 'We would probably say how amazing Slade are now.'

'Slade say something to you about being British,' Alexis Petridis says. 'Like Madness, a bit naughty, lads down the pub, a few drinks; but we're basically good people and we like to have a laugh. We're all in it together. There's something really potent about that, much less easily definable about Slade than it is about Madness, or Oasis or about unity between other bands that do that kind of thing. I can't quite put my finger on what it is about their music in all their songs that makes you feel that way, but it does, and it works.'

'Somebody once said that Slade were one of the last bands, apart from Queen, where you knew all four members of the band,' Paul Cookson says. 'The fan in me says, "I want the world to see how good Slade are, even at this age." I want them to be seen as being as good as Queen or the Stones because they would be live. There's no question about that. But also, it's not going to happen.'

'Over and above all the great hit singles, the showmanship, Noddy's voice, Dave's outfits, Jim's skill, Don's resilience, 'Merry

Xmas' and all the rest, at heart they were simply a knockout live band,' says Chris Charlesworth. 'That's what drew me to them really. By the time they became famous they'd played hundreds of gigs night after night, and you can't beat that sort of experience in the real world of rock'n'roll, the world where instead of appearing on a televised talent contest you gig regularly for at least a couple of years, make a living doing it, before seeing the inside of a recording studio.'

This is something echoed by premier Slade historian Chris Selby: 'They were a group who seemed to look at whoever else was on the bill, and would say, "well done dear, that was really good but this is how it should be done." BOOM!'

'It was an honour and a privilege to have worked with Slade,' John Punter concludes. 'They are still one of my favourite bands and to have had the opportunity to work with them was awesome. I think we made some great music together – I hope the "boyz" think so too.'

'They definitely were friends,' says Frank Lea. 'I've worked with lots of bands but I've never come across anything like that. Everything about the band is unique. They were incredibly professional, and everything had be to right. Everything about the live shows had to be meticulous. I was always around. I roadied, I became Chas Chandler's partner, then I played with the band, I mean, fucking hell, what else could I do? I've known the band since they were 13 years old. I've seen the band played hundreds of times and never got bored once: it was always exciting."

'I know many famous designers have made stuff for rock'n'roll bands, who had a reputation before that,' Steve Megson says. 'Rock stars have gone to them, and it's enhanced their reputation. I was just a kid at art college, working with some mates. That's what it was. Me working with some mates. Mates who I was really pleased that were making it. I loved it when they got to number one, and we had parties in my dad's pub.'

* * *

'When I look at the career of the band, it was unfortunate we split up, but it does happen. I never wanted to give it up,' Dave Hill said.

'Always have to look at what made the greatness … the success and brilliance of the time, gotta remember we were living in black-and-white world in the sixties, but when colour hit the box, people like me and Marc Bolan, it was a field day.'

Slade remain well thought of, especially in the industry, and for Don Powell, that is down to some simple facts: 'We did have a lot of love, especially with TV producers, radio producers. I think a lot of it was because when we were lucky enough to start to get TV and radio, we respected it. We had this thing the four of us, we were never late. We had an opportunity given to us and we weren't gonna piss on it. I think that gave us a lot of respect.'

The power, the musicianship, the clothes and finally, the charismatic presence of Noddy Holder out front: 'A Slade show was an event,' Holder wrote. 'We wanted to make the band and audience as one, with no mental barrier between us.'

There is no doubt that the magic of Slade was all four working together in unison and harmony. Slade's unity, and remarkable self-belief saw them through; as Jim Lea said when he first went on to *Top of the Pops*: 'I looked at this, and I thought, we can take this, we can do this.'

* * *

There is a parallel universe one could briefly visit, in which it is Slade, not Queen, that Bob Geldof, Harvey Goldsmith and Maurice Jones select and put on at a key moment of Live Aid. Opening with a truncated 'Rock and Roll Preacher', the band then blitz into 'Cum On Feel the Noize', 'Far Far Away' (in which the band ease off, ticking over, while Holder emotes, Springsteen-style: 'Although Ethiopia is far, far away, today it is close'), 'Run Runaway', 'Mama We're All Crazee Now' and end with a medley of 'My Oh My' and a fabulously unseasonal 'Merry Xmas Everybody'. A rush-released greatest hits collection is issued, and the band capitalise on their appearance by finally making proper inroads in the States in the wake of Quiet Riot's Top 10 version of 'Cum On Feel the Noize'. In 2022, they begin their final farewell tour to support their biopic *Feel the Noize*, before headlining Glastonbury on the Sunday night. Sadly, it was never to be.

In writing this book, I realised that it was an utter love-letter to times past; that even in the arc of its writing, people were leaving us; venues that once were, are flattened; groups long parted. Beyond that, it was a world without the internet, mobile phones, overplanning. In these days of rampaging knife crime, there's almost a nostalgia for that old-fashioned almost theatrical yobbism, based around football and flat-roofed pubs. Because of the fact they remained intact, and ended when they did, Slade are emblematic of this period; of black and white turning into Technicolor and Panavision, yet still retaining predominantly the colours brown and orange. And so, they never really outgrew that time and their image.

So, whatever happened to Slade? Perhaps the final irony is that their original name, The 'NBetweens, is exceptionally apt for the group they became – in between genres, in between fan groups, too English for America and when they 'got serious', they were in between the sombre music heads and their teenybop fans; their film was too grim for the majority of their followers, yet unseen by those who should have seen it; in between the class divide of the music industry; they were the real thing, and, as a result, somehow almost totally eclipsed by others who were far less popular than them in the day.

So, thank heavens, then, for Christmas. The whole crazee world is less than a year away from hearing them again.

Afterword
By Jim Moir

I heard Slade on Radio One when they did 'Get Down and Get With It': I remember thinking this is my kind of thing. I can clearly recall walking to school with that ringing in my ears. Another moment was buying 'Gudbuy T'Jane'. What was really great about them was that they didn't really fit in with the glam rock thing; they didn't look right and maybe that was part of their appeal. There were no airs and graces or ponciness going on there. I think that's what people could see as well, what you saw was what you got. They were enormously successful, more than anyone else at that time.

Years later, I wanted to do a *Coronation Street* in the West Midlands, turning pop stars into soap opera characters. So, Slade lived there. Black Sabbath were next door; Duran Duran were the new young tearaway kids who'd just moved in. We'd dress in the Slade uniform and go on holiday – I just thought it would be funny. We never thought too deeply about any of these things. I thought Bob would look better as Dave Hill, and I sounded more like Noddy. We made it all up – we didn't really know much about Slade at all, so we developed all of those characters. When I did meet Noddy, he said it was so close to the truth. So, we judged the books by their covers and applied it – it seemed to work out really well.

It ended up as a bit of revival for Slade, I think we did them a favour!

Jim Moir, Kent, spring 2023

Bibiliography

Altham, Keith. *The PR Strikes Back*. Blake, London, 2001.

Anderson, Paul 'Smiler' and Mark Baxter. *Scorcha! Skins, Suedes and Style from the Streets 1967–1973*. Omnibus Press, London 2021.

Betrock, Alan. *The I Was a Teenage Juvenile Delinquent Rock'n'Roll Horror Beach Party Movie Book: The Complete Guide to the Teen Exploitation Film: 1954–1969*. Plexus, London, 1986.

Brackett, David (ed.). *The Pop, Rock and Soul Reader: Histories and Debates* (third edition). Oxford University Press, Oxford, New York, 2014.

Brown, Pete. *Clubland – How the Working Men's Club Shaped Britain*. Harper North, Manchester, 2022.

Buck, Paul. *Performance – A Biography of the Classic Sixties Film*. Omnibus Press, London, 2012.

Buckley, David. *Strange Fascination – David Bowie: the Definitive Story* (revised and updated edition). Virgin Books, London, 2005.

Cann, Kevin. *David Bowie: Any Day Now – The London Years: 1947 – 1974*. Adelita Ltd, London, 2010.

Charles, Tony. *Slade in 1975 and 1976*. The Pouk Hill Press, Poland, 2022.

Charles, Tony. *Slade in 1977 and 1978*. The Pouk Hill Press, Poland, 2022.

Charlesworth, Chris. *Feel The Noize! An Illustrated Biography*. Omnibus Press, London, 1984.

Cookson, Paul. *Touched By the Band of Nod: The Slade Poems*. A Twist in the Tale, Retford, UK, 2016.

Edmundson, Ian and Chris Selby. The Noize – The Slade Discography – Revised and Updated Second Edition. Available via Amazon, UK, 2021

Essex, David. *A Charmed Life*. Orion, London, 2002.

Ertegun, Ahmet. *'What'd I Say?' The Atlantic Story: 50 Years of Music*. Orion, London, 2001.

Gambaccini, Paul, Tim Rice and Jo Rice. *UK Top 1000 Singles*. Guinness Books, London, 1988.

Geldof, Bob with Paul Vallely. *Is That It?*. Pan Books, London, 1986.

Hann, Michael. *Denim and Leather: The Rise and Fall of the New Wave of British Heavy Metal*. Constable, London, 2022.

Hepworth, David. *1971 – Never A Dull Moment*. Bantam Press, London, 2016.

Hill, Dave. *So Here It Is – The Autobiography*. Unbound, London, 2017.

Hodgkinson, Will. *In Perfect Harmony – Singalong Pop in '70s Britain*. Nine Eight Books, London, 2022.

Holder, Noddy with Lisa Verrico. *Who's Crazee Now?*. Ebury Press, London, 1999.

Holder, Noddy. *The World According to Noddy – Life Lessons Learned In and Out of Rock and Roll*. Constable, London, 2014.

Hoskyns, Barney. *Glam! Bowie, Bolan and the Glitter Rock Revolution*. Faber & Faber, London, 1998.

Jenkinson, Philip and Alan Warner. *Celluloid Rock – Twenty Years of Movie Rock*. Lorrimer, London, 1974.

Johnson, Brian. *The Lives of Brian*. Michael Joseph, London, 2022.

Kutner, Jon and Spencer Leigh. *1000 UK Number One Hits.* Omnibus Press, London, 2005.

Larkin, Colin. *The Virgin Encyclopedia of Popular Music* (Concise fourth edition). Virgin, London, 2002.

Massey, Howard. *The Great British Recording Studios.* Hal Leonard Books, Milwaukee, 2013.

McDonnell, Evelyn. *Queens of Noise – The Real Story of The Runaways.* Da Capo, Boston, 2013.

O'Hara, Helen. *What's She Like – A Memoir.* Route, Pontefract, 2022.

Palin, Michael. *Diaries 1969–1979: The Python Years.* Weidenfeld & Nicolson, London, 2006.

Palmer, Tony. *All You Need Is Love: The Story of Popular Music.* Weidenfeld & Nicolson and Chappell, London, 1976.

Parker, Alan G. and Steve Grantley. *Cum On Feel the Noize! The Story of Slade.* Carlton Books, London, 2006.

Peel, John and Sheila Ravenscroft. *Margrave of the Marshes.* Bantam Press, London, 2005.

Peel, John and Sheila Ravenscroft. *The Olivetti Chronicles: Three Decades of Life & Music.* Bantam Press, 2008.

Powell, Don and Lise Lyng Falkenberg. *Look Wot I Dun – My Life in Slade.* Omnibus Press, London, 2013.

Powell, Don and Lise Lyng Falkenberg, illustrated by Mark Millicent. *The Adventures of Bibble Brick.* (Self published), 2022.

Quatro, Suzi. *Unzipped.* Hodder & Stoughton, London, 2007.

Radcliffe, Mark. *Reelin' In the Years: The Soundtrack of a Northern Life.* Simon and Schuster, London, 2011.

Rees, Dafydd and Luke Crampton. *Q Encyclopedia of Rock Stars.* Dorling Kindersley, London, 1996.

Reynolds, Simon. *Shock and Awe: Glam Rock and Its Legacy.* Faber & Faber, London, 2016.

Rice, Tim, Jo Rice and Paul Gambaccini. *The Guinness Book of Number One Hits*. Guinness Publishing, Enfield, 1988.

Robbins, Ira A. (ed.). *The All-New Trouser Press Record Guide* (third edition). Collier Books, New York, 1989.

Ross, Jonathan. *The Incredibly Strange Film Book*. Simon & Schuster, London, 1993.

Sandbrook, Dominic. *State of Emergency, The Way We Were: Britain 1970–1974*. Allen Lane, London, 2010.

Sandbrook, Dominic. *Seasons in the Sun: The Battle for Britain 1974–1979*. Allen Lane, London, 2012.

Savage, Jon. *1966 – The Year the Decade Exploded*. Faber & Faber, London, 2015.

Shail, Robert. *Stanley Baker – A Life in Films*. University of Wales Press, Cardiff, 2008.

Smith, Sid. *In the Court of King Crimson – An Observation Over Fifty Years*. Panegyric Publishing, Buckinghamshire, 2019.

Southall, Brian. *The A–Z Of Record Labels* (second edition). Sanctuary Publishing, London, 2003.

Spence, Simon. *When The Screaming Stops: The Dark History of the Bay City Rollers*. Omnibus Press, London 2016.

Stanley, Bob. *Yeah Yeah Yeah: The Story of Modern Pop*. Faber & Faber, London, 2014.

Thompson, Ben (ed.). *Ban This Filth! Letters from the Mary Whitehouse Archive*. Faber & Faber, London, 2012.

Tremlett, George. *The Slade Story*. Futura Publications Ltd, London, 1975.

Turner, Alwyn W. *Crisis? What Crisis? Britain in the 1970s*. Aurum, London, 2008.

Wale, Michael. *Slade Nobody's Fools*. Music Sales, London, 1976.

Walker, John. *Halliwell's Film Video & DVD Guide 2006*. Harper Collins, London, 2006.

Walker, John. *Halliwell's Who's Who in the Movies 14th Edition.* Harper Collins, London, 2001.

Newspapers and Magazines

Many publications, including: *Metro; The Times; The Sunday Express; The Independent; Billboard; The Mirror; Q; Mojo; New Musical Express; Clash Magazine; The Guardian; The LA Times; Uncut; Newsweek; People Magazine; Classic Rock Presents Prog; USA Today; Entertainment Weekly; Record Collector.*

All other publications referenced in text.

Internet

Main Slade pages

1966 And All That
https://www.facebook.com/Slade1966/

1969 And All That
https://www.facebook.com/blocoboy/

From Roots... To Boots
http://sladestory.blogspot.com

The Official Slade Page
www.facebook.com/OfficialSladeBand/?locale=en_GB

Slade Are For Life – Not Just For Christmas
https://www.facebook.com/Sladeforlife/?locale=en_GB

Slade Discography
https://www.sladediscography.co.uk

Slade Fan Club http://www.sladefanclub.com/
uploads/7/6/6/0/7660950/2676319_orig.jpg

Slade In England
http://www.sladeinengland.co.uk

Slade Live
https://sladelive.weebly.com

Slayed (and forum)
www.slayed.co.uk

Dave Hill Slade
https://www.davehillslade.com

Don Powell
http://www.donpowellofficial.com

Jim Lea
http://www.jimleamusic.com

Noddy Holder
http://www.noddyholder.com

Dave Hill:
http://www.telegraph.co.uk/finance/personalfinance/
fameandfortune/9563138/Slades-Dave-Hill-Most-of-our-earnings-went-
on-tax.html

https://www.birminghammail.co.uk/news/local-news/dave-hill-from-
slade-talks-about-his-roots-128854

https://www.theguardian.com/music/2021/mar/08/slade-guitarist-
dave-hill-stroke-depression-glam-rock

Noddy Holder:

Back To School
https://www.business-live.co.uk/economic-development/slades-
noddy-holder-goes-back-3922671

Merry Xmas
https://www.theguardian.com/music/2015/nov/26/noddy-holder-
people-think-i-live-in-a-cave-all-year-and-come-out-in-december-
shouting-its-chriiisstmaaasss

Potholes
https://www.dailystar.co.uk/news/latest-news/113421/Wayne-
Rooney-s-house-builder-fixes-the-road-for-Noddy-Holder

Very Best Of interview
https://www.loudersound.com/features/slade-the-long-gudbye

Bibiliography

Who's Crazee Now Interviews
https://web.archive.org/web/20050405014451/http://www.
soundchecks.co.uk/articles/noholder.html

Jim Lea:

Jim Lea Music
https://www.facebook.com/JimLeaMusic

http://bigboyzbignoize.blogspot.com/2005/06/jim-lea-biography.
html

https://www.shropshirestar.com/entertainment/music/2018/07/08/
slades-jim-lea-tells-his-own-cancer-story/

https://www.thefreelibrary.com/Interview+Jimmy+Lea%3A
+I'll+be+Jim,+like+it+or+not.-a060515704

Don Powell:
http://www.donpowellofficial.com

*   *   *

Brumbeat
http://www.brumbeat.net/aslade.htm

ATV Today
https://www.macearchive.org/films/atv-today-04011973-new-home-
dave-hill-slade

Black Country
http://www.smabs.co.uk/projects/blkcoun/mappingtheblackcountry.
pdf

Black Country Beats
https://www.wolverhamptonart.org.uk/whats-on/black-country-
beats/

Dave Kemp
http://www.davekempandslade.com/xmas-1983.html

Bailey's Nightclub Watford
https://kajafax.co.uk/2011/04/30/kajagoogoo-watford-and-baileys-nightclub/

Jack Baverstock
https://vinylmemories.wordpress.com/tag/jack-baverstock/?fbclid=IwAR1LAB_BN-H8vFSXY0sKhjFJ-rQkpZMboAL7IIO4Z9UJ_GqmOO0Sg5dY1o4

https://vinylmemories.wordpress.com/2020/10/10/a-personal-history-of-the-british-records-business-88-dick-leahy-pt-1/

https://www.popmatters.com/totally-wired-paul-gorman-excerpt

https://philipsrecords.wixsite.com/history/fontana-records

https://thestrangebrew.co.uk/interviews/peter-daltrey-chelsea

Biff Byford
www.loudersound.com/features/the-10-greatest-festival-experiences-of-my-life-by-saxons-biff-byford

California Ballroom, Dunstable
http://www.california-ballroom.info/bands/slade.htm

'Coz I Luv You'
https://web.archive.org/web/20121208032109/http://www.guardian.co.uk/music/2011/jun/11/slade-number-one

Chas Chandler
http://justbackdated.blogspot.com/2014/01/chas-chandler-1938-1996.html

https://www.independent.co.uk/news/people/obituaries-chas-chandler-1329256.html

http://justbackdated.blogspot.com/search/label/Slade

Cheap Trick
https://web.archive.org/web/20111028195802/http://blogcritics.org/music/article/music-review-cheap-trick-the-latest1/

https://www.youtube.com/watch?v=uu_3ZRm_pWw

Dangerous Minds
https://dangerousminds.net/comments/slade_proto_punk_heroes_
of_glam_rock

Def Leppard
http://www.deflepparduk.com/2017newsaug167.html

Don Powell accident
http://sladestory.blogspot.com/1973/07/

Earls Court
http://www.sladeinengland.co.uk/Press/live%20reviews/Slade%20
Earls%20Court%20Charlsworth%201973.htm

Fake news
http://worldposttimes.com/world-news-/royal-family-announces-st.
html

Fanfare For Europe
www.wsc.co.uk/stories/getting-into-europe-the-1973-common-market-
match/

Feud
http://www.dailymail.co.uk/tvshowbiz/article-3374311/Poisonous-
feud-merriest-Christmas-hit-earns-fortune-two-Slade-s-stars-ZILCH.
html#ixzz4lgWiP9i9

Fontana Records
http://www.philipsrecords.co.uk/Fontana%20Records.html

Obscure Bands of the 50s and 60s
http://forgottenbands.blogspot.com

Grange Pub Bilbrook
https://www.youtube.com/watch?v=8sTQTtpDvoY

Girlschool
https://www.getreadytorock.com/rock_stars/girlschool.htm

John Peel – The Bangin' Man
https://twitter.com/johnpeel3904/status/1463148520463024130/
photo/2

King Crimson
ttp://www.sladescrapbook.com/cuttings-1977.html

Lanchester Arts Festival
https://www.festivival.com/history/lanchester-arts-festival-1972

Les Perrin
https://www.jonimitchell.com/library/view.cfm?id=2317

Mallory Park
www.radiorewind.co.uk/radio1/fun_days.htm

Maurice Jones
https://www.expressandstar.com/news/2009/11/10/mogul-behind-live-aid-gig-dies-at-64/

https://www.birminghammail.co.uk/news/local-news/meet-the-hidden-face-behind-live-243929

'Merry Xmas Everybody'
https://www.theguardian.com/music/2016/dec/22/its-christmas-best-festive-songs-chosen-slade-neil-diamond

https://www.theguardian.com/music/2015/dec/03/mariah-carey-slade-and-the-watersons-the-songs-that-make-it-feel-like-christmas

New Victoria, NME
http://www.sladeinengland.co.uk/Press/live%20reviews/slade_New_Vic_75.htm

Pouk Hill greenbelt threat
https://www.expressandstar.com/news/environment/2021/10/30/hands-off-our-pouk-hill-says-noddy-holder/

Pret A Manger
www.campaignlive.co.uk/article/pret-manger-brings-noddy-holder-celebrate-christmas-july/1721401

Record Collector
http://recordcollectormag.com/reviews/whatever-happened-to-slade-well-bring-the-house-till-deaf-do-us-part

Richard Cox/Derby
https://www.tonyrcox.co.uk/?p=452

Roger Allen
https://www.expressandstar.com/news/local-hubs/

wolverhampton/2017/07/24/wolverhampton-music-supremo-roger-allen-dead-at-76-/

Samantha's
https://ninebattles.com/2023/04/10/samanthas-club-new-burlington-street-what-clubs-and-venues-do-you-remember-in-london/

Slade Alive reissue
https://www.expressandstar.com/entertainment/lifestyle/2017/09/18/noddy-holder-it-was-a-non-stop-merry-go-round/

Slade in Flame
http://www.bbc.co.uk/blogs/markkermode/2012/08/film_club_-_slade_in_flame.html

http://www.reelstreets.com/films/slade-in-flame-aka-flame

http://bigboyzbignoize.blogspot.com/2005/06/slade-in-flame.html

Slade On Stage
https://thequietus.com/articles/32483-slade-on-stage-review-quietus-subscribers

Slady
https://www.sladyworld.com

Southend-on-Sea Police
http://essexpolicemuseum.org.uk/the-law-archive/n_7004lw.pdf

Stage Door Canteen
http://www.stagedoorcanteen.co.uk/ww2-history.html#stagedoorcanteenlondon

Stratford Place
http://www.sladefanclub.com/london-sightseeing.html

Sue Wilkinson
https://archive.org/stream/smash-hits-1980-08-21/smash-hits-1980-08-21_djvu.txt

Suzan Holder
https://harpercollins.co.uk/blogs/authors/suzan-holder

Swin Obituary
https://www.expressandstar.com/news/local-news/2015/12/04/
tributes-as-man-who-oversaw-the-rise-of-slade-dies-after-cancer-battle/

Syracuse/ZZ Top
http://www.sladeinengland.co.uk/Press/live%20reviews/Slade%20
Live%20Syracuse%20NY%201975.html

Tear Into The Weekend
https://www.discogs.com/release/9987304-Noddy-Holder-Pepsi-
Anthem-Tear-Into-The-Weekend

Trouser Press
https://trouserpress.com/slade-autodiscography-with-drummer-don-
powell/

The Trumpet
https://www.thetrumpet-bilston.com/history

https://www.midlandspubs.co.uk/staffordshire/bilston/trumpet.htm

Tupholme Abbey
www.heritagelincolnshire.org/resources/learn-about-tupholme-abbey

Walsall Town Hall
https://www.expressandstar.com/news/local-hubs/
walsall/2017/11/08/noddy-holder-remembers-first-walsall-gig/

Warrington Guardian
https://www.warringtonguardian.co.uk/news/1082344.noddy-holder-
holds-court-sitting-amid-the-austere-bustle-of-a-radio-station-canteen-
his-achingly-familiar-cheeky-grin-provides-a-surreal-edge/

Wolverhampton
www.wolves-beat.co.uk/html/wolverhampton_people_f-j.html

Wolverhampton scene
http://www.historywebsite.co.uk/articles/InBetweenTimes

Wolverhampton
http://www.wolves-beat.co.uk/html/wolverhampton_people_f-j.html

Zine-On-A-Tape/Andy Savage/Noddy Holder
www.soundchecks.co.uk/articles/noholder.html

Rocks Back Pages
1971
Slade/1971/Phil Symes/Disc and Music Echo/Slade: When Their Hair Finally Grew/08/10/2016 18:00:25/http://www.rocksbackpages.com/Library/Article/slade-when-their-hair-finally-grew

1973
Kent, N. (1973) 'Slade: The Kidz Are All Right'. New Musical Express. Slade. Retrieved April 15, 2023, from http://www.rocksbackpages.com/Library/Article/slade-the-kidz-are-all-right

Lanchester Arts Festival
Billy Preston, Chuck Berry, Pink Floyd, Slade/1972/Tony Stewart/New Musical Express/Chuck Berry, Pink Floyd, Billy Preston, Slade: Locarno Ballroom, Coventry/08/10/2016 18:02:15/http://www.rocksbackpages.com/Library/Article/chuck-berry-pink-floyd-billy-preston-slade-locarno-ballroom-coventry

Murray, C. (1972) Big Red Cars, Little White Chicks And The Chuck Berry Lick. Cream. Chuck Berry. Retrieved April 15, 2023, from http://www.rocksbackpages.com/Library/Article/big-red-cars-little-white-chicks-and-the-chuck-berry-lick

Lillian Roxon
Roxon, L. (1973) 'A Rock Critic's Rough and Reddy Life'. New York Sunday News. Rod McKuen, Helen Reddy, Slade. Retrieved May 8, 2023, from http://www.rocksbackpages.com/Library/Article/a-rock-critics-rough-and-reddy-life

Slade Alive!
Slade/1972/Jon Tiven/Rolling Stone/Slade<i>: Slade Alive!</i>/08/10/2016 17:30:14/http://www.rocksbackpages.com/Library/Article/slade-slade-alive

Slade/1972/Lester Bangs/Phonograph Record/Slade: <I>Slade Alive!</I> /08/10/2016 17:36:54/http://www.rocksbackpages.com/Library/Article/slade-islade-alivei-

Slade/1972/Metal Mike Saunders/Phonograph Record/Slade: <i>Slade Alive!</i> /05/01/2017 17:32:35/http://www.rocksbackpages.com/Library/Article/slade-slade-alive-

Slade in Flame
Slade/1975/Simon Frith/Let It Rock/Slade: <i>Slade In Flame </i>(Polydor)/08/10/2016 18:02:32/http://www.rocksbackpages.com/Library/Article/slade-slade-in-flame-polydor

Slade/2002/Rob Chapman/unpublished/Slade/04/01/2017 15:46:59/http://www.rocksbackpages.com/Library/Article/slade-4

Superyob
Altham, K. (1973) "Slade: Superyob". New Musical Express. Slade. http://www.rocksbackpages.com/Library/Article/slade-superyob

Pete Townshend
Murray, C. (1973) 'Pete Townshend part 2: If The Who Split We'd Really Have To Own Up'. New Musical Express. The Who. Retrieved April 15, 2023, from http://www.rocksbackpages.com/Library/Article/pete-townshend-part-2-if-the-who-split-wed-really-have-to-own-up

YouTube

The Bardney Festival
https://www.youtube.com/watch?v=ql8rbw7htu4
https://www.youtube.com/watch?v=VnasJ9UGjeI
https://www.facebook.com/watch/?v=597369350758221

Blessings In Disguise
https://www.youtube.com/watch?v=38N-Ajs0LGY

BBC Radio Scotland Interview 2022
https://www.youtube.com/watch?v=9A5C-Xa7MUw

Brumbeat: Rocks Family Trees
https://www.youtube.com/watch?v=Wz2VlL8ZKNM

Hancock's Half Hour: The Publicity Photograph
https://www.youtube.com/watch?v=FCnOEtrjSow

I Won't Let It 'Appen Agen
https://theartsdesk.com/new-music/reissue-cds-weekly-slade

It's Slade
https://www.youtube.com/watch?v=OSmgmPHtnTk

Bibiliography

Jonathan Ross 2003/Noddy
https://www.youtube.com/watch?v=jwpotoLW9V0

Perseverance
https://www.youtube.com/watch?v=45R-c7TIWMg

Winterland concert
https://www.youtube.com/watch?v=aqcpx2K2SVA

Facebook
https://www.facebook.com/Sladeforlife

General Reference
www.allmusic.com
www.bbc.co.uk
www.discogs.com
www.rocksbackpages.com
en.wikipedia.org

Sleevenotes
Altham, Keith. *The Slade Box*. Salvo Records, 2006.
Charlesworth, Chris. *Slayed?* Polydor Records, 1972.
Charlesworth, Chris. *Sladest*. Polydor Records, 1973.
Charlesworth, Chris. *Wall of Hits*. Polydor Records, 1991.
Charlesworth, Chris. *Greatest Hits – Feel the Noize*. Polydor Records, 1997.
Dome, Malcolm. *Caravan: Who Do You Think You Are?*. Madfish Records, 2021.
Ellen, Mark. *When Slade Ruled the World 1971–1975*. BMG Records, 2015.
Epstein, Dan. *In for a Penny: Raves & Faves*. Shout! Factory, 2007.
Hamblett, Mike. *Therapy* (James Whild Lea). Jim Jam Records, 2009.
Howells, Johnny. *The Genesis of Slade*. TMC Records/Cherry Red, 1996.
Houston, Bob. *Sladest*. Polydor, 1973.
Ingham, Chris. *The Amazing Kamikaze Syndrome*. BMG Records, 2022.
Ingham, Chris. *B-Sides*. Salvo Records, 2007.
Ingham, Chris. *Nobody's Fools*. BMG Records, 2022.
Ingham, Chris. *Slade in Flame*. Salvo Records, 2015.
Ling, Dave. *Beginnings/Play It Loud*. Salvo Records, 2006.
Thomas, Keith C. *Slade II – Keep On Rockin'*. Prestige, 1995.

Interviews
1. Jonathan 'Chas' Chandler 13/10/16
2. Dave Kemp 27/1/17
3. Chris Charlesworth 28/11/17, 11/4/23
4. Ray Shulman 21/11/16
5. John Dummer 12/11/17
6. Don Powell 9/11/17, 4/12/17
7. Steve Megson 24/3/18
8. Chris Carr 4/4/18
9. Chris O'Donnell 24/4/18
10. Richard Loncraine 24/4/18
11. Andy Scott 16/7/18
12. Mike 'Emperor Rosko' Pasternak 3/3/18
13. Stephen Cross 13/11/21
14. Tim Rice 26/11/21
15. Alan O'Duffy 7/2/22
16. Kevin 'Billy' Adams 8/2/22
17. Paul Cookson 8/2/22
18. Gered Mankowitz 11/2/22
19. Steve Mason 9/1/23
20. Helen O'Hara 12/1/23
21. Irving Martin 13/1/23
22. Michael Hann 16/1/23
23. Jerry Ewing 18/1/23
24. Steve Hammonds 19/1/23
25. Wendy Solomon (Jem Lea) 23/1/23
26. Danie Cox (Gobby Holder) 25/1/23
27. John Taylor 27/1/23
28. Nick Van Eede 29/1/23
29. John Steel 1/2/23
30. Ian Edmundson 3/2/23
31. Andrew Birkin 10/2/23
32. John Martin (The Big Figure) 11/2/23
33. Phil Kinrade 11/2/23
34. Tim Fraser-Harding 11/2/23
35. David Stubbs 13/2/23
36. Bill Nelson 14/2/23
37. John Barker 14/2/23

38. Andy Miller 16/2/23
39. Sandy Lieberson 23/2/23
40. Alexis Petridis 23/2/23
41. Gavrik Losey 24/2/23
42. John Halsall 10/3/23
43. Frank Lea 15/3/23
44. Francis Rossi 16/3/23
45. Jim Moir 24/3/23
46. Dave Ling 26/3/23
47. Len Brown 7/4/23
48. Markus Birdman 8/4/23
49. Andre Jaquemin 10/4/23
50. Gary Crowley 12/4/23
51. John Maher 13/4/23
52. Martin Baker 16/4/23
53. Lady Ellen Baker 17/4/23
54. Bob Geldof 21/4/23
55. Liz Lenten 24/4/23
56. Suzi Quatro 28/4/23
57. Steve Gregory 28/4/23
58. Andy Fairweather Low 29/4/23
59. Terry McCusker 2/5/23
60. Nick Heyward 3/5/23
61. Stu Rutter 10/5/23
62. Phil Simner 10/5/23
63. John Punter 11/5/23
64. Jon Astley 12/5/23
65. David Graham 12/5/23
66. Jim Fry 16/5/23
67. Mick Gallagher 22/5/23

With sincere thanks to Chris Charlesworth for use of Chas Chandler and Jim Lea's 1980s interview tapes from *Feel the Noize!*.

Mark Blake for the invaluable use of his transcripts of interviews with Noddy Holder, Dave Hill, Jim Lea and Don Powell from July 2019 for *Planet Rock* magazine.

Dave Ling for his permission for use of Noddy Holder *Classic Rock* 307 interview.

Jill Adam at *Louder Than Words* for permission for use of interview with this writer and Don Powell 11/20.

Bethany Williams at Wolverhampton Art Gallery for use of the Jim Lea and Don Powell interview undertaken by this writer, 6/8/22.

Slade Selected UK Discography

(For full, exhaustive discography, please consult Selby/Edmundson's
The Noize)

1) ALBUMS

AMBROSE SLADE
Beginnings
Fontana STL 5492, May 1969
Side One: Genesis / Everybody's Next One / Knocking Nails into My
House / Roach Daddy / Ain't Got No Heart / Pity the Mother
Side Two: Mad Dog Cole / Fly Me High / If This World Was Mine /
Martha My Dear / Born to Be Wild / Journey to the Centre of Your
Mind

SLADE
Play It Loud
Polydor 2383 026, November 1970
Side One: Raven / See Us Here / Dapple Rose / Could I / One Way
Hotel / The Shape of Things to Come
Side Two: Know Who You Are/ I Remember/ Pouk Hill / Angelina /
Dirty Joker / Sweet Box

Slade Alive!
Polydor 2383 101, March 1972
Side One: Hear Me Calling / In Like a Shot from My Gun / Darling
Be Home Soon
Side Two: Know Who You Are / Keep On Rocking / Get Down and
Get With It / Born to Be Wild

Slayed?
Polydor 2383 163, December 1972
Side One: How D'You Ride / The Whole World's Goin' Crazee /
Look At Last Nite / I Won't Let It 'Appen Agen / Move Over
Side Two: Gudbuy T'Jane / Gudbuy Gudbuy / Mama Weer All Crazee
Now / I Don' Mind /Let the Good Times Roll

Old New Borrowed and Blue
Polydor 2383 261, February 1974
Side One: Just Want a Little Bit / When the Lights Are Out / My
Town / Find Yourself a Rainbow / Miles Out to Sea / We're Really
Gonna Raise the Roof
Side Two: Do We Still Do It / How Can It Be / Don't Blame Me / My
Friend Stan / Everyday / Good Time Gals

Slade in Flame
Polydor 2442 126, November 1974
Side One: How Does It Feel / Them Kinda Monkeys Can't Swing /
So Far So Good / Summer Song (Wishing You Were Here) / O.K.
Yesterday Was Yesterday
Side Two: Far Far Away / This Girl / Lay It Down / Heaven Knows /
Standin' on the Corner

Nobody's Fools
Polydor 2383 377, March 1976
Side One: Nobody's Fool / Do the Dirty / Let's Call It Quits / Pack
Up Your Troubles / In for a Penny
Side Two: Get On Up / L.A. Jinx / Did Ya Mama Ever Tell Ya /
Scratch My Back / I'm a Talker / All The World's a Stage

Whatever Happened to Slade
Barn Records Ltd. 2314 103, March 1977
Side One: Be / Lightning Never Strikes Twice / Gypsy Roadhog /
Dogs of Vengeance / When Fantasy Calls / One Eyed Jacks with
Moustaches
Side Two: Big Apple Blues / Dead Men Tell No Tales / She's Got
the Lot / It Ain't Love But It Ain't Bad / The Soul, The Roll and the
Motion

Slade Alive Vol Two
Barn Records Ltd. 2314 106, October 1978
Side One: Get On Up / Take Me Bak 'Ome / My Baby Left Me / Be /
Mama Weer All Crazee Now
Side Two: Burnin' in the Heat of Love / Everyday / Gudbuy T'Jane /
One-Eyed Jacks / Cum On Feel the Noize

Return to Base
Barn Records Ltd. NARB 003, October 1979
Side One: Wheels Ain't Coming Down / Hold On to Your Hats /
Chakeeta / Don't Waste Your Time (Back Seat Star) / Sign of the
Times
Side Two: I'm a Rocker / Nut Bolts and Screws / My Baby's Got It /
I'm Mad / Lemme Love Into Ya / Ginny, Ginny

Till Deaf Do Us Part
RCA RCA LP 6021, November 1981
Side One: Rock and Roll Preacher (Hallelujah I'm On Fire) / Lock
Up Your Daughters / Till Deaf Do Us Part / Ruby Red / She Brings
Out the Devil in Me
Side Two: A Night to Remember / M'Hat M'Coat / It's Your Body Not
Your Mind / Let the Rock Roll Out of Control / That Was No Lady
That Was My Wife / Knuckle Sandwich Nancy / Till Deaf Resurrected

Slade on Stage
RCA RCALP 3107, December 1982
Side One: Rock and Roll Preacher / When I'm Dancin' I Ain't
Fightin' / Tak Me Bak 'Ome / Everyday / Lock Up Your Daughters
Side Two: We'll Bring the House Down / A Night to Remember /
Gudbuy T'Jane / Mama Weer All Crazee Now / You'll Never Walk
Alone

The Amazing Kamikaze Syndrome
RCA PL 70116, December 1983
Side One: Slam the Hammer Down / In the Doghouse / Run
Runaway / High and Dry / My Oh My / Cocky Rock Boys (Rule O.K.)
Side Two: Ready to Explode: i: The Warm Up ii: The Grid iii: The
Race iv: The Dream / (And Now – The Waltz) C'est La Vie / Cheap
'n' Nasty Luv / Razzle Dazzle Man

Rogues Gallery
RCA PL 70604, March 1985
Side One: Hey Ho Wish You Well / Little Sheila / Harmony /
Myzsterious Mizster Jones / Walking on Water, Running on Alcohol
Side Two: 7 Year Bitch / I'll Be There / I Win, You Lose / Time to
Rock / All Join Hands

Crackers – The Christmas Party Album
Telstar STAR 2271, November 1985
Side One: Let's Dance / Santa Claus Is Coming to Town / Hi Ho
Silver Lining / We'll Bring the House Down / Cum On Feel the Noize
/ All Join Hands / Okey Cokey / Merry Xmas Everybody
Side Two: Do You Believe in Miracles / Let's Have a Party / Get Down
and Get With It / My Oh My / Run Runaway / Here's To... (the New
Year) / Do They Know It's Christmas? / Auld Lang Syne – You'll
Never Walk Alone

You Boyz Make Big Noize
RCA PL 71260, April 1987
Side One: Love Is Like a Rock / That's What Friends Are For / Still
the Same / Fools Go Crazy / She's Heavy / We Won't Give In
Side Two: Won't You Rock With Me / Ooh La La In L.A. / Me and
the Boys / Sing Shout (Knock Yourself Out) / The Roaring Silence /
It's Hard Having Fun Nowadays

2) SELECTED COMPILATIONS

Sladest
Polydor 2442 119, September 1973
Side One: Cum On Feel the Noize / Look Wot You Dun / Gudbuy
T'Jane / One Way Hotel / Skweeze Me, Pleeze Me / Pouk Hill / The
Shape of Things to Come
Side Two: Take Me Bak 'Ome / Coz I Luv You / Wild Winds Are
Blowin' / Know Who You Are / Get Down and Get With It / Look At
Last Nite / Mama Weer All Crazee Now

Beginnings of Slade
Contour 6870 678, December 1975
Side One: Born to Be Wild / Genesis / Martha My Dear / Ain't Got
No Heart / Roach Daddy / Everybody's Next One

432

Side Two: Fly Me High / If This World Was Mine / Pity the Mother / Knocking Nails into My House / Mad Dog Cole / Journey to the Centre of Your Mind

Slade Smashes
Polydor POLTV 13, November 1980
Side One: Cum On Feel the Noize / My Friend Stan / Far Far Away / Coz I Luv You / Everyday / Gypsy Roadhog / Thanks for the Memory (Wham Bam Thank You Mam) / The Bangin' Man / In for a Penny / Skweeze Me, Pleeze Me
Side Two: Mama Weer All Crazee Now / Look Wot You Dun / Take Me Bak 'Ome / Let's Call It Quits / Give Us a Goal / Merry Xmas Everybody / How Does It Feel/ My Baby Left Me / That's Alright Mama (Medley) /Get Down and Get With It / Gudbuy T'Jane

We'll Bring the House Down
Cheapskate Records SKATE 1, March 1981
Side One: We'll Bring the House Down / Night Starvation / Wheels Ain't Coming Down / Hold on to Your Hats / When I'm Dancin' I Ain't Fightin'
Side Two: Dizzy Mamma / Nuts Bolts and Screws / My Baby's Got It / Lemme Love Into Ya / I'm a Rocker

Slade Greats
Polydor SLAD 1, May 1984
Side One: Cum On Feel the Noize / My Friend Stan / Far Far Away / Coz I Luv You / Everyday / Thanks for the Memory (Wham Bam Thank You Mam) / The Bangin' Man / Skweeze Me, Pleeze Me
Side Two: Mama Weer All Crazee Now / Look Wot You Dun / Take Me Bak 'Ome / Let's Call It Quits / Merry Xmas Everybody / How Does It Feel? / Get Down and Get With It / Gudbuy T'Jane

Wall of Hits
Polydor 511 612-1, November 1991
Side One: Get Down and Get With It / Coz I Luv You / Look Wot You Dun / Take Me Bak 'Ome / Mama Weer All Crazee Now / Gudbuy T'Jane / Cum On Feel the Noize / Skweeze Me, Pleeze Me / My Friend Stan
Side Two: Everyday / Bangin' Man / Far Far Away / Let's Call It Quits / My Oh My / Run Run Away / Radio Wall of Sound / Universe / Merry Xmas Everybody

Greatest Hits – Feel the Noize
Polydor 537 105-2, January 1997, CD
Get Down and Get With It / Coz I Luv You /Look Wot You Dun /
Take Me Bak 'Ome / Mama Weer All Crazee Now / Gudbuy T'Jane/
Cum On Feel the Noize / Skweeze Me, Pleeze Me / My Friend Stan /
Everyday / Bangin' Man / Far Far Away / How Does It Feel / In for
a Penny / We'll Bring the House Down / Lock Up Your Daughters /
My Oh My / Run Runaway /All Join Hands / Radio Wall of Sound /
Merry Xmas Everybody

The Slade Box – A 4CD Anthology 1969–1991
Salvo SALVOBX 401, September 2006, 4-CD
Disc One: Born to Be Wild / Roach Daddy / Wild Winds Are Blowing
/ The Shape of Things to Come / Know Who You Are / Pouk Hill /
One Way Hotel / Get Down and Get With It / In Like a Shot From
My Gun (Live) / Coz I Luv You / Look Wot You Dun / Take Me Bak
'Ome / Wonderin' Y / Mama Weer All Crazee Now / Gudbuy T'Jane
/ The Whole World's Goin' Crazee / I Won't Let It 'Appen Agen /
Cum On Feel the Noize / I'm Mee I'm Now And That's Orl / Skweeze
Me, Pleeze Me / Kill 'Em at the Hot Club Tonite / My Friend Stan /
Merry Xmas Everybody

Disc Two: When The Lights Are Out / We're Really Gonna Raise the
Roof / How Can It Be / Everyday / The Bangin' Man / She Did It to
Me / Far Far Away / So Far So Good / How Does It Feel / Thanks for
the Memory (Wham Bam Thank You Mam) / In for a Penny / Can
You Just Imagine / Let's Call It Quits / When The Chips Are Down /
Nobody's Fool / L.A. Jinx / Gypsy Roadhog / Be / It Ain't Love But It
Ain't Bad / Burning in the Heat of Love / My Baby Left Me – That's
All Right

Disc Three: Give Us a Goal / Rock'n'Roll Bolero / It's Alright Buy
Me / Ginny Ginny / Sign of the Times / Not Tonight Jospehine /
Okey Cokey / Don't Waste Your Time (Back Seat Star) / We'll Bring
the House Down / Wheels Ain't Coming Down / Night Starvation /
When I'm Dancin' I Ain't Fightin' / Knuckle Sandwich Nancy / Lock
Up Your Daughters / Rock and Roll Preacher / Til Deaf Do Us Part
/ Ruby Red / A Night to Remember / (And Now The Waltz) C'est La
Vie / My Oh My / Keep Your Hands Off My Power Supply

Disc Four: Don't Tame a Hurricane / Ready to Explode / Run Runaway / Two Track Stereo One Track Mind / All Join Hands / Little Sheila / 7 Year Bitch / Leave Them Girls Alone / Myzsterious Mizster Jones / Do You Believe in Miracles / Still the Same / Gotta Go Home / That's What Friends Are For / You Boyz Make Big Noize / Ooh La La In L.A. / We Won't Give In / Let's Dance '88 / Radio Wall of Sound / Universe

B-Sides
Salvo SALVOCD 203, February 2007, 2-CD

Disc One: One Way Hotel / C'mon C'mon / Do You Want Me / The Gospel According To Rasputin / My Life Is Natural / Candidate / Wonderin' Y / Man Who Speaks Evil/ I Won't Let It 'Appen Agen / I'm Mee I'm Now And That's Orl / Kill 'Em At The Hot Club Tonite / My Town / Don't Blame Me / She Did It To Me / O.K. Yesterday Was Yesterday / So Far So Good / Raining In My Champagne / Can You Just Imagine / When The Chips Are Down / L.A. Jinx / Forest Full Of Needles

Disc Two: Ready Steady Kids / O.H.M.S. / Daddio / It's Alright Buy Me / Not Tonight Josephine / Funk Punk & Junk / Keep Your Hands Off My Power Supply / Don't Tame A Hurricane / Two Track Stereo One Track Mind / Here's To The New Year / Leave Them Girls Alone / Mama Nature Is A Rocker / My Oh My (Swing Version) / Gotta Go Home / Don't Talk To Me About Love / Wild Wild Party / You Boyz Make Big Noize (Instrumental) / Lay Your Love On The Line / Red Hot

Live At The BBC
Salvo SALVOCD 211, September 2009, 2-CD

Disc One: Coming Home /The Shape Of Things To Come / See Us Here / Know Who You Are / My Life Is Natural / Coloured Rain / Man Who Speaks Evil / Move Over / Omaha / Sweet Box / Nights In White Satin / It's Alright Ma, It's Only Witchcraft / Raven / Gudbuy Gudbuy / Getting Better / Darling Be Home Soon / Let The Good Times Roll / Dirty Joker / Get Down And Get With It / Wild Winds Are Blowing /JINGLES: "Radio I, Where The Best Music's On" / "Everyday The Sounds We Play On Radio I" / "This Is Radio I, We're All Having Fun" / "We're Slade!"

Whatever Happened to Slade?

Disc Two: LIVE AT PARIS THEATRE: Introduction / Hear Me
Calling / In Like A Shot (From My Gun) / Look Wot You Dun / Keep
On Rocking / Move Over / Mama Weer All Crazee Now / Lady Be
Good / Coz I Luv You / Take Me Back 'Ome / Get Down And Get
With It / Good Golly Miss Molly

When Slade Rocked the World 1971–1975
Salvo SALVOBX 412L, November 2015

LPs

Slade Alive!
Side One: Hear Me Calling / In Like a Shot from My Gun / Darling
Be Home Soon
Side Two: Know Who You Are / Keep on Rocking / Get Down and
Get With It / Born to Be Wild

Slayed?
Side One: How D'You Ride / The Whole World's Goin' Crazee /
Look at Last Nite / I Won't Let It 'Appen Agen / Move Over
Side Two: Gudbuy T'Jane / Gudbuy Gudbuy / Mama Weer All Crazee
Now / I Don' Mind /Let the Good Times Roll
Old New Borrowed and Blue
Side One: Just Want a Little Bit / When the Lights Are Out / My
Town / Find Yourself a Rainbow / Miles Out to Sea / We're Really
Gonna Raise the Roof
Side Two: Do We Still Do It / How Can It Be / Don't Blame Me / My
Friend Stan / Everyday / Good Time Gals

Slade in Flame
Side One: How Does It Feel / Them Kinda Monkeys Can't Swing /
So Far So Good / Summer Song (Wishing You Were Here) / O.K.
Yesterday Was Yesterday
Side Two: Far Far Away / This Girl / Lay It Down / Heaven Knows /
Standin' on the Corner

CD

Disc One: How D'You Ride / The Whole World's Goin' Crazee
/ Look at Last Nite / I Won't Let It 'Appen Agen / Move Over /
Gudbuy T'Jane / Gudbuy Gudbuy / Mama Weer All Crazee Now / I
Don' Mind /Let the Good Times Roll / Hear Me Calling / In Like a

Shot From My Gun / Darling Be Home Soon / Know Who You Are / Keep On Rocking / Get Down and Get With It / Born to Be Wild

Disc Two: Just Want a Little Bit / When the Lights Are Out / My Town / Find Yourself a Rainbow / Miles Out to Sea / We're Really Gonna Raise the Roof / Do We Still Do It / How Can It Be / Don't Blame Me / My Friend Stan / Everyday / Good Time Gals / How Does It Feel / Them Kinda Monkeys Can't Swing / So Far So Good / Summer Song (Wishing You Were Here) / O.K. Yesterday Was Yesterday / Far Far Away / This Girl / Lay It Down / Heaven Knows / Standin' on the Corner

SINGLES
Coz I Luv You / Look Wot You Dun
Take Me Bak 'Ome / Cum On Feel the Noize
Skweeze Me, Pleeze Me / Merry Xmas Everybody
The Bangin' Man / Thanks for the Memory

FLEXI
Slade Talk To *19* Readers

Feel The Noize – The Singlez Box
BMG BMGCAT 311BOX, September 2019, 10 7-inch set
Single One: Coz I Luv You / My Life Is Natural
Single Two: Take Me Bak 'Ome / Wonderin' Y
Single Three: Mama Weer All Crazee Now / Man Who Speeks Evil
Single Four: Gudbuy T'Jane / I Won't Let It 'Appen Agen
Single Five: Cum On Feel the Noize / I'm Mee, I'm Now, An' That's Orl
Single Six: Skweeze Me, Pleeze Me / Kill 'Em at the Hot Club Tonite
Single Seven: My Friend Stan / My Town
Single Eight: Everyday / Good Time Gals
Single Nine: Far Far Away / O.K. Yesterday Was Yesterday
Single Ten: Night Starvation / When I'm Dancin' I Ain't Fightin'

Cum On Feel the Hitz
BMG BMGCAT 464DLP, September 2020 (2-LP)
Side One: Get Down and Get With It / Coz I Luv You /Look Wot You Dun/ Take Me Bak 'Ome / Mama Weer All Crazee Now /Gudbuy T'Jane

Side Two: Cum On Feel the Noize / Skweeze Me, Pleeze Me / My Friend Stan / Everyday / The Bangin' Man / Far Far Away
Side Three: How Does It Feel / Thanks for the Memory / In for a Penny / Let's Call It Quits / We'll Bring the House Down/ Lock Up Your Daughters
Side Four: My Oh My / Run Runaway /All Join Hands / Myzsterious Mizster Jones / Radio Wall of Sound / Merry Xmas Everybody

Cum On Feel the Hitz
BMG BMGCAT464DCD, September 2020 (2-CD)
CD One: Cum On Feel the Noize / Skweeze Me, Pleeze Me / Mama Weer All Crazee Now / Coz I Luv You / Take Me Bak 'Ome / Gudbuy T'Jane / My Friend Stan / Far Far Away / My Oh My / Everyday / The Bangin' Man / Look Wot You Dun / Thanks for the Memory / Run Runaway / We'll Bring the House Down / In for a Penny / Let's Call It Quits / How Does It Feel / All Join Hands / Get Down and Get With It / Radio Wall of Sound

CD Two: Lock Up Your Daughters / My Baby Left Me: That's Alright / Gypsy Roadhog / (And Now the Waltz) C'est La Vie / Myzsterious Mizster Jones / Ruby Red / Do You Believe in Miracles / Wheels Ain't Coming Down / 7 Year Bitch / Still the Same / The Shape of Things to Come / Know Who You Are / Nobody's Fool / Burning in the Heat of Love / Give Us a Goal / Ginny Ginny / Sign of the Times / Knuckle Sandwich Nancy / Ooh La La In L.A. / That's What Friends Are For / We Won't Give In / Merry Xmas Everybody

All the World Is a Stage

BMG BMGCAT 728BOX, September 2022
Slade Alive!
Hear Me Calling / In Like a Shot from My Gun / Darling Be Home Soon / Know Who You Are / Keep on Rocking / Get Down and Get With It / Born to Be Wild

Slade On Stage
Rock and Roll Preacher / When I'm Dancin' I Ain't Fightin' / Tak Me Bak 'Ome / Everyday / Lock Up Your Daughters / We'll Bring the House Down / A Night to Remember / Gudbuy T'Jane / Mama Weer All Crazee Now / You'll Never Walk Alone

Alive! At Reading

Take Me Bak 'Ome / When I'm Dancin' I Ain't Fightin' / Wheels Ain't Coming Down / Somethin' Else – Pistol Packin' Mama – Instrumental Jam – Keep It Rockin' / You'll Never Walk Alone (Noddy Holder & Crowd Version) / Mama Weer All Crazee Now / Get Down and Get With It / Merry Xmas Everybody (Crowd Version) / Cum On Feel the Noize / Born to Be Wild

Live At The Hucknall Miners Welfare Club

Dizzy Mamma / Night Starvation / Take Me Bak 'Ome / Wheels Ain't Coming Down / Lemme Love Into Ya / Everyday / Somethin' Else – Purple Haze – Pistol Packin' Mama – Keep A Rollin' / When I'm Dancin' I Ain't Fightin' / Gudbuy T'Jane / Get Down and Get With It / You'll Never Walk Alone / Mama Weer All Crazee Now / Merry Xmas Everybody / I'm a Rocker / Born to Be Wild

Live at the New Victoria

Them Kinda Monkeys Can't Swing / The Bangin' Man / Gudbuy T'Jane / Far Far Away / Thanks for the Memory (Wham Bam Thank You Mam) / How Does It Feel / Just A Little Bit / Everyday / O.K. Yesterday Was Yesterday / Raining in My Champagne / Let the Good Times Roll / Mama Weer All Crazee Now

3) SELECTED IMPORTS

Stomp Your Hands, Clap Your Feet
US, Warner Bros. Records BS 2770, February 1974

Side One: Just Want a Little Bit / When the Lights Are Out / Find Yourself a Rainbow / Miles Out to Sea / We're Really Gonna Raise the Roof

Side Two: Do We Still Do It / How Can It Be / Don't Blame Me / Everyday / Good Time Gals

Keep Your Hands Off My Power Supply
US, CBS Associated Records, April 1984

Side One: Run Runaway / My Oh My / High and Dry / Slam the Hammer Down / In the Doghouse

Side Two: Keep Your Hands Off My Power Supply / Cheap 'N' Nasty Love / Can't Tame a Hurricane / (And Now – the Waltz) C'est La Vie / Ready to Explode: i: The Warm Up ii: The Grid iii: The Race iv: The Dream

Get Yer Boots On: The Best of Slade
US, Shout! Factory DK 34008, March 2004, CD
Get Down and Get With It / Coz I Luv You / Look Wot You Dun /
Take Me Bak 'Ome / Mama Weer All Crazee Now / Gudbuy T'Jane
/ Cum On Feel the Noize / Skweeze Me, Pleeze Me / My Friend Stan
/ Merry Xmas Everybody / Everyday / Bangin' Man / Far Far Away /
How Does It Feel / Run Runaway / My Oh My

In for a Penny: Raves and Faves
US, Shout! Factory 826663-10481, April 2007, CD
Shape of Things to Come / C'Mon C'Mon / Sweet Box / In Like a
Shot from My Gun / Wonderin' Y / How D'You Ride / Move Over /
Don't Blame Me / Do We Still Do It / When The Lights Are Out /
Them Kinda Monkeys Can't Swing / Thanks for the Memory (Wham
Bam Thank You Mam) / In for a Penny /Let's Call It Quits /Burning
in the Heat of Love

4) SINGLES

AMBROSE SLADE
Genesis / Roach Daddy (Fontana TF 1015, 5/69)

SLADE
Wild Winds Are Blowing / One Way Hotel (Fontana TF1056, 10/69)
Shape of Things to Come / C'mon C'mon (Fontana TF 1079, 3/70)
Know Who You Are / Dapple Rose (Polydor 2058 054, 9/70)
Get Down and Get With It / Do You Want Me/The Gospel According
to Rasputin (Polydor 2058 112, 5/71, No 16)
Coz I Luv You / Life Is Natural (Polydor 2058 155, 10/71, No 1)
Look Wot You Dun / Candidate (Polydor 2058 195, 1/72, No 4)
Take Me Bak 'Ome / Wonderin' Y (Polydor 2058 231, 5/72, No 1)
Mama Weer All Crazee Now / Man Who Speeks Evil (Polydor 2058
274, 8/72, No 1)
Gudbuy T'Jane / I Won't Let It 'Appen Again (Polydor 2058 312,
11/72, No 2)
Cum On Feel the Noize / I'm Mee, I'm Now An' That's All (Polydor
2058 339, 3/73, No 1)
Skweeze Me, Pleeze Me / Kill 'Em at the Hot Club Tonite (Polydor
2058 377, 6/73, No 1)
My Friend Stan / My Town (Polydor 2058 407, 9/73, No 2)

Merry Xmas Everybody / Don't Blame Me (Polydor 2058 422, 12/73, No 1)

Everyday / Good Time Gals (Polydor 2058 453, 3/74, No 3)

The Bangin' Man / She Did It to Me (Polydor 2058 492, 6/74, No 3)

Far Far Away / O.K. Yesterday Was Yesterday (Polydor 2058 522, 10/74, No 2)

How Does It Feel / So Far So Good (Polydor 2058 547, 2/75, No 15)

Thanks for the Memory (Wham Bam Thank You Mam)/Raining in My Champagne (Polydor 2058 585, 5/75, No 7)

In for a Penny / Can You Just Imagine (Polydor 2058 585, 11/75, No 11)

Let's Call It Quits / When the Chips Are Down (Polydor 2058 690, 1/76, No 11)

Nobody's Fool / L. A. Jinx (Polydor 2058 716, 4/76)

Gypsy Roadhog / Forest Full of Needles (Barn Records Ltd. 2014 105, 2/77, No 48)

Burning in the Heat of Love / Ready Steady Kids (Barn Records Ltd. 2014 106, 4/77)

My Baby Left Me – That's All Right / O.H.M.S. (Barn Records Ltd. 2014 114, 10/77, No 32)

Give Us a Goal / Daddio (Barn Records Ltd. 2014 121, 3/78)

Rock'n'Roll Bolero / It's Alright, Buy Me (Barn Records Ltd. 2014 127, 10/78)

Ginny Ginny / Dizzy Mama (Barn Records Ltd. BARN 002, 3/79)

Sign of the Times / Not Tonight Josephine (Barn Records Ltd. BARN 010, 10/79)

Okey Cokey / My Baby's Got It (Barn Records Ltd. BARN 011, 12/79)

SIX OF THE BEST – Night Starvation / When I'm Dancing, I Ain't Fightin'/I'm a Rocker / Don't Waste Your Time / Wheels Ain't Coming Down / Nine to Five (S.O.T.B. SUPER 45 3, 6/80)

ALIVE AT READING '80 - When I'm Dancing, I Ain't Fightin' / Born to Be Wild / Pistol Packin' Mama / Keep A Rollin' (Cheapskate CHEAP 5, 9/80, No 44)

XMAS EAR BENDER – Merry Xmas Everybody (Slade and The Reading Choir) / Okey Cokey / Get Down and Get With It (Cheapskate CHEAP 11, 11/80, No 70)

We'll Bring the House Down / Hold on to Your Hats (Cheapskate CHEAP 16, 1/81, No 10)

Wheels Ain't Comin' Down / Not Tonight Josephine (Cheapskate CHEAP 21, 3/81, No 60)

Knuckle Sandwich Nancy / I'm Mad (Cheapskate CHEAP 24, 5/81)

Lock Up Your Daughters / Sign of the Times (RCA RCA 124, 9/81, No 29)

Ruby Red / Funk Punk and Junk (RCA RCA 191, 3/82, No 51)

Ruby Red / Funk Punk and Junk/Rock and Roll Preacher (Live Version)/ Tak Me Bak 'Ome (Live Version) (2 x 7-inch, RCA RCAD 191, 3/82)

(And Now – The Waltz) C'est La Vie / Merry Xmas Everybody (Live & Kickin') (RCA RCA 29, 11/82, No 50)

Okey Cokey / Get Down and Get With It (Speed SPEED 201, 12/82)

My Oh My / Merry Xmas Everybody (Live & Kickin')/ Keep Your Hands Off My Power Supply (RCA RCA 373, 11/83, No 2)

Run Runaway / Two Track Stereo, One Track Mind (RCA RCA 385, 1/84, No 7)

All Join Hands / Here's To... (RCA RCA 455, 11/84, No 15)

7 Year Bitch / Leave Them Girls Alone (RCA RCA 475, 1/85, No 60)

Myzsterious Mizster Jones / Mama Nature Is a Rocker (RCA PB 40027, 3/85, No 50)

Myzsterious Mizster Jones (Extended Version) / Mama Nature Is a Rocker / My Oh My (Piano & Vocal Version) (12-inch, RCA PT 40028, 3/85)

Do You Believe in Miracles / My Oh My (Swing Version) (RCA PB 40449, 11/85, No 54)

Do You Believe in Miracles / My Oh My (Swing Version)/Santa Claus Is Coming to Town/Auld Lang Syne / You'll Never Walk Alone (2 x7-inch, RCA PB 40449 D, 11/85)

Do You Believe in Miracles / My Oh My (Swing Version)/Time to Rock (RCA PT 40450, 11/85)

Do You Believe in Miracles / My Oh My (Swing Version)/Time to Rock / Santa Claus Is Coming to Town / Auld Lang Syne / You'll Never Walk Alone (12-inch, 'Slade Xmas' double pack, RCA PT 40450D, 11/85)

Still the Same / Gotta Go Home (RCA PB 41137, 1/87, No 73)

Still the Same / Gotta Go Home / The Roaring Silence / Don't Talk to Me About Love (21st Anniversary double pack, RCA PB 41147D, 1/87)

Still the Same (Extended Version) / Gotta Go Home (12-inch, RCA PT 41138, 1/87)

That's What Friends Are For / Wild Wild Party (RCA PB 41272, 4/87)

That's What Friends Are For / Hi Ho Silver Lining / Wild Wild Party / Lock Up Your Daughters (Live) (12-inch RCA PT 41272, 4/87)

You Boyz Make Big Noize / Boyz (Instrumental) (Cheapskate BOYZ 1, 6/87)

You Boyz Make Big Noize (Noize Remix) / You Boyz Make Big Noize (Instrumental Boyz Version) / You Boyz Make Big Noize (The USA Mix) (12-inch, Cheapskate T BOYZ 1, 6/87)

We Won't Give In / Ooh La La In L.A. (Cheapskate BOYZ 2, 11/87)

Let's Dance (1988 Remix) / Standing on the Corner (Cheapskate BOYZ 3, 11/88)

Let's Dance (1988 Remix) / Far Far Away / How Does It Feel / Standing on the Corner (CD single, BOYZ CD3, 11/88)

Radio Wall of Sound / Lay Your Love on the Line (Polydor PO 180, 10/91, No 21)

Radio Wall of Sound / Lay Your Love on the Line / Cum On Feel the Noize (12-inch, PZ 180, 10/91)

Radio Wall of Sound / Lay Your Love on the Line / Cum On Feel the Noize (CD single, PZCD 180, 10/91)

Universe / Red Hot / Merry Xmas Everybody (Polydor PO 189, 11/91)

Universe / Red Hot / Gypsy Roadhog / Merry Xmas Everybody (12-inch Polydor, PZ 189, 11/91)

Universe / Red Hot / Gypsy Roadhog / Merry Xmas Everybody (CD single, Polydor PZCD 189, 11/91)

5) FLEXI-DISCS

The Whole World's Going Crazee / MIKE HUGG: Bonnie Charlie (33rpm with *Music Scene* magazine) (Polydor/Sound For Industry SFI 122, 10/72)

Slade talk to *Melanie* readers (with *Melanie* magazine) (Lyntone LYN 2645, 9/73)

Slade exclusive to all *19* readers (with 19 magazine) (Lyntone LYN 2797, 2/74)

Acknowledgements

To Jules and Flora Easlea. Baby, baby, babies! Every day, I love you more.

To Nick and Fi Maslen, John Chadwick – that's what friends are for.

To the memory of Dave Kemp with sincere thanks to Barbara Kemp.

To Chris Selby, Ian Edmundson and David Graham for defining what true fans can be. The research that is out there is astonishing, and it has been an honour to reference and fact check with it, and them. To everyone who keeps the Slade flame alive.

To David 'Baz' Barraclough – your patience and excellent humour really is to be revered and cannot be appreciated enough.

To Chris Charlesworth for his support and wise counsel and opening many doors.

To all at Omnibus Press – Claire Browne, Greg Morton, Giulia Senesi, David Stock, Dave Holley.

To Holly Lippold, you made all the difference.

To Michelle Hickman aka 8bitnorthxstitch for her fabulous work, honoured that you are in the book.

Thanks to all those who agreed to be interviewed: Kevin 'Billy' Adams, Jon Astley, Lady Ellen Baker, Martin Baker, John Barker, Markus Birdman, Andrew Birkin, Len Brown, Chris Carr, Jonathan

'Chas' Chandler, Chris Charlesworth, Paul Cookson, Danie Cox, Stephen Cross, Gary Crowley, Ian Edmundson, John Dummer, Jerry Ewing, Andy Fairweather Low, Tim Fraser-Harding, Jim Fry, Mick Gallagher, Bob Geldof, David Graham, Steve Gregory, John Halsall, Steve Hammonds, Michael Hann, Nick Heyward, André Jacquemin, Dave Kemp, Phil Kinrade, Frank Lea, Liz Lenten, Sandy Lieberson, Dave Ling, Richard Loncraine, Gavrik Losey, John Maher, Gered Mankowitz, Irving Martin, John Martin, Steve Mason, Terry McCusker, Steve Megson, Andy Miller, Jim Moir, Bill Nelson, Chris O'Donnell, Alan O'Duffy, Helen O'Hara, Mike 'Emperor Rosko' Pasternak, Alexis Petridis, Don Powell, John Punter, Suzi Quatro, Tim Rice, Francis Rossi, Stu Rutter, Andy Scott, Chris Selby, Phil Shulman, Ray Shulman, Phil Simner, Wendy Solomon, John Steel, David Stubbs, John Taylor, Nick Van Eede.

My love and deep respect to all who politely declined.

Sincere thanks to Jill Adam, Lady Ellen Baker, Martin Baker, John Barker, Duff Battye, Mark Baxter, Will Birch, Joe Black, Mark Blake, Mark Brennan, Martin Brooks, Paul Buck, Zal Clemenson, Declan Colgan, Paul Conroy, Danie Cox, Imogen Clark, Dave Clarke, Tim Daines, Andy Delaney, Malcolm Dome, Peter Eden, Richard England, Brit Felmberg, Gaby Green, Ian Gittins, Kevin Godley, Steve Hammonds, Lee Harris, Sara Harding, Chris Hewlett, Jane Hitchen, David Homer, Sandie Homer, Barney Hoskyns, Zoë & Dylan Howe, Jakko Jakszyk, Andre Jacquemin, Phill Jupitus, Julian Kindred, Phil Kinrade, Frank Lea, Steve Machin, John Maher, Joel McIver, Mick Middles, Gary Moore, Andrew Morgan, Lyane Ngan, Laura Page, Michael Parker, Mark Paytress, Donald Rice, Chris Roberts, Hikaru Sasaki, Henry Scott Irvine, Joel Selvin, Dave Shields, Sylvie Simmons, Slady, Sid Smith, Miguel Terol, Wendy Solomon, David Stark, Jon Wallinger, Adam White, Bethany Williams, Lois Wilson, Andrew Winter, Olav Wyper.

Thanks deep and wide: Chrissie Absalom, Steven & Sharon Absalom, Beth Absalom, Ellie Absalom, Dr Absalom, Mr Whitton and forthcoming attraction, Pete Barry, Kate & Ian Batcock, Tad Blower, Kelly Buckley, Suezy Burridge, Tom Burgess, The Bushes, Dearest Liz Carr, Steve & Sarah Carr, Johnny Chandler & co, Dave & Jo Collins, Carolyn & Lauren Cooper, Paul & Tina Cotgrove, Val

Cutts, Ray and Ashley Dalton, *DORNANS*, Dave & Fi Dulake, John
Earls, Glenn, Mandy, Sierra, Savanna and Vinni Easlea, Big Billy
Edwards, *FARRUGIA*, Simon Fowler, Karen Gabay, Haircut 100, Mick
Houghton, Bruno Irace, Katie Kash, Mark Lancaster, Lucy Launder,
Paul Lester, Oliver Lippold, Owen Lloyd, Virginia Loveridge, Yvette
Lyons, Kris Maher, Mitchell & Jurga & Jurgen, Big Jimmy Moonraker,
Syd Moore, Josie Moore and the Moore massive, Ian & Jacqui Pile,
Grant Philpott, Lisa Power, Sarah & Geoff Raggett, Nigel Reeve, Brian
Regan, Joy & Steve Robins, Sweet rockin' Lily Robins, Maia Robins,
Sue Ryder and family, Phil Savill, Emmie Schurer, Siouxsie Stalker,
Wadey & The Cats, Erin West, Bel Withers, Mark Wood & John
Geddes, Ondie & Carl Woods.

To Middle Age Spread (Grown Up Disco For Those Unafraid To Dance):
We are still here, what a scene – Adam Hasan, Alastair Johnson and Dan
Newman – http://www.the-middle-age-spread.co.uk

To FM Switch Off/The Tarmey Brothers we almost brought the house
down. Well, caused someone to partially close a window: Graham
James Brown, John Suckling, Julie Grigg, Alan Taylor and our Syd
figure Phil Short. To Wendy, Nathan, Katy, Amelia, Isaac, Steve,
Sally and the extended.

To the West Midlands network keeping me clued up: Jodi Allen, Liz
Baker, Dr Clive Holmwood, Phil Simner, and honorarily Sarah Tsang
and Jeanette Wyre.

To the happy reacquaintance in the past few years of Simon Ford,
Dave 'Bandana' Smith and Trevor Stoneman, who with Bernie Brown,
Rod Easlea, Andrew Johnstone & Phil Short were the beginning of all
this.

www.shipfullofbombs.co.uk

To the good cats at UMR, Decca, Demon, Sony, Warner and Cherry
Red.

To all at *Mojo*, *Prog* and *Record Collector*.

To KUBE, the Leigh scene and the Wolstanton Cultural Quarter.

Hair by Pammy Playle.

To Leah Ford, the future will never be the same, but it still can be bright.

Gudbuy T'Jane!

Mark Ford, Paul Carr, Ian Ryder, Malcolm Dome, Mick Hutson – you beautiful creatures.

To all those not here, and the list it grows monthly, miss you very much.

Index

Index

454

Index

Index